7.9.21
$27.95

D0856465

Keeping Those Words in Mind

How Language Creates Meaning

Max Louwerse

Prometheus Books

Guilford, Connecticut

(PB) Prometheus Books

An imprint of The Rowman & Littlefield Publishing Group, Inc.
4501 Forbes Boulevard, Suite 200,
Lanham, Maryland 20706
www.rowman.com

Distributed by NATIONAL BOOK NETWORK

British Library Cataloguing in Publication Information Available

Library of Congress Cataloging-in-Publication Data

Names: Louwerse, Max, author.
Title: Keeping those words in mind : how language creates meaning / Max Louwerse.
Description: Lanham, MD : Prometheus Books, [2021] | Includes bibliographical
    references and index. | Summary: "By examining how our brains process language
    and find patterns, the intricacies of the language system itself, and even scientific
    breakthroughs in computer science and artificial intelligence, Keeping Those Words
    in Mind brings a brand new and interdisciplinary explanation for our ability to extract
    meaning from language."—Provided by publisher.
Identifiers: LCCN 2020046347 (print) | LCCN 2020046348 (ebook) | ISBN
    9781633886506 (cloth) | ISBN 9781633886513 (epub)
Subjects: LCSH: Psycholinguistics.
Classification: LCC BF455 .L68 2021 (print) | LCC BF455 (ebook) | DDC 401/.9—
    dc23
LC record available at https://lccn.loc.gov/2020046347
LC ebook record available at https://lccn.loc.gov/2020046348

♾™ The paper used in this publication meets the minimum requirements of American
National Standard for Information Sciences—Permanence of Paper for Printed Library
Materials, ANSI/NISO Z39.48-1992.

Contents

Prologue   v

 1 Words   1
 2 Language   17
 3 Guess   39
 4 Training   63
 5 Instinct   81
 6 Network   99
 7 Grounding   119
 8 Shortcut   137
 9 Patterns   163
10 Sound   185
11 Order   203
12 Company   227
13 Bootstrapping   251
14 Avenues   275

Notes   285
Acknowledgments   313
Bibliography   317
Index   339

Prologue

$\mathcal{O}$nce upon a time there was an ant. Just an ordinary ant. That ant went on a mission for a walk on a beach. Any beach. The tiny little ant walked with perseverance and dedication over the sandy beach, with almost-insurmountable sand hills it had to conquer. The tiny little ant moved one way, then moved another way, finding a route and then soon looking for an alternative one. The ant took a detour, quickly circumventing an obstacle and crisscrossing across the beach, determined to accomplish the major achievement of crossing the large sand plane. And what an achievement that is for a tiny little ant!

When observing the path of the ant, we see an incredibly complex and carefully thought-out route on a massive spatial map of the beach. From our point of view, the ant demonstrates very complex behavior. We can try to map out the behavior and see all kinds of patterns and deviations from those patterns. We could ask ourselves the question of how a tiny little ant is able to cross a beach and how it has acquired such complex behavior.

Perhaps the ant has been carefully trained by its ant parents how to cross a large surface. Father and mother ant have shown the tiny little ant how to cross a beach, and by repeating this behavior over and over again, the tiny little ant has now mastered beach-crossing skills. The tiny little ant's parents rewarded their child with sugary nectar after it accomplished the task. Or perhaps the tiny little ant was born with a beach-crossing instinct. As with any other ant in the world, maybe our tiny little ant was born with a brain attuned to this kind of beach-crossing behavior. Despite its small brain size, the tiny little ant's brain stood the test of evolutionary time and specialized in beach-crossing behavior.

Another explanation for our tiny little ant mastering the complexity of beach crossing comes from the massive computations the ant is able to make when crossing a beach. The tiny little ant takes in information, distributes these pieces of information to the desired output, and learns over time how to cross the beach. It computes one route, estimates its performance of choosing an alternative route, and carefully weighs the probabilities of which route is the best option to select. Slowly but surely, the ant builds a network of optimized probabilities that allows it to crisscross the sandy beach in an efficient way.

Yet another explanation as to how the tiny little ant is able to cross the beach is that the ant simulates the routes by making use of its magnificent memory skills. The ant imagines how to cross the beach by simulating its leg and body movements. It is aware of its own body, is immersed in its environment, and embodies its route. The head and body of the ant allow for conquering certain sand hills, but not others, and by being aware of itself and its environment, the ant is able to perceptually simulate any route on any beach. Basically, the tiny little ant does not observe the route; it is *part* of the route.

But there may be another explanation that complements the explanations mentioned thus far. That explanation, however, does not lie in training, instinct, network, or embodiment. It lies outside the tiny little ant's brain or the brains of the tiny little ant's parents! The behavior of crossing the beach indeed looks complex. But perhaps the complex behavior our tiny little ant demonstrates reflects the complexity of the environment in which it finds itself.[1]

This book is not about tiny little ants and is not about beaches. Neither is this book about beach-crossing behavior. This book is about words and how we keep them in mind. It is about language and how it creates meaning. Metaphorically speaking, this book is about a beach and how it creates a path. And we, we are the tiny little ants.

• *1* •

Words

Take, for example, the "faculty" of language. It involves in reality a host of distinct powers. We must first have images of concrete things and ideas of abstract qualities and relations; we must next have the memory of words and then the capacity so to associate each idea or image with a particular word that, when the word is heard, the idea shall forthwith enter our mind. We must conversely, as soon as the idea arises in our mind, associate with it a mental image of the word, and by means of this image we must innervate our articulatory apparatus so as to reproduce the word as physical sound. To read or to write a language other elements still must be introduced. But it is plain that the faculty of spoken language alone is so complicated as to call into play almost all the elementary powers which the mind possesses, memory, imagination, association, judgment, and volition.

—William James[1]

*A*s soon as Bill Lowery left his home, he realized something was wrong. He had woken up like any other morning, said good morning to his wife and his son, and joined them for breakfast. It had been an early morning. The night before he had studied hard on a list of medical terms and their meanings for a sales pitch that day, dozens of new products from stethoscopes to electroencephalographs to sphygmomanometers. At least the names of products were accompanied by their pictures, so that memorizing the names was tedious yet manageable. While shaving in front of the bathroom mirror, Bill tried to cram the last few words in his mind by mentally linking the words to their pictures.

Getting into his car, Bill's neighbor mentioned to him the exciting news that his encyclopedia had a litter of nine dogs. Bill first assumed he had

1

misheard, after all, the coffee had not quite woken him up yet. But when he arrived at work, he walked to his desk and heard his junior co-workers joking about teaching old dogs new trumpets. Bill guessed he was just slightly confused, perhaps because of all that memorizing of words and their meanings the night before. He struggled throughout the morning, but around lunchtime, he realized that it was not that he had misheard his neighbor, nor that he had misunderstood his co-workers, but that something more serious was going on. Waiting for the elevator to arrive for his lunch break, Bill's colleague asked him: "Do you know a good place to have some dinosaur?" Bill knew all too well that dinosaurs do not get served for lunch, and he was also too aware his colleague hardly ever joked. Now he was quite certain something was wrong. Even more confused than he already had been so far, Bill stepped into the elevator, and while going down to the main floor, he overheard his colleagues being involved in an animated conversation.

> "Man, the Dodgers teeth the Giants last name. They almost lost it too if sacks hadn't hit that luggage running home in the night."
> "Oh, I'm a saddle deserts try saying man anyway, but her son movies absolutely candles."

Bewildered, Bill realized the meaning of words so common to him now seemed to be slipping away. Words that used to be meaningful started to become meaningless. What once seemed so obvious was now so confusing. For Bill, language had become an intricate spaghetti of words and word meanings. What used to be a simple connection between linguistic symbols and what these symbols refer to was now a broken connection between words and their meanings. From one day to the next, *encyclopedia* started to mean "Labrador," *trumpets* "tricks," and *dinosaur* "lunch." The words and the world had lost their sense for him. Bill was lost in words.

Bill Lowery is the main character in "Wordplay,"[2] for me one of the most memorable episodes of the *Twilight Zone* series, a television sequence that brought together science fiction, suspense, and psychology. Imagine waking up one morning, and what you always thought was a word for an object is no more. How would you communicate with your loved ones? When would you find out that words do not carry the meanings you were used to? What if you enthusiastically say "Good morning!" to your neighbor when you head off to work, and she looks back quizzically and responds, "Oxygen mask to feet too!" You get in your car and slow down for the red stop sign you see every morning at the house block on your way to work that reads in white block letters: *SPROUT*. You order your morning coffee, and the cashier completes the transaction saying "One flower, February." When you arrive at work, your colleague asks you with genuine interest "how colorless your green ideas were" and when you ask her what she means, she responds friendly: "But do they sleep furiously?" In other words, what if the anguish of the needle swims to plates with volcanoes that sniff over the mud? What if the ship of the macaroni does not jump along the table? Would the nozzle of freedom banana ships to escape from nobody's dolphin anguish? I guess you get the comma.

Toward the end of "Wordplay," Bill realizes the world has gone linguistically mad, or rather that Bill himself has. Nobody understands what he means, and Bill does not understand what the world means. In the last scene of the episode, Bill looks desperate. His linguistic world has collapsed. He sits on the bed in his son's bedroom wondering how to make sense of the word mess. How would he reconnect these words to their right meanings again? He then finds his son's picture book, the one any child and parent are so familiar with. Bill opens the picture book, points at the picture of a dog and carefully reads the word underneath the picture: *Wednesday*. *Wednesday* apparently means "dog." Bill starts to relearn language, linking all the words of his now-meaningless vocabulary to all the concepts and actions that used to make it meaningful.

When I watched the "Wordplay" episode for the first time, I was first and foremost intrigued. I tried to imagine the confusion when you suddenly realize that what seems to be so common is suddenly so foreign. The sounds that Bill heard came through, he was able to make words out of those sounds, and he was even able to arrange those words in a grammatical structure. What failed was Bill's ability to always assign the right meaning to those words. Sometimes he seemed to get it right, and other times he got confused. How would Bill's mind make sense out of words that used to be so common to him, and how do we, humans, do this?

In addition to being intrigued, I was also alarmed. How would we know that Bill was wrong, and the people who talked to him were right? What if my mind had started to lose the linguistic reality because the word *dinosaur* does actually mean an opportunity around 12 o'clock in the afternoon to have a midday meal? How can I know the words in my mind actually make sense? How did I know that the meaning of *coffee cup* is the same meaning my wife gives to the same linguistic symbols? Perhaps the connotations she has with a coffee cup (she prefers tea) are very different from the meaning I assign to a coffee cup (I am an avid coffee addict).

How would I know that the meanings of the words in my mind were the *right* meanings? And if they were not the right meanings, when would I find out that I had gone linguistically mad? Perhaps the utterances I used in my conversations with the intention of saying one thing were perceived by my environment as saying something totally different. Perhaps my friends and family just tried to make sense out of my words, but the sense they made was different than my sense. How would I know? The "Wordplay" episode kept me awake at night. It kept me thinking for a while. In fact, it kept me thinking for an entire academic career, as a linguist, as a psychologist, as a cognitive scientist, and as an artificial intelligence researcher.

7 BILLION BILL LOWERYS

"Wordplay" may seem like fiction, with the fictional character Bill Lowery, in an episode of a science fiction series, but there are people in a situation similar to Bill's. Actually, there are many of them. Approximately 353,000 new people every single day experience what Bill Lowery experienced. These people struggle finding the right meaning for the words they hear. In fact, their condition is even worse than Bill's—or perhaps theirs is better, depending how you look at it. Whereas Bill knew the word but found a wrong meaning being assigned to it, these 353,000 people hear random sound combinations in unfamiliar words and have no idea what meaning belongs to these sound combinations. Each of these 353,000 people see somebody staring them in the eyes and uttering sound sequences, but they have no idea what those sounds mean. The condition these people struggle with today will be experienced by another 353,000 people tomorrow. And another 353,000 individuals the day after tomorrow.

Such a linguistic virus may sound worrisome, but the good news is that the condition of the 353,000 individuals experiencing this daily improves over time, for every single one of them. Soon they do not even notice they had difficulty attaching meaning to words, and after several months, their loved ones notice obvious signs of improvement. After two years the condition is typically gone. And after several years, these people do not even recall ever having had a condition similar to that of Bill Lowery. They don't have any recollection of the difficulty extracting meaning from words.

As if the 353,000 new cases of people experiencing symptoms similar to Bill Lowery's were not already worrisome enough, the situation is actually considerably worse. There is an epidemic of this condition among some 7 billion people worldwide at one point in their lifetime, who had difficulty assigning meaning to words. Each one of them was once challenged with the task of extracting meaning out of sound combinations, finding meaning behind words such as *encyclopedia*, *dinosaur*, and *Wednesday*. These 7 billion people encountered the experience of not being able to link words to their meaning; they then mastered that skill and kept those words and meanings in mind.

And you were one of them. Yes, that's right! One day you were one of those 353,000 people who were confronted with some random sound sequences that turned out to be language. And the good news is that you overcame the struggle and now belong to the group of 7 billion people who managed to make sense out of words and their sounds.

Any baby, born anywhere in the world, was once confronted with combinations of sounds that were initially meaningless, but later became very meaningful. Around 350,000 newborns every day hear people in their environments, most notably their happy parents, utter seemingly random sounds and will try to make meaning out of what later turn out to be words in their language. When these newborns become able to make meaning out of those sounds, they start using those sounds to communicate meaning to others. And after they acquire these speech-comprehension and speech-production skills, many—but not all—years later acquire the skill of assigning meaning to the representations of these sounds in the form of written characters when learning how to read. How do they do this? How do they keep all those words in mind?

IT'S PERSONAL

I have been fascinated by language, I must admit. I find it fascinating to hear somebody speak, utter sound combinations from which it turns out to be possible to extract meaning. I find it fascinating that the scribbles you are currently perceiving allow you to make sense of what I am trying to say. Imagine you were asked to explain to somebody who does not yet speak or is unable to speak how to articulate the sound of a word: "Place your tongue against the back of your front teeth, then move your tongue down while you form the vowel sound [u], then hit the edges of the back of your tongue against the back of your upper teeth, then push air through your front teeth, and close the airstream suddenly by hitting the tip of your tongue against your front teeth. That's how you pronounce the word *thirst*." Speech pathologists who train patients who suffered from a stroke that impaired their speech abilities need to go over these steps. Slowly but surely, the patient relearns how to pronounce the sounds of each word. But any four-year-old is able to pronounce words without any such instructions. It comes natural to them.

I have been fascinated by the chunking process of getting words out of the long stream of sounds. The average speaker does not stop and pause at each and every word, but rambles on, gluing one word against the other. Sometimes that glue seems like superglue, making it almost impossible to disentangle the words of the speaker. And yet, we typically have little difficulty getting the right words and the right meaning out of the person who is talking to us.

I have also been fascinated with the process of getting the shapes presented on a blank page into words into sentences into discourse. If you look at each of these shapes we call letters, there is nothing really that tells us what the meaning of these letter combinations is. We are even able to do this when the shapes are not consistent, for instance with different fonts or different kinds of handwriting. We fixate on a page with printed letters, scramble them together, and read from one page to the next.

But perhaps I have been most fascinated by how we get meaning out of language. For me knowing the meaning of a word is the heart of communication. The sentence may seem grammatical, and the intentions of the speaker may seem so right, yet without understanding the meaning of the word, communication falls apart, as the Bill Lowery episode shows. But with this fascination for the meaning of words come questions. How do we learn the meaning of words? How are we able to remember all those words and their meanings?

I have been playing games with language. I sometimes play the predict-the-word game with myself. Can I predict the next word of a speaker when she starts to pause midway through a sentence? Often I think I am right. I guessed the word the speaker intended to say. But how am I able to know without crediting myself with some telepathy power (which I am sure I do not have). Or I try to predict the word that would follow at the end of the sentence. Whenever I am reading a book, and the sentence has not ended at the end of a page, I play the game of guessing what the remainder of the sentence will look like on the next page. Again, often I think I am right in my predictions, but then I also quickly realize this might be a confirmation bias (we often like to be right, and anytime we are, we would like to emphasize our success and ignore our failures).[3]

"Wordplay" started my fascination with language, cognition, and computation. I went to college and was captivated by the fact that language could move people. I wondered how arbitrary combinations of sounds and letters could make people happy, sad, or disgusted. How is it that some word combinations on a page can bring somebody to tears, whereas other word combinations can nail somebody to their seat and—page after page—immerse them in the story they read. I started to get interested in the structure of stories.[4] Researchers had come up with grammars for stories, just like grammars for sentences.[5] And indeed, when you look at fairy tales, detectives, thrillers, James Bond movies, and Disney movies, they all follow a somewhat-regular storyline, whereby a happy situation is disturbed by a villain, whom the hero then fights in the climax of the story, after which the happy situation returns (or is even happier than before with the hero having found his true love)—words that form meaningful sentences that are somewhat predictable, that form meaningful stories that are somewhat predictable.

When I started my PhD, I wondered how we give meaning to texts. I studied how the human mind processes long sequences of words in texts. But I also wondered whether what the human mind does can be implemented in an artificial mind. Might it be possible that computers can understand language the same way humans do? I ran psychological experiments in which I asked participants to press a key each time they processed a word, in order to find out how fast it took for them to understand each word in a text; I ran experiments in which I monitored people's eye gaze when they read a story.[6] I carefully monitored what people were looking at when reading a sentence and how many milliseconds they fixated on each word. It would help me understand how people extracted meaning from language. But it also helped me to build computational algorithms that would mimic the processes humans go through when comprehending language.

When I became a professor, I worked on intelligent tutoring systems, computers that could teach students topics such as conceptual physics and computer literacy through conversations.[7] The computer heard the student say something, processed the information by extracting meaning from the student's utterances, and responded to it in natural language. The computer did not know what the student was going to say, how the student was going to say it, but yet was able to respond in a natural way to the student. In the meantime, it adjusted its pedagogical moves to the student it was talking to. By building these artificial intelligence algorithms, I was part of a team of researchers that developed conversational agents that had conversations with their human users, without knowing in advance what a user would say. We found that not only did these human-computer interactions yield human-like conversations, but they also led to students learning from these interactions.

I have also had the opportunity on a range of other projects to investigate mental representations of language. Do we think in words, in pictures, in sounds perhaps? And how much meaning can be extracted from language? I had the opportunity to conduct experiments tapping into psychological processing when participants processed language. We monitored how fast people read by measuring button-press responses. We used eye-tracking technologies to see what pupil movement people made. We asked people to wear caps with electrodes that recorded brain activity in order to understand how information travels through the brain when people process language. And we built computer models that incorporated the information we found in experiments. We wondered about mental representations. How do we capture the meaning of a word in our mind? Is there a little homunculus, a tiny little mini-me that whispers the meaning of a word we read or hear? And who informs this homunculus? Another mini-me? The question of how humans get meaning out of language has haunted me since first watching "Wordplay."

GAVAGAI

There are some 6,500 languages spoken in the world, though some two thousand languages only have less than a thousand speakers. Imagine being a linguist who specializes in foreign languages. Your university sends you out on a mission in a rain forest far, far away to study the unknown language of a tribe. After a long flight, you arrive in the foreign country and travel for days to finally encounter the tribe. You set up camp a safe distance from the tribe and assemble your camera and directional microphone, ready to collect the language data for your mission. You sit down with your notebook, headphones secured to your head, and listen to the natives talking to each other. All you hear are sounds that are very foreign to you. Until something exciting happens. A rabbit scurries by, and the native says "Gavagai." You immediately write down in your notebook the words "Rabbit" or "Look, a rabbit." This is only a tentative translation that needs to be checked, as you do not know whether the native said "animal," "white," or "rabbit." In hindsight, you realize the native could have meant a large number of things. He could have meant "Hey guys, dinner!" "That's so cute!" "That's not a canary!" or "Look, a monkey!" (if the native happened to have poor eyesight).[8]

One way to find out what *gavagai* means is by asking the native. You draw a picture of a rabbit and walk up to the native. Now remember, you do not speak the language. You could look at the native and observe his gestures when watching the picture of a rabbit. This is, of course, tricky. You may be able to rule out some potential meanings, but the native may gesture that the picture means "gavagai" while you still do not know whether he means "rabbit," "animal," or "white." Moreover, gestures turn out to be confusing. Even for the societies whose languages we do know, gestures can mean a variety of things. The V-sign in the United States might mean peace, but in the United Kingdom, Australia, and South Africa, the same gesture with the back of the hand facing the other person is quite insulting. And the same is true for the native and the gestures he makes. You cannot make sense of them.

But you are in luck. In asking "Gavagai?" in the presence of the picture of a rabbit, the native responds with "evet" and "yok." And the native has said these two words often enough for you to conclude that these mean "yes" and "no," but you have no idea which is which. You can try to echo the native's words. If he says "evet" more often than "yok," you may conclude that "evet" means "yes." You may also try to respond yourself with either "evet" or "yok" to the native's remarks. The word that does not result in an angry native is the better candidate for "yes." But really, your efforts all result in working hypotheses. They are estimated guesses on the true meaning of words, making you wonder: Do we really understand each other, and how do we know?

The gavagai problem was posed by Willard Van Orman Quine, an influential American philosopher and logician of the twentieth century.[9] The problem exemplifies that an infinite number of hypotheses about word meaning are possible given the word that is given, a problem that any language-learning child is confronted with. But how does the child know what to guess as the meaning of a word?

In fact, we can take the gavagai example a step further. A child hears somebody say "gavagai!" The expression could be rather meaningless, as when somebody's is sneezing. No need to extract meaning out of the sneezing— the sound is totally arbitrary and should not be further interpreted. But let's assume that *gavagai* constitutes some linguistic expression.[10] Has the child heard the sentence "gav a guy" or the word *gavagai*? And if the child heard the word *gavagai*, would this refer to what the child sees when hearing the word *gavagai* or perhaps to the speaker, who meant "My throat hurts!" or "I am bored!" And if the word refers to the rabbit scurrying by, does *gavagai* mean a verb (as in *run*), an adjective (as in *fluffy*), or a noun (as in *rabbit*)? And do we actually know the intention of the speaker when uttering the word *gavagai*? Was the speaker asking, "Is that a rabbit?" commanding, "Fetch the rabbit!" solemnly saying, "Pray for all rabbits!" or simply making a statement, "That's a rabbit!"

The gavagai example brings up the important question of how a language-learning child is able to assign the right meaning to the right word. How is a child able to keep those words in mind?

TRAINING, INSTINCT, NETWORK, AND GROUNDING

Imagine you wake up one morning, like Bill Lowery did, and you are lost for words. Or you are in the middle of the rain forest listening to the foreign sounds and gestures of the native. Or imagine you wake up like one of the 353,000 newborns today, who need to assign meaning to words. What would you do? How do you know the meaning of words? Granted, as a baby you do not have much of a choice, but still, what can you do? How do humans acquire language, assigning meaning to seemingly random sounds? Over more than a century, scientists from different disciplines, ranging from linguistics to psychology, from philosophy to anthropology—and later—from computer science to artificial intelligence, have investigated this question and have provided various answers. These answers tell us something about our communicative system called language, about our thought processes in the mind, our mental machinery called the brain, and how silicon chips might simulate these processes.

One answer as to how children learn the meaning of words may come from training. When a baby carefully utters "baba," her parents look with full anticipation and excitement, encouraging the child to say more. The environment, the child's parents, motivate the baby and steer her in the right linguistic directions. When the first "mama" is uttered, parents have become ecstatic. By receiving these pieces of positive feedback—"Yes, that is right! Good job: ma-ma!"—and by mimicking behavior from the environment—"mmmma-mmma"—the child learns how to speak. She may start out with a blank slate, but by turning on their vocal apparatus, by hearing so many words in their environment, and by getting all the praise for every utterance the child expresses, she slowly but surely starts to acquire natural language.

Humans learning language is not very different from dolphins performing tricks in the water. When dolphins jump out of the water, make a pirouette, and dive back into the deep end, they are rewarded with sardines. They learn because of rewards. Children will unlikely learn verbal behavior with sardines or other fish as a reward, but the reward of being comprehended may suffice. Corrections in their verbal performance—"No that is not a rabbit. That is a tiger"—or rewards—"Yes, yes, that is a rabbit, rabbit. Good job!"—will help children make their linguistic pirouettes. The praise from their caregivers helps some 353,000 children every day learn the meaning of words.

But words are hardly ever uttered in isolation. Usually, we hear or read words in sentences, and those sentences determine the meaning of a word. So rather than asking questions about the meaning of *gavagai*, we should first better understand the bigger picture of how children understand language, how they understand the grammar of a sentence. The ability of early language users to understand grammatical structures is shared across the world. Whether the child is born in the United States, China, India, or Brazil, children are all able to pick up on the grammatical structure and recreate new grammatical sentences. It almost seems like the human brain has an instinct for language. The idea that the answer for language acquisition lies in the human brain, rather than in the environment, is interesting because any child across the world is able to acquire language no matter how little or how much linguistic stimuli the environment provides and how much feedback is provided. We therefore must be born with a language instinct.

The brain as an explanation for language acquisition is interesting, but really what children do when learning the meaning of words is perform computations on input and output, just like computers. In artificial intelligence, artificial neural networks are used for this purpose. Their structure is similar to that of a human brain. Large amounts of input—numbers, pictures, words, sounds, and any other data—are pushed through pathways in the network's architecture. At the end of the pathways, output awaits. So perhaps the human brain is like a computer. Words are the input, and meaning is the output. By continuously being exposed to a word and its meaning, a child over time forms a fast track in their neural network to link the word to its meaning. It takes some training in the beginning, with some mistakes being made, but over time, the tracks become stronger and stronger. It is almost like the unbeaten path in the woods. Initially, there is no path, but over time—with more and more data walking over the paths—the paths become clearer, and a fast track emerges.

But neither the training nor the instinct nor the network computations as an answer to how we keep those words in mind are the answers provided by the case of Bill Lowery or the gavagai example. Bill Lowery dealt with the situation by sitting down, desperately picking up his son's picture book, and linking each individual word to its corresponding meaning. Obviously, we do not learn words from picture books, but it is perfectly plausible that we learn the meaning of words by linking the word to its object in the outside world ("*That* is a rabbit," our parents point out to us when we—as two-year-olds—wonder about the animal in front of us). It makes sense that learning the meaning of words can be described as bringing their corresponding pictures to mind, by grounding the word in perceptual experiences.

Think of any concept that you can think of, and there likely is a picture that accompanies that word. If you think of your favorite color, you don't think of the words *red* or *blue*—if these happen to be your favorite color—but you mentally see the actual color. The word *firecracker* goes with the perceptual simulation of a large audible bang in your mind; when you read *needle*, you might perceptually simulate the sharp end touching your skin. Or consider the word *lemon*. You may mentally see the yellow color; you may mentally feel the rubbery skin when touching a lemon. But you also mentally taste the lemon. When you read that I cut a lemon in half, then took one half in my right hand, opened my mouth, and took a bite out of that lemon, it is likely that saliva pools in your mouth while you "feel" the sour taste in your mind. It is as if the meaning of words is synonymous to the perceptual simulations of those words.

These four explanations—training, instinct, network, and grounding—have been commonly provided as explanations of how we keep those words in mind, how humans are avid language users seemingly effortlessly acquiring language at a young age.

THE ELEPHANT IN THE ROOM

We keep those words in mind by training our linguistic skills and being re-warded on our path to linguistic success. Or by taking advantage of the part of our brains that specialize in language, a uniquely human language instinct. Or by the computational machinery in our minds that crunch the input to the output. Or by linking the word to the perceptual interpretation.

There are many scientific studies outlining these explanations, and many popular science books summarizing the findings. All these other books have already provided answers to how humans keep words in mind, and why humans excel in language. We acquire language *because* we undergo the training, we have the brains, and we take advantage of the computations or form perceptual interpretations. But this book will not advocate one of these answers. Instead it will advocate a complementary alternative, one that has not been paid attention to enough, and has implications for linguistics, psychology, and artificial intelligence alike.

Let me emphasize that I would be the last person to argue the four explanations for knowing language given in the literature are in any way wrong. I think these explanations are to different degrees true and backed up with extensive scientific evidence.[11] I am simply arguing that there is one aspect to language behavior that is not addressed sufficiently in the linguistic, psychological, and artificial intelligence literature. And that aspect turns out to be the elephant in the room. A big one. A giant elephant that we often tend to ignore. Before I define that elephant in the room, let me illustrate the logic that comes from the explanations for knowing language.

Imagine you just signed up for an experiment in which I present you with a sequence of two symbols, *x* and *o*. These symbols are presented in a sequence, and at the end of the sequence, you are asked to choose which of the two symbols is most likely to follow that sequence on the position of a question mark. Ready?

x o x o x o x o x o x o x o x o x o x o ?

That was easy. You most likely would put an *x* in the position of the question mark. Every *x* is followed by an *o*, which is followed by an *x*. So if the sequence ends with an *o*, it is no rocket science to guess the next symbol to be an *x*. Another sequence is not too complex either:

X O O X O O X X O O O X X O O O X X X O O O O ?

You would most likely choose an *x*. Every *n* number of *x*'s is followed by *n+1* *o*'s, whereby the number of *x*'s increases by one after being repeated once. We can ask ourselves the question of how you have been able to choose the correct answer. You could have received a reward for your performance: a sardine (as in the case of the dolphin earlier) or the praise from an excited parent (as in the case of a language-learning child). You could also have guessed the *x* correctly because you just have an *x-o* instinct you were born with. You are able to manipulate *x*'s and *o*'s in different constructions, and you are equally successfully able to extract such construction when you see them. Or you have computed the probabilities of *x*'s and *o*'s by having run a series of computations and estimated the likelihood of an *o* following an *x*. Or you may have attached pictures to the *x*'s and *o*'s or imagined placing the *x*'s and *o*'s on a spectrum based on this mental *x-o* spectrum. Indeed, getting to the conclusion of the sequence may have come from training, instinct, computation, or grounding. But let me get back to the elephant in the room, by considering one final sequence of *x*'s and *o*'s. What is the next symbol at the end of the sequence, an *x* or an *o*?

X O O X X X O X O X O X X O O X O O X X X X O X X ?

Guessed it? Did you select an *x* or an *o*? You couldn't choose? Why not? If you got stuck, I don't blame you. The question is, why didn't you come up with an answer like you did with the other two sequences of *x*'s and *o*'s. Was it the training, your instinct, the computations, or your perceptual simulations that let you down? Of course not! Even though these four explanations may have played some role, the reason you could not complete the sequence is simply because there was no obvious pattern in the data!

Completing (or not completing) the sequence of symbols was possible because of the sequence of symbols itself! The same logic can be followed for assigning meaning to words, and for language acquisition at large. The four proposals that have commonly served as explanations for language processing seem to have inverted cause and effect. What has often been considered as the cause for the language system is really the effect of the language system. Training, instinct, computation, and perception help to *discover* language, just like the sequence of symbols allows for being discovered.

I am not the first who would like to draw attention to the language system, and the reversing of cause and effect in the explanation for how humans are so good at language. Terrence Deacon in his dazzling book *The Symbolic Species* already asks for our attention to the language system.

> There is another possibility that has been almost entirely overlooked, and it is the point of the remainder of this chapter to explore it. I think [many linguists] have articulated a central conundrum about language learning, but they offer an answer that inverts cause and effect. They assert that the source of prior support for language acquisition must originate from *inside* the brain, on the unstated assumption that there is no other possible source. But there is an alternative: that the extra support for language learning is vested neither in the brain of the child nor in the brains of parents or teachers, but outside the brains, in language itself.[12]

But Deacon does not explain how meaning can be extracted from the language system itself, because his message gets lost in the neurobiology, evolutionary theory, and semiotics of symbolic thought. Deacon argued that humans, and no other species, have a unique capacity for symbolic thought. That capacity is not the consequence of the evolution of the brain but is equally the consequence of the language system. According to Deacon, brain and language coevolved.[13] The idea of the language system playing a role in language acquisition and language processing puts an exciting new perspective on how we keep those words in mind!

Language as an explanation for language acquisition? That seems like putting the linguistic cart before the cognitive horse. And yet this is exactly what this book will argue. I will demonstrate that what seems to be an arbitrary communication system, with arbitrary characters and sounds that become words, and arbitrary meanings for those words, actually is a well-organized system that has evolved over tens of thousands of years to make communication as efficient as it is. What is needed for humans to acquire language is for humans to recognize and discover the patterns in our communication system.

This book is about the ant and the beach from the prologue. This book is about Bill Lowery finding meaning again for the words that got lost. This book is about gavagai and the rabbit that scurries by. This book is about the elephant in the room.

I'll take you on a journey through the language system, our human brain, our human mind, and will look at artificial minds. That journey will take you to linguistics, the discipline that studies language; to cognitive psychology, the discipline that studies the human mind; to neuroscience, the discipline that studies the human brain; but also to artificial intelligence and computer science, disciplines that study artificial minds. You will see how many predictions you can make solely on the basis of the organization of the language system. You will see that we do not need much more than an ability to pick up patterns, in order to be able to understand and produce language.

It sometimes helps if the introduction of a book includes some cues with regards to its organization. As a writer, I am hesitant to provide such cues, but as a reader, I know how welcome they may be. Chapter 2 ("Language") provides an introduction to the language system, Chapter 3 ("Guess") to the psychology of language. After these introductory chapters, four chapters—chapter 4 ("Training"), chapter 5 ("Instinct"), chapter 6 ("Network"), and chapter 7 ("Grounding")—will be devoted to explaining how we keep those words in mind, how humans acquire language so fast and use it so well. Chapters 8 ("Shortcut") and 9 ("Patterns") place these four explanations in perspective and pave the way for a fifth explanation, outlined in the following four chapters. Chapters 10 ("Sound"), 11 ("Order"), and 12 ("Company") give examples of how language creates meaning and how this could serve as an explanation on how we keep those words in mind. Chapter 13 ("Bootstrapping") provides a theoretical framework for this explanation, and for the findings discussed in the previous three chapters. Finally, chapter 14 ("Avenues") places the book in a broader framework by arguing that fundamental research may sometimes look like it is stuck in an ivory tower, but hardly ever is.

• 2 •

Language

There is a decided advantage in beginning our investigation of language by restricting our attention to the form and behavior of words, since the essential phenomena in the dynamics of words are far more clearly apparent and readily apprehended than those of the smaller or larger speech-elements.

—George Kingsley Zipf[1]

*W*e can ask the question how we keep those words in mind, as the first chapter did, but how many of those words are we actually talking about? How many words does the average person know? A thousand? Five thousand? Perhaps as many as ten thousand? Even more than that?

Let's try to answer this question by placing it in perspective. An average one-year-old knows about twenty words, and a two-year-old knows about 250 words. I guess it is safe to assume you know more than 250 words. Now, a three-year-old knows about one thousand words, and by the time the child goes to school, her vocabulary has grown to two thousand words. We can also safely assume that the number does not consistently multiply tenfold over time as is the case with the one- and two-year-olds, quadruple as is the case with the two- and three-year-olds, or double as is the case with the three- and five-year-olds. If that were to be the case, it would mean that you know at least double the number of words you knew last year.

Even though any parent knows that their five-year-old is already quite talkative, how does our vocabulary size compare with that of a five-year-old? Perhaps estimating our own vocabulary size by comparing it with that of a five-year-old is awkward. We now know the lower bound, some two thousand words, but we do not know the upper bound, which must be much higher.

Works—but he didn't. If we double (or triple) the size of the *Collected Works*, the number of words increases until it plateaus at approximately thirty-five thousand words that he knew but didn't use. So the estimate of the number of words Shakespeare knew (but did not yet use) consists of the original more than thirty thousand words he used in his work, plus the thirty-five thousand he did not use but could have used had he written more, totaling no less than sixty-five thousand words!

We already concluded that Shakespeare was a linguistic magician. The number of about sixty-five thousand word types he knew is thus impressive but may not apply to the average person, people like you and me. All we know is that the estimate for our vocabulary size lies somewhere between that of a five-year-old (some two thousand words) and that of Shakespeare (some sixty-five thousand words). How would we then measure the number of words we know, as people who use language but will never write a literary masterpiece that will be remembered for hundreds of years?

Researchers estimate the vocabulary size of a third grader to be about two thousand words and that of a seventh grader to be around 4,760 words.[6] These numbers are impressive in the sense that a seventh grader knows about 14 percent of the vocabulary of Shakespeare. The only problem is that other researchers estimate the number of words more in the line of twenty-five thousand for a third grader and fifty-one thousand for a seventh grader! These findings demonstrate two things: first, it shows researchers do not always agree when it comes to estimates, and secondly, that when they make estimates, the range between estimates can be large.

Let's look at the total number of words we know in more detail. A group of colleagues of mine conducted an experiment with over two hundred thousand participants.[7] Interestingly, they did not ask the participants how many words they knew, but instead came up with a very clever approach. They presented participants with a random list of one hundred words, 66 percent real words and 33 percent words that looked real, but did not exist. The invented words such as *mirm*, *molk*, and *muntence* could have been part of the English language—whereas a word like *grzgremrz* could not. For one, I would not know how to pronounce the word and would think it is a representation of some kind of sneeze sound, a non-English sneeze. The reason the research team came up with these foil words was to counter a problem in their experiment: when asking participants whether they know a word, participants can easily fool the researchers (consciously or unconsciously) by saying they know a word even if they actually don't. And this is where the foil words came in.

To correct for overconfidence, the proportion of times that participants said they recognized a nonword as a word was subtracted from their score for recognizing a word as a word. The "fooling score" was subtracted from the "actual score." This had a number of advantages. It kept the participants on their toes because they could not have known the included words because they were invented. Also, including nonwords controlled for participants who tried to fool the experimenters. By presenting these long word lists and correcting for overconfidence, the researchers estimated that a twenty-year-old knows around forty-two thousand words and a sixty-year-old around forty-six thousand. This would mean that we know about forty thousand to fifty thousand words. Quite impressive, I think!

However, the estimates of forty thousand to fifty thousand words did not include multiword expressions. *Washing machines* and *salad spinner* were not included. Let's estimate that these multiword expressions cover around 10 percent of the total vocabulary. This raises the counts for the twenty-year-old to forty-six thousand and the sixty-year-old to fifty-two thousand words! But even this number is an underestimate, as names and acronyms were not included in the experiment either. It is difficult to make estimates on the number of names (including *Bill Lowery, Shakespeare, Tolkien*) and acronyms (including *YOLO, ASAP, FAQ*) that we know, but databases have been constructed with the names of eleven thousand famous people, so it would be fair to increase the vocabulary size to fifty-seven thousand to sixty-three thousand words. This means that we—you and I—know about the same number of words that William Shakespeare knew, a total of sixty thousand different words![8]

Obviously, these vocabulary sizes are only estimates. There are various factors that will influence the count, such as whether somebody is an avid reader who reads one novel every week, or dislikes reading unless it is absolutely necessary, or the readers who read the *Lord of the Rings* trilogy four times, and those who argue you might save yourself some time by watching the *Lord of the Rings* movies. And what do I actually mean by "knowing a word" in the first place? Is recognizing a word as an actual word in a language the same as being able to give a definition of the meaning of a word? And is guessing the meaning of a word when reading the same as knowing how to use the word in language production? And what does it mean if somebody "knows" more than one language? Does a non-native speaker of English know double the number, because for every English word, she also knows the translation? Or one can raise the question about the relationship between the number of words and their meanings—speaking a different language may double the number of words, but not the number of meanings. The point here is not so much whether you should be proud beating the vocabulary size of a five-year-old or honored your vocabulary size is not that much different from that of Shakespeare or Tolkien; the point is that what we commonly take for granted—the words and those meanings that naturally come to us—should not at all be taken for granted, because our vocabulary size is truly astonishing.

WORD MEANING

If you were already exhilarated by the number of words you know, I have more good news to share. The estimate of the number of words was based on the number of different sequences of characters printed on a page, thereby assuming that each word has one meaning. But that is not quite the way we know the meaning of a word. After all, a word can easily have more than one meaning, and should thus be counted as different words that look the same, but are in fact different. Let's think of some: a soccer *ball* and a Cinderella *ball*, a rock *band* and a rubber *band*, a flying *bat* and a baseball *bat*, a filing *cabinet* and a government *cabinet*, lighting a *match* and a boxing *match*, to *lie* about your whereabouts and to *lie* on a bed, being *kind* and a *kind* of fish, a cherry *pit* and digging a *pit*, a high *pitch* and a baseball *pitch*, the British *pound* and a *pound* of meat, a *mole* on her face and a *mole* under the ground, a horse *race* and the human *race*, left or *right* and the human *right*, a wedding *ring* and phone *ring*, a shoe *sole* and a fillet of *sole*, the *spring* that arrives and a coiled *spring*, a law*suit* and a man's *suit*, a restaurant *tip* and the *tip* of the tongue, the *trunk* of an elephant and the *trunk* of the car, shoes on your *feet* and twenty-four inches in two *feet*, the back*yard* and three feet in one *yard*. These are all words with more than one meaning.

You may argue that these are carefully selected examples of some special words in the English language. But this is not at all true. If I open the Oxford English dictionary on any random page—as you can see, I am rather old-fashioned when it comes to books—I do not find one single entry word with just one meaning. On the contrary, every word entry lists far more than one meaning, and we generally know at least some of those. There are clearly some true record holders in terms of the number of meanings they have. The word *set* has 464 meanings, *run* 396 meanings, *go* 368, *take* 343, *stand* 334, *get* 289, *turn* 288, *put* 268, *fall* 264, and *strike* 250 meanings. The word *set* is the winner for English. In fact, the word is listed as a Guinness World Record. I will not fill the next pages with the hundreds of meanings of the word *set*, but let's take a subset (no pun intended).

1. put, lay, or stand (something) in a specified place or position. *"Delaney set the mug of tea down."*
2. put or bring into a specified state. *"The Home Secretary set in motion a review of the law."*
3. adjust (a clock or watch), typically to show the right time. *"Set your watch immediately to local time at your destination."*
4. harden into a solid or semi-solid state. *"Cook for a further thirty-five minutes until the filling has set."*

5. (of the sun, moon, or another celestial body) appear to move towards and below the earth's horizon as the earth rotates. *"The sun was setting and a warm red glow filled the sky."*
6. (of a tide or current) take or have a specified direction or course. *"A fair tide can be carried well past Land's End before the stream sets to the north."*
7. start (a fire). *"The school had been broken into and the fire had been set."*
8. (of blossom or a tree) form into or produce (fruit). *"Wait until first flowers have set fruit before planting out the peppers."*
9. sit. *"The rest of them people just set there goggle-eyed for a minute."*
10. a group or collection of things that belong together or resemble one another or are usually found together. *"A set of false teeth."*
11. the way in which something is set, disposed, or positioned. *"The shape and set of the eyes."*
12. a radio or television receiver. *"A TV set."*
13. a collection of scenery, stage furniture, and other articles used for a particular scene in a play or film. *"Sponsorship was necessary to defray the costs of building and painting the set."*
14. an arrangement of the hair when damp so that it dries in the required style. *"A shampoo and set."*
15. a cutting, young plant, or bulb used in the propagation of new plants.
16. a young fruit that has just formed.
17. the last coat of plaster on a wall.
18. the amount of spacing in type controlling the distance between letters.
19. the width of a piece of type.
20. group (pupils or students) in sets according to ability.

Some of these meanings may seem archaic, some more modern, others too subtle, perhaps artificially increasing the total number to 464 meanings. If you feel that the meanings that seem too archaic should be dismissed, or the differences between some of the other meanings seemed too subtle, keep in mind that there were another 440 to choose from! It is obvious that many words do not have that many meanings. The word *the* for instance "only" has twenty-five.

Now let's assume of all the sixty thousand words you know, you do not know all of their meanings—464 in some extreme cases—but only two. It is then fair to say that you may know sixty thousand printed words, but you know 120,000 word-meaning relations. The amount of language you know measured in words was already astonishing, but when measured in word-meaning relationships, it just became even more astonishing.

If you managed to identify the subtleties in meaning—for instance, pointing out that some of the meanings seemed too subtle—you showed the ability of placing meaning in context. And if you managed to place meaning in context, you showed evidence of mastering the relations between meaning, so-called semantic relations. Those semantic relations are interesting, because they are part of the language we know, and yet are far less obvious than the number of words that we can count. For instance, we know when two words overlap in meaning (e.g., *happy* and *glad*)—so-called synonyms—when words have an opposite meaning (e.g., *happy* and *sad*)—so-called antonyms—and when the meaning of a word is a component of that of another word (e.g., *ecstatic* is a kind of *happy*)—so-called hyponyms. Simply put, the antonym of *synonym* is *antonym*, the hypernym of *hyponym* is *hypernym*, and the hyponym of *hypernym* is *hyponym*. *Meronym* is a meronym of *holonym* and *holonym* is a holonym of *meronym*. The point is not to confuse you with some originally ancient Greek words that you can now add to your already sixty-thousand-word vocabulary, but to highlight the fact that the words we know have different meanings and those meanings share relations that you know (regardless of the terminology that may come with it).

You can try this out yourself: take any word, and think of the first new word that comes to mind. Undoubtedly that word has similarities in the meaning with the initial word you came up with. That is, words and their meanings are not independent entities, but they are part of a larger network of interconnected meanings. For any of the words you read, you are able to estimate their semantic relations. This means that the sixty thousand words you know with their sixty thousand meanings you know operate in a network of $60,000 \times 60,000 = 3,600,000,000$ meanings. If we follow the argument that a word has at least two meanings, the network of word-meaning relations increases to $120,000 \times 120,000 = 14,400,000,000$. That is 14.4 billion word-meaning relationships that are part of the language you know![9]

You could immediately object that this calculation seems rather absurd. It seems silly that any two words have a semantic relationship. Let's take two random words, say *dog* and *spaghetti*, and it is difficult to argue that these two words have a semantic relationship. But the fact that you do know that their semantic relationship is weak proves my point. Moreover, a semantic relationship may seem weak, but often you can easily think of semantic associations that show two semantically unrelated words are not that unrelated altogether. You may have watched Disney's *Lady and the Tramp* and recall the scene in which the two dogs romantically eat a spaghetto (a single noodle of spaghetti). No matter how farfetched two words may seem in meaning, you are able to make up a semantic relationship. Finally, the computations are based on two meanings per word, even though we have seen that many words have more than one meaning. If we assume that a word carries three meanings, the network of word-meaning relationships consists of a total of more than 32 billion connections! The question of how much language we know starts to yield an even-more-impressive answer.

WORD STRUCTURE

By now we have established that our vocabulary size is quite astonishing: sixty thousand words with well over 120,000 meanings that operate in a network of billions of word-meaning relations. But it is worthwhile to make another distinction by introducing the concept of *lemma*, the head word. When we look at a lemma, we see that many lemmas look the same but carry different meanings. When we look up the word *break*, we find different meanings (a total of more than eighty). But there are a range of derivations and inflections of a word. That is, we may know the different meanings of the word *break* as in *my girlfriend and I are on a break*, and *there was a major break in the glass*, and *we went to Florida on Spring Break*, but also the verb *break* as in *I break the glass, I break up with her*, and *I break a new record*. But we have only looked at the five-letter word *break*. The plural of the word *break* (*breaks*) has not yet been counted, and neither has the third-person singular of the verb *break*: *breaks*. And I have not even mentioned the word *broke*, the past tense of *break* (which also happens to be an adverb, as in *I am broke*), or the past participle of the verb *break*, *broken* (which also happens to be an adverb, as in *I am broken*, as well as an adjective, as in *I have a broken heart*). These different forms of the word are important, for you have no difficulties pointing out the ungrammaticality of *he break, yesterday I breaks, there were major break in the glass*, or *my girlfriend and I are on a breaks*.

You may argue that the differences between the first-person conjugation *break* and its third-person *breaks*, as well as the singular noun *break* and its plural *breaks*, should not be taken as separate words in our vocabulary, because they share so much overlap. The fact is, however, that you have the ability to distinguish between the subtleties in meaning between these words, and that in itself adds to your already-impressive language skills.

Word structure, called "morphology" in linguistics, is important for language, not only to determine whether word combinations are grammatical, or to make a plural out of a singular word, but even to form new words. The verb *create* has a form for the third-person singular (*he creates*), can have a past tense (*created*) and a progressive form (*creating*), and we can create a noun out of it (*creation*), which can of course also become plural (*creations*). The same verb can also be extended to *re-create* (and hence *re-creates, re-created, re-creating, re-creation* and *re-creations*).

Let's take this a step further. Take for instance the word *antidisestablishmentarianistically*. It is likely you have never heard this word (in which case you can add it to your sixty-thousand-word vocabulary), and it is equally likely you will never hear it again. But you can assign meaning to this word. Let's break the word apart into so-called morphemes. You probably know the word *establish*, "to put in place." If you know the word *establish*, you can guess what *dis-establish* means, namely, ending the established status of an entity. From here, you can guess what *dis-establish-ment* means, because you are making a noun out of a verb. *Disestablishment* has the more specific meaning of the separation of church and state. *Anti-dis-establish-ment* is not surprisingly the opposition to *disestablishment*. *Antidisestablishmentarian* is an opponent of disestablishment. The movement of the opponent of disestablishment is called *antidisestablishmentarian-ism*. The person in that movement is an *antidisestablishmentarian-ist*, who thus acts *antidisestablishmentarianist-ically*.

The English example already looks quite intimidating, but some other languages like Dutch beat the complexity of *antidisestablishmentarianistically*. A word such as *kindercarnavalsoptochtvoorbereidingswerkzaamhedenplannen* would make a Dutch speaker pause, but not choke. The word means the preparation activity plans for a children's carnival procession. The word *kindercarnavalsoptochtvoorbereidingswerkzaamhedenplannen* can be broken down into smaller parts: *kinder* (*children*) *carnavals* (*possessive of carnaval*) *optocht* (*procession*) *voorbereidings* (*possessive of preparation*) *werk* (*work*) *zaamheden* (*activities*) *plan* (*plan*) *nen* (*plural*).

So even if you do not know a word, being exposed to that word still allows you to extract meaning out of that word. Conversely, morphology in language also allows us to create new words on the fly, words that do not exist in a dictionary. For instance, if you use Twitter, you send *tweets* (neither word existed fifteen years ago). These tweets can be *retweeted* (another word that did not exist until recently). If a tweet gets retweeted, it apparently is *retweetable* (just added another nonexisting word you know). If a tweet does not get retweeted, it is rather *unretweetable* (and another one). As a *tweeter* on Twitter, it may be worthwhile to know when a tweet becomes unretweetable, because it then allows you to estimate the *unretweetability* of your tweets (and yet another new word). Any attempt to go against the unretweetability of your tweets can be considered efforts in favor of *anti-unretweetability* (plus one). And voila, you just added another few words to your vocabulary. Want to try another few for Facebook, Instagram, LinkedIn, or other social media?

But we can take things even further. Let's assume there are 24 percent nouns, 28 percent verbs, 15 percent adjectives, and 23 percent adverbs in the

English language. These estimates differ considerably in the literature, with some arguing there are 37 percent nouns, but this is what I computed myself from a large corpus of English text. We earlier estimated that we know about sixty thousand words. Taking the percentages of word categories and the estimated vocabulary size we know, we can estimate that we know 14,400 nouns, 16,800 verbs, and 9,000 adjectives. If we consider the word forms of these words, we end up with some interesting computations. If we know the lemmas of 14,400 nouns, we also know their plural forms, totaling the number of nouns we know to 28,800 nouns. If we know 16,800 verbs, we know not only the stem of the verb (e.g., *break*) but also the third person (e.g., *breaks*), the past tense (e.g., *broke*), and the past participle (e.g., *broken*), even though these word forms can have different variations (*talk, talks, talked, talked* versus *am, are, is, was, were, been*). We thus know some 16,800 × 3 = 50,400 verb forms. Of the nine thousand adjectives we know, we know not only the original adjective (e.g., *happy*), but also its comparative (e.g., *happier*) and superlative (e.g., *happiest*). Sometimes this superlative looks very much like the original adjective (e.g., *important, more important, most important*) and sometimes very different (*little, less, least*). Let's assume we know the adjective's two additional forms: its comparative and superlative. That brings us to 9,000 × 3 = 27,000 adjectives. That means that of the 40,800 nouns, verbs, and adjectives that we know, we should add some 65,400 word forms, doubling the number of words we know, again warranting the question: How do we keep those words in mind?

SENTENCE STRUCTURE

We started this chapter looking at the number of words we know, extended that investigation to the number of word-meaning combinations we know, and extended that yet further to the number of word forms we know. But words hardly ever occur in isolation! Language almost always has words accompanied by other words in sentences: A. Word. By. Itself. Means. Little. At least compared to words combined into a sentence. But a sentence is considerably more than a sequence of words. Let's take the following sentence: *The young woman saw a magnificent gorilla with binoculars.* This sentence consists of two noun phrases—[*the young woman*] and [*a magnificent gorilla*]—a verb phrase [*saw*], and a prepositional phrase [*with binoculars*]. That may sound very technical, but it is important in our production and comprehension of sentences. For instance, imagine somebody expressing this sentence; it is more likely that they place an "uhm" or other small pause just before or after these phrases than in the middle of the phrases. *The young woman . . .*

uhm . . . saw a magnificent gorilla with binoculars is more likely than *the young . . . uhm . . . woman saw a magnificent gorilla with binoculars*. These phrases are thus not artificial word combinations but form units. And that is important because we can form new sentences from this original sentence: *She saw him with binoculars. With binoculars she saw him. It was a gorilla she saw with binoculars. Did she see a gorilla with binoculars? Did the young woman see him with binoculars?* Moreover, these units in themselves can grow. *A very young woman saw a very magnificent gorilla with spectacular binoculars. A very young woman out there in the jungle saw a very magnificent gorilla with a silver back with spectacular binoculars that she had bought especially for this trip. A very young woman aged twenty years, out there in the jungle, all by herself, suddenly saw a very magnificent, large, and seldomly spotted gorilla with a silver back, the leader of a large group of gorillas, with her spectacular, high-end binoculars that she had bought earlier especially for this trip in the Specular Binocular Store on Fifth Avenue.* Knowing just a few words allows us to create multiple sentences.

Even if we keep the word count within a sentence consistent, we can extract multiple meanings of a sentence. Take, for instance, the young woman, named Mary, watching a gorilla with binoculars in the following sentence: *Mary saw a gorilla in pajamas with binoculars on a mountain.* This sentence alone can mean:

1. Standing on a mountain while she was wearing her pajamas, Mary saw a gorilla with her binoculars.
2. While she was wearing her pajamas, Mary saw a gorilla that was standing on a mountain with her binoculars.
3. Next to a pair of binoculars that were lying there on this mountain, Mary saw a gorilla while she was wearing her pajamas.
4. Standing on a mountain while she was wearing pajamas with binoculars printed on them, Mary saw a gorilla.
5. While she was wearing pajamas with binoculars printed on them on a mountain, Mary saw a gorilla.
6. Standing on a mountain, with her binoculars Mary saw a gorilla in pajamas.
7. Standing on a mountain, Mary saw a gorilla in pajamas with binoculars printed on them.
8. Mary saw a gorilla in pajamas with binoculars printed on them on a mountain.

If you have heard too much about Mary and the gorilla she saw by now, let's take another example from Dan Jurafsky and James Martin's *Speech and Language Processing*,[10] not the easiest read, but perhaps the best introduction to computational linguistics. Imagine you heard the sentence *I made her duck*. We know the meaning of the individual words in that sentence, may even recognize some ambiguities, but this sentence alone can generate five different meanings. Five meanings! Let's try them out:

1. I cooked waterfowl for her benefit (to eat) (I made her duck rather than Caesar salad).
2. I cooked waterfowl belonging to her (I made her duck, not mine).
3. I created the (plaster) duck she owns (I made her duck, after I had broken it).
4. I caused her to quickly lower her head or body (I made her duck when I found out that the ceiling was pretty low).
5. I waved my magic wand and turned her into undifferentiated waterfowl (I made her duck not frog, as I initially intended as a Harry Potter wannabe).

Language users hardly have any difficulty distinguishing between the meaning of these sentences. Not only do we know sixty thousand words, but also we often know multiple meanings of these words, increasing our vocabulary size. Moreover, we know the semantic relations between these words—meanings that add to the unique meaning we assign to individual words. In addition, we are able to assign multiple meanings to sentences for which the meaning of the individual words is the same.

SOUNDS

As a reader, you have a relatively easy task. The characters of a word are clearly printed on a white background. There is little doubt whether you read *pig* or *big*, *nineteen* or *ninety*, *man* or *ma'am*. But when you listen to a speaker uttering these words, you deal with a considerably higher level of complexity. It is true that as a hearer, intonation helps to guide you. Yet in conversation, you hear bursts of sounds being sent to you, and your task is to make meaning out of those sounds.

What I mean is this: If you did not speak a word of Chinese, Italian, or French, and you listened to a speaker of those languages and were asked to identify where a word starts or ends, you would not be able to do so. Sure, you could make an attempt when somebody speaks slow-ly and clear-ly, pau-sing, be-tween each and e-ve-ry word. But that's not the way people speak. They speak rapidly, with no pauses between words, where the last sound of a word already gets absorbed in the first sounds of the next word.

And yet, a speaker (or rather listener) of English is generally able to listen to that speech stream, identify the words from these bursts of sounds, morphologically analyze these words, place them in the syntax of the sentence, and assign meaning to these words and their sequence all within a few hundred milliseconds, because by the time you have identified the meaning of one word, the speaker has already moved on five words.

The sound of the words, the phonemes, are studied by phonologists. At school we learn about the grammar of sentences, but hardly about the grammar of sounds. And yet sound grammar is just as important (if not more important, for without the grammar of sounds, there would be no grammar of sentences). Because of this grammar of sounds, we know what a word is and what it is not. A word starting with *zcsrqcq-* will more likely be a combination of typos or a very foreign word than it is an English word.

The five meanings of the written sentence *I made her duck* I mentioned earlier may have been hard enough, but imagine you heard the sound combinations of this sentence. In that case, you may have actually heard[11]:

1. I mate or duck.
2. I'm eight or duck.
3. Eye maid; her duck.
4. Aye mate, her duck.
5. I maid her duck.
6. I'm aid her duck.
7. I mate her duck.
8. I'm ate her duck.
9. I'm ate or duck.
10. I mate or duck.

Listeners will rapidly be able to identify the right combination of words and assign the correct meaning to the combination, because they know so much language.

Earlier we saw that some words are spelled the same but sometimes sound different or carry very different meanings. Similarly, there are words that sound the same, are spelled differently, but carry very different meanings. These are so-called homophones, such as—to take a small number of examples from a large list: *ad* or *add, aisle* or *I'll* or *isle, allowed* or *aloud, ate* or *eight, eye* or *I, brake* or *break, but* or *butt, buy* or *by* or *bye, cite* or *sight* or *site, coarse* or *course, colonel* or *kernel, flea* or *flee, flew* or *flu, gays* or *gaze, genes* or *jeans, hear* or *here, heard* or *herd, knight* or *night, knot* or *not, know* or *no, knows* or *nose, mail* or *male, missed* or *mist, morning* or *mourning, muscle* or *mussel, naval* or *navel, pair* or *pear, pause* or *paws, peace* or *piece, profit* or *prophet, rose* or *rows*, *seas* or *sees* or *seize*, *there* or *their* or *they're*, *waist* or *waste*, *wait* or *weight*, *weather* or *whether*, and *your* or *you're*.

There are few language users who struggle during a conversation because of a homophone cacophony, and yet we do know the sound similarities and meaning differences between these words. It is amazing how much language we know! Even before you went to school and learned your grammar, even before you started to speak, you already had an impressive vocabulary and were able to form sentences grammatically!

LANGUAGE USE

By now, I have covered all aspects to language: its sounds, its grammatical structure at the word level as well as at the sentence level, and its meaning. Language users have no difficulty with all these aspects of language, which makes them linguistic magicians. As if the magic were not enough, they can do even more with language. They *use* it.

Imagine I asked you out for dinner. We are sitting in a restaurant, opposite one another, discussing how many words humans know. The entrees have been served. I am looking for the salt shaker, which stands closest to you, and ask you, "Can you please pass me the salt?" You respond, "Yes, of course," and continue eating your entrée. According to the phonology, morphology, syntax, and semantics of my question, there is nothing wrong with my statement. In fact, you yourself have faithfully answered my question whether you have the ability to pass me the salt. As you politely answered me, you do have that ability. But that was not really what I intended to ask.

Now imagine that same scenario, but now I make sure that what I say matches what I intend to say. We are at that same dining table, and entrees have been served. The salt shaker is on your side of the table, and I would need a little bit of salt. To match what I intend to say and what I say, I now command you in a loud and clear voice, to ensure there are no misunderstandings, "You pass me the salt, *now!*" It is likely you would look me in the eyes, throw your napkin on the table, move your chair back, stand up, and leave the restaurant, murmuring, "What's up with that guy! How rude!"

The point is that what language means is not always what it means when it is used. We generally have little problems with this, even though I often need to be reminded to be less sarcastic. When somebody asks me on a Monday how I feel, I too often respond, "Still breathing!" or "Is it Friday yet?" None of these responses are incorrect phonologically, morphologically, syntactically, or semantically, but what the utterances mean are different than what I intended to say. Of course, I am still breathing (otherwise I would not have been able to answer the question); of course it is not Friday (it is Monday). However, my colleagues immediately get the point of what I intended to say when I frantically run past them from meeting to meeting.

In the 1960s, researchers argued that when we use language, we implicitly sign a contract between each other.[12] I signed that contract when I started writing for you, and you signed that contract when you began reading this book. That contract consists of multiple clauses. For instance, in the contract, I promise to tell the truth. If by the end of this chapter, I told you that nothing I said was actually true, you feel rather betrayed. Imagine that I said Shakespeare wrote not 31,534 words but 1,124 different words; you'd have every reason to feel mad. Why would I purposefully give you a different number than the actual number if we signed the contract that I would always tell the truth? If I met you on the street and you asked me for the directions to the nearest restaurant, and I told you to take a right, then a left, then straight ahead, and then another right, even though there was no restaurant, it would not make sense. The deal is that I tell the truth, and you do the same.

Another clause in the implicit contract we signed states that I will not say more than I need to say, but not less than I need to say either. Imagine you pass by me on the street and quickly say, "Hey, how are you?" I stop you, preventing you from walking on, and answer:

> That is a very good question. I woke up around 7 o'clock in the morning, and first went to the bathroom. Then I took a shower and shaved myself. I got dressed, put on my shoes, and went downstairs, where I brewed coffee in the kitchen. I then got some cereal, put it in a bowl, poured some milk over it, and started to eat. Obviously with a spoon. Eating cereal without a spoon is somewhat inconvenient. I then drank a cup of coffee, no milk some sugar. For a while now, I have been trying to lower the amount of sugar I take in my coffee, but so far I have not been very successful. I finished the coffee and went back upstairs to brush my teeth. I have one of those automatic toothbrushes. They are pretty useful, in my experience. I rinsed my mouth with water, wiped my mouth with a towel, and turned off the bathroom lights. I guess I mentioned that I turned them on earlier? Anyway, I went back downstairs and got my laptop and left the house, carefully locking the door. I am rather neurotic when it comes to locking the door, but I will tell you about that later. I then got in my car, started the engine, and drove off. You know, first taking a left, then that roundabout, and then straight ahead, until the traffic lights. When I arrived at work, I bumped into you. Well that's my day so far. Also want to hear about yesterday?

A little too much information for a passing-by how-are-you?

Now imagine the scenario that we are having dinner—after I had showed you the directions to the restaurant and you passed me the salt. You captivatingly ask me: "That book of yours is fascinating. Tell me more about it!" and I respond, "It's about words," returning to my dinner and not saying any more about the book. A little too little information for that question, for the clause we signed in the contract is to say enough, not too much, not too little. The napkin might again be thrown on the table, and you might again walk out angrily.

A third clause in the contract states that I will communicate orderly and unambiguously. After the dinner we had, we order dessert. The ice creams get served and look very appetizing. After taking a bite, I look very pale, which brings you to ask, "Is everything okay?" I simply respond, "Sure, no worries, just a simple sphenopalatine ganglioneuralgia." I could have responded, "Brain freeze!" but I just broke another clause of the contract.

The final clause is perhaps the most important, as one can argue that it encompasses the other three clauses: be relevant. After all, in considering how much language we know, I was standing at a taxi stand, when I met a friend of mine with a penguin. I told my friend he should take the animal to the zoo. My friend responded, "Already been there, but he didn't like it!" If this joke did not quite fit the relevance of my argument, you just got the point.

SEXTILLION SENTENCES

The question of how much language we know was initially answered at the word level. We concluded that we know at least sixty thousand words. Taking into account a language's lexical semantics, this is an underestimate, for one word can have more than one meaning. Taking into account a language's morphology, this is an underestimate, for we can create new words on the fly. Taking into account a language's syntax, this is an underestimate, for words should not be considered in isolation but in sequences. Taking into account pragmatics, it is an underestimate, for we should consider language in use. But arguing that a concrete estimate—sixty thousand words—is an underestimate does not help us much further how much language we actually know. Instead of asking how many words we know, let's rephrase the question in how many sentences we know, ignoring morphology and lexical semantics for the sake of the discussion.

How many sentences do we know? One can argue that the answer is "infinite" because to any sentence, we can add another subordinate clause. For instance, Virginia Woolf's essay "On Being Ill" counts 182 words.

Considering how common illness is, how tremendous the spiritual change that it brings, how astonishing, when the lights of health go down, the undiscovered countries that are then disclosed, what wastes and deserts of the soul a slight attack of influenza brings to view, what precipices and lawns sprinkled with bright flowers a little rise of temperature reveals, what ancient and obdurate oaks are uprooted in us by the act of sickness, how we go down into the pit of death and feel the water of annihilation close above our heads and wake thinking to find ourselves in the presence of the angels and harpers when we have a tooth out and come to the surface in the dentist's arm-chair and confuse his "Rinse the Mouth—rinse the mouth" with the greeting of the Deity stooping from the floor of Heaven to welcome us—when we think of this, as we are frequently forced to think of it, it becomes strange indeed that illness has not taken its place with love and battle and jealousy among the prime themes of literature.

We can easily add to these 181 words a subordinate clause starting with "even though there are several literary works in the twentieth century that actually do use illness as a prime theme," adding up the total to 201. But these are the exceptions from literary authors. Even though we may be able to generate endless sentences, how many sentences do we actually know? How many sentences can we comprehend? Earlier we saw that *Mary watched magnificent gorillas with her binoculars* generated at least eight different syntactic constructions. Let's look at this a bit further. As an illustration, let's assume that a sentence can maximally have three words: a noun, a verb, and a noun. And that our vocabulary consists of only six—rather than sixty thousand—words: three nouns (*John, Mary,* and *Jane*) and three verbs (*hits, beats,* and *hugs*). From this rather limited vocabulary of six words and the limited grammar of three words, we can generate twenty-seven different sentences.

1. John hits John.
2. John hits Mary.
3. John hits Jane.
4. John beats John.
5. John beats Mary.
6. John beats Jane.
7. John hugs John.
8. John hugs Mary.
9. John hugs Jane.
10. Mary hits John.
11. Mary hits Mary.
12. Mary hits Jane.
13. Mary beats John.
14. Mary beats Mary.

15. Mary beats Jane.
16. Mary hugs John.
17. Mary hugs Mary.
18. Mary hugs Jane.
19. Jane hits John.
20. Jane hits Mary.
21. Jane hits Jane.
22. Jane beats John.
23. Jane beats Mary.
24. Jane beats Jane.
25. Jane hugs John.
26. Jane hugs Mary.
27. Jane hugs Jane.

The calculation to get to twenty-seven sentences is relatively simple: we choose three words in three positions, so the permutations are $3 \times 3 \times 3 = 3^3 = 27$. But this is a simplification. We know sixty thousand words and hardly produce three-word sentences. (Except this one.)

Let's dig a little deeper into how many sentences we can interpret. What would happen in actual language where we have more than three nouns, three verbs, and three-word sentences? To answer that question, we first need to get a sense of the number of words in a sentence. We know that the average sentence length is fifteen to twenty words, so let's assume that the sentences in our language can be a maximum of twenty words. We are then able to know sentences consisting of three words up to sentences consisting of twenty words, but not longer. This is, of course, a simplification, because the *average* number of words is fifteen to twenty, and many sentences exceed the maximum of twenty words (and in an extreme case like the Virginia Woolf sentence, 181 words).

It would be too simple to argue that we only have maximally twenty words. After all, we do not have twenty articles like *the* and *a*, and we do not have twenty prepositions like *on*, *up*, and *above* either. A good cocktail of word categories we tend to use is 19 percent noun, 27 percent verb, 6 percent adverb, 3 percent adjective, 21 percent pronoun, and 7 percent preposition, and the remaining 15 percent consists of determiners, coordinators, modals, subordinators, and adverbial particles.[13]

With these percentages, we can now estimate the number of nouns, verbs, adjectives, adverbs, and other categories in a three-word sentence, four-word sentence, five-word sentence, up to a twenty-word sentence, our maximum sentence length. So let's start calculating the numbers. Bear with me. Based on the likelihood of finding a noun, verb, and pronoun in a sentence, we can expect one noun, verb, and pronoun in a three-word sentence. Recall that we have 14,400 nouns at our disposal, 16,800 verbs, and some pronouns, which translates to over 30,000 noun, verb, and pronoun combinations. A ten-word sentence is then estimated to have two nouns, three verbs, one adverb, two pronouns, and one preposition. This means that the possible permutations of a ten-word sentence are over 4,741,000,000,000 sentences. That is quite an impressive number of sentences we are able to recognize!

But we are not there yet. If we add the number of permutations from a three-word sentence to a twenty-word sentence, we end up with interpreting over 5,000,000,000,000,000,000,000 sentences without difficulty! But still we are not close to an accurate estimate. After all, so far we have assumed that the order of the word classes in a sentence remains constant. This is obviously not the case. So let's simplify the situation again and assume that there are only two variations of word order in a sentence, like *yesterday John did kiss Mary* and *John did kiss Mary yesterday*. For the sake of discussion, we are ignoring alternative orderings like *did John kiss Mary yesterday?* If we only take two-word order variations into account, we can safely assume that we know at least 10,000,000,000,000,000,000,000 sentences, or 10 sextillion sentences!

Let's place this number in perspective. There are currently 7.7 billion people in the world. That is 7,000,000,000 people. We would not even recognize their faces, let alone their names. We know 1,000,000,000,000 times more sentences than there are humans in the world!

Here is another comparison to the astonishing number of sentences that we know. There are about 2 trillion (2 million million) galaxies in the observable universe.[14] If we assume some 100 billion stars per galaxy, the total number of stars in the observable universe is 2 sextillion (or 2,000,000,000,000,000,000,000 stars). We know more sentences than we can observe stars in the universe around us!

Or if we take another dramatic example, and compare the number of sentences we know to the number of sand grains in the Sahara Desert.[15] There are about twenty grains of sand along a centimeter, so $20^3 = 8,000$ grains of sand in a cubic centimeter. This means that we count about 8 billion grains of sand per cubic meter (about thirty-five cubic feet). Given the actual sandy surface of the Sahara Desert, excluding the rocky parts, the estimated number of grains of sand in the Sahara Desert is not that far apart from the number of sentences we know. Admittedly, I have not meticulously counted the exact number of sentences we know, and neither have I meticulously counted the exact number of grains of sand in the Sahara Desert. Nevertheless, the conclusion that the number of sentences (given the constraint of a maximum of ten words) even approximates the number of grains of sand in the Sahara Desert is nothing short of astonishing!

COMPUTING THE NUMBERS

Calculations of tens of thousands of words, billions of semantic relations, and sextillion sentences may come across as academic. My point here is that the number of words, or rather the number of sentences, that we can keep in mind is astounding. Had I simply stated that we know as many sentences as there are grains of sand in the Sahara Desert, you may have ridiculed the comparison. The empirical evidence, however, shows the numbers are not as far off as they may have seemed initially.

We started out the chapter with the question of how much language we know. With Shakespeare using some thirty thousand words, your estimate was likely not much higher than that amount, unless you had strong literary ambitions rivaling those of Shakespeare. But it turns out that we know more words than Shakespeare used in his collected works. In fact, if we estimate the number Shakespeare knew and not only the words he used, the estimate of the number of words *you* know is on par with those Shakespeare knew. But we know more words than that. We can form new words on the fly, as social media demonstrates on an almost-daily basis. If we then consider the number of meanings one word can have, the number of word forms that a word has, the meaning combinations of words have in a sentence, and the situation context in which these words are expressed, we can conclude that we know an astonishing amount of language. And we do not know words in isolation. We know them in sentences, in context. When estimating the number of sentences you know on the basis of the number of words we know, the estimate exceeds the number of stars in our galaxy and the number of grains of sand in the Sahara Desert!

How many words we keep in mind is impressive, but how we do this is at least as impressive. Let's have a closer look at what happens in our mind when our eyes glance over the shapes presented on these pages in the next chapter.

• 3 •

Guess

And remember too that there is a continuous series of transitional cases between that in which a person repeats from memory what he is supposed to be reading, and that in which he spells out every word without being helped at all by guessing from the context or knowing by heart.

—Ludwig Wittgenstein[1]

*W*hat you are doing right now is nothing short of miraculous. Your eyes pick up different shapes that form letters on a light background. Some of these letters are presented in capitals, some in lower case, some in bold, and some in italics. The shapes all differ from each other, and yet you manage to find coherence in them. The font in which these letters are presented does not matter. If you read a book in another font, or even if you read a handwritten text, nothing really hinders you in rapidly picking up the shapes to form letters that form words. And you are not even aware of these letters. You quickly turn sequences of letters into words. These words may be ones you know, or ones that come close to ones that you know. You somehow assign meaning to these words, often considering more than one possible meaning, and effortlessly link the possible meaning for one word moving on the next one and assigning meaning on the basis of the accumulated meaning in a sentence.

Something similar is going on for speech, except that the shapes of letters your eyes pick up are now contours of sounds you hear, sound combinations that you form into words into meaning. In contrast to reading, when listening to speech you do not have the opportunity to go back to the words you already processed to double-check you are still on the right track. Your fate of comprehending speech lies in the mouth of the speaker you are listening to.

That process, whether we are reading or listening, is so effortless that we are not aware of it. It comes to us almost naturally. It's like walking. As soon as you are conscious about what you are really doing when you walk—lift your foot, leaving the front of your foot to the ground; then bend your knee; move your leg forward; then hit the ground with the back of your foot, and let the front of your foot follow—you will stumble and fall. For processing language, it is pretty much the same. As soon as you start reading a word by its letters or carefully listen to the sounds of speech, you stumble and fall. It's better not to think about it.

How do we process language? If the number of words we know is astonishing and the process of understanding the meaning of words so miraculous, what goes on in our mind when we listen to speech or read language? Let's focus on the reading process for now. When we read the words of a page, it seems that we focus on the first character of a word and read the second character until we have seen all the letters and have identified what the word is. We then look up the meaning of that word in our mental dictionary, which consists of about sixty thousand entries, and move on to the first character of the next word, collecting the letters until we read the end of the word, identify it, and look it up in our mental dictionary. Gradually we then cover all the words in a sentence left to right, and move from the top to the bottom of the page down, gluing together the meanings of each word.

According to this explanation, we apparently try to capture the meaning of the word in some kind of dictionary that is lying around on our mental bookshelves. From the previous chapter, we know that our mental dictionary consists of over sixty thousand entries. How is that mental dictionary then organized? It may seem that the organization of our mental dictionary is similar to that of an ordinary dictionary we have been used to—that is, if our mental dictionary is organized like the Oxford English or Merriam-Webster dictionaries, organized alphabetically by entry. That would mean that when we read the word *orange*, we skim through our mental dictionary until we hit the *O* section and look up the word *orange*, retrieve its meaning, and move on. Consequently, words in the *A* section—like *apple*—would take very little time to find, whereas *orange* would take quite a while—fourteen sections further in our alphabetically ordered dictionary. There is, however, no evidence whatsoever that words that start with an *A* take less time to process than words that start with an *O*. In other words, when comparing *apples* and *oranges*, the differences are limited, at least with regards to an alphabetically organized mental dictionary.

Perhaps, then, our dictionary is not organized like a good old-fashioned dictionary, but is organized by content. That makes sense, as intuitively it feels that words such as *the*, *because*, and *us* are processed in a different part of our dictionary than words such as *apples* and *oranges*. Perhaps our mental dictionary has at least two parts, a part consisting of words that are primarily grammatical in nature, and a part that consists of words that are primarily content related. The grammatical words are somewhat meaningless—it is odd to ask what *the* means—but we can look them up in the dictionary nevertheless. Content words are very meaningful—it is not strange at all to ask you what the word *orange* means.

This distinction between grammatical items and lexical items is supported when considering language acquisition with lexical item words being acquired before grammatical item words. The first word of a child is not *because, but,* or *and*. Instead, it falls in the lexical item category. The category of *mummy, daddy,* and *doggy*. And grammatical items are processed considerably faster than lexical items, another reason for a two-part dictionary.

But this does not quite solve the mental dictionary problem either. The advantage may be that you do not have to scan through the entire dictionary, but the question remains how many categories the dictionary has. Do we read a word and categorize it as grammatical or lexical and then open either of the two bags? And how are these bags organized? Moreover, are there two parts of the dictionary? Or more than two? Within the grammatical items, we can find articles (*the, a*), pronouns (*I, you, he, she, it*), conjunctions (*and, because*), auxiliary words (*may, must, will*), and prepositions (*on, over, under*). And for the lexical items, the number of categories seems endless: *Apples* and *oranges* may fall under the fruit category; there is undoubtedly a vegetable category, or perhaps a dinner category, which is considerably different from the cars category, which is very distinct from the kitchen utensils, ocean, jungle, books, emotions, places, persons, computer, bathroom, factory, furniture, time, music, body parts, politics, children television characters, tea flavors that are minty, shoes without laces that you can wear comfortably in the summer categories.

There is another problem with any mental dictionary. What do we do when we read words such as *refuse* (as in garbage) and *refuse* (decline to accept), or *tear* (as in ripping apart) and *tear* (as water coming from your eyes)? We pronounce the words very differently, and we typically don't get confused when reading those words. Perhaps we do not only have a dictionary in which we look up the words we read, but also one for the words we hear. That would allow us to disambiguate garbage from declines, and physical consequences of temper tantrums from the emotional consequences. Getting to the meaning of words in our mental dictionary, we basically have a reading route and a hearing route, as well as a grammatical and content route[2]—multiple routes through our mental dictionary to get to the meaning of a word.

How do we know whether a word is stored in the mental dictionary in the first place? Imagine you read an uncommon word, say *zygote* (which means the union of the sperm cell and the egg cell, if you didn't know). Do you first go through the entire mental dictionary, section by section, until you reach the end and then come to the conclusion the word was not in there? Or worse, a word that really does not exist, such as *distrum*, you would look up in your mental dictionary, and you would then be left with a string of characters that remains meaningless after you concluded that it does not appear in your mental dictionary (and, really, in no dictionary at all)? That does not seem to be the case!

In fact, when you read the word *qwrtpl* rather than *zygote* or *distrum*, it takes you no effort at all to reject this sequence of letters as a word candidate for your mental dictionary. But it is odd to reject a word like *distrum* as a candidate of the mental dictionary before you have checked it in your mental dictionary. Unless we keep the entries of the sixty thousand words but not yet their meanings in consciousness. But given that the amount of information that we can keep in consciousness is limited, that seems a waste of cognitive resources.

We like words. Processing a combination of single letters takes more time when these letters do not appear in a word than when they do. James McKeen Cattell, the very first professor in psychology in the United States, estimates that it takes twice as long to read random letter combinations compared to letter combinations of actual words.[3] Words somehow seem to have some glamour to the reader. There is a word-superiority effect,[4] and that word superiority effect is strong. When we guess there might be a pattern of a characters or sound forming of word, we readily jump on it linguistically.

If we read a word and look it up in our mental dictionary—alphabetically or otherwise, and extract the meaning from a matching word, it suggests that if we cannot find a match, we do not try attempting to extract its meaning and reject it as a candidate. Consequently, major problems will occur with any *typoo* we *expereince* in a text. If the word is not present in the mental dictionary, and even does not sound like a word that is actually present in the mental dictionary (such as *typoo* and *expereince*), we should not be able to know its meaning. But we do. It seems as if we look at a word, guess how it might fit our mental dictionary, and guess its meaning. It seems as if we have an estimated mental representation of an estimated meaning of an estimated word in our mind.

The idea of carefully reading a word letter by letter, and reading a sentence word by word, while looking up a word in a mental dictionary, is not quite what we do when reading. We do not look at each letter of a word and process every word on a page, and thus don't look up each and every word in the mental dictionary. It is not even the case that you read left to right, top to bottom. This may be the overall pattern, but if we use special equipment to carefully monitor the eye gaze of a reader, our fixations on the words of a page more look like jumps between several words, sometimes a jump back, and sometimes a jump forward. More like a hop, skip, and jump than a smooth scan from word to word.[5] It may seem as if reading is a precise process that involves exact, detailed, sequential perception, whereby readers identify letters and words, and slowly but surely build these smaller language units up to larger language units. But this is a misconception. Instead, readers partially use minimal language cues from the perceptual input and the expectations of the reader.

Let me give an example. One of the most well-known books in linguistics is Noam Chomsky's *Aspects of the Theory of Syntax*, a book cited about forty thousand times the last time I counted. The preface of the book starts with the following two sentences.

> The iedea taht a lagnauge is baesd on a sytsem of rlues detemriinng the itnerpretatoin of its ifninietly many setnecnes is by no maens noevl. Well oevr a cetnury ago, it was epxressed with raesonalbe clairty by Wihleml von Hubmoltd in his fmauos but raerly sutdeid intordutcion to geenarl lignusitics.

Well, not exactly. The sentences have been taken from the preface of the book, but the letters of the words I jumbled up. Despite the fact that few of the words make sense, or are words in the first place, we tend to manage to reconstruct the words and their meanings fairly well on the bases of the guesses we make. We read the incoming information that is available, make predictions on what the word could be, and take it from there. For this same reason, we often do not even recognize typos in the text, because we have already guessed the word and moved on to the next one.

One may argue that in the above example, a lot of the grammatical words, words like *the, is, on, a, of, it*, are not altered. That is correct. Apparently, these grammatical words make up the syntactic glue of the sentence that allows us to reconstruct the jumbled words. But even when we take the grammatical words out and leave the remainder of the words intact—and even though the sentences are severely handicapped—it is still possible to extract some of the gist out of them through guessing the glue between the words.

> Idea language based system rules determining interpretation infinitely sentences by no means novel well century ago expressed reasonable clarity Wilhelm von Humboldt famous rarely studied introduction general linguistics.

If you happen to disagree, let me ask you whether the sequence of words in this example is more than the sum of its parts, the sum of individual meanings of a word. I think it is. But one could rightly argue that the word order in the example above helps us to reconstruct the gist of the sentences. But even jumbling up all the words within a sentence still allows us to play the psycholinguistic guessing game—granted, one that starts to become somewhat annoying. The meaning of individual words and the confidence that the words belong to the same sentence allow us to reconstruct aspects of the information.

> The of idea its determining interpretation based a language a system means no of sentences novel. infinitely that rules the is many is on by well ago, his general century famous but to reasonable was with introduction clarity it over von a linguistics Humboldt in Wilhelm by studied expressed rarely.

Again, the sentence is a mess, but as long as we work under the assumption that these sentences were intended to be meaningful, we are able to get the gist out of the sentences. And leaving the sentences intact but changing the order also leads to a perfectly acceptable opening of the preface of a book, except that a bit more mental work is needed than the original order of sentences.

> Well over a century ago, it was expressed with reasonable clarity by Wilhelm von Humboldt in his famous but rarely studied introduction to general linguistics. The idea that a language is based on a system of rules determining the interpretation of its infinitely many sentences is by no means novel.

On the basis of minimal information, readers make predictions that are confirmed, rejected, or refined during the reading process. Reading is a psycholinguistic guessing game in an interaction between thought and language.[6] We will find evidence for this throughout this book. It seems that regardless of whether they are sequences of letters, words, or sentences, we guess our way through the reading process, picking up from the language what we can and reconstructing from memory what we have. Psychologists call this bottom-up and top-down processes, or data-driven and theory-driven processes.[7] We take in the environment and apply our background knowledge to make the minimal information we take in as coherent as possible. The more we are exposed to the information we take in and the more we have practiced filling in the gaps of the information we take in, the more successful we are in the guessing game. Frequency of the information we are exposed to thus matters, as do the regularities in the structure of the information.

One may argue that presenting the passage four times makes it no surprise any reader is able to reconstruct the original meaning of the passage. But this is exactly my point. The more we are exposed to pieces of the puzzle, the better we are able to put the puzzle together. It's like when you are wearing glasses. As any owner of glasses has experienced, you frequently lose them. So without your much-needed glasses, you need to find your glasses. You search through the house in the most obvious places, the places where you use them most frequently. They do not reveal to you the place where your glasses can be found, but the place where the glasses are most likely to be found based on past experiences. When you finally find your glasses, everything suddenly makes sense. What used to be foggy in your search, now can be explained in minute detail: "Of course, when I placed my glasses on the cabinet right next to the door late last night!"[8] Or, when to be consistent with the foggy sentences presented earlier: "Of course, the idea that a language is based on a system of rules determining the interpretation of its infinitely many sentences is by no means novel!"

WORDS

I am actually not so certain that language comprehension is just a guessing game. The guesses we make when we comprehend language are not random, not as random as when we guess whether a coin flip ends with heads or tails. In language comprehension, we make estimated guesses. It is as if we form hypotheses based on past observations. The more observations, the better our hypotheses.

Imagine that you read the sentence "Yuo cna porbalby raed tihs." You don't make random guesses on what the words might mean; you make *educated* guesses. These educated guesses are based on the assumption that you are ultimately dealing with actual language and that it does not take too much cognitive effort to unscramble the information you read (and if it does, you might fall back to the conclusion you are not dealing with actual language). So presenting you with "oyu nca ypbolrab drea shti" will not make the educated guessing game much fun, as it would take too much cognitive effort likely making you conclude that the puzzle is unsolvable. So in the guessing game of language comprehension, we make some assumptions. We assume we are dealing with language, and we therefore assume there is structure in the data. And we can assume there is structure in the data on the basis of our past observations; the more the merrier. The sentence "Yuo cna porbalby raed tihs" is considerably easier to read than "bilboimnaaics are caaplbe of arpepeehdning prhaesooliges," simply because you are more familiar with words like *you*, *can*, *probably*, *read* and *this*, than you are with words like *bibliomaniacs*, *capable* or *apprehending* and *phraseologies*. We basically estimate the posterior probability of a word and sentence on the basis of prior probabilities of that word and sentence.[9] We mentally compute the likelihood of a word on the basis of how often we have encountered the word. Similarly, we compute the likelihood of a sentence on the basis of how often we have encountered the structure of that sentence. And together they allow us to make decent educated guesses.

What helps in our educated guesses is that language is pervasive. We cannot ignore words. Take for instance the situation of watching your favorite Netflix series with closed captioning accidentally on. It is impossible to ignore the subtitles at the bottom of the screen, despite the fact that it is certain that the subtitles transcribe what is being said. Compare this to when you switch the subtitles to a language that is not (or is less) known to you. In that situation, it becomes much easier to ignore the subtitles. We are accustomed to our language.

The best example of pervasiveness of language comes from the most well-known experiment in psychology that led to the Stroop effect, named after John Ridley Stroop in 1935.[10] The Stroop effect should have been called the Jaensch effect, after Erich Jaensch,[11] who reported the effect six years before Stroop. But *Stroop effect* apparently sounded better. In the Stroop experiment, participants see color words presented in different colors and are asked to name the color (ignoring the word). Below is a black-and-white version of the Stroop effect. Just name as quickly as possible the color (white, grey, or black) of the font, ignoring the word that is given.

As you see, that turns out to be quite a challenge. Each time you think you manage, the word in question yells at you in despair: "Read me! Comprehend me!" Language comes so natural to us that it is extremely difficult to ignore it, probably because we are so used to it.

What then determines the comprehension of a word? Among several candidates that could determine word processing, the frequency of a word is the absolute winner. The word *apple* is simply processed faster than a word like *unintelligibility*, because the word *apple* occurs more frequently in language. The problem with frequency is that, though it is the best predictor for the speed of word processing, it is also a proxy for a number of alternative candidates. One such candidate is word length. Shorter words tend to be more frequent (or frequent words tend to be shorter).[12] When we consider shorter nouns like *time, year, way, day, thing,* and *man* and shorter verbs like *say, get, make, go, know,* we process them considerably faster than longer nouns like *mispronunciation, acknowledgment, procrastination,* and *professionalism* or longer verbs like *authenticate, counterbalance,* and *recapitulate.* And the latter are far less frequent than the former.

Also processed faster are concrete words like *apple* and *orange,* at least when compared to abstract words like *freedom* and *unintelligibility.* If a rating test were conducted in which participants were asked how concrete or abstract a word was, the resulting ratings would provide a decent estimate of how easy it is to comprehend a word. The problem, however, is that concrete words are also shorter than abstract words, so perhaps it is not so much the concreteness that determines the speed at which they are processed, but the word length—or the word frequency, as we know that shorter words tend to be more frequent.

Those words that are acquired at a younger age are also processed faster. If one were to make a list of the words that young children use and a list of the words adults use, the age of acquisition of a word is a good predictor of how fast the word is comprehended. A word like *ball* children acquire much earlier than a word like *philosophy.* But *philosophy* is also more abstract than *ball.* And the word is longer. And is less frequent.

Whether the meaning of a word is a member of a category or the category itself also determines the speed with which it is processed. Category words like *dog* are processed faster than members of the category dog, like *Golden Retriever* or *Pitbull Terrier.* But again, the members of the category also tend to be more concrete, and tend to be longer, and tend to be more frequent.

Moreover, different categories of words are processed faster or slower. Animate words (*dog, cat, woman*) tend to be processed faster than inanimate words (*kitchen, freedom, lake*). But the animacy of a word might also be explained by the concreteness of the word, which in turn might be explained by the length of the word, which in turn might be explained by the frequency of the word.

Let's summarize. We understand words faster than nonwords, words that look and sound the same faster than words that look or sound dissimilar, words that are acquired earlier faster than words acquired later, words that fit a syntactic construction faster than words that don't, concrete words faster than abstract words, category words faster than member words, animate words faster than inanimate words, words that are similar in meaning faster than words that are dissimilar in meaning, shorter words faster than longer words. And what these effects all seem to have in common is *frequency*. Words that are recognized fast tend to be short, acquired earlier, concrete, animate, meaningful . . . and more frequent.

So what is it about frequency? Obviously, things you encounter more are more frequent. Frequent words also have a higher likelihood of being used in a variety of situations. It seems that if we see, hear, feel, smell, or taste objects more, we tend to use them more in language. Those are more likely to be objects that are concrete and animate, and are basic categories more than members of a category. And these are probably also the objects and therefore the words that children acquire first. An interdependency of relations between aspects that help us keep those words in mind.

Now, we can compute the factors that determine the comprehension of words in isolation, as we did for frequency, word length, concreteness, age of acquisition, and category membership. But that limits us in the factors we can evaluate. For instance, imagine that we want to investigate whether the sound of a word has an effect on comprehension, or the grammatical category. To determine what affects the processing of a word, it is often useful to use two words. If the second word is read faster because of the first word, it is assumed that the two words have some relation. The first word primes the second word. From these experiments, we know that if you read two words that look like each other (*cough* and *dough*) the first word primes the second word. If two words do not look but sound like each other (*tribe* and *tripe*), again, the first word primes the second word. If words share meaning (*intelligent, unintelligent, intelligible, intelligibility*), the words also prime one another, also when they do not look or sound like each other (*buy* and *bought*). If two words make a grammatical syntactic combination (*angry* and *cup*), the adjective primes the sound (but the effect is not found for two nouns like *anger* and *cup*).[13]

So the organization of our mental dictionary is complex. It is based not only on letters but also on sounds, as well as on syntax and on meaning. When we read two words that have a similarity in meaning, the words prime one another. The word *coffee* primes the word *tea*, but it does not prime the word *dog*.[14] This is even true for people who speak multiple languages. If you speak both French and English, *cat* is processed faster when you read *dog* but also when you see the French equivalent for *dog*, *chien*.[15] If these various aspects affect the comprehension of a word, it demonstrates that the metaphor of simply looking up in an alphabetically organized mental dictionary is rather problematic.

IT'S FAST

We read a word on average in 240 milliseconds. If 240 milliseconds do not sound that fast, imagine this. If any of us were presented with a green circle on a screen that we know will turn red, and we are asked to press any button on our keyboard as quickly as possible when the green circle turns red, we would not be able to do this faster than approximately 240 milliseconds.[16] So in this situation, we only need to respond to one simple stimulus (a change from green to red), and we know exactly what to expect (red). And that simple task takes us 240 milliseconds. In that simple task, it will be difficult to keep up with the 240 milliseconds response time for each stimulus that gets presented. After a hundred items or so, we will start showing some fatigue. But not so when we are listening to speech or reading language. In what you are doing right now, it takes no effort to glance from word to word and access its meaning, as you have done for over two thousand words already in this chapter alone.

How do we measure how quickly we understand a word? Scientists used to use tachistoscopes, a piece of equipment that presents a word for a specified amount of time.[17] More commonly now, scientists use reading time techniques that let the participant be the judge. They present participants with a word on a screen and ask them to judge as quickly as possible whether a word is an actual word or not. Or they ask participants to name the word they see. Button presses are an easy way of obtaining information about the cognitive processes involved when we read a word.

A more sophisticated way that provides more detailed information is by using eye tracking technologies. Over the years, eye trackers have been around in many different types. There are eye trackers with contact lenses with wires glued on that monitor the minutest movement. There are also eye trackers that are far less intrusive. In many eye trackers, a small beam of infrared light is projected onto the eye, and the reflection is recorded. Any changes in the movement of your eyes are thus captured. In the early days, participants were asked to put their forehead against the eye-tracking system, clench their teeth on a bite bar to keep their head stable, and then read a text "naturally." More modern eye trackers sit still on a table, and all you need to do is read from a computer screen while the eye movements are recorded from a distance in a webcam fashion. When compared to specially prepared contact lenses and bite bars, this results in more natural reading if you ask me.

Eye-tracking techniques tell us that whenever we fixate on a word, our eyes come to a rest on a word for a few hundred milliseconds. During this brief fixation time, the eyes capture some seven to nine characters—and not the characters of every word, but the characters of some words. For instance, we often do not fixate on grammatical words like *the*, *is*, or *and*, but we somehow take these words for granted. We do fixate on most of the content words, but not for long. In fact, our eyes don't fixate on a particular spot for too long at all. Or rather, they can't. Very brief jerky eye movements, so-called "saccades," help us to jump from one fixation to the next. These saccades last some ten to thirty milliseconds and are therefore too fast for us to pick up any visual information from the page, unless it is very blurry information.[18] The saccadic eye movements seem to jump approximately ten letters and move forward to what comes next, but also backward. Whereas the majority of eye movements move forward, some 10–15 percent of our eye movements move backward,[19] as if they try to bring a word that we already read back into memory. But we typically do not notice these backward or forward moves.

On average, we read some three to six words per second, some two hundred to four hundred words per minute. But this depends on a variety of factors: the presentation of the text, its font and color, and the reading skills of a reader. It also depends on the text genre. My best guess is that it takes approximately 220 milliseconds per word you fixate on in the current book, but compared to this book, an easy narrative text might save you some twenty milliseconds per word, while a physics or biology text may cost you some forty milliseconds extra per word. So if you skip all coffee or bathroom breaks, and continue reading the words presented to you here, you should be able finish this book in approximately seven hours. Just keep on reading!

How much information do we pick up during an eye fixation on a word? This is a difficult question to answer, because it depends on how much information we can get on the left and the right of the point of the word. How much the part of the eye that can focus—the foveal area—takes in, and how much the areas around the fovea take in, the parafoveal and the periphery. Cognitive psychologists Keith Rayner and George McConkie—best known for their groundbreaking eye-tracking research—came up with a clever solution to identify the perceptual scan. They made the words people looked at gaze contingent. When somebody looked at a word, the other words changed, and when the person moved to the other words, the one word changed. Now if Rayner and McConkie changed the other words to *x*'s and people did not notice these *x*'s, the unchanged words were part of the perceptual span. If, on the other hand, a word changed to *x*'s and the participant noticed the change, it exceeded the perceptual span. In one study, they found that readers are using ten to eleven positions from the fixation point. This basically means that readers do not see more than two to three short words at a time. Larger words cannot be seen at once! Even though when you look at a word, you are pretty convinced of the nature of the other words, the gaze-contingent studies demonstrate that you cannot be convinced. If these words changed to *x*'s (if they stayed outside the ten to eleven positions away of what you focus on), you wouldn't notice a thing![20]

In another experiment, Rayner used not *x*'s to replace the word, but shape and letter substitutes. For instance, participants read the sentence: *The king watched the traitor from his throne*. But instead of *traitor*, the word *teacher* was used, which was both syntactically and semantically a good substitute. Other substitutes were nonwords with the first and last letter being correct, and everything else looking the same (*tcaobcr*), the first and the last letter being the same, and everything else not looking the same (*tiffrir*), or the first and the last letter as well as everything else looking but not being the same (*fcaobcn*). Readers did not recognize that a letter string was not a word when they fixated on more than three to four character positions to the left of the beginning of that string. But what was particularly striking is that the substitute word *teacher* was treated very similar as the target word *traitor*. It is difficult to visualize what participants were able to see, because the presentation changed as a function of the eye gaze, but let me give it a try. Participants saw the sentence "The king watched the traitor from his throne."

The king watched the traitor from his throne.	Original sentence
xxx xxxx xxxxxxx the traitor from xxx xxxxx	periphery replaced by x's
The king watched the teacher from his throne.	periphery replaced by semantic information
The king watched the fcaobcn from his throne.	periphery replaced by visually similar nonword
The king watched the tiffrir from his throne.	periphery replaced by visually dissimilar nonword

Source: **Rayner and McConkie (1977).**

When participants focused on the word *watched*, both visual and semantic inconsistency resulted in higher fixation times, suggesting that information away from the word they fixated on, words in their periphery, was taken into account. However, the peripheral information was limited to seven to twelve characters for visual information and one to six characters for semantic information. But most interestingly, the semantically similar words, but not the nonwords, behaved most like the original word, as if the mind somewhere in the eye's periphery processed information it had not really intended to.

Another interesting finding from these studies is that the perceptual span was not symmetrical. It extended far more to the right of the fixation point than to the left. The asymmetric span covering more of the information that is coming up for readers of English (and Dutch, German, and French) is reversed for languages that are printed from right to left, such as Hebrew.[21] For Chinese and Japanese, very similar results have been found, both for horizontal and for vertical presentation of the letters.[22] What these findings show is that the mind is thinking ahead when reading. The mind is guessing the nature of the word not only on the basis of visual information but also particularly on syntactic and semantic information, and does that with more forward looking than backward looking. The educated guessing game.

Let's illustrate this a bit more. First of all, the evidence that the sentence order and the semantic organization of words matter is obvious when we compare a "normal" sentence like "The quick brown fox jumps over the lazy dog" with "dog lazy the over jumps fox brown quick the." But this may say more about the presentation of words in a sentence than your ability to make predictions on the word that follows the next word. Let's therefore do a little experiment and test this yourself. Below, I have presented a list of words. Now put a sheet of paper over the top line and move it down. How well would you be able to predict the next word, that is, without fixating on the word, looking it up in your mental dictionary, accessing its meaning, and then moving on to the next word? Now try it the other way around. Move your sheet of paper from the bottom to the top and see how this changes how to process each and every word. My guess is that it takes considerably longer reading from bottom to top than from top to bottom, and not because of the direction you are reading things in (which is unnatural for English speakers anyway, because we tend to read from left to right).

The	based	rules
idea	on	is
that	a	by
a	system	no
language	of	means
is		novel.

What this example shows is that we apparently do not read each word separately and look up its meaning, but we make predictions on the words we encounter, an accumulated prediction based on past experiences we have with the frequency of words and sentence structures.[23] This explains why we struggle with sentences like

The swimmers drowned in the lake were not found until the next morning.
The general presented copies of the report was aware of the problems.
The government plans to raise taxes were defeated.
The investigation revealed the error resulted from gross negligence.

These sentences led you up to a syntactic path you are familiar with (swimmers drowned in the lake; the general presented copies; the government plans to raise taxes; the investigation revealed the error), but suddenly you were led astray on the path you followed, and you had to walk back, taking a new path. These sentences are called garden-path sentences, and in the 1970s, publications in linguistics blossomed with linguists-turned-gardeners. Garden-path researchers tried to explain why we stumble over the syntactic structure of these sentences and wander on (what turns out to be) the wrong path. For instance, they defined rules that stated that humans prefer those syntactic structures that were simplest in their grammatical complexity. Or they explained these cognitive trip-overs by the erroneous linking of the incoming information to the most recently processed information. Some interesting syntactic theories were proposed. But the meaning of words often trumped the syntactic structures. The following two garden-path sentences are identical in syntactic structure, and yet you undoubtedly have less difficulty with the second than with the first one.[24]

The doctor examined asked the patient about his recovery.
The patient examined asked the doctor about his recovery.

So if we add a bit of context to the sentences presented above, we can make better guesses. For instance, if we go back to the sad news about "the swimmers drowned in the lake were not found until the next morning," a little context allows us to not be led astray anymore.

The search crew had searched all night for the swimmers that had gone missing in the lake. The swimmers drowned in the lake were not found until the next morning.

And that is good news to us, language users. Just like we are hardly ever being presented with words in isolation, we are hardly ever being presented with sentences in isolation. Words and sentences typically appear in context. A while back, I conducted an eye-tracking experiment with a graduate student on confusing garden-path sentences like the ones above.[25] In addition to using the original sentences, we also used sentences with some added context, some specific context, and some overall context. In all cases with context being added we were able to guide the reader off the garden path, with the eye-tracking data showing that all initial confusion was basically gone. Participants did not experience any difficulties if language was presented in its natural habitat, in context.

Or take another psycholinguistic experiment that looked at whether people remembered the sentence itself or the meaning of the sentence.[26] Participants read the following sentence as part of their experiment instructions.

When you score the results, do nothing to your correct answer but mark carefully those answers which are wrong.

The participants had no idea they were participating in a recall experiment. To their surprise they were presented with snippets from the sentence and asked whether or not they had actually read each snippet. For instance, they were asked whether they had read *your correct* or *correct your*, while another group was asked whether they had read *mark carefully* or *carefully mark*. The difference between the two groups was that the former group was presented with a change in meaning, whereas the other group was presented a snippet that did not change in meaning, only in the exact wording. The change-in-meaning group scored 100 percent correct, while the change-in-form (but not in meaning) group performed considerably lower, at only 50 percent accuracy.[27] Our memory for the exact wording of a sentence seems to vanish, whereas the memory for the gist remains.

Or in yet another experiment,[28] participants read a long series of sentences and were later asked which sentence they had seen. For instance, the series of unrelated sentences included *The window is not closed*. The multiple-choice test included the following four sentences:

The window is not closed.
The window is closed.
The window is not open.
The window is open.

The first sentence was the sentence participants had read, and perhaps unsurprisingly, that was the one they best remembered. But when they made a mistake, things got interesting. The exact wording of the second multiple-choice answer and the syntactic structure of the third one came closest to what participants had seen before. But most people chose the fourth one, the sentence that was closest in meaning, not closest in wording or syntactic structure.

So familiarity with the language itself seems to be important, as we have seen in the scrambled letters from which we are able to reconstruct words. The structure of the sentence seems to be important, as we have seen in the garden-path sentences. And the context seems to be important, as we have seen in the findings from priming experiments and the findings that we can reverse garden-path effects on the basis of the context the sentences are placed in. But in all these cases, meaning matters.

This gives me the opportunity to introduce you to the world of discourse psychology. Psychologist Walter Kintsch and his team asked participants to read eighteen short texts. After reading these texts, all participants had to do was to identify whether they had seen a sentence presented to them or not. Pretty simple. However, the sentences they were shown either came directly from the text they had seen (copied and pasted), were paraphrases (with some minor word choice and sentence structure differences), or were inferences (possible conclusions drawn from a sentence but not explicitly stated). A mini-text like "It was a wonderful day. Joan put down her towel and baked in the sun for half an hour" would have a paraphrase of the first sentence, as in "She spread out her towel," and an inference of the second sentence, as in "She lay down on her towel." When participants were tested immediately after having read the texts, they best remembered the original sentences, followed by the paraphrases, and said they had not seen the inference sentences. After forty minutes, the differences between original sentence and paraphrase was basically gone. And after two days, participants could hardly distinguish between the original, the paraphrase, or the inference sentences.[29] It is the familiarity with the language, the sentence structure, and the linguistic context that help us in our guessing game.

But it even seems to be the case that background information helps us in our guessing. Last night my wife and I went to a nearby restaurant. We waited to be seated, and when the waiter arrived, I gave the reservation name, and the friendly waiter guided us to our table. We ordered drinks and then looked on the menu. It was difficult to make a choice, but we ordered our appetizer and entrée. A wonderful dinner indeed. Afterward, we ordered a dessert: chocolate fudge. The waiter got our coats and gently held the door open for us. When we got back to our car, we noticed that the windshield was frozen, and we had to scrape off the thin layer of ice.

I bet you are not deeply upset with me. Why would you? I just told you about my evening last night, and you are not deeply upset with me for not having paid the bill. Of course we paid the bill (and added a tip), but it is basically part of a restaurant script we all have in our minds, which includes—even if is not explicitly mentioned—paying the bill. You just filled in the blanks on the basis of a restaurant script that you apparently have in mind.[30] For many scenarios, we already anticipate what is going to happen next. Or we know what objects and items are present. If in my story I had mentioned that the waiter arrived at our table with a corkscrew, you would have hardly paid attention to it. But if the waiter arrived at our table with a screwdriver, you might be surprised. Similarly, if I had told you that I entered the restaurant, ordered the dessert, was guided to the table, and waited to be seated, the story is almost ungrammatical (unless of course you glanced over this example, made some educated guesses, and didn't even get the ungrammaticality).

Scientists have argued that like the grammar of a sentence we are all familiar with from school, there is also something like a story grammar. Vladimir Propp, in the early part of the twentieth century, studied the story structure of Russian fairy tales. He found out that there is a pattern to these stories. It commonly starts with a general situation where nothing in the world could go wrong. A queen and a king, who have a daughter, and all is well. Suddenly something happens. A witch shows up, a dragon is ruining the peaceful and quiet life, or some other villain fits the axis of evil. For instance, the princess might get kidnapped. Then there is some climax in the story. The hero (stereotypically the male prince) shows up and fights a dragon. When everything almost seems to be lost, the hero wins nevertheless. And after the resolution of the climactic conflict, the situation gets back to normal, or gets even better, with everybody living happily ever after (and the prince and princess obviously getting married).

If this sounds too much like a fairy tale, take any James Bond movie, any Disney movie, any Harry Potter, Lord of the Rings, or Star Wars movie, and you will find evidence for these story grammars. Obviously, you will also find them in their original books. The reader or moviegoer would leave the cinema rather disgruntled if James, Elsa, Harry, Frodo, or Luke lost the battle. They may almost lose it, but we anticipate a happy ending, and some disruption, otherwise the movie would not be exciting enough.

What does this have to do with keeping those words in mind? Well, let's recap. We started out with a word-superiority effect with language users making words not out of a concatenation of individual letters, but guessing the word on the basis of some of its letters. We then moved onto sentences, which are not understood as a concatenation of words, but involve guestimates too. Similarly, we guestimate the story line in texts, stories, and discourse, as we don't just read the concatenation of sentences.

So we started out this chapter with the idea that the reading process is something like the following: "Reading is a precise process. It involves exact, detailed, sequential perception and identification of letters, words, spelling patterns, and large language units." But we basically ended up with "Reading is a selective process. It involves partial use of available minimal language cues selected from perceptual input on the basis of the reader's expectation. As this partial information is processed, tentative decisions are made to be confirmed, rejected, or refined as reading progresses." Language processing is a(n educated) guessing game.[31]

LISTENING

The guessing game called reading is difficult. Most children have not captured reading before they turn six. No wonder, with the wiggly shapes on a white background that need to be translated to sensible information. Yet reading can take advantage of a number of pieces of information that hearers do not have. At least the shapes of the letters on a page are clustered. Sequences of letters are nicely separated from other sequences with a space, a comma, a period, or other punctuation markers. In reading, it is clear when one word stops and another word starts—the spaces between words guide you along the way. It is also clear when one sentence stops and the next one starts—punctuation markers and capitals will tell you. And the reader reads at her own pace. If the reading goes too fast, she can slow down. If the reading is too slow (or the content too boring), she can speed up. If the reading becomes complex, the reader can go back and reread words or entire sections.

The hearer, on the other hand, has considerably less to work from. Her guessing work is rather amazing. In speech, words are not separated by distinct pauses but are laced together in one continuous airstream, making it difficult to determine when they start and when they end. Sentences are not marked by punctuation markers or capitals, making it difficult to determine when a sentence has ended and when a new sentence has started. And if you had lost track of words and sentences, there is no opportunity to go back to what has been said. There is no opportunity for regressions to previous words, let alone to what was said a while back. The hearer is fully dependent on what the speaker provides to her right here, right now.

And even what the speaker says is difficult. Imagine hearing the words *ball*, *bill*, *able*, and *rob*. The *b*'s in all four words sound slightly different. How would you know as a language user that they belong to the same sound, the *b*? And to make matters worse, even if you had learned that the four words have slightly different *b* sounds, these sounds change when placed in context. When you read out loud *I rob burglars*, *I rob plenty of people*, *I rob ten people*, or the most politically correct *I rob nobody*, the assumption is that the word *rob* is the same, but in all four examples, the last sound of the word *rob* is pronounced differently. Yet most people have little difficulty bringing back the small variations of the sound of the word *rob* to the same word (and call the police).

Talking about police, it is a crime in linguistics to equate the hearing process with the reading process. We have just seen that there are important differences between reading language and hearing speech. Even though one can consider hearing speech to be more natural—children automatically learn how to communicate, but they have a much harder time learning to read—it is easier to study the reading process and more convenient to understand what's going on. Equipment like eye trackers or button-press options provide easy tools to measure what's going on, and because in reading—and less so in listening—the participant has full control on how fast she reads, whether she wants to jump forward or jump back, there simply is more experimental literature on reading than on hearing language. And many of the effects that have been found for reading words apply to hearing words. For instance, as in written language, in speech there seems to be a word superiority effect with phonemes being detected more quickly in words than nonwords.[32] And as in written language, in speech we consider word candidates when reading through a sentence, and reconstruct words if they contain a typo.

In an experiment by psycholinguist Mike Tanenhaus and his team, participants looked at four pictures: a picture of a cup used in chemistry classes, a picture of an insect, a picture of a loudspeaker, and a picture of a carriage.[33] You guessed it, that of a beaker, beetle, speaker, and carriage. They presented participants with the word *beaker*, while the eye gaze of the participants was recorded. Basically, the experimenters wanted to determine whether the activation of the meaning (the picture) was based on the sound of the word or the rhyme of the word. In the first 200 milliseconds after participants heard the word *beaker* being pronounced, the fixations hit all the pictures proportionally the same. But around 200 milliseconds, a change could be observed. The unrelated word *carriage* lost in the fixation race. It was not looked at, and all attention went to the other three pictures. Beetle and beaker both got quite some fixations. Speaker was still in the race but was losing out to beetle and beaker, and unsurprisingly, after 400 milliseconds, it became obvious who won the fixation race: beaker.

This experiment showed that phonological information at the start of the word activates several candidates with similar sounds, but also candidates for which the sound is similar not at the start but at the end of the word. Translated to our mental dictionary example, apparently we do not only look at the *B*-section of the mental dictionary because other candidates whose beginning sound the same, but also, albeit briefly, at the -*EAKER* section for candidates that have a similar word-sound ending.

So apparently language processing is incremental: when we hear a word, we immediately make educated guesses about potential candidates that match the incoming information. Words that sound similar are not entirely ruled out as candidates for the guessing, and even words that have semantic associations are candidates. We form multiple hypotheses based on our prior observations.

And we form our educated guesses quickly. In an experiment similar to the beaker experiment, participants heard the word *hammer* and looked at the picture of a hammer presented on the screen, but they also looked at the picture of a nail. And when they heard the word *hammock* the same happened. Even *hammock* made us make an educated guess that what participants really heard was *nail*. Similarly, when participants heard something similar to the first two phonemes of *lock* and *logs*, they were eager to also look at *key* and *wood* (but not at *deer* or *apple*).[34]

And as in reading, we are sometimes so convinced of our educated guesses that we make up words when we hear a sentence. In one famous psychology experiment, participants heard:

> The state governors met with their respective legislatures convening in the capital city.

But when the *s* in *legislatures* was replaced by a cough, 95 percent of the participants did not even hear the cough. The remaining participants did hear a cough, but did not know where it had occurred. Similarly, when participants heard the sentences

> The *eel was on the orange.
> The *eel was on the axle.
> The *eel was on the shoe.
> The *eel was on the table.

where the * was a cough, participants clearly heard *peel*, *wheel*, *heel*, and *meal*. They made educated guesses and restored the phoneme that was missing.[35] We basically hear what we want to hear. Like reading, listening is a guessing game. And it is likely that listening is even more of a guessing game than reading is. After all, in reading, you the reader are in control. You can speed up, slow down, look back, and look forward. In listening, you are dependent on the person delivering the language to you at her speed. If you were not sure about the sound signal, you would have to guess (unless you want to annoy your conversational partner with a continuous repetition of "What did you say?").

And just like in reading, context plays a critical role in the memory of spoken sentences. In fact, the more interactional a sentence is, the better we remember the sentence. A sentence like "I think there are two fundamental tasks in this study" is grammatically correct in about every way. The words exist and are common; the grammar of the sentence does not include anything unusual. For a sentence like "I think you've made a fundamental error in this study," the same is true, except that the interactional content is considerably higher. In addition to the meaning of the sentence itself, I am also including *you* in the conversation. When a group of researchers investigated the recall of sentences expressed in a luncheon meeting some thirty hours after that meeting took place, memory for the interactional sentences was considerably higher than the sentences with less interactional information. Memory for language was good; memory for language in use was better.[36]

WITH THE SPEED OF MIND

Both in reading written language and in hearing spoken speech, our mind rapidly and effortlessly extracts the meaning of the language it experiences. The speed with which this process takes place is astonishing, with less than a quarter of a second to process an average word. But the process is considerably more astonishing if you take into account that it is not so much the letters that we process, but the word. And not so much the words that we process, but the sentence. And not so much the sentence that we process, but the discourse. It is as if two mental processes work in tandem. One process, a bottom-up process, picks up any useful information it can find. It does not consider all information to be useful, but is selective. It jumps from one potentially useful language resource to the next. Another process, a top-down process, does just the opposite. It does not care too much about the incoming information, but has a mind on its own. It fills in blanks, it corrects what it thinks is incorrect information (regardless of whether it is right in doing so), and it is happy to make guesses about a word, sentence, or story as soon as it finds any piece of evidence in favor of it. Obviously, one cannot do without the other. The top-down process needs input to base its guesses on. Meanwhile the bottom-up process would not work without a process that at some point in time decides there is sufficient information to make a decision on the incoming language.

In the previous chapter, we have seen that we are able to keep some sixty thousand words in some sextillion sentences in mind. In this chapter, we have seen that this is not at all a static process, but a very dynamic process in which we put the pieces of the puzzle together and guess in an educated way what the puzzle is about—a puzzle that consists of the structure of the word (its morphology), the sound of a word (its phonology), the sentence structure (its syntax), the meaning of the word (its semantics), and the context (its pragmatics). And we are guessing not only the word but also the language and context leading up to that word. In reading and listening, we look (and hear) forward to predict what will come next. And we are doing all that in the 240 milliseconds we spent on processing a word.

Now the big question that has kept linguistics, psychologists, anthropologists, artificial intelligence researchers, computer scientists, and philosophers alike occupied in the last few centuries is how we are able to do this. How do we keep those words in mind? Let's have a closer look at some of the answers to that question.

• *4* •

Training

The amount of reinforcement accorded the verbal behavior of a particular speaker varies from community to community and from occasion to occasion. A child reared in a family which reinforced generously is likely to possess such behavior in great strength and will talk upon almost any occasion. A child reared in the absence of such reinforcement may be relatively silent or taciturn. . . . In a situation designed to resemble an interview of an experiment on verbal habits, the experimenter shapes up the behavior of his subject simply by giving some slight "sign of approval" contingent upon a selected property of behavior.

—B. F. Skinner[1]

*A*lready at a very young age, she learned how to use sign language. When she was a little over one year old, she had acquired four signs that she understood fairly well already. Close to celebrating her second birthday, she was able to produce her first sign combinations, like *gimme sweet* and *come open*. About a year later, the number of signs had accumulated to over thirty, a number that then tripled in only a year. On her third birthday, her language skills had gotten to a level where she was able to sign her first sentences, which started to become longer than just two words, sentences like *you me go out* and *you me go out hurry*. With these sentences she had shown to already have acquired some basic grammar, slowly but surely, with actual syntactic combinations. She had shown to be able to vary the subject, object, and action of the sentence, syntactic combinations that pretty much looked the same as those any other baby would make, except she would make them in sign language.

Many of the signs she acquired were initially imitations from the signs her caregivers made, signs such as *sweet, flower, toothbrush,* and *smoke.* But she also created new signs. When she saw a swan for the first time and didn't know the sign for *swan* yet, she created a sign, that of *water bird.* Or when she didn't remember the sign for *bib,* she made up a sign herself, drawing a square on her chest. And like every other child, she generalized the information she learned. For instance, when she played with a padlock and a key, she learned that the sign for the padlock key could also generalize to other keys, like an ignition key. Over time, she was able to learn approximately 350 signs and used a selection of them in the sentences she signed.

Her name was Washoe, and Washoe grew up in a trailer with a five-thousand-square-foot yard. The trailer was equipped with a kitchen, living room, and bedroom, couch, refrigerator, and bed. Washoe seemed to be a happy kid, even though she had lost both of her parents. Her past was sad. She was captured by the U.S. Air Force for research for the U.S. space program and brought from West Africa to the United States, in Nevada. When she was five years of age, she moved to Oklahoma, where she lived in the Institute for Primate Studies. Washoe was a chimp who took part in a research experiment on animal language acquisition, and Washoe was the first nonhuman to learn American Sign Language (ASL).[2]

Allen and Beatrice Gardner, Washoe's trainers, understood that the vocal apparatus of chimps is not quite the same as that of humans. In the 1950s others had tried to teach spoken English to Viki, a chimp that was brought up in the home of her caregivers.[3] Careful speech therapy whereby Viki's lower jaw was manipulated to make her utter the sounds she was taught did not have the expected success. After six years of training, Viki was not able to produce sound combination that extended beyond *mama, papa, cup,* and *up.* Even though the fact that Viki was unable to speak could be interpreted as evidence that chimps are unable to acquire human language, it more likely indicates something else. Chimps simply do not have the vocal apparatus to produce the sounds of human speech. So perhaps chimps are able to learn human language, but can't be expected to produce speech.

Instead of being taught spoken language, Washoe was taught sign language. And Washoe did well. She was able to remember hundreds of signs, as evidenced by using them spontaneously for two weeks in a row and as demonstrated by the vocabulary tests she passed successfully. And she was able to teach sign language to others. When Loulis, a chimp who was not taught sign language by humans, joined the group Washoe was in, Loulis was able to learn his first sign from Washoe after being only a week in her company.

Another chimp, Nim Chimpsky, tongue-in-cheek named after the linguist Noam Chomsky, was trained at Columbia University by Herbert Terrace and some sixty teachers.[4] Nim learned about 125 signs in the first four years of his life. Nim also created sentences, but Terrace was concerned with the sentence constructions Nim created. Human children may start out with small two-word sentence (*mommy cookie*), but they steadily make their sentences longer (*mommy always bakes cookies, but daddy makes dinner*). Nim did not get much further than a sign and a half on average. Like Washoe, these sign combinations covered subject, verb, and object, like *play me, tickle me, eat Nim*, and *me eat*. If sentences were getting longer, they were on the level of *play me Nim, tickle me Nim, eat Nim*, and *banana Nim eat*. They basically added the word *Nim* to the word *me*. And while it was amazing that chimps like Nim were able to produce such sentences, Terrace found that many of the signed utterances were basically imitations from the trainers. About 40 percent of all sentence Nim generated were simple copies or reductions from what the trainer signed to the chimp. Only a small 10 percent were spontaneous utterances. The language-acquisition progress Nim made even dampened the enthusiasm of Terrace himself. Nim did not really seem to be able to acquire syntactic constructions human children rapidly made.

I am not in a position to comment on the ethics behind these studies given the zeitgeist of the 1960s. Raising a chimpanzee in a home environment deprived of any of its own species, teaching the chimp more human things than chimp things, and abandoning these chimps when a research project is over, may raise some eyebrows.[5] The 2011 documentary *Project Nim* does not make the viewer excited about the life of the main character, Nim Chimpsky. But if I try to ignore these aspects and simply look at the findings of the various studies that aimed to teach chimps human language, then no matter how optimistic we look at the words these chimps acquired and about the sentences they were able to form, their human language abilities were still a far cry from the many words human children effortlessly acquire. Yet knowing the mechanisms with which humans acquire language and with which nonhumans may is important, as it sheds light on the more general question of how language may be acquired.

BEING HUMAN

The question of whether nonhuman animals have language goes back to the question of how different nonhuman animals are from humankind. Eighteenth-century Swedish botanist, zoologist, and physician Carl Linnaeus, who is best known for his classification system of 4,400 species of animals and 7,700 species of plants, struggled exactly with that question. Where would you place chimps in the taxonomy of mammals? Close to humans or rather far away from them in the classification system? In the first edition of his *Systema Naturae*, he placed humans, sloths, and monkeys in the same category, which he labeled *Anthropomorpha* (or "human shaped"). But in the later editions of the classification system, he replaced *Anthropomorpha* with *Primate*, and included lemurs, monkeys, and humans in the same category. The genus Homo of the order Primates were divided into *homo diurnus* (man of the day) and *homo nocturnus* (man of the night). Humans fell under *homo diurnus*, orangutans under *homo nocturnus*.[6]

The struggle to understand whether primates—as we now know are our closest ancestors—are human or not goes back further. In the mid-seventeenth century, the Dutch anatomist Nicolaas Tulp had seen a young chimp from Angola in the menagerie of the Prince of Orange. He observed that the face of the animal looked like that of a human, and the ears and chest too were human-like, and so were its limbs. Interestingly, the animal was able to walk upright. And the similarities did not stop in the appearances of the animal. Its behavior was also very human. The animal wiped its mouth after drinking from a can, slept with its head on a pillow, and covered itself under a sheet. He therefore called the animal *Ourang-Outang sive homo sylvestris* (Ourang-Outang or wild human).

Another Dutchman, Jacobus Bontius, who worked as a physician in Java, one of the Dutch colonies at the time, came to a similar conclusion as Tulp. Bontius was convinced that Ourang-Outangs were furry versions of human females. In his *Natural and Medical History of the Indies*, he wrote in Latin that the Javanese claimed that the Ourang-Outang was actually able to talk. The fact that they generally didn't is not because they couldn't. In fact, they carefully kept their mouth shut and did not *want* to talk because they were afraid of being forced to work. Ourang-Outangs were basically human and could talk.

At the turn of the seventeenth century, a young male chimp was captured in Angola and brought to England, where it was displayed in a freak show in London. The chimp had incurred various injuries from his long journey to Europe, and due to infection, he sadly died in captivity three months later. Edward Tyson, England's foremost anatomist in the seventeenth century, seized the opportunity to dissect the chimp and concluded it had many human characteristics. Tyson made a list tallying the similarities and the differences the chimp in front of him had with humans. He concluded that the animal walked upright, its brain showed remarkable similarities to that of a human, and the animal had speech organs. But neither he nor anybody else had heard the animal speak, and he therefore concluded the creature must have lacked the spiritual qualities needed for language. Consequently, it was not human.

Lord Monboddo, an important jurist in eighteenth-century England, came to a different conclusion. He argued that chimps are part of the human species. They walk erect, build shelters, use sticks to defend themselves, and are in principle able to speak. And he proposed something interesting that may have served as a research proposal predating the research proposals regarding Viki, Washoe, and Nim by some two hundred years. Lord Monboddo argued that in order to know whether chimps are human, we should try an experiment where we investigate whether a chimp can be taught to speak. The creature needs to be young in order to participate in such an experiment, and Lord Monboddo was fairly convinced the experiment would in fact succeed, and the chimp would speak like a human. Importantly, he added, if the experiment would fail, it would not mean that the hypothesis of animals being able to use human language had to be given up. After all, articulation was difficult for anybody, chimps not excluded. Moreover, savages like chimps are naturally very lazy, and it might therefore be the case that they may not care to acquire language, even though they could.[7]

I don't think chimps are any lazier than the human primates. I often think (and will argue later) that it is humans who are considerably lazier, taking shortcuts whenever they can. Lord Monboddo's first argument, however, is a valid one, in light of the language research on primates. The vocal apparatus of chimps and other primates cannot be taken as an argument that chimps could not acquire language. And for that reason, Allen and Beatrice Gardner as well as Herbert Terrace used sign language. There are, however, species that have a vocal apparatus similar to that of humans. And this species is so different from humans that any human language ability they show would raise interesting questions about animal cognition at worst and evidence for animals being able to acquire human language at best. Grey parrots are such a species.

By far the most famous grey parrot is Alex. Alex was a grey parrot that was able to understand and produce human language. Irene Pepperberg taught Alex language.[8] After obtaining her master's degree in chemistry and her PhD in chemical physics, both at Harvard, she pursued her research in animal psychology at Purdue University after she read up on the sign language studies with chimps. At a local pet store, she asked the owner to choose a bird for her, to avoid any later accusations of her carefully selecting a specific bird that stood out in language abilities. The pet store owner chose Alex. Alex was taught different objects. In the thirty years Alex was trained, he was able to label more than fifty objects, seven colors, five shapes, and quantities from one to six, and was able to identify, request, and refuse some one hundred different objects. Alex understood relative size, the notion of absence, and the difference between *same* and *different*. A simple computation tells us Alex was able to understand the meaning of more than ten thousand linguistic constructions.

In one of the conversations with Alex,[9] Pepperberg shows Alex a square shape cut out of wool and asks Alex: "What matter?" Alex does not hesitate, answering, "Wool!" Pepperberg praises Alex, and continues with the same object, now asking "What shape?" Alex answers, "Four corners." When presented with two keys, different in color and size, and being asked "how many?" Alex responds, "Two!"—immediately followed by the question "Go back?" Pepperberg wants Alex to continue the experiment, and Alex tries a different trick, stalling the experiment by asking, "Have some water?" When shown a smaller and a larger green key and being asked "what color bigger?" Alex responds, "Green."

You could argue that the guessing rate is pretty high when only two objects are shown. But when Alex is shown a tray of fifteen objects, consisting of six blue blocks, two green blocks, four blue toy cars, and three green toy cars, things get more complex. There are now five green objects and ten blue objects, there are seven cars and eight blocks. But the combinations do not bother Alex. When asked, "How many green blocks?" Alex responds, "Two!"

One major deficiency Alex had was discussing his favorite object matter, that of paper. He was simply unable to discuss it. We could come up with far-reaching cognitive conclusions on Alex's linguistic "disability" of discussing materials made from paper. There may, however, be an easier explanation. When you don't have lips, pronouncing the word *paper* is simply not that easy.

The cognitive skills of Alex are impressive and make one reconsider animal cognition. But no matter how impressive, Alex's linguistic skills were not humanlike. Sure, there were interesting similarities, but Alex did not acquire language the same way humans do or use language the same way humans do. The question is perhaps not whether they could, but why they would.

LEARNING

Understanding how we can teach animals language requires an understanding of how animals learn. And to be clear, by *animals* I do not just mean chimpanzees and grey parrots, but also the human type. In the late nineteenth and very early twentieth century, psychologists were convinced that there was only one way to understand the human mind, and that way was through introspection. It basically worked as follows: You thought about your own thoughts and emotions and wrote them down in verbal reports so that others would be able to analyze them further. Reviewing your own mental processes would inevitably reveal an understanding of mental processes in general. A group of psychologists disagreed and strongly argued that psychology is a purely objective experimental branch of natural science and should adopt an approach that is objective and experimental. It would not be possible to investigate the processes going on inside the mind, but it would be possible to observe the behavior of the mind, not through introspection, but through carefully defined behavioral experiments.

In these early experiments, these psychologists, who called themselves behaviorists, investigated reflexive behavior in animals.[10] One such reflexive behavior is salivation. Most dogs salivate when they see meat. And when they do not see meat, but instead hear a particular sound—say, a bell—they do not salivate. American psychologist John B. Watson in the United States, but before him the Russian physiologist Ivan Pavlov, investigated whether a dog would be able to make the association between a bell, which would not result in the dog salivating, with the meat that would make the dog salivate. They made a sound just before showing a dog some meat. And even though the sound initially had no effect on the dog, the dog indeed learned to link the sound to the meat. Soon by only producing the sound, the dog would salivate. And even when the sound was not identical to the sound that was paired with the meat but was similar, the dog was able to learn how to generalize the pairing over different kinds of sounds. That association turned out to be powerful for a range of behaviors.

For humans, making these associations turned out not to be much different either. A small child, John B. Watson called him "little Albert," loved rats. When little Albert was shown the fluffy white animal, he showed all signs of affection. But then, just before the small white rat was shown to little Albert, a loud noise was made that frightened the toddler. Albert soon made the association between the friendly little animal and the scary sound. Presenting the friendly, fluffy rat without the frightening sound was enough to make Albert cry. And worse, the effect generalized over other objects. Whereas before, Albert had shown no fear of other furry objects, he now was frightened by a rabbit, a furry dog, and a seal-skin coat. Even a Santa Claus mask with white cotton balls in the beard was enough for Albert to cry.

If you think only hungry dogs and little toddlers would fall for associating two stimuli so that a neutral stimulus would yield a reflexive response, you are wrong. You can as easily be fooled into liking or disliking a stimulus. It happens to you on a daily basis, through television, billboards, and social media. Only seeing the red logo of Coca-Cola will make you thirsty (in fact, only thinking of it will already make you want to grab an ice-cold glass of Coca-Cola to quench your thirst, with or without the salivating). And the same is true for the picture of a juicy hamburger with tomato and lettuce on a wonderful-looking sesame seed bun. Mouthwatering. Or the clean logo of an apple (with one small bite taken out). You visualize iPhones or MacBook, and crave standing in hour-long lines to get the most recent piece of equipment with that logo.

For another real-life example, let me turn back the clock a few years. It does not happen frequently anymore, at least not with my computer (although the fear is still there), but there was a time that Windows computers spontaneously crashed. While you were working, a bright blue screen might pop up with the message "An error has occurred and Windows has been shut down to prevent damage to your computer." Your computer had crashed, and there was a high likelihood that your data was gone. Just gone. Hours of work deleted. And that was only if the operating system was able to pick up where you had left off. Basically, the bright-blue screen deserved its name: "Screen of Death." You did *not* want to experience the panic when that screen popped up! A common practical joke at the time was to see whether one could create a "little Albert" effect in the audience during presentations. Somewhere in the middle of your slide deck, you included a slide of the Screen of Death. It worked like a charm. If your audience had fallen asleep, showed signs of disinterest, or you were just curious what it would take for your audience to get something close to a heart attack, this one slide would do the job. You presented the Screen of Death, and all the little Alberts in your audience gasped in a state of panic.

The downside of the salivation or fear experiments is that they focus on passive behavior of the animal. Even though the animal—human or not—had associated one stimulus with another, there was little the animal itself needed to do. One could argue that salivation or being frightened hardly counts as "intelligent" behavior. To find out whether animals show signs of intelligence in active behavior, Watson placed a rat in a cage to perform a particular action. The small cage contained only a lever. There would not be much else for the rat to do than to walk around, explore the box, and perhaps accidentally press the lever. But as soon as the rat accidentally hit the lever, it received food. The rat soon associated pressing the lever with food. It had learned that pressing the lever meant food and pressed the lever more and more.

B. F. Skinner, the most-cited[11] and perhaps least understood[12] psychologist of the twentieth century, extended these experiments with a rat in a box pressing a lever to a maze in which the rat had to make specific turns to receive the food. Initially, the rat was lost in the maze, running around and accidentally finding the exit. But when food was awaiting, the rat learned to find the route through the maze. The rat was reinforced to find the exit of the maze with a reward and worked harder to get through the maze in anticipation of the reward.

Skinner soon got tired of fetching the rats each time they had managed to reach the end of the maze and developed a device that better allowed for observing the animal's behavior. The device looked like a cage and consisted of a loudspeaker, lights, a lever, an electric grid (to provide shocks), and most important for the rat, a food dispenser. Skinner found that learning a behavior could take place in four ways. If he wanted the rat to press the lever, he would either give the rat a reward, so that the rat would press the lever more to get more food, or the rat would press the lever more to be punished less. If the rat received shocks through the electric grid, but the shocks were removed once the rat pressed the lever, it learned really fast to press the lever. If Skinner wanted the rat to do the opposite, not pressing the lever, he would simply have the rat learn the opposite. If the rat pressed the lever, it would receive a shock, or would not get the food it wanted. This way Skinner was able to control the behavior by making it more likely to occur or less likely to occur. He could monitor when to give the food and how often, when to give shocks and how few. Skinner was able to become the puppet master of the behavior of his puppet, the Guinea pig (or rat).

When you want an animal to learn a behavior in the outside world to perform it, you might have to wait for a very long time. The rat in the cage will sooner or later press the lever with little else to do in the cage, but what if you wanted your dog to learn to roll over? In order for your dog to perform this behavior, you could patiently wait for the moment to arrive for your dog to roll over and then reward your pet (I would not recommend the alternative Skinner proposed: starting shocks that are later removed). Another way of making your dog roll over would be to reward your pet for any behavior that resembles the first steps to rolling over. For instance, your pet happens to start to lie down, and you reward it for lying down. Every successive approximation, every step that would get you closer to the ultimate desired action of rolling over, you use as a reward. And over time, by shaping the rolling over, your pet learns this new behavior.

Skinner argued that learning is associative.[13] Behavior, any behavior, can be learned by its consequences, the feedback from the environment. All you need is stimulus and a response—say, food and pressing a lever, or food and rolling over—and have the animal associate the two. The reward follows the response and increases the likelihood the response gets repeated. This way, animals—humans or not—do things that have positive consequences and stop doing things that have negative consequences.

Any parent knows that this often (but not always) works like a charm. "If you do your homework, you can have more screen time." "If you do your homework, you don't have to do the dishes." Just like the rat in the cage, your child may need a few reminders, but over time the new behavior will be learned. I often need to remind myself that so much experimental evidence has shown that since association techniques result in a desired behavior, it can only be a matter of time before my own children are perfectly well-behaved, will do their homework without any reminders, and that I do not have to set any limits on screen time. One day, hopefully soon, the association might have taken place.

The story goes that the technique of associating behavior with a reinforcer also works for psychology professors teaching Skinner's theory. Apparently, they too behave like rats. In a large lecture hall, students had agreed their professor would be an ideal Guinea pig for an experiment they concocted. The students decided to pay lots of attention to the lecturing professor when he was standing on one side of the podium. But as soon as the professor moved to the other side of the podium, they pretended to not pay much attention, in fact started to look bored. Initially not much changed, except that the students stuck to their plan. Pretended attention or no attention to the lecture depended on where the professor stood. It took a while for the professor to get the mental food from his students, but over time he learned the behavior that by standing on one side of the auditorium he got what he desired: attention from his students. He too had mastered associative learning.

VERBAL BEHAVIOR

What do pressing a lever, rolling over, electric shocks, and food have to do with language? Aren't our linguistic skills very different than pressing levers and rolling over? Not so much for Skinner. Language use is also behavior, as he explained in his 1957 book titled *Verbal Behavior*. The irony of the book written by a behaviorist is that it did not consist of any experiments. The book is all theory, and it is not an easy read, not even by academic standards. Skinner proposed a theory based on all the experimental work he had done. That theory stated that we learn language the same way we learn all other kinds of behavior, through rewards and punishments, through reinforcement.

So when a child is in the presence of a duck and the parent says, "That's a duck! Can you say duck?" and the child repeats, "Duck," the parent enthusiastically responds with "That's right!"—a positive reinforcement, the verbal substitute for the food the rat and the dog received for pressing a lever or rolling over. Over time, the child will say "duck" without the echoing prompt from her parents.[14] The child has learned to associate the word *duck* with the actual waterfowl through the reinforcements made by the parent. Or when the child says, "Bababababa," the parents will not quite repeat the expression, but as soon as the child starts to utter, "Mommy," the child is reinforced in her behavior: "Yes, that's mommy!" The child saying "babababa" provides enough reinforcement for the child to continue uttering sounds, but when the patterns of the sounds become more meaningful (at least to the parent), the child gets all the reinforcement she needs to become a fluent language user.

Most verbal behavior happens between speakers, whereby the speaker provides the stimulus (the verbal lever) and the listener the response (the verbal food). For instance, the child may have heard the word *push*. When she sits on the swing and says, "Push," she gets reinforced in using the word, if the word results in being pushed. By learning to associate the word *push* with the pushing of the swing, the child gets what she wants.

Whether or not the speaker is a child and the listener is a parent, many real-life situations help you learn verbal behavior. When the speaker requests or commands something and the listener complies, you know which request would give what you want (sometimes saying "please" helps, sometimes not). When the speaker asks something and the listener answers, the speaker has learned how to formulate questions. When the speaker gives advice or warns, and the listener follows the advice or warning, the form in which the advice or warning is given depends on the intended effect. When the speaker asks for attention and the listener attends to them, the speaker has learned how to get attention (eye contact will do, as with the example of the lecture hall, or raising hands may do). When we read *d-o-g* and somebody says, "Dog," or when we hear "dog" and then type "dog," we may have made the desired association. In all these cases, the verbal behavior of the speaker is reinforced by the listener, sometimes the listener being the speaker herself. For Skinner, language is action; language acquisition is training.

And just like with the generalization and discrimination of tones that will lead to the dog salivating, the generalization and discrimination of sounds will lead to a positive or negative reinforcement of the verbal behavior. A sound that is similar but not the same may lead to a response, telling the child that the sound belongs to the same category. But a sound that may have sounded the same, now leading to a correction or lack of attention, will have become a discriminant stimulus. Similarly, when the child learns *green circle* and *red square*, she is able to recombine generalizations like *green square* and *red circle*.

For the structure of sentences, things are pretty much the same. An ungrammatical sentence like *The store runs the boy* does not get reinforced in this order, but does get reinforced by its grammatical order, and we therefore tend to use the grammatical order more.[15] If a speaker has heard "the boy's gun," "the boy's show," and "the boy's hat," "the boy's _____" is available for any other combination.[16] In exactly the same way, the speaker learns to use the -*s* at the end of a verb when it is preceded by a noun.

So children seem to learn verbal behavior through interactions with their environment and being reinforced in their verbal behavior. Children are born with innate cognitive tendencies like abstraction and analogy, but their mind is otherwise a tabula rasa, a blank slate. Over time, they learn language, by associating the intention behind the sentence of a speaker with the effect in the listener. And this makes sense. Children imitate their parents, and when they do, they get rewarded, either by explicit praise, or at the very least by being shown signs of comprehension. Each time we see that somebody understands us, it could be seen as a reinforcement of the verbal stimulus.

Remember Nim Chimpsky, the chimp that learned sign language? Nim was able to sign many words and sentences by being reinforced, by being given a reward for the signs he created. And remember Alex, the grey parrot trained by Irene Pepperberg? Alex got rewarded and punished for successful and unsuccessful verbalizations. Pepperberg used a clever method related to the reinforcement technique advocated by Skinner.[17] Pepperberg was concerned that Alex would not so much learn the verbal behavior, but would only learn the verbal behavior specifically related to the reward. Rather than having Alex be the person experiencing the reward or punishment, Pepperberg made Alex the observer of the reward or punishment. Two trainers played along with the learning. When one of the trainers got an association right, she got extensively praised, and when she got an association wrong on purpose, she got ignored by the other trainer. That seemed to work. Alex did not pick up on the reinforcement to himself, but the reinforcement he observed from others.

There is much to be appreciated about Skinner's work, and his work on verbal behavior is no exception. Language is acquired, maintained, and extended the same way other behavior is. Just like pressing a lever or rolling over is an intentional action, for Skinner using language is an intentional action. Communication and language are basically nothing more than speaker and listener behavior, behavior that is learned, maintained, and extended through reinforcements. So when the speaker asks for the salt, and the listener responds by passing the salt, there is an association between the verbal behavior of the speaker and the action of the listener.

In a way, Skinner was almost twenty years ahead of his time, twenty years before the philosopher J. L. Austin in his *How to Do Things with Words* introduced the field of pragmatics.[18] Austin argued that we need to distinguish between what is said and meant, what is intended with it, and what happened as a result. Skinner demonstrated how to do things with words, how to link intention to effect, how to study language not in theory but in practice, in action. In a way, Skinner was paving the way for the field of pragmatics, the field of language use, well before it was even created.

In the field of pragmatics, the notion of action ladders is popular.[19] When we use language—when we do things with words—we build actions onto one another. For instance, if you want to ask the barista at Starbucks how much a latte costs, you first seek eye contact. As a function of that execution of behavior of seeking eye contact, you get the attention of the shop keeper. The reinforcement of eye contact through attention allows you to present a signal. You open your mouth and utter some speech, and the barista identifies this signal (she recognizes you uttering an English sentence). The identification of the signal reinforces you to speak. Based on the recognition of the signal, she also recognizes the meaning of what you say. Your intention of your speech act is to propose something to the barista (a question), and the barista considers that proposal. This dance of execution of behavior and attending to it, presenting a signal and the identifying of it, the signaling of something and the recognition of what is meant, and the proposing of something and the consideration of the proposal—this action ladder—to me looks very Skinnerian in nature.

Hardly any scientists today would dare to mention Skinner or behaviorism with regards to the psychology of language.[20] It is a no-go because of one review that changed the field of psycholinguistics in the late 1950s. In response to Skinner's theory outlined in his book *Verbal Behavior*, some very positive reviews appeared from some very respectable researchers.[21] But one review has been remembered best, one that made people remember the book for all the wrong reasons.[22] The review was written by Noam Chomsky, a young linguist at the time who later turned out to dominate the field of linguistics in the latter part of the twentieth century. Chomsky's review of Skinner's ideas outlined in his book was far from positive. In fact, the only one positive thing Chomsky said about *Verbal Behavior* was buried in a footnote. The review was damaging and influenced the way behaviorism was remembered by psycholinguists.

Chomsky argued that children are not taught language, the way Skinner proposed, but acquired language themselves. According to Chomsky, parents hardly ever rewarded children for the grammaticality of sentences, and therefore it was at least mysterious as to how children were able to know what was a grammatical sentence and what was not without getting the reinforcement needed to learn this verbal behavior. Besides, the linguistic stimuli children were exposed to consisted of speech fragments, disfluencies, and snippets of information, certainly not the rich linguistic environment that would be needed to learn the verbal behavior described by Skinner. In fact, the experiments with animals to acquire verbal behavior are perhaps the best example that humans do not learn language that way, Chomsky argued. Neither chimps nor grey parrots would come close to the ability that only our human species has, the uniquely human ability of acquiring language. Chomsky's criticism was pretty much an advertisement for the way he viewed humans to understand language, as we will see in the next chapter.

Somewhat surprisingly, Skinner brushed off the criticism and never quite responded to the review, and neither did fellow behaviorists, at least not for a while.[23] But when behaviorists finally started to respond, by then anything that even remotely reminded cognitive psychologists and psycholinguists of behaviorism had become very suspect.

The criticism had much to do with a different perspective on what linguists thought they were supposed to study. Charles de Saussure, one of the most prominent linguists, proposed a distinction between language as a system of abstract, systematic rules and conventions and language use. De Saussure illustrated this distinction with a game of chess. You can look at chess as the rules behind playing the game. But you can also look at chess as the moves a chess player makes when playing the game. De Saussure introduced the distinction in the early part of the twentieth century, predating both Skinner and Chomsky. Skinner's view on verbal behavior was very much similar to the moves the chess player makes; Chomsky, however, was more interested in the rules behind the game.

The Skinner-Chomsky feud—or rather Chomsky's criticism of Skinner's approach, for Skinner never responded—is not an academic discussion. It brings us to the heart of how to keep those words in mind—or how we keep those chess moves in mind, to follow De Saussure's analogy. For instance, the question we can ask is how somebody learns the game of chess. One answer may be that we just jump into a game. We make a move and see what move our opponent makes. If we win a game, we made the right moves. If we lose a game, we made the wrong moves, with each individual move leading up to a reinforcement or a punishment. We are basically trained in playing chess by simply doing it. No prior knowledge is needed. We start out with a blank slate and act on the moves being made.

Somebody can object that learning chess this way is silly. There is nobody who starts playing chess without being explicitly told what the rules are behind the chess game. A chess player starts out not with a blank slate but with some existing knowledge of the game of chess. This knowledge consists not of a sequence of individual moves but of the rules behind those moves. It would make much more sense to learn the rules rather than individual moves, as the number of possible moves is incredibly large. Let's assume that each chess player has only two options for any move she makes, and let's assume that the average chess game has some forty moves. The number of options for a player would be 2^{40}, which is over a trillion. But this would be an extreme underestimate, as there are typically some thirty moves to choose from, leading to some 10^{60} combinations.[24] Learning each of these moves would be impossible, whereas relying on rules seems a bit more manageable. According to the U.S. Chess Federation, the game of chess has ninety-one rules[25]—still a lot, but at least a number that consists of only two rather than sixty-one digits.

Just like chess players do not get the continuous reinforcement they may need, children often do not receive the reinforcement needed to build their verbal behavior. Parents are often so excited about their children saying the first sentences that they do not care *how* it is said, but *that* it is said. So if their child utters an ungrammatical sentence, no parent will correct the child, pointing out that the grammar is not quite perfect. And yet the child has no difficulty acquiring grammar. They will generate sentences they have never heard before by applying the rules of the language system. And even if the parent corrects the child, any parent knows that their offspring can be stubborn, as shown in the following dialog.

Child: Want other one spoon, daddy.

Father: You mean, you want the other spoon?

Child: Yes, I want to other one spoon, please daddy.

Father: Can you say "the other spoon"?

Child: Other . . . one . . . spoon.

Father: Say "other."

Child: Other.

Father: "Spoon."

Child: Spoon.

Father: "Other spoon."

Child: Other . . . spoon. Now give me other one spoon?[26]

ANIMAL COMMUNICATION

Let me return to where I started out this chapter. Whenever I mention to my students that animals do not have language, there are always several students forcefully protesting. Clearly, their dog or cat understands what it means to lie down. And what about dogs barking at each other or cats meowing to other felines—wouldn't that be communication? Don't animals communicate?

Of course animals communicate. Perhaps the most commonly used example of animals giving meaning to words in the wild is that of vervet monkeys. Vervet monkeys live in the southeastern part of Africa. They use some thirty-six words, or rather sounds. Three of those are alarm calls used to warn the other vervet monkeys of predators. One of them is a call that warns the fellow vervet monkeys of a snake, another is one that warns them of a leopard or other large animal, and the third is for a predator coming from the sky, like a bird of prey. The fellow vervet monkeys look to the trees, the ground, or the sky when they hear the respective calls, showing signs of comprehension. And they pass these calls on to others, so the vervet monkeys further away are also warned of the predator.

For vervet monkeys, the three calls are intended to warn the fellow vervet monkeys that a predator is approaching. They do not use the call for any other purpose. There is no evidence the vervet monkeys sit down at night and use the same calls to tell how a predator a while back happened to approach them, or evidence that they use the call to tell each other scary bedtime stories. For the vervet monkey, the intention behind using the call is intrinsically linked to the call itself. And that is very different from the way humans use language. I can command, "Quiet!" when I demand silence; request, "Quiet?" if I would like others to please be quiet; or say, "Quiet . . ." when it is finally quiet and I am expressing the relief of a quiet environment. But I can use *quiet* in many different ways. I may tell you that I almost became very quiet a while back when I heard about the accident that could have occurred. To make a long story short, apparently humans have unpaired the intention of the utterance and the meaning of the utterance. One advantage of this unpairing is that it saves memory. Children do not need to memorize each word and its intention, but can recycle language and intentions.[27]

Was Skinner plain wrong in his proposal that we acquire language by reinforcing verbal behavior, the same way all animals learn behavior? The evidence shows that we cannot simply conclude that. Language learners learn from their environment. If the linguistic environment is not that rich, it affects language performance. For instance, if we assume that babies hear some two hundred to three thousand words per hour, we can compute that by the age of three, babies from lower-income families have heard somewhere between 1 million and 15 million fewer words than babies from higher-income families. And this turns out to have an effect on later vocabulary growth rate, vocabulary use, and IQ test scores.[28]

Language users rely on context, as we have seen in the previous chapter. What may look difficult actually becomes quite easy if sufficient context is provided. And, as we have seen in the previous chapter, language learners rely on frequencies. Furthermore, we adjust our language as a consequence of reinforcement, as can be shown, for instance, in the groups we hang out with. The language I use with friends in a pub is rather different from the academic prose I use in scientific articles—all in line with verbal behavior (and verbal behaviorism).

Learning chess means learning the rules behind chess. But learning the rules is not enough to be a decent chess player. You will have to practice. Each move you make and each move your opponent makes shape you in becoming a better chess player. The frequency of moves and whether you win or lose certainly have an impact on your chess-playing behavior. So if learning chess means learning the rules behind chess, the question is where those rules come from. For chess we can rely on somebody telling us what the rules are, or carefully reading through the rules. But for language comprehension, it is not even clear what the rules are.

And that brings us back to how we keep those words in mind. We absolutely keep them in mind by training. By reading and listening to words in different contexts, we are better able to keep them in mind. But apparently training is not the only answer.

· 5 ·

Instinct

It seems clear that many children acquire first or second languages quite successfully even though no special care is taken to teach them and no special attention is given to their progress. It also seems apparent that much of the actual speech observed consists of fragments and deviant expressions of a variety of sorts. Thus it seems that a child must have the ability to "invent" a generative grammar that defines well-formedness and assigns interpretations to sentences even though the primary linguistic data that he uses as a basis for this act of theory construction may, from the point of view of the theory he constructs, be deficient in various respects.

—Noam Chomsky[1]

*H*umans have a knack for language. But where does that knack come from? The previous chapter argued that the answer might lie in the environment in which we train our language abilities. But perhaps we need to look for an answer somewhere else, inside ourselves, in our brains. Perhaps we are so good at language because we simply have the linguistic brains for it. Perhaps we are born with a language-acquisition device, or language instinct, that allows us to not put any effort into learning language, but enables us to acquire language effortlessly and automatically. That language instinct may be similar to the instinct spiders have when knowing how to spin webs. Spiders do not spin their webs because somebody told them, but simply because they have spider brains.[2] Humans with their human brains have a language instinct they are born with.

The idea of language acquisition being innate has dominated linguistics and psychology for over half a century. Before, researchers argued we are born with a blank slate and need to acquire language through the interactions with the environment, as the previous chapter discussed. Nativists argue language acquisition relies not on nurture but on nature. The nativist fire was ignited by linguist, cognitive scientist, philosopher, and political activist Noam Chomsky in the 1950s, but the torch was passed to many followers, most notably popularized by Steven Pinker in his book *The Language Instinct*. Rather than children starting out with a blank slate when they are born, nativists argue they are born not with a general-purpose computer module but with a module that is located in the human brain designed to do what humans are so good at: language processing. To quote Chomsky:

> To say that language is not innate is to say that there is no difference between my granddaughter, a rock and a rabbit. In other words, if you take a rock, a rabbit and my granddaughter and put them in a community where people are talking English, they'll all learn English. If people believe that, then they believe that language is not innate. If they believe that there is a difference between my granddaughter, a rabbit, and a rock, then they believe that language is innate.[3]

Apparently, the claim that there is such a thing as a language instinct seems rather undisputable. Clearly, even though I do not know her, Chomsky's granddaughter is very different than a rabbit or rock. So that ends the discussion. But I guess it would also shut down any discussion without the proper arguments. And I am not quite ready to shut down any discussion.

Let's turn back time to the 1950s and see how the view that a language instinct must be an explanation for language processing came about. Since 1957 the nonsensical sentence "colorless green ideas sleep furiously" has become sensical. In that year, Noam Chomsky published the book *Syntactic Structures*, a decade ago selected by *Time* magazine as one of the one hundred most important nonfiction books ever written, together with such illustrious works as Stephen Hawking's *A Brief History of Time*, Milton Friedman's *Capitalism and Freedom*, and Martin Luther King Jr.'s *Why We Can't Wait*[4]—impressive company for a book on language that counted only 117 pages. In the book, Chomsky argues that despite the fact that the colorless-green-ideas sentence is nonsensical, any speaker of English would agree that the sentence is grammatical, in contrast to a sentence like "furiously sleep ideas green colorless." Indeed, we, avid language users, have little difficulty distinguishing a grammatical sentence from a nongrammatical one. And it is not meaning that matters when it comes to understanding language but grammar, according to Chomsky. Grammatical structures are so intuitive to us, and the acquisition of these structures is so similar in children across the world, that there can hardly be any other conclusion than that grammar must be deep-rooted in our mind, so the argument goes.

According to Chomsky, understanding grammaticality based on the meaning of words is futile. Chomsky built on the work of his advisor, Zellig Harris, whose work tried to identify a mathematics of language.[5] Just like a computer program—the first transistorized computer was developed four years before the publication of Chomsky's book—language might be seen as a computer program with an initial state and a final state. The computer runs through sequences of states, adding a word during each transition, ultimately ending up with a final state: the sentence. The interesting aspect of this is that these sequences may also consist of loops, allowing for recursion in language. Let me illustrate that.

Consider the function $x = a$ (+ x), which reads as "we have a variable and that variable consists of another variable either with or without that same original variable." Based on this function, we can generate a potentially infinite number of combinations, such as a (because that is what x is minimally) and ax (if we take into account the minimal version of x and the optional additional x, which could be a). But we can also create *aax*, *aaaaax*, and *aaaaaaaax*. Now let's not use a and x as letters, but as variables, as placeholders for words. For instance, a is "old" and x is "man." We can now generate "old man" but also "old old man" and "old old old old man." Not very creative and not worthy of any literary praise. But interesting nevertheless, because we can generate a large number of sentences on the basis of only a few variables. If we now use a and x as syntactic categories, things become even more interesting. For instance, let's say that $x = a$ (+ x) now means "Noun Phrase = Adjective (+ Noun Phrase)." We are now able to generate "wise sincere grumpy old man" (minimally one, maximally infinite, and in this case three adjectives and one noun). Let's extend our rule system a bit more and assume that we have the following linguistic rules:

Sentence = Noun Phrase + Verb Phrase
Noun Phrase = (Preposition +) Determiner + Noun
Verb Phrase = Verb (+ Noun Phrase)

We have identified that a sentence must consist of a noun phrase and a verb phrase, and that the former must consist of a determiner and a noun and could consist of an additional preposition. The latter must consist of a verb, but may also consist of a noun. Three simple rules. But our linguistic software can now generate sentences such as "the man walks on the pavement in the park in downtown of the city in the county of the district of the state of the country on the continent of the world." With some simple software rules, we are able to generate a possibly infinite number of sentences, perhaps as many as sextillion! And those sentences are recursive. They reuse elements allowing for interesting reiterations of syntactic rules. Very long sentences like this specific example that shows how humans are able to generate an almost infinite number of sequences of words we typically call "sentences" in disciplines such as linguistics, but certainly not limited to linguistics, as disciplines like computer science and artificial intelligence are also very familiar with them, using a systematicity in a rule system for language that Chomsky proposed in *Syntactic Structures*, the book published in 1957 that turned out to be groundbreaking in the field of language research, and that affected many other fields in research because of the rules it outlined, capturing the structural regularities in language, including English but also many other languages that are or were spoken.

The rules can be used in building syntactic trees from sentences. So underlying the sentence "colorless green ideas sleep furiously" is the following tree structure.[6]

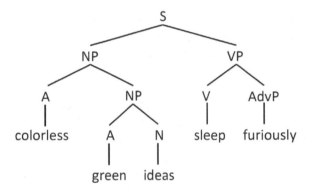

This structure tells us a lot about language. First, it shows which linguistic units belong to one another. The adverb *furiously* says more about the verb *sleep* than about the noun *ideas*. The "ideas" are "green" and the "green ideas" are "colorless." The evidence for this structure comes from a variety of pieces of evidence. It is far more likely that a speaker pauses between the branches high up in the tree than branches further down. So a speaker might say "colorless green ideas . . . ehm . . . sleep furiously," demonstrating these structures are psychologically intuitive. But perhaps even more importantly, we move units around when we form different sentences rather than the elements within the units. So I might ask, "What are the green ideas?" and you may respond "colorless." Or "what sleeps furiously?" and you may respond, "The colorless green ideas." Even forming questions follows transformational rules. Any speaker of English knows that if you want to form a question like "Did the colorless green ideas sleep furiously?" you basically put the original sentence in the past tense—"colorless green ideas slept furiously"—add the auxiliary verb *did* to the sentence—"colorless green ideas did sleep furiously"—and move the auxiliary verb to the beginning of the sentence. We know this because we have the grammatical rules in our mind, as we have the transformational rules in our mind.

Chomsky's proposal of a mathematical theory of communication, a software for language processing, needs to be seen in a broader context, a computational context. At a summer workshop at Dartmouth College in 1956, the field of artificial intelligence was born, when John McCarthy coined the term. MIT professors John McCarthy and Marvin Minsky, Carnegie Mellon professors Allen Newell and Herbert Simon, and IBM researcher Arthur Samuel attended the workshop.

That same year, another discipline—cognitive science—was born.[7] A Special Interest Group in Information Theory symposium was held on September 11, 1956, at MIT. The symposium included a paper by psychologist George Miller on human memory and the storage of information, one by Allen Newell and Herb Simon on a complex information-processing system, and one by Chomsky on formal grammars. Both the workshop at Dartmouth and the one at MIT were surrounded with enthusiasm on understanding the human mind in light of the advance of computers. Instead of the human mind being a black box that only functions in response to the environment, the human mind—like a computer—had independent thought processes, goal states, and memory and was able to execute plans.

There was excitement about human minds as well as about the artificial minds. By investigating human minds, we would learn more about artificial minds, and by building artificial minds, we would learn more about human minds. I often need to remind colleagues and friends that artificial intelligence has been around for quite a while, and that many of the developments in AI would probably not have taken place were it not for the developments in cognitive science.[8]

According to nativists like Noam Chomsky and Steven Pinker, language instinct turns out to be the answer as to why children are able to acquire language so well. What else can explain why every child, anywhere in the world, regardless of socioeconomic status or cognitive skills, is able to acquire language without a problem—assuming there are no factors detrimental to normal upbringing of the child, such as neglect or abuse? What else can explain how children are able to acquire language rapidly? Already before they turn 10, children are fluent in their native language. This is particularly interesting, because later on in life, it seems to be so much more difficult to acquire a new language.

So we could say that language is acquired fast and seems to have an age-dependent critical period during which it is automatically acquired. It is automatic, indeed, as we don't have a choice in language acquisition. I can choose whether or not to learn how to ride a bike or how to swim. But for language acquisition, it is different. I cannot bail on acquiring language. Whether I like it or not, I am equipped for acquiring language. I do not even need special instructions—as most children do when learning how to ride a bike or how to swim—and do not need any special encouragements. My parents never promised me money for acquiring language, as they did for coming home with an acceptable grade report. (I never made much.) Language is not learned on the basis of reinforcements and punishments, the argument goes. Language is acquired by children all over the world, at a similar speed, in similar phases, in more or less the same way.

And given that children all over the world, despite their different socio-economic status, despite the differences in their upbringing and education, all learn language in pretty much the same way, we must assume that there is some universal grammar underlying all languages in the world. Such a universal grammar may, for instance, consist of a particular structure such as the subject of the sentence preceding the verb. An extensive study[9] that investigated the word order of 5,252 languages in the world found that an astonishing 83 percent either had a subject-object-verb (SOV) order or a subject-verb-object (SVO) order. The SOV order can be found in languages like Japanese, Korean, Persian, and Turkish; the SVO order in languages like English, Spanish, and Chinese. Other languages, like Dutch and German, double-dip. They use SOV in their subordinate clauses and SVO in their main clauses. Despite the fact that languages could choose six different orders, almost 4,500 languages prefer either SVO or SOV word orders. No special International Committee of Linguistics was ever put in place to prescribe the use of subjects, verbs, and objects, and no world committee of linguistics ever prescribed the SVO or SOV structure. The strong preference for that order must suggest evidence for a universal grammar.

But if the argument is that language has a single set of rules from which all grammatical sentences in a language can be derived, why do languages look so different from one another? The answer is that what may seem different at the surface is ultimately the same when considering what lies beneath. That abstract knowledge of a language—and that's really what counts in the universal grammar—can be seen in the deep structure of a sentence. Take for instance the sentence "Juliet was kissed by Romeo." Even though the sentence looks different on the surface, at a deeper, more abstract level, it really is the same as the sentence "Romeo kissed Juliet." Or take the sentence "flying planes can be dangerous." The sentence can mean different things at a deeper, more abstract level. If you have not taken any flying lessons, for most of us the conclusion is simple: flying planes can be dangerous. But as for radiographic drones, the conclusion for those of us standing on the ground is the same: flying planes can be dangerous. The surface structure of a sentence is one thing; the deep structure of a sentence is another. And it is the deep structure that ultimately counts in this theory.

This universal grammar hidden in the deep structure of sentences is what maps language to grammar. That universal grammar, also called language-acquisition device,[10] can be seen as a mental switchboard that has a sequence of switches that need to be turned on or off. All the language-learning child needs to do is to turn on and off switches for the grammar it acquired. For instance, imagine a child becoming a speaker of Spanish. For her it is easy to turn on the pronoun-drop switch so that you can generate the sentence "*Ve este tronco? Sería Bueno para la fogata. Está completamente seco* [See this log? Would be good for the campfire. Is completely dry]." But for a child learning English, the pronoun-drop switch should be turned off, so sentences with a pronoun can be generated, such as "Do you see this log? It would be good for the campfire. It is completely dry." These switches, or parameters as Chomsky calls them, is a universal aspect of language. The language-learning child sets these parameters as they are exposed to language, thereby constraining the possible shapes of the grammar the child tries to acquire. Languages across the world must have a universal grammar because children across the world acquire language in such similar ways.

Steven Pinker would take the universal grammar to apply not only to sentences, but also to words. Similar to sentences, we have intuitive rules in our mind for word structure. Take for instance the word *Trumpianisms*.[11] Three years ago, then-President Trump accidentally tweeted, "Despite the constant negative press covfefe." *Covfefe* was a misspelling of *coverage*, but the word became an internet meme. *Covfefe* became a Trumpianism, one of several Trumpianisms. Without this explanation for a word you likely have never heard before, you would probably have had little difficulty getting to the meaning of *Trumpianism*. You would assume that *Trumpianisms* is likely to be plural, and *Trumpianism* would be singular. You would probably also be able to peel off the *-ism* from *Trumpianism* and conclude I was referring to something rather Trumpian. And if I asked what something Trumpian would be referring to, you would likely respond that it would refer to Trump. As with the sentence tree structure, the word tree structure would look something like this:

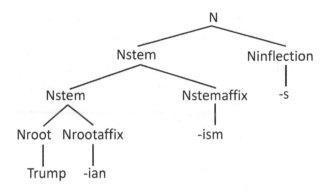

These rules—whether applicable to sentences or words—are intuitive to us. They are part of our language instinct. So if humans have a language-acquisition device, a universal grammar, a language instinct, that may be the conclusion. But what are the arguments arriving at that conclusion?

POVERTY OF THE STIMULUS

An important argument why our knack for language cannot come from anything other than a language-acquisition device or language instinct is that there is nothing else. It would be tempting to think that children learn language by simply memorizing the sentences their parents speak. We already know that the repertoire of sentences parents could choose from is some 10 sextillion. A child could have a fast learning strategy that allows for imitating every sentence that her parent has ever uttered. However, the language-acquiring child is able to speak sentences she has never heard before. And more importantly, the linguistic environment the child learns from is rather poor. There is a poverty of the linguistic stimulus.

Imagine that the child needs to learn what is a correct grammatical sentence and an incorrect ungrammatical sentence. She hears slips of the tongue ("The sky is shining"), sentence fragments ("Good job!"), and simplified sentences ("Wanna cookie?"). She hears incomplete sentences ("What I wanted to say really is . . . ah, never mind!") and disfluent sentences ("Can you . . . can you . . . can you help?"). For both incomplete and disfluent sentences, listen to somebody on the telephone, and mark how often the speaker uses an actual grammatical sentence. Not that often. Or think about how most people talk to babies: high pitch, lots of nonsense words, simplified syntactic structure with verbs and determiners being skipped ("Doggie gone!")—what some have called Motherese.[12] Compared to the sentences we are familiar with, and the ones a child will be able to produce, sentences are shorter, articulation is clearer, speech rate is lower, there are many repetitions, and so on. Because the stimulus children hear is so poor, it is remarkable that they are able to start generating full-fletched grammatical sentences and do not start to speak like their parents speak to them, in Motherese. Despite the poverty of the stimulus, children are able to acquire language and produce grammatical sentences that they have never heard before. Because of the poor quality of the stimuli, children cannot learn grammar from the stimuli themselves; they must have a generative grammar, a language instinct, at least according to some.

CRITICAL PERIOD

Further evidence for a human-specific biological capacity for language comes from a critical period during which language is acquired automatically. Humans have an optimal period for first language acquisition before the teen years. After the critical period, a fully complex language system will not develop. Evidence for a critical period in which language acquisition takes place comes from a study that investigated Chinese and Korean immigrants' language-acquisition skills of English.[13] The socioeconomic background and exposure to English were controlled for. The ages of arrival in the United States were between three and thirty-nine. A grammaticality judgment test showed that those who arrived between ages three and seven had a performance that was the same as for native speakers of English. After the age of seven, performance dropped to 94 percent for those who arrived between eight and ten, dropped further to 87 percent for those who arrived between eleven and fifteen, and dropped to 77 percent for those who arrived between seventeen and thirty-nine.

The fact that the immigrants performed at native-speaker level only if they learned the English language between three and seven years old shows evidence for a critical period. But this study is for those who learned a second language. What we would really like to know is whether there is a critical period for language acquisition in children who learn their native language. And that study seems impossible, or unethical at least. It would not be possible to deprive children of language and see whether—after the presumed critical period—they are able to learn language after all.

Sadly enough, there are cases—fortunately only very few—where children have been deprived of language. The most notable, sad case is that of Genie. Genie was born in 1957. From about the age of twenty months, Genie had been isolated in a small, closed room and was physically punished by her father if she made any sounds. Neither her father nor her older brother ever spoke to Genie, and there was no radio or television in the house. The mother was forbidden to spend more than a few minutes with Genie during feeding. I will not describe more details of Genie's very sad case, other than to emphasize that she was deprived of language during what can be presumed as a critical period in which she would be able to acquire language. Genie was rescued when she was thirteen years and nine months old. When admitted to the hospital, Genie was a painfully thin child who appeared to be six or seven years younger than her age. Susan Curtiss, who documented Genie's language development, gave examples of the speech she was later able to produce after being taken care of in foster homes.[14]

- Applesauce buy store.
- Man motorcycle have.
- Genie full stomach.
- Want Curtiss play piano.
- Father hit Genie cry long time.
- Mama have baby grow up.

Genie had not mastered grammar.

Another case of a child raised in a language-deprived environment is Chelsea. Chelsea was diagnosed as being retarded and emotionally disturbed. In reality, Chelsea was hearing impaired. When she was diagnosed as such and was fitted with hearing aids, she began acquiring language in her early thirties. Intensive training allowed Chelsea to speak, but her language was without syntax or morphology—for example[15]:

- The small a the hat.
- Richard eat peppers hot.
- Banana the eat.
- The boat sits water on.
- Combing hair the boy.
- The woman is bus the going.
- The girl is come the ice cream shopping buying the man.
- Daddy are be were to the work.

The ungrammatical sentences are the consequence of language not being acquired during the critical period for language acquisition. And native language acquired after the critical period, the argument goes, cannot be as grammatical as native language acquired during the critical period. Presumably the sad cases of Genie and Chelsea showed this all too well.

LINGUISTIC BRAINS

Evidence for a universal language instinct would ideally come from evidence for a genetic basis of language. We could, for instance, investigate language disorders in several generations of a family. If a language disorder is consistent across generations and if there is a neurological basis for a language instinct, then we should be able to identify the genetic basis through genetic glitches across the generations. Those glitches are then assumed to be associated with DNA, providing a biological basis for language. In the early 2000s, there was excitement in the language research community. A British family suffered from being unable to understand complex sentences and lacked syntactic organization in producing sentences. They placed words in the wrong order. A specific gene was found in the language disorders,[16] a stretch of code on chromosome 7, named FOX2P. The biological basis for the language instinct was found!

But the FOX2P gene could only be part of the answer. First of all, the fact that a language disorder in a family could be attributed to a mutated gene is one thing, but assuming that this gene is therefore responsible for normal development is another. Secondly, the FOX2P gene also showed to be related to the lungs, gut, and heart.[17] But perhaps most importantly, the FOX2P gene was not reserved for humans; it could also be found in other species. And that posed a problem. If the argument is that the language instinct is not found in any other species, and the FOX2P gene is the biological basis for the language instinct, then the gene is not to be found in other species. However, the evidence did show that the FOX2P gene is responsible for the fine motor control of bird song, and perhaps there is a strong similarity between bird song and human speech and language.[18]

But is there nothing in the brain that would suggest a language instinct? Well, I am not sure whether brain structures would demonstrate a language instinct per se, but it is the case that specific areas are more active in language processing than other areas. It would be a mistake to not think the entire brain is active in language processing (the same mistake as to think that we only use a small portion of our brain, as you sometimes hear at parties). Whenever we listen to speech or read, many parts of our brain are active: your motor and sensory cortex (the "hairband" over your ears), your visual cortex (the very back of your head), but most active in language processing are the areas that cover your forehead and your ear, the left side specifically. For about 90 percent of right handers, language processing takes place in the left hemisphere, and for about 50 percent of left-handers, it is processed in both hemispheres or even in the right hemisphere. And digging a little deeper in language areas, two areas stand out. One is called Broca's area, the other Wernicke's area.

Broca's area is named after nineteenth-century French physician, anatomist, and anthropologist Pierre Paul Broca. In 1861, Broca described a patient who had a stroke. The patient then had difficulties speaking. Pronouncing words, whistling, and singing were still relatively normal, but speaking sentences turned out to be extremely difficult. But his language-comprehension skills were still intact. He was able to understand speech. After the patient had passed away, Broca found that a specific part of the brain had damage. Later, some eight patients with similar language impairments had damage in the same area of the brain, an area that is now called Broca's area, around the left temple of the brain. Below you see an example of patient M.E. (initials are used to protect the privacy of the patient).[19]

> Ah . . . Monday . . . ah Dad and Paul and Dad . . . hospital. Two . . . ah, doctors . . . and ah . . . thirty minutes . . . and yes . . . ah . . . hospital. And, er, Wednesday . . . nine o'clock. And er Thursday, ten o'clock . . . doctors. Two doctors . . . and ah . . . teeth.

The speech of the patient we can still follow, but the grammaticality of the sentences seems to be the problem. The sentence structure is impaired.

Wernicke's area is another area in the brain that plays a central role in language processing. As you may have guessed, Wernicke's area is also named after the scientist who first linked the area to the language impairment, nineteenth-century German neurologist and psychiatrist Carl Wernicke. A group of his patients who had a stroke had no problems with the production of language, as with Broca's aphasia patients, but did struggle with the comprehension of written and spoken language. A well-known example of speech by a Wernicke's aphasia patient is that of C.B., who was shown a picture of two children stealing cookies out of a cookie jar while their mother's back was turned:

> Well this is . . . mother is away here working her work out o' here to get her better, but when she's looking, the two boys looking in the other part. One their small tile into her time here. She's working together and one is sneakin' around here, making his work an' his further funnas his time he had.[20]

What the cases of Broca's and Wernicke's aphasia show is that apparently the brain has areas dedicated for particular functions, language processing being one of them. More specifically, the heart of Wernicke's area is formed by the planum temporale. The planum temporale is reported to be five times larger in the left hemisphere than in the right hemisphere.[21] Perhaps the planum temporale is the language organ we have been looking for? In one study, brain activity was compared in three-month-old infants when presented with normal speech and reversed speech when they were awake and when they were asleep. The language areas that are active in adults, including the planum temporale, were also active in infants, despite the fact that they were not able to speak or presumably understand language.[22]

In another brain-imaging study, German native speakers were presented with Italian and Japanese samples and with an artificial language that violated the rules of a universal grammar. The results of the brain-imaging experiment showed that Broca's area was involved in the acquisition of syntactic rules of the universal grammar (Italian and Japanese) but not for the artificial grammar. Perhaps Broca's area, then, is the neurologically missing piece of the language instinct?[23]

UNIVERSAL GRAMMAR

The idea of humans having a universal language, a language-acquisition device, a language instinct has dominated linguistics for decades. But if the universal grammar is so universal, it should be easy to identify the elements of that grammar. We may argue that coming up with a unified universal grammar is not that easy because there may be small differences across languages, but according to Chomsky, the principles of universal grammar are really exceptionless.[24] Despite hundreds of scientific articles that discuss a universal grammar, a handbook of universal grammar does not exist, not even seventy years after the concept was introduced. And that is rather surprising if it forms the backbone of our uniquely human language instinct. Luckily some linguists have made proposals on what a universal grammar would look like. But when ten[25] of these proposals are compared, none of them are the same. They vary in almost every aspect!

But perhaps we should really look not at the elements of universal grammar but at the general principles, such as the ordering of subject-verb-object in languages. Did we not conclude that almost 4,500 languages either had SVO or SOV order in their deep structure? That would surely constitute some universality. Indeed, it is noteworthy that 83 percent of all languages use two out of the six word-order options. But when language *families* are considered, the number drops to 70 percent. Moreover, examples of languages for all six word-order combinations can be found.

One of the most central arguments for a universal grammar was the poverty of the stimulus. Children are never exposed to the grammatical sentences they are able to generate. But the argument can be made that there is not a poverty of the stimulus but a richness of it. Studies that looked at the actual quality of child-directed speech found something in stark contrast to a poverty of the stimulus argument. Out of the 1,500 sentences spoken to children, only one sentence—that's right, less than 0.1 percent—was ungrammatical. And even though some have argued that the fact that parents ask more questions and use more imperatives than in conversations we have, which consist of more declarative sentences, is evidence in favor of a poverty-of-the-stimulus argument,[26] others have argued that the less-is-more approach that parents take, starting with simpler utterances and slowly but surely building on to more complex utterances, in fact helps children to acquire language![27]

We may also place comments in the margin on the argument that children acquire language at an amazing speed. If children are able to learn language between three months and five years, one can object that they actually had an earlier head start, as studies have shown that children already acquire linguistic information while being in the womb.[28] Perhaps not so much complex syntactic information or semantic information, but certainly information about intonation of speech that may in turn affect at least grammar. Besides, what is *fast*? Five years and three months (or six years if you count the information the fetus acquires in the womb) may be fast, but everything is relative. Most babies take their first steps sometime between nine and twelve months and are able to walk around by the time they are fourteen or fifteen months old. So within six months, they are able to walk.[29] Or babies who begin to learn to swim between six and eighteen months old will take around one to two years to learn to be safe in the water. I am not comparing walking or swimming with language acquisition, but place six years in the context of other skills being acquired by babies, and the question can be raised what *fast* is.

But at least the cases of Genie and Chelsea demonstrate a critical period for language acquisition, don't they? Well, not really. UCLA professor Victoria Fromkin led a team of linguists who conducted the research on the language development of Genie. One of her graduate students, Susan Curtiss, did the testing and recording of Genie. Genie's case has been used as evidence in favor of a critical period, but the researchers themselves wrote a paper titled "The Development of Language in Genie: A Case of Language Acquisition Beyond the 'Critical Period,'" the abstract of which reads:

> The present paper reports on a case of a now-16-year-old girl who for most of her life suffered an extreme degree of social isolation and experiential deprivation. It summarizes her language acquisition which is occurring past the hypothesized "critical period" and the implications of this lan-

guage development as related to hemispheric maturation and the development of lateralization.[30]

But let's assume that the original researchers documenting Genie's case had it all wrong. There is the case of Chelsea. Chelsea performed poorly on tasks in which grammar was involved but did well on tasks in which vocabulary was involved. But again, the researcher reporting the Chelsea case, Susan Curtiss, does not argue for a critical period, but points out something different. She states, "In cases where the child and her language learning mechanisms are normal, but the language learning circumstances are not . . . one finds relatively intact grammar acquisition alongside more problematic pragmatic development . . . and, some researchers argue, lexical development as well."[31]

Both Genie and Chelsea were severely deprived of environmental stimuli altogether. In both cases, deficient cognition was reported, and it is at least problematic to attribute problems Genie and Chelsea had in acquiring grammar in isolation, separate from all the other problems they had to conquer.

Then there is the argument in favor of a language instinct because humans have language, and other species do not. That is true, as far as we know. We can consider the language-learning experiments as evidence that other species, regardless of all the efforts trainers put in, are unable to learn humanlike language. That is the linguistic glass being half empty. But the conclusion that animals do not learn humanlike language—and therefore humans have a language instinct—is a conclusion that is drawn too quickly. We could also argue that despite all the differences, it is miraculous that animals are able to acquire some basic meaning to words and grammatical structures in the first place. To follow Pinker's argument, "We should be impressed, first and foremost, that research on . . . grammar [in animals] is even possible!"[32]

And why would the fact that animals do not acquire human language be evidence for a language instinct? Perhaps it should be an argument for the role of the environment these animals live in. After all, there are clearly differences between animals living in the wild and animals living in captivity. Environment apparently matters.

An overview study that carefully analyzed 3,448 sign utterances from five chimpanzees (among them Washoe) came to the conclusion that chimps primarily use signs for objects and actions; they do not demonstrate evidence for semantic or syntactic structure in combinations of signs. If there were longer combinations of signs, they showed repetition. In short, sign use showed differences with child language, let alone adult human language.

Let's go back to Herbert S. Terrace, who taught the chimpanzee "Nim Chimpsky" language. Even though Terrace's original hypothesis was that animals learned verbal behavior the way humans learned verbal behavior, through conditioning, as we have seen in the previous chapter, his results ultimately confirmed Chomsky's view that language is uniquely human.[33] Nim's grammar was not human grammar. But recently, Terrace reached a somewhat different conclusion. In *Why Chimpanzees Can't Learn Language and Only Humans Can*,[34] Terrace didn't argue for a language instinct—even though his results may have suggested to others that this should be argued. Instead he argued that Nim couldn't learn language because he couldn't create sentences because Nim couldn't even learn words. It was not just the absence of grammar that distinguished Nim's language skills from those of humans'. Nim was not able to use words and name objects. Terrace argues that words, as much as grammar, are the cornerstones of language.

A final argument made by nativists for a universal grammar was the hypothetical language-acquisition device, the location of the language instinct in the brain. All the neuroscience evidence suggests that our language organ must be housed in the left hemisphere.[35] But there is a dominance for the left side also in birds and even in frogs, and we had just concluded that other species do not have language.[36]

If we look deeper in the left hemisphere, we might conclude that at least humans process language in Broca's and Wernicke's areas. That must then be the location of the language organ. If we consider Wernicke's area, perhaps the plenum temporale is the place to look. But Wernicke's area can also be found in great apes.[37]

The FOX2P gene might still be reason for excitement. The genetic basis for language might lie in this gene. Well, it turns out that the FOX2P gene seems to be related to the inability of coordinating motoric movements to form sounds. The gene can also be found in mice, an animal lacking the language instinct (the one named Mickey being excluded).[38]

There has been a lot of discussion on the language instinct. Whether or not the environment of the child is linguistically rich or poor, whether the argument for a poverty of the stimulus may be difficult or easy to make, there are few who would deny that children are able to extract syntax out of the language exposed to them. And whether children are relatively quick or relatively slow in acquiring language, whether the argument for a critical period may be difficult or easy to make, the way children are able to acquire language simply is remarkable. Whether parrots or chimpanzees are able to be taught language skills is an ongoing discussion of the linguistic glass being half empty or half full. In any case, this line of research has taught us a lot about animal cognition, and has at least humbled us in our bragging about our superior cognitive skills. And whether we have a language organ, a module in the brain specifically equipped for language processing or not, nobody would deny that one needs to have the brains—the human brains—to acquire language.

Yet what I have never been able to get my head around is the argument that meaning does not matter, that it is syntax that is the magic. To me syntax and semantics are intrinsically intertwined. The meaning of words determines the way syntactic constructions are formed. It is harder to read the sentence "The culprit killed the victim" than "The victim killed the culprit," even though both sentences are equally acceptable in terms of their syntax. And as I argued in chapter 3, if syntax is leading readers astray along a garden path, the syntactic confusion can be quite readily remedied by providing meaningful context.

But perhaps most importantly, I have never quite been able to understand nativists in the logic that language regularities bring us to a language instinct. I find it intriguing to see there are mathematical structures to language—despite the many exceptions to these structures across languages. But if there is a mathematics to language, why does there need to be a language organ? If there are regularities in language, why would that need to be governed by mental parameters? Why might the answer to why humans have language while other species do not be found somewhere else, outside of the language-acquisition device, outside of the language instinct, in language itself? It is not that arguing in favor of a language instinct is wrong; it just seems incomplete, perhaps as incomplete as arguing that language can only be acquired through training.

· 6 ·

Network

These models assume that information processing takes place through the interactions of a large number of simple processing elements called units, each sending excitatory and inhibitory signals to other units. In some cases, the units stand for possible hypotheses about such things as the letters in a particular display or the syntactic roles of the words in a particular sentence. . . . Thus a hypothesis about the identity of a word, for example, is itself distributed in the activations of a large number of units.

—James McClelland, David Rumelhart, and Geoffrey Hinton[1]

Let's talk canaries. What do you know about them? If you asked me this question, I would answer that canaries are birds. That they have wings and fly. They are often yellow. They have a beak. They eat bird seed. And because canaries are birds, I know they are animals, and therefore they are animate. They are often held in a bird cage as a pet. And one instance of a canary I know is called Tweety, and she is chased by a cat, Sylvester. An answer like that.

It is not my objective to start this chapter giving an exposé of the serinus canaria forma domestica, also called the domestic canary, but to ask a different question. A question not about what we know about canaries, but about *how* we know what we know about them. What is the nature of the representation of canaries we have in our mind? This question is most central to the cognitive sciences, as well as to computer science and artificial intelligence. After all, if we know how the meaning of a word is embedded in a network of meanings, we might be able to build computer programs that can answer questions. And the artificial minds of these computer programs might operate in a similar way as our human minds, and thus help us in the answer to our question of how we keep those words in mind.

Researchers trying to answer the question of what the nature of the representation of canaries (and any other concept) we have in our mind is have proposed that we understand the meaning of the word *canary* through semantic networks, networks of meanings of words. One instantiation of such a network is a hierarchical network that places concepts in relation to one another by placing semantic relations between them.[2] For instance, we know that canaries are birds, as are ostriches and penguins, and that birds are animals. Meanwhile, birds distinguish themselves from mammals, three instances of which are humans, cats, and whales.

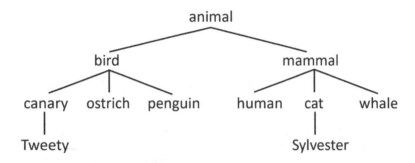

The advantage of this representation is that we only need to know the properties of the higher-level categories to automatically know the properties for the lower-level categories. Animals eat and breathe; birds thus eat and breathe, and so does Tweety. The semantic network excels in cognitive economy: I don't need to know all the features for a word. All I need to know are the features of the concept word the word in question falls under (its hypernym), so that Tweety inherits the features from *canary*, *canary* inherits the features from *bird*, and *bird* the features from *animal*.

This hierarchical semantic network seems to be an easy way to think about our conceptual world: a hierarchical model of all the concepts we have in our minds, related to all the words in our mind. And the hierarchical semantic network is not only theoretically interesting but also empirically supported. When participants are presented with sentences like "Canaries can sing" (a property low in the network linked to the concept low in the network), "Canaries have feathers" (a property medium-high in the network linked to the concept low in the network), and "Canaries have skin" (a property high in the network linked to the concept low in the network), the time it takes them to decide whether the sentence is true or not is higher with the increasing levels in the network. The sentence "Canaries can sing" takes hardly any time to verify, "Canaries have skin" takes the longest to verify, and

"Canaries have feathers" falls right in between. Words seem to be organized hierarchically in memory, as shown in several experiments.[3]

But despite its charm, there are some challenges with the hierarchical model. For instance, where do we place ostriches and penguins? We could place them at the level of birds, but are ostriches really at the same level as canaries and robins? Or should there be a subdivision of levels? I don't know about you, but to me canaries are more like robins than like ostriches or penguins. And what do we do with the platypuses? A platypus has a beak and lays eggs, and thus definitely belongs to birds (the ostrich camp of the birds, as platypuses do not fly). But a platypus swims and thus belongs to fish. But a platypus biologically is a mammal, though mammals don't lay eggs and platypuses do. Perhaps the platypus is an exception to the birds, fish, and mammals, but an exception that does mess up the hierarchical network.

I guess you can always find exceptions to every rule, and perhaps ostriches, penguins, and platypuses are the exceptions to the bird rule (with sincere apologies to the ostriches, penguins, and platypuses for singling them out!). But the hierarchical semantic network poses more problems. How do we deal with concepts that are difficult to consider in terms of a hierarchical network? Where do we place a cobblestone? Cat litter? Street? Dust? There are so many concepts that are difficult to put in a category overlooked by another category. A hierarchical network can hardly be the entire story how words are placed in a semantic network.

Several researchers realized exactly that and considered an alternative to a hierarchical network as a representation to how we keep those words in mind. Instead of thinking about a hierarchy where one concept inherits the features of another, perhaps we should think about a semantic network in terms of prototypes. We then have prototypical concepts in our mind, and we match different concepts to the prototype. Let's say that a canary is a prototypical bird. We could then still categorize an ostrich as a bird, but not a prototypical one, because it deviates from the prototypical canary. Basically, what we do over time is average all instances of birds and find the common denominator. The common denominator of the concept bird is then more likely to be like a canary than an ostrich.[4]

Or perhaps we have a semantic network that is not so much based on a prototype or an instance of a prototype, but a network based on the theories we form, some kind of theory theory.[5] On the basis of the world we view around us, we build mini-theories with facts about the concepts we learn. These mini-theories are like encyclopedia entries that fill themselves with the beliefs about what makes a concept a member of a category. These theory theories are subject to change and evolve over time, the more we learn about a particular concept. The idea of a theory theory may be interesting—well—in theory, but does not quite help to put our finger on the exact information we have in our minds. Perhaps we should not see our semantic network as a network of interrelated concepts, but simply as a list of features affiliated with a concept. For instance, a canary is [+*bird*, −*mammal*, +*fly*], a penguin is [+*bird*, −*mammal*, −*fly*], and a dog is [−*bird*, +*mammal*, −*fly*].

While identifying features for canaries may be a simple and elegant solution, there are some challenges. How many features should a concept actually hold, and how are we tracing down all these features? Should canary actually consist of *[+bird, −mammal, +fly, −swim, +swing, −bark, −meow, −growl, −wood, −plastic, −paper, −food, +beak, −nose, −square, +small, −large, +yellow, −green, −fur, +feathers, −rectangular, −triangular, −tail, −engine]*? That list may be almost endless. But perhaps canaries are just incredibly complex concepts for which it happens to be difficult to identify features. It may be the case that the number of features to identify for a concept like bird is difficult. There are different kinds of birds: some that fly, some that don't, as is the case of a canary and a penguin; some that possess bipedalism, walking on two legs, others hopping, as is the case for an ostrich and a canary.

Then let's take an easy concept, that of bachelor. That concept seems so simple. If I ask you for the features of a bachelor, it is easy to name two primary features: [−*married*, +*male*]. Bachelors tend to be male (otherwise they would be bachelorettes), and they are not married. Simple as that. But even the simple concept of bachelor turns out not to be that simple. Take Billy. Billy is a ten-year-old kid who likes baseball. Billy has a crush on Jennifer, his classmate. Billy qualifies as a bachelor, because he is both male and unmarried. But anybody would object that Billy cannot be qualified as a bachelor. Bachelors tend to be adults. So the feature list for bachelors is [−*married*, +*male*, +*adult*].

Now take Paul. Paul is an unmarried adult male, who has been living with his girlfriend for the last three years. Their relationship is happy and stable. Paul would certainly qualify as a bachelor, because he is not married and is an adult male. But here again, we can object that Paul is not quite a bachelor. Bachelors also need to be available, and Paul is not. Or meet Bernard. Bernard is an unmarried adult male; he does not have a partner. Bernard is a monk living in a monastery. Bernard matches all bachelor criteria and yet is not the most obvious bachelor. So perhaps our feature list needs to be extended to [−*married*, +*male*, +*adult*, +*available*].

And what about Charles? Charles is a married adult male, but he hasn't seen his wife for many years. Charles is dating and hopes to find a new partner. Charles is [+*married*, +*male*, +*adult*, +*available*]. Whenever I ask in my classes whether Charles would qualify as a bachelor, the entire class tends to be split. Whereas male students are easily convinced that Charles qualifies as a bachelor, I generally tend to get strong objections from female students: "Charles a bachelor? He is a cheater!"

To settle the discussion whether Charles is a bachelor (in which case we need to adjust our feature list) or a cheater (in which case we don't have to adjust our feature list), let's settle for Charles being a cheater. But what do we do with Dallin? Dallin is a married adult male, but he lives in a culture that encourages men to take two wives. Dallin is dating hoping to find a new partner. Dallin would definitely qualify as a bachelor according to our feature list, yet few of us would really call Dallin a bachelor. So even a seemingly simple concept like bachelor turns out to be complex.

Perhaps we should abandon hierarchical networks, prototype theories, feature theories, and theory theories altogether. They all seem too rigid for an understanding of the richness of the meanings we have in mind for a concept. Abandoning a proposal is, of course, easy. But proposing an alternative is difficult. Not long after the hierarchical semantic network was proposed, an improved version appeared[6]: a semantic network with interconnected nodes. Now robin, canary, and platypus can all be connected to one another, though with different strengths. Sylvester is connected to Tweety, Tweety to Big Bird, Big Bird to yellow and to beak (as is Tweety).

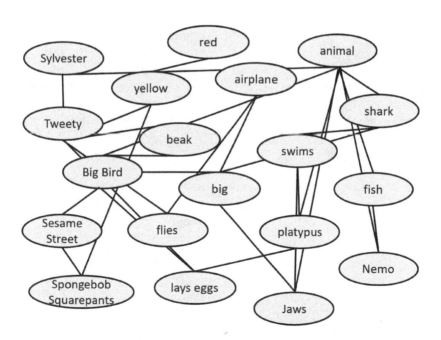

This network seems to nicely represent our knowledge, as it does justice for the many relations that exist between words as well as the many relations we could think of.

The idea of a semantic network of interconnected nodes was of interest not only to psychologists but also to computer scientists. For computers, it is notoriously difficult to understand the meaning of a concept. And understanding the meaning of a concept is important, for instance, in information retrieval. Imagine searching the internet for the meaning of *canary*, where else would you find this meaning than in the concepts related to canaries?

In the field of computer science, several attempts have been made to build a semantic network. One such attempt is WordNet,[7] an initiative that aimed to build a database of words and the semantic relationships between them. WordNet was initiated in 1985 by psychology professor George Miller at Princeton. Miller was getting tired of the toy examples presented in the psychology literature (examples such as the canary example used in this chapter, I guess) and started to develop a lexical database, initially of forty-five nouns and their relations. Those initial nouns ended up with a semantic network for English that now consists of 155,327 nouns, verbs, adjectives, and adverbs. And WordNet grew beyond English. It rapidly expanded to about two hundred languages. Many computer scientists and cognitive scientists have helped to develop WordNet, identifying each and every relation, relationships such as hypernym (the umbrella term of a hyponym), the hyponym (an instance of a hypernym), a coordinate term (two words that share the same hypernym), a meronym (words that have a part-of relationship), and a holonym (the opposite of the part-of relationship). Let's take our canary example again. In WordNet we find the following hypernyms for *canary*[8]:

a canary is a finch
    is an oscine
        is a passerine
            is a bird
                is vertebrate
                    is a chordate
                        is an animal
                            is an organism
                                is a living thing
                                    is a whole unit
                                        is an object

But *canary* also has a hyponym itself, the "common canary." And if you thought I could put the canary to rest, *canary* also has a range of sister terms from *goldfinch* to *crossbill, bullfinch, cardinal, honeycreeper,* and dozens of other feathery friends.

WordNet has proven to be a great resource for computer scientists. For instance, WordNet has been used for IBM Watson, a question-answering computer system that allows its users to ask questions in natural language. Watson then answers back. In 2011 Watson beat *Jeopardy!* champions Brad Rutter and Ken Jennings and won the first prize of $1 million. You can imagine that for a computer to answer a *Jeopardy!* question, the system needs to understand a word by taking all its semantic relations into account in order to come up with an answer. And a computational implementation of a semantic network like WordNet can be of help.

Indeed, WordNet is a fabulous resource! But it has also taken lots of effort and perseverance for WordNet researchers to build this massive lexical database. And yet for most of us, we have these relationships in our mind—granted, perhaps not of passerine being an oscine being a finch. How do we, language users, get those meanings in our mind, without homunculus programmers carefully crafting the relationships in our mind, or taking the 16MB database file and having it read by our brains?

And these are just single words. And as argued before, when it comes to language, we hardly ever use words in isolation, out of context. Cognitive psychologist Walter Kintsch and text linguist Teun van Dijk understood this all too well.[9] They tried to build an abstraction of the meaning of a sentence. Such an abstraction was needed. It is difficult to think of the concept canary as a specific canary in the pet store, the canary in my neighbor's house, the canary I saw in my daughter's picture book, and the canary I saw in the Warner Brothers cartoon; the semantic network consists of an abstraction of all those specific canaries.

Similarly, it is difficult to think of different meanings of the sentence "Juliet was kissed by Romeo," "Romeo kissed Juliet," "A kissing took place between Romeo and Juliet," "It was Romeo who kissed Juliet." As with the common denominator of the instances of canary, it's easier to think about a common denominator for the kissing event done by Romeo to Juliet. Something like KISSING (ROMEO, JULIET). These abstractions of sentences were called propositions. A story or text could thus be presented like a propositional network. And by using these propositional networks, van Dijk and Kintsch were able to get insight in how humans understand texts, how they remember the gist of the text (they recall the most important propositions), and how we summarize text.

With the success of WordNet, other computational linguistic tools emerged. FrameNet focused on semantic frames, similar to propositions, consisting of a conceptual structure describing an event, relation, object, and the participants in it.[10] And VerbNet, a database of English verbs that links their syntactic and semantic patterns.[11] The advantage of propositions, and VerbNet and FrameNet as tools, is that they moved beyond the word level. But they still required manual work. Humans had to interpret the sentences and rewrite these sentences into propositions, and then link the propositions to one another in a network. The question of how language users understand sentences and propositions so easily—while computers have so much difficulty with it, relying on carefully crafted databases—has not been answered.

But there was another problem. Much of what is not presented in language is used in our mental representation of the language. Let's use *Romeo and Juliet* as an example. When Romeo is exiled, Juliet is supposed to marry Count Paris. When Juliet asks to delay the marriage, her mother refuses. She then goes to Friar Laurence and asks for advice. Friar Laurence has an idea. He offers Juliet a potion that will put her into a deathlike coma for forty-two hours. The Friar promises to send a messenger to inform Romeo, who can then return when Juliet awakens. All this information can be presented in carefully crafted propositions that are interconnected. But when we understand this text, there is so much that is not in the text, but is in our mind, that making inferences based on propositions is hard. For instance, we know that if a person were dead, they would not have to marry anyone. Or we know that if someone drinks a fatal dose of poison, they immediately die. Or that if one believes that the love of his life has just died, then he is likely to feel overwhelming sadness and hopelessness. That if someone dies, they stay dead. So how do we know all these pieces of information, without them being given in the text?

Psychologists have struggled with this question, but for a computer scientist, this question was equally difficult to answer. An initiative like WordNet is great to develop a semantic network of words, but how do you deal with commonsense information, inferences? How could a computer reason like a human? Around the time George Miller started WordNet to map out the meaning of words, Douglas Lenat began an ambitious project to code the millions of pieces of knowledge that make up human common sense. The project was dubbed Cyc and is an inference engine and a database of statements.[12] All these pieces of knowledge were entered by a staff of human supervisors. As of today, over 25 million such general rules have been codified and formally represented.

So if you ask the question "When she takes the feign-death potion, does Juliet believe Romeo will believe she is alive during the time she is in suspension?" Cyc will answer:

Yes. If, at time T1, an agent's model of a subject's beliefs at time T2 includes a proposition, then the agent believes at T1 that the subject believes the proposition at T2.

At the time of Juliet's taking of the feign-death potion, Juliet has a model of Romeo's beliefs at the time of Juliet's being in suspension after taking the feign-death potion that includes the proposition that Juliet is a living thing.[13]

Even though Cyc is an incredible repository of common knowledge, we can ask why it takes a team of many, many coders thirty-five years to implement 25 million commonsense rules, many of which come naturally to any child.

Now whether a semantic network is hierarchical, whether some words are more prototypical than others, whether we have lists of features in our mind when thinking about a word, or whether semantic networks are simply a large collection of interconnected units, the real question is how they come about. WordNet has taken years of manual work identifying the many semantic relations between the words. And WordNet only looks at words, not even sentences. Cyc does move beyond sentences, but still has required large teams of supervisors entering information for years. And we, avid language users, do not require any manual work to understand the relationships between words and sentences, and the inferences we make on the basis of those words and sentences. It comes naturally to us. How do we keep those words in mind?

NEURAL NETWORKS

Perhaps for an answer to how semantic networks operate, we need to look deeper at the human brain. In the previous chapter, we looked at the brain in terms of hemispheres and language areas, but perhaps we should dig a little deeper into the brain to better understand what is happening within these areas.

The human brain consists of some 100 billion biological cells, called neurons. These neurons are responsible for the transmission and retention of information in the brain. They look a bit like a tree with a stem and branches. These "branches" of neurons are called dendrites (from the Greek word *tree*) and receive information from other neurons. Every neuron is connected to some one thousand other neurons. You can only imagine what an incredible network of 1 trillion connections looks like. That massive neural network has quite some benefits.

Our thoughts seem to go extremely fast. In chapter 2 ("Language"), I already discussed how fast we process language, but one can argue that picking up the words from a page or picking up the sounds from speech takes up some time in itself. The process of thinking—after the letters projected onto our retina or the sounds that have hit our ears' hair cells—seems to go even faster. Thinking about it, I can think a thousand thoughts with the speed of light, at least so it seems. The speed with which information in neurons travels varies in speed as a consequence of the width of the neuron. Some neurons travel between 150 and 250 miles an hour, while others make it to only one to four miles an hour. But even the 150–250 miles an hour is rather slow, when compared to the speed of light, light traveling about 670,000,000 miles per hour!

Now the distance traveled, of course, makes a difference. For instance, the distance a signal needs to travel determines its reaction time (the movements of your hand are faster than the movements of your foot). But on a larger scale, this is even more true. The distance a signal travels within your brain is considerably smaller than the distance lights need to travel in the universe. But there is another reason my thoughts *seem* to keep up with the speed of light, and that reason is important for the brain's neural network as well as for the way we process language.

If the brain were to process information step by step, speed matters. If our neurons were to work like a domino challenge, toppling one domino stone after the other, the process would be rather slow. The sequence of one neuron firing to the next one would make it impossible to read the word *dog* while thinking about my own dog. But in contrast to the way computers work, the brain's neurons do not send signals in serial, step by step, but in parallel. Compare it with the outbreak of the flu. It is not the case that when I have the flu and sneeze, one other person gets the flu, who passes the virus on when she sneezes, and so on, resulting in one large chain of virus spreaders. As we have experienced all too well with the spreading of the COVID-19 virus, one person might infect ten others simultaneously, who—not waiting for one another—spread the virus even further, resulting in a large pattern of virus activation. But back to the brain: with the trillion connections in the brain, a signal can travel across these connections simultaneously. The speed with which a signal travels is not that important, but the spread of parallel activation is.

When I say that neurons fire information to other neurons, it is tempting to think one neuron holds an entire concept. A grandmother cell that holds the memories of my grandmother. Or a Jennifer Aniston neuron that, for example, fires when the *Friends* television series is shown. Although the argument has been made for a grandmother cell or Jennifer Aniston neuron[14] for specific kinds of processing, for instance, in the case of facial recognition, overall the idea of holding information is a misconception. There is no "canary" neuron, or a "yellow" and "fly" neuron. Instead, the electrical signal that travels through a neuron is an all-or-nothing signal. The neuron fires, or it does not. Information the way we understand it, such as the concept of "canary," is not the information in one neuron but a pattern of activation across a bunch of neurons that are active in a network. So canaries in the brain may be represented as 101011011011—indeed, like computer code, where a concept is also stored on your hard drive as a sequence of 1s and 0s. This is at least true for the electrical signal of neurons, not quite for the chemical signal. The chemical signals are graded and modifiable in the neurotransmitters that flow between the connections between neurons, the synapses.[15]

PILE OF SAND

Now let's have a closer look at the way neurons in a network operate, in order to better understand the functioning of a neural network in the brain, and the developing of an artificial version of it in computers. To introduce you to the world of neural networks, let me illustrate with a pile of sand. That's right, I am comparing your brain to a pile of sand. Just as an analogy.

When you pour water on the pile of sand, the water flows in all directions. There are no pathways yet that determine how the water flows over the pile, but this changes the second time you pour water over the pile. Then some initial channels start to form. Water might still spill between channels, but it is not the case that water flows in all possible directions any longer. Instead, it starts to be canalized. The more water is poured over the pile of sand, the more the water deepens the channels. There is less water being spilled across channels, and water finds its way more quickly to the end of the pile.

This analogy shows a few things. At first, there are not really any connections (any channels) in the pile of sand, but over time the pile of sand "learns" which channels carry the water and how deep the channels need to be. Moreover, whereas water initially is flowing in many different directions, when channels are formed, the water flows efficiently and quickly to the end of the channel. The deeper the channel, the more the pile of sand has learned how to distribute the water. And finally, if one of the water channels in the pile of sand gets blocked, the water will make use of other channels to get to the bottom of the pile. It's not that the flow of water stops, or the pile of sand breaks down, but that the flow of water finds new ways of distributing itself over channels, with the depths of the channels adjusting as a function of water making use of them.

Now imagine that the water you pour over the pile of sand consists of different colors. There is one bottle with blue water, a bottle of red water, and a bottle of yellow water. As any child with a coloring book knows, blue and yellow mix to a green color, and blue, yellow, and red to a brown color. But the mix of colors depends on two things: the amount of color you pour into the mix, and the colors themselves you pour into the mix. In our pile of sand example, it depends how much of the yellow bottle or the blue bottle you pour over the pile, but also how deep the channels are. More colored water of one color with a channel that runs deeper will have more a prominence for a particular color than channels that do not run too deep (too much yellow, and you will get very light green). Now the channels that come together determine the outcome. That is, blue and yellow dye will give green, but if these channels mix with red, you get brown. So the depth of the channel (how wide and deep a channel is) and the amount of dyed water (one spoonful or two spoonfuls) matter in the output (or should I say outpour) of the water on the pile of sand.

Still with me? Now let's call the amount of dyed water "input unit." We have blue, yellow, and red water, so three input units. And let's call the depth and width of the channels "weights." If dyed water runs through a channel, the input unit thus has a weight, in our example three input units each with their own weights. Now let's say that the color that is formed (by the dyed colors) is called the activation. We can now say that the sum of activation of the output unit (the final color) is determined by the sum of all the units that input to it (the three colors) and the weights (the channel depth and width).

If the amount of dyed water and the depth of the channels in the pile of sand were to be predetermined, it is relatively easy to obtain a green color. But the magic of neural networks is that they learn how much dyed water and how deep the channels need to be entirely by themselves. The way they do this is by providing feedback into the system, a process that is called *back-propagation*. Initially, we just pour dyed water onto the pile of sand, not taking care how much yellow, blue, and red water we pour down. The channels also differ in depth. At the end of the pile of sand, we compare the color that is obtained with an ideal color green. If there is a mismatch, the error gets computed between what we got and what we wanted to have, and we adjust the channel accordingly (apply weights to the connections). Ultimately, after enough training, the perfect color green runs down the pile of sand. Next time we pour dyed water over the pile of sand, we obtain the color that the system was trained on.

There are many reasons why the analogy between a neural network and a pile of sand does not work. But I hope this example helps in understanding at least two things. First of all, the example is supposed to help you understand that we can start out with a blank slate—a pile of sand that has never had any water poured over it. Over time the system learns how patterns—channels—are formed based on the data—the water—sent through the pile of sand system. The weights of the network get adjusted based on the information that flows through the network. And that makes neural network pretty powerful. You do not have to continuously tell the network what is right and what is wrong; instead, in a training phase the network is told what is right and what is wrong ("No, this becomes too brown!" "No, no, the green is a little too light!" "No, not quite, now the green is too dark!") but is then able to learn by itself. Even if it gets new information, for instance a new color, based on the rules it has learned it is able to make its own decisions.

I also hope the pile of sand example helps in understanding how the system—our pile of sand—distributes information over the network—the channels of water that are formed. The more data that is sent through the network, the stronger the channels become. That means that if you pour too little or too much dyed water over the pile of sand, you might still be able to recover the green color. In fact, even if somebody comes along and blocks some of the channels on the pile of sand, the system does not collapse, but redistributes the information, strengthening the channels that have been formed already. Other channels may now take over and still carry the colors of the water through to the output color.

ARTIFICIAL NEURAL NETWORKS

Neural networks are in the brain. But we can also recreate them in a computer. These artificial neural networks, or connectionist models, basically work the same way as the neural network in the human brain. There are input units (in our pile of sand analogy the blue, yellow, and red color) and output units (in our analogy the green color). The channels that are formed have branches. Each time there is a new collection of branches, we can identify a layer. Simple neural networks only have one or two layers, but more sophisticated neural networks have many different layers, so-called hidden layers. These hidden layers distribute information over channels, so that patterns of activation in the network form information.

Neural networks, and particularly artificial neural networks, were extremely popular from the 1950s through the 1990s. "Cybernetics," as artificial networks were called in the 1940s–1960s, were very popular with the first computers to see daylight. "Connectionism" in the 1980s–1990s triggered enthusiasm as computers really seemed to mimic the human brain. Whether it concerned recognizing pictures, understanding handwriting, or performing speech recognition, neural networks were the answer!

They also seemed to be extremely powerful, as I found out during my PhD studies. When I was experimenting with artificial neural networks myself, I was determined to find out whether I would be able to create summaries of stories. I had collected several stories and their summaries and trained a large neural network to summarize the stories. Some initial tests worked pretty well, so I was excited. Because I knew that the network would take up a lot of computing power, I decided it was safest to start running my analyses on Friday night and have it run throughout the weekend. As soon as I started running the network, the activation units lit up, and patterns of activation were sent through the network. These colorful fireworks in themselves were worth running the analysis! These were the days that you had to dial in to the internet, so I would not be able to consistently monitor the network's progress online.

Monday morning, I got on my bike and cycled to the campus, hopeful to find some really cool results. I was met by the IT expert in the department, and he did not look happy. The network I ran had basically disrupted all internet traffic. It had taken up so many resources that it took a while before things in the department were back to normal. But despite the computational power outage my analysis had cost, the results looked pretty cool!

The first neural networks were introduced in the 1950s, accompanied by a lot of excitement. The July 8, 1958, issue of the *New York Times* stated, "The Navy revealed the embryo of an electronic computer today that it expects will be able to walk, talk, see, write, reproduce itself and be conscious of its existence." Contrary to human embryos, embryos of electronic computers apparently need more time in their life cycle, as seventy years later the electronic embryos with their artificial minds are not able to walk, talk, see, write, reproduce themselves, and be conscious of their existence.[16] But a lot of progress has been made in the meantime.[17]

Ross Quillian, who proposed the semantic networks we started out with, already emphasized that semantic networks could be seen as neural networks,[18] but it took until the 1980s for research in artificial neural networks to really take off. When I look to my right, I see two volumes of a book featured on my bookshelf: a blue one and a brown one. They are the two volumes that for me best define the field of cognitive science. The spines of the books read *Parallel Distributed Processing: Explorations in the Microstructure of Cognition, David E. Rumelhart, James L. McClelland, and the PDP Research Group* (PDP stands for parallel distributed processing). The two-volume book includes chapters by all prominent connectionists at the time (and many of today). It questions what it is that makes people smarter than computers, and then answers this question by describing the massively parallel architecture of the human brain. The book provided not only the foundations of what is called deep learning today but also models of perception, memory, language, and thought. James McClelland extended the line of PDP work for semantic cognition two decades later.[19]

Let's look at these artificial neural networks for semantic cognition a bit more. Typically, these networks have input units—where information goes in—and output units—where information comes out. Imagine the following artificial neural network, with three input units and one output unit.

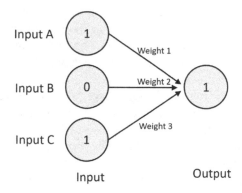

Each of these units can only have one value, 1 or 0, on or off. For each of the combinations of the input—for instance, 1, 1, 0; 0, 1, 0; or as depicted, 1, 0, 1—the output can be either 0 or (as depicted) 1. Let's assume that the network's task is to determine whether a set of features is a bird or not. Input A is whether or not the concept has a beak (yes = 1 and no = 0), input B is whether or not the concept flies (yes = 1 and no = 0), and input C is whether or not the concept is yellow (yes = 1 and no = 0). The output of the network is whether or not we are dealing with a bird (yes = 1 and no = 0).

The magic of the network starts with the weights. For each of the input units, there are weights for the output unit. The weights basically give the importance of an input unit for the output unit. Importantly, the weights can be adjusted, and this allows for the network to be trained. Imagine that we encounter Tweety, and we need to determine whether Tweety is a bird or not. Tweety has a beak, flies, and is yellow, and some supervisor (a judge, teacher, parent, or homunculus in our brains) or backpropagation tells us that Tweety is a bird. Before ever having encountered a bird, the weights (weight 1, 2, and 3) are set to a random number; each of the input units are randomly important. But now we know that the pattern 1, 1, 1 yields a 1 (a bird), and we can start adjusting the initially random weights. We can reinforce the weights and increase them. All units turn out to be important. Next, the network evaluates a yellow airplane. The pattern 0, 1, 1 is sent through the system, and the supervisor evaluates the concept as not being a bird. The weights can now be adjusted based on the error. Apparently, *yellow* and *fly* are not as important for something to be a bird as *beak* is. Weights 2 and 3 get downgraded, weight 1 upgraded. When the concept of a redbird is sent through the system, *beak* and *fly* get upgraded, and *yellow* downgraded further.

The advantage of this distributed representation is that we do not need a representation for a yellow Tweety that can fly, a red Tweety that cannot fly, or any of the other six units we would need, but we can now summarize all combinations in only three units (that can be on or off).

Needless to say, this is an oversimplification of an artificial neural network. Typically, these networks have a large number of input units as well as a series of output units. But importantly, they have something in between input and output units. As with my analogy of the pile of sand, these networks generally become more efficient and more powerful if pathways can be formed. These pathways become possible through one or more layers of hidden units, units that are neither input nor output units but moderating units that operate in the background; they are hidden. The input, hidden, and output units are like the sensory neurons, interneurons, and motor neurons in the human central nervous system. The sensory neurons pick up information from the environment; for instance, they "feel" you are picking up a rose for your loved one. The motor neurons activate muscle movements so that your hand jerks away whenever your sensory neurons feel a thorn on the stem of the rose you are picking up. Your sensory neurons and motor neurons are trained so that whenever something sharp is felt in the input, the output is a jerking away. What about the interneurons then? The interneurons sit between the sensory and motor neurons and communicate information between them in the central nervous system.

It may seem this is a rather inefficient system. Evolution apparently has not quite taken its course. After all, one would hope that if something really sharp is picked up, an immediate message is sent out to the motor neurons to drop whatever is picked up.

The opposite turns out to be true. By having these interneurons in the network, far more flexibility and efficiency emerge. If you feel something sharp or hot, it may be a signal to drop it—for instance, when touching a piece of broken glass or picking up a hot pan from the stove. But in many cases, it depends whether one should drop what is being picked up. Without interneurons, the floor of your local Starbucks would be a complete mess.

So a more sophisticated artificial neural network—but still an oversimplification—looks like the one presented below. It has three input units, four hidden units, and two output units. Unsurprisingly, it has far more opportunities to form activation pathways through the network. There are several advantages of having these hidden units, including not messing up the floor with hot coffee. Imagine that some of the input information is handicapped; say, for example, we observe Tweety from the back, after she fell in a can of red paint, and is consequently unable to fly. Because pathways have already been formed, we might still be able to identify Tweety as a bird. Or take character recognition: The network may be trained on *a, b, c, d . . . x, y,* and *z.* But now the *a* looks like an *q* and can thus not be recognized. The word *apple* is now an unknown nonsense word. However, thanks to the pathways being formed based on input, the network might be able to reconstruct the word *apple.*

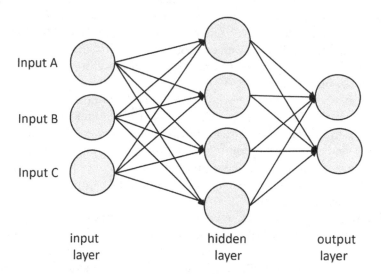

input layer   hidden layer   output layer

So let's take the idea of an artificial neural network even a step further yet and consider more input units, more hidden units, and more output units—and several thousand connection weights between all these units. For instance, we could take some concepts—say, some trees like a pine and an oak, some flowers like a rose and a daisy, some birds like a robin and a canary, and some fish like a sunfish and a salmon. We can also list a series of attributes, like whether the concept can grow, move, swim, or fly, whether it has bark, petals, feathers, or scales, and whether it is pretty, tall, living, or red. So we have a network with concepts as input units and input units with a bunch of hidden units that connect input to output. What the network is supposed to do, among other things, is to learn that canaries can move, grow, fly, and swim. And it can if we tell the network when it got it right in its patterns of activation and when it got it wrong. The purpose is not so much to find out whether a canary is a canary, but to measure what the network learns to "know" in terms of activation patterns.

The connection weights gradually adjust based on this feedback. So the network starts with random activation throughout the network "thinking" canaries swim and have gills, but gradually the more it learns, it finds out that birds and fish are different from one another. And the advancement of these patterns of activation is of interest to semantic cognition. For instance, we know that children acquire larger semantic distinctions first, before these distinctions become more fine-tuned. So when a child is around eight months old, they can distinguish between animals and furniture, but they are not quite able to make distinctions between fish and birds or tables and chairs.[20] Those distinctions emerge later. Networks show an identical development. The network starts out in a state where plants, trees, birds, and fish are alike. Then slowly but surely it moves categories apart, first the plants and trees away from the fish and birds, but later also the plants from the trees and the fish from the birds. And only then it starts to form distinctions between each of these categories. In a way, the computational development of the artificial mind mimics that of the cognitive development of the child's mind.

The network also learns which attributes are particularly important for a concept and which are useful to know but not necessary to know. If the network knows that flying is very important for the concept of a bird, it also knows that feathers and wings tend to be important, more so than the color yellow. Similarly, the network knows which attributes are important for different categories, just like children know that the color of a food item is more important than its shape, but that shape is more important for toys than color is.[21] So size is important for the category of plants and trees but not for the fish and birds, whereas brightness is important for the animals, but not for the plants.

Using these networks, we can see how new attributes introduced to the network generalize to specific features of a concept or groups of concepts. Or we can evaluate what would happen if the network suffers from progressive semantic impairments like dementia. Specific features in the network disappear first, followed by more intermediate features. Gradually, over time, the damaged artificial mind shows similar deterioration as the aging human mind.

In the 1980s, artificial neural networks seemed to be as hip as they could be. Doing connectionism was cool. Then in the 1990s, the paradigm shifted. Perhaps because connectionism seemed to be overpromising what it would be able to do, enthusiasm dampened. Computer power and the availability of enough data (there was not enough big data) made connectionism an academic exercise, with little real-world applications.

Even though scientists are typically not known for their branding and marketing, with regards to neural networks, they did an excellent job. They rebranded artificial neural networks and connectionism as "deep learning," and suddenly the excitement was back. Today, the number of courses on neural networks, machine learning, and reinforcement learning are countless. Any time you hear *AI*, it seems that what is meant is *deep learning*.[22] Self-driving cars can only operate with sophisticated deep learning whereby networks are trained on the environment: What is a road, What are different roads, What is a traffic sign, and How does a traffic sign distinguish itself from a pedestrian? For recognizing fingerprints on your smart phone, deep learning is used; for facial recognition, again the algorithm is a neural network. Speech recognition? Neural networks.

It is difficult to compare biological neural networks with artificial neural networks. We could compare them in terms of the number of neurons. The 86 billion neurons in the human brain with some 100–1,000 trillion synaptic connections will outperform artificial networks with some 160 billion parameters for the high-end performing neural networks. But size shouldn't matter.

The architecture of an artificial neural network is also very different than the biological counterpart. In artificial neural networks, information moves from one hidden layer to the next, whereas hidden layers in the human brain are hardly layers but vast dimensions of interconnected neurons.

American poet James Whitcomb coined the phrase "When it walks like a duck and swims like a duck and quacks like a duck, it must be a duck."[23] For artificial neural networks, one could argue the same. If the architecture of an artificial neural network looks like a biological neural network, it trains like a biological neural network, and it performs like a biological neural network, then it must be a biological neural network. But that conclusion comes a bit too fast. If it looks like a duck, quacks like a duck, but needs batteries, it may not be a duck after all.

One of the main questions I am struggling with while being impressed by the opportunities artificial neural networks provide does not so much concern the architecture, the processes, or the efficiency, but concerns the training and the data. In the field of artificial neural networks and machine learning, there is considerable enthusiasm about what is called reinforcement learning. The learning is reinforced by rewards. Every time the system is on the right track, you reinforce or potentially punish it. And that takes us back to chapter 4 ("Training"), where we concluded that cannot quite be the full story of how humans learn.

But I have a bigger concern that is related. How does the network know what is right and what is wrong, and what are the units in the network? In the simple example I gave earlier, there are some dozen features given for a concept. Okay, this is a simple example. But how many features should then be defined? How many features should be given for a canary, and where do these features come from in human cognition?

And finally, for artificial neural networks, it does not matter too much whether the units are random or structured. Whether I train the network on whether the pixels in automated image recognition are highly structured or not does not matter too much for the functioning of the network. Sure, it may operate a bit faster, but so far, no other advantages have been reported. And the question can be raised whether the same is true for language.

So in addition to training and instinct, perhaps networks are not the ultimate answer either as to how we keep those words in mind. As with training and instinct, network is undoubtedly part of the answer, but not the complete answer. Perhaps we should look further.

· 7 ·

Grounding

It can also be maintained that it is best to provide the machine with the best sense organs that money can buy, and then teach it to understand and speak English. That process could follow the normal teaching of a child. Things would be pointed out and named, etc. Again, I do not know what the right answer is, but I think both approaches should be tried.

—Alan Turing[1]

*T*he man sat calmly in his chair looking at the table in front of him. The room was sober with very little furniture in it, just a chair and a table. Not that he needed much more, but a room with no windows and very little furniture is just that, sober. The man couldn't see much more than the four walls around him. One side of the room had a letterbox, with a large sign hanging right above it that read *input*. The other side of the wall had a similar letter box that clearly read *output*. On the table, just in front of the man in the chair, lay a ledger. When the man studied the ledger, he found Chinese character combinations in the left column. In the right column he also found Chinese character combinations, but different ones. It seemed that the Chinese character combinations on the left had something to do with the combinations on the right. The task the man had received was simple. He had to wait for a note with Chinese characters written on it being passed on to him through the *input* letterbox. He then had to find the right sequence of Chinese characters in the left column ledger with the corresponding Chinese characters in the right column, write them down on a blank note, and put them in the *output* letter box. Basically, the man's job was to translate Chinese character sequences into other Chinese character sequences. He was translating Chinese into Chinese. The only problem was that the man did not speak a word of Chinese. He did not know the language at all. He was essentially locked up in a Chinese room.

The argument, now famously called the Chinese room argument,[2] is this: If the man in the Chinese room translates a sequence of arbitrary Chinese symbols into another sequence of arbitrary Chinese symbols, then does the man really understand Chinese? In a way this is what a Chinese speaker does, for instance, when answering a question. He receives a question in Chinese as input, searches through his long-term memory for an answer, and produces an answer in Chinese as output. But is he able to process the Chinese language and answer questions in Chinese just like a native speaker of Chinese does?

Most of us would agree the man in the Chinese room does not capture any knowledge of Chinese. The man just translates random foreign characters into other random foreign characters without understanding. The symbols he receives and produces are all Greek to him, or rather, Chinese.[3]

Now imagine taking this example one tiny step further. There is no room, there is no man, and hence there is no human mind. Instead, there is an artificial mind. A computer. The artificial mind does not receive Chinese characters, but combinations of *1*s and *0*s. All the artificial mind does is translate a sequence of 1011011 into another sequence of *1*s and *0*s, say, 001101100. If you agreed that the man in the Chinese room does not understand a word of Chinese, but instead he is crunching characters, you will also have to agree that the artificial mind is crunching numbers. For the artificial mind, let's call those numbers *bytes*. The argument—the Chinese room argument—is that artificial minds cannot understand the translation from number combinations into other number combinations. And consequently, computers cannot be shown to have a mind. They can never understand the meaning of language, because all they do is translate characters into other characters. So if the man in the Chinese room does not demonstrate language understanding, and if computers operate much like the man in the Chinese room, we will have to conclude that the network explanation for keeping those words in mind described in the previous chapter needs to be dismissed. Because neural networks do exactly that: they translate sequences of *1*s and *0*s into other sequences of *1*s and *0*s just like the man in the Chinese room does.

The Chinese room argument could be perceived as the argument that computers cannot think. But that's not at all what the argument is about.[4] If a computer is defined as something that can carry out computations, then every human is a computer. And every computer can thus think. Instead, the argument is that computation in terms of symbol manipulation—the translation from Chinese symbols into other Chinese symbols that are meaningless for the man in the Chinese room—does not guarantee thinking. More is needed than symbol manipulation.

Basically, the Chinese room argument is based on two claims, one related to meaning, the other to simulation. What the Chinese room argument tells us about meaning is that rules are not the same as meaning. Syntax is not the same as semantics. The man in the Chinese room is perfectly able to apply rules, as is a computer able to run a program, but this is very different from understanding semantic content. I can write computer code that says that if canaries fly, they move; or if canaries sleep, they dance; or if canaries bark, they abandon. The computer code will be perfectly able to process an occurrence of a barking canary into an abandoning canary, but it does not mean that the computer is able to understand the notion of canaries barking and abandoning. And similarly, the Chinese Room shows that simulation is not the same as duplication. It may simulate the cognitive processes of the human mind, but that would not mean that it has those cognitive processes. The simulation of digestion on a computer would, after all, be very different from a computer actually digesting pizza or beer.[5]

The Chinese room argument is a thought experiment introduced by the philosopher John Searle in 1980. The point of the argument here is to raise the question, *What constitutes extracting meaning from language?* And, according to Searle, the answer does not lie in the symbol manipulation that artificial neural networks do. Indeed, the Chinese room argument has major consequences for symbol manipulation systems that computers are. If the Chinese room argument is valid, and for now we are going to assume it is, then fields of natural language processing and computational linguistics, as well as artificial intelligence, can at best do something that may look like linking symbols from an input letter box to an output letter box, but would not come close to human language processing. It also means that the computer as a metaphor for language processing is flawed and we would not be able to learn much from it.

Others, in addition to Searle, such as the cognitive scientist Stevan Harnad, used a similar, less claustrophobic analogy than a Chinese Room with no windows. Imagine that you arrive in a foreign country not speaking the language of that country. All you have is a dictionary with words of that foreign country that are explained in other words of the language spoken in that foreign country. You can feel relieved having the dictionary to your disposal, but all you can do is translate words into other foreign words, which can be translated into other foreign words. Upon leaving the airport, you see a sign on the street in the language you do not speak, look up its meaning in your dictionary, find a sequence of symbols that do not make sense, look them up, and find another sequence of symbols that do not make sense. You basically end up in a symbolic merry-go-round—similar to the cabin fever of the Chinese Room, an inescapable, symbolic merry-go-round.

What is needed is something that gets you out of the circularity you are in, and that something is the outside world. The arbitrary symbols need to be grounded to something in the outside world for the words to make sense. The meaning of the word dog is not the symbol 狗 or the sequence 101110111. Instead, the meaning of the word dog is the image of a four-legged animal with a tail, the sound of the barking, the smell of a dog, the petting, in short the perceptual simulations of a dog. That is its meaning.

In the 1600s, the philosopher René Descartes argued that there is a clear distinction between our mind and our body. Mind and body may be connected, but the mental processes of the mind should be seen as very separate from the functions of the body. Consciousness and self-awareness are part of the mind and should be clearly distinguished from the brain. Indeed, the rational mind was divine and operated independent from the body—almost similar to the argument several centuries later that the logical computer could operate independently from an embodiment, and similar to the argument that the brain is a digital computational device separate from the body.

In contrast to this notion of a mind separate from a body, or dualism, researchers in the late twentieth century argued in favor of embodied cognition. In the previous chapter, we looked at considering words as part of a semantic network, organized as a hierarchy, as a set of features, as prototypes or instances, as a theory or otherwise. And that seemed to work well. We could look up the word *chair* in our semantic network and find that a chair is a piece of furniture, that it has four legs and a seat, with a support for the person's back, and that there are many instances of chairs, such as an arm chair, a barber chair, a rocking chair, and a wheelchair. That constitutes our knowledge of a chair. But embodied cognition researchers argue this rather computational view is a complete misconception of the human knowledge we have of a chair because in that notion of chair, the concept is nonembodied.

According to an embodied cognition account, the meaning of the word *chair* is not what is in the semantic network, whether it is hierarchical, prototypical, or feature-like. It is not a neural network where *1*s and *0*s constitute the concept of a canary or a chair. Instead, a chair is the set of affordances, things you can do with a chair: you can sit on a chair, you can use it to stand on when changing a light bulb, you can use it as a bookshelf or a table, you can lift it, you can use it to smash a window, and if you see a snake, you can use it to flick the snake away. These are the things we know about chairs without being told or taught, but these affordances we happen to know because of the perceptual experiences we have with *chair* in the real world. Let me illustrate with another example:

Imagine you have 500 bricks. If you throw one off a plane, how many will you have left? I guess the answer to that question is not too difficult: 499.

Here is another question. How do you put an elephant into a refrigerator? You may answer that's not possible. But the answer is that you open the refrigerator door, put the elephant inside, and close the door!

Let's follow up with yet another question. How do you put a giraffe into a refrigerator? You may argue that you open the refrigerator door, put the giraffe inside, and close the door. But you are wrong. You open the refrigerator door, take the elephant out, put the giraffe in, and close the door!

Enough about refrigerators. Imagine the following. The whole jungle was invited to the lion's party, but someone didn't show up. Who is it? Well, of course, the giraffe, because he was inside the refrigerator!

Now, an old granny wants to cross a crocodile-infested river. But somehow, she crossed the river safely. How? She could cross it safely because there were no crocodiles!

If you say that this does not make sense, because the river was crocodile-infested, you forgot about the fact that the crocodiles went to the lion's party!

But even though the granny was safe swimming across the crocodile-infested river, she tragically died. You wondered how? You thought the crocodiles ate her? Not really. The brick thrown off the plane hit her head.

Imagine understanding this series of riddles with the semantic and propositional networks I talked about in the previous chapter. That would be quite a challenge! The five hundred bricks minus 1 might be doable, but for all the other riddles, there is so much common knowledge tucked away that it would be hard how a strictly symbolic mind would understand the series of riddles. You have to understand that elephants do not fit in refrigerators, that there would not be enough space for the giraffe in the refrigerator unless an elephant is taken out. You need to perceptually simulate the story about the granny being killed, and that in popular stories crocodiles commonly kill humans, including grannies, but that if those crocodiles were all gone, even grannies could not be eaten. Basically, you would have to perceptually simulate the information in order to understand the joke. Embodied cognition theorists would argue not only that for the understanding of jokes we need perceptual simulation, but also that we need it for understanding the meaning of words. Or rather, they would argue cognition is embodied.

The notion of an embodied cognition questions symbol manipulation the way I described how we keep those words in mind in the previous chapter. Symbol manipulation through networks, artificial or not, demonstrates syntactic processes, but not semantic processes. But embodied cognition also questions the notion that grammar is independent of meaning, the way I described it two chapters ago. Remember Chomsky arguing that what counts in linguistics is an understanding of the grammar behind the sentence "colorless green ideas sleep furiously," independent of the meaning of that sentence? Embodied cognition theorists made the opposite argument, that grammar is dependent on meaning. Chomsky's mind-as-a-computer paradigm was replaced by a mind-as-body.[6]

Many embodied cognition theorists have made the strong claim that computers will never be able to understand the meaning of words.[7] The reason is that words are abstract, amodal, and arbitrary.[8] Words can refer to a procedure, a relation, a node, or a specific object. They have a high level of abstraction. Words are also amodal because it is unclear what sensory modality is involved in their perception. Sure, we read words with our visual modality or listen to words with our auditory modality, but that is basically it. Regardless of the modality in the meaning of the word, any word is spoken or written, and that makes them amodal. And words are arbitrary. There is no fixed relationship between the sound of a word and its meaning. We can even change the word without changing its meaning. If all English speakers would agree today that we call a toothbrush a canary, all is well. It may take a little practice assigning the new word to its old meaning, but we'll get used to it.

Pictures, sounds, touches, smells, and tastes are not amodal, abstract, or arbitrary. They have direct links to their auditory, tactile, olfactory, or gustatory experiences. They are concrete, modal, and fixed. The picture of a canary means a canary, not a procedure or relation, just a canary. Pictures are concrete representations. Pictures cannot be heard; they are always seen. They are modal representations because of the relation the picture has with a specific modality. And the meaning is fixed, not arbitrary. No matter how hard we may try to agree the picture now represents something else, it will always represent a canary.

Contrary to pictures, words are abstract, amodal, and arbitrary. They therefore cannot carry meaning without embodiment, without perceptual simulation. And because computers do not have eyes, ears, tongues, noses, or any other senses, computers will never be able to understand language the way humans do, at least according to many embodied cognition theorists. So much for fields such as computational linguistics, artificial intelligence, and computer science! Any computer model of language understanding—say, an information-retrieval system like Google or an interaction system like IBM

Watson—may look like human language comprehension, but it is not. The findings from the computational disciplines may correlate with human performance, but they say nothing about the actual extracting of meaning the way humans do, according to the embodied cognition argument. Remember the claim from the Chinese room argument: simulation is not duplication; what may look like digestion is not digestion itself, and what looks like language comprehension may not be the comprehension of language.

Much of the evidence for a network explanation as to how we keep those words in mind comes from computational models—for instance, in the development of an artificial neural network. Much of the evidence for a perceptual simulation explanation as to how we keep those words in mind comes from experimental evidence.[9] Computer scientists and artificial intelligence researchers advocating a neural network explanation argue that embodied cognition theorists are not even able to be precise in their definitions and operationalizations; after all, they have not implemented their ideas in a computational implementation. Experimental psychologists, on the other hand, advocating a perceptual simulation explanation, argue that those symbolic manipulation researchers will never be able to approximate human cognition in their computer models.

MONKEY SEE, MONKEY DO

In the 1990s, a group of neuroscientists in northern Italy, between Genoa on the west and Venice on the east, studied how neurons in the brains of macaque monkeys control their movements.[10] These researchers at the University of Parma inserted electrodes in the brains of the macaque monkeys and found that specific neurons fired in the motor cortex of the brains of these monkeys when they performed a particular action. So far, this was hardly spectacular. Already in 1937 Wilder Penfield had described how different parts of the body are arranged in the human motor and sensory cortex,[11] with different areas of the body being dedicated to different parts of the cortex. The more complex sensory or motor connections are, the more the amount of cortex being devoted to it, resulting in a very large cortical area devoted to hands, lips, and face, and very little cortical area devoted to neck, arm, and shoulder.

So finding different neurons firing for different actions was not spectacular. But finding the same neurons firing for observing an action as for performing an action was spectacular indeed. Apparently the macaque monkey's brain was set up in such a way that doing was the same as perceiving. Whether mirror neurons can also be found in humans turns out to be a more difficult question to answer.[12] There is at least a lot of research showing evidence for mimicry. For instance, when you stick out your tongue to a baby, it is likely the baby sticks out her tongue to you. And when you smile, the baby smiles.[13]

There is also evidence from the social cognition literature. In one "monkey see, monkey do" study, monkeys were substituted for humans. Two participants were sitting in front of each other in an experiment room. Unbeknownst to the other, one of the participants was actually a confederate, somebody who was an experimenter wolf in participant sheep coat. The task the confederate had in one half of the experiments was to increasingly rub his face. In the other half of the experiment, the confederate was to increasingly shake his foot. What the experimenters were really interested in is whether the actual participant would shake his or her foot or rub his or her face more often as a function of the confederate rubbing his face or shaking his foot. And that's exactly what they found.[14]

In my own lab we did a similar experiment, albeit without confederates. We recorded participants while they were communicating with each other on a specific task. One of the participants had a map in front of them with a route that guided them along a number of landmarks. The other participant had the same map, but with no route drawn on it. Actually, the map was not the same. In order to trigger some discussion, some of the landmarks did not match on the two maps. We collected thirty hours of communicative data: eyebrow movements, mouth movements, whether a participant touched his or her face, and of course also their speech. All that information got carefully transcribed.

In one study we investigated whether participants were actually copying each other's behavior. And they did. Not a little, but a lot. They copied the words the other person was using—if one person said "okay," the other person was more likely to say "okay."[15] They copied their eyebrow movements—if one participant moved her eyebrow up, the other was more likely to do this. They even copied hand movements—if one person touched his or her face, the other was more likely to do this. They matched their behavior across all the channels we could look for, and they did that increasingly. The more they talked to each other, the more they behaved like the other. It seems as if our words, gestures, and facial expressions become tightly coupled when we are engaged in dialogue. We start to function as one embodied system, rather than two.[16]

There are, in fact, immediate consequences to these findings that you can take advantage of. If you have ever served as a waiter or waitress in a restaurant or bar, or even better, if you are serving as a waitress or a waiter, here is some free advice on how to increase your tip money: copy the behavior of the customer. In a social cognition study,[17] a group of researchers looked at whether mirroring customers would increase tip size. The waitresses either mimicked a customer by literally repeating their order, or they did not. "A Cabernet Sauvignon, please, and a glass of water." "Of course, sir, a Cabernet Sauvignon and a glass of water." Those waitresses who mimicked their customers received much larger tips. So the advice is simple: do what your customer does, and see your tips increase. Apparently we like each other more as a consequence of copying each other's behavior. Copyists—rather than opposites—attract.

What is true for reenactment of behavior also seems to be true for reenactment of language. In one experiment,[18] participants saw sentences like "Courtney handed you the notebook" or "You handed Courtney the notebook," "Andy delivered the pizza to you" or "You delivered the pizza to Andy." The difference of interest between these sentences was that they conveyed a movement away from you as a comprehender (you giving something to somebody) or toward you as a comprehender (something being given to you). In addition, participants also saw nonsense sentences. Their task was to identify whether a sentence made sense or not by pressing a "yes" or "no" button. Nothing spectacular so far. But the buttons were not placed in front of the participants as a regular keyboard, but as a keyboard rotated 90 degrees. That is, in half of the trials, the "yes" button was away from the participant; in the other half of the trials, the "yes" button was toward the participants. It turned out that in most of the cases, participants were faster responding to "toward" sentences when the button was closer to them, and to "away" sentences when the button was further away, as if participants reenacted the meaning of the sentence when judging its sensibility.

Or when participants were presented with a sentence conveying a left-turning motion (as in "Dave removed the screw from the wall" or "Eric turned down the volume") or a right-turning motion (as in "Jane started the car" or "Louis sharpened the pencil").[19] This time, participants listened to the voice of somebody reading out the sentences and made sensibility judgments by turning a knob in front of them to the left or the right. You guessed it: clockwise movements were faster for the right-turning sentences, whereas counterclockwise movements were faster for the left-turning sentences. Again, participants must have reenacted the meaning of the sentence they heard.

Remember from chapter 5 ("Instinct") that most language processing takes place in the left hemisphere, around Broca's area and Wernicke's area? When I mentioned this previously, I hastened to say that language processing doesn't *only* occur in these areas of the brain, but instead that activation can be found across the brain. One such area turns out to be the motor cortex. In one study,[20] the brains of participants were scanned with an MRI scanner, a piece of medical imaging technique device that looks like a small tunnel you are sent through while pictures are made of the anatomy and the physiological processes of your brain. The participants heard words like *kick*, *pick*, and *lick* while they were scanned—three verbs that are related to foot movements, hand movements, and tongue movements, and that are similar in word length and in sound.

Now when the group of researchers monitored what happened in the brain when participants were exposed to these three verbs, they found something remarkable. The verb related to foot movement activated the part of the motor cortex involved in kicking. The verb related to hand movement activated the part of the motor cortex involved in picking. And, you guessed it, the verb related to tongue movement activated the licking part of the motor cortex. The motor cortex being involved in language processing is difficult to explain if language processing were merely a translating of symbols into other symbols. But if language processing requires a reenactment of the meaning it conveys, such as foot, hand, or tongue movements, then one would expect that areas in the motor cortex are active. And that turns out to be the case. So even though we already knew that more parts of the brain are involved in language processing than just Broca's area and Wernicke's area, what is peculiar is that those parts of the brain involved in reenacting the meaning of the verbs are also involved. It is as if cognition is for action.

In another innovative study where the brains of participants were scanned, participants were presented with a list of words and were asked to memorize their meaning—some forty words, so the task was not much beyond the homework that an average high school student gets when studying a foreign language. Two days later, the same participants were asked to come back for a recall task, the analogous high school exam, except that for the participants in this experiment, their brains were scanned again and the recall task was considerably simpler than that of a high school student. Participants were only asked whether or not they had seen the word presented to them. All participants got an A.

Now the experiment was not that much about remembering words. Critical to the experiment was that participants memorized words either with pictures or with sounds. For instance, the word *dog* was learned with a picture of a dog or with the sound of a dog barking. What was perhaps not so surprising is that the meaning of the word was remembered through the picture or the sound of the word. However, what was surprising was that the modality-specific memory was also used during recall.[21] When we remember words, we store those memories together with the modality in which we learned them.

Embodied cognition even lies in the wrinkles of one's face.[22] In one experiment, only middle-aged female participants were allowed, and only those middle-aged female participants ready to undergo a treatment with injections of botulinum toxin A (BTX) in corrugator supercilii muscle for the treatment of glabellar lines. In nonmedical terms, the participants were ready to undergo a Botox treatment to remove wrinkles in their face. As you may know, Botox paralyzes muscles, at least for a while, reducing wrinkles. A side effect, however, is that it also blocks facial expressions. And for a study investigating embodied responses to language, these participants are particularly interesting before and after the Botox treatment.

Participants read angry sentences like "The pushy telemarketer won't let you return to your dinner," happy sentences like "The water park is refreshing on the hot summer day," and sad sentences like "You hold back your tears as you enter the funeral home." Participants read the sentences while their response times were recorded before they underwent the Botox treatment and afterward. Before the treatment, they were able to use their facial expressions like most of us, and response times were "normal." However, after the Botox treatment, reading these emotional sentences took considerably longer, as if the participants were hampered by their body in understanding these emotions. Beauty is only skin deep; embodied cognition is apparently deeper.

PERCEPTUAL SIMULATIONS

Remember reading that detective, that thriller, or that romantic novel? When we are reading, it often feels as if a movie were being played in front of our eyes. A series of experiments have shown that this is indeed the case. The experiments all have basically the same design. The experimenter presents the participants with a sentence accompanied by a picture that matches or mismatches the sentence presented. In one series of experiments, participants read the sentence "A ranger saw an eagle in the sky" or "A ranger saw an eagle in a nest" followed by a picture of either an eagle with its wings spread out or an eagle in a nest. Response times were faster for pictures matching the content of the sentence than for pictures not matching the content.[23]

In another series of experiments, participants read the sentence "The carpenter hammered the nail into the wall," accompanied by a picture of a nail presented horizontally or vertically. The horizontally oriented pictures were comprehended faster than the vertically oriented pictures, but the opposite was true for the sentence "The carpenter hammered the nail into the floor." The researchers concluded that the only explanation for this finding is that language comprehension requires perceptual simulations, in this example of the visual kind.[24]

When participants saw the sentence "You are driving a car" and were asked whether a word like *steering wheel* was part of the sentence, participants were faster responding to *steering wheel* than *tire*, with the opposite being true for the sentence "You are washing a car." The explanation, according to the researchers, is that when you read the sentence that you are driving a car, you perceptually simulate that sentence, and the steering wheel is more visually present than the tires are. But when you read the sentence about washing a car, it is easier to see the tires in your mind's eye than the steering wheel. Apparently it is not only the visual information presented in the sentence but also the perspective described in the sentence.[25]

Still not convinced? Well, let's consider an experiment in which participants grounded information without being asked to ground it.[26] They took part in an eye-tracking experiment. Their eye movements were carefully recorded with an eye tracker, so the experimenters knew exactly what participants were looking at on a computer screen and where their eyes moved to over time. Participants thought they participated in an experiment in which they read some texts while their eye gaze was recorded; the experiment was broken up into parts with a break in between. The experimenters, however, were interested in not so much what happened before and after the break, but during the break itself. They monitored what the participants' eyes were doing during the break after having read one of the texts below.

Imagine that you are standing across the street from a 40 story apartment building. At the bottom there is a doorman in blue. On the 10th floor, a woman is hanging her laundry out of the window. On the 29th floor, two kids are sitting on the fire escape smoking cigarettes. On the very top floor, two people are screaming.	Imagine you are standing at the top of a canyon. Several people are preparing to rappel down the far canyon wall across you. The first person descends 10 feet before she is brought back to the wall. She jumps again and falls 12 feet. She jumps another 15 feet. And the last jump, of 8 feet, takes her to the canyon floor.
Imagine a train extending outwards to the left. It is pointed to the right, and you are facing the side of the engine. It is not moving. Five cars down is a cargo holder with pink graffiti sprayed on its side. Another six cars down is a flat car. The train begins to move. Further down the train you see the caboose coming around a corner.	Imagine a fishing boat floating on the ocean. It's facing leftward from your perspective. At the back of the boat is a fisherman with a fishing pole. The pole extends about 10 feet to the right beyond the edge of the boat. And from the end of the pole, the fishing line extends another 50 feet off to the right before finally dipping into the water.

Source: **Spivey and Geng (2001).**

As you can see, in some of these texts, an upward motion is described, and in other texts, a downward motion is described. In yet another text, a leftward motion is described, in another a rightward motion—just like the quadrants presented here, with the upward and downward in the top two cells, and the leftward and rightward motion in the bottom two cells. Participants made eye movements in the expected direction of the story. Apparently the story participants had seen was acted out by their eyes.

The evidence of activating perceptual simulations in language comprehension is not limited to one specific modality. There is evidence that a shift in modalities makes a comprehender a bit confused. In experiments in which participants were presented with sentences like "Apples can be green," they were followed with "Apples can be shiny" or "Apples can be tart." When participants were asked whether the property names of the concept belonged to the concept or not, the researchers found something interesting. If the content of the sentences stayed in the same modality, participants were quite fast in responding—for instance, when a visual sentence was followed by another visual sentence. But when a visual sentence was followed by a sentence denoting another modality—for instance, a gustatory sentence—it took participants longer to respond, apparently because they needed to switch between modalities.

EMBODIED METAPHORS

In the previous chapter ("Network"), I raised the question of how concepts relate to one another, what our conceptual system looks like. It also became obvious that it is difficult to answer that question. We may be able to build hypothetical semantic networks as examples, or even build computational implementations for applications. But there might be another way to shed light on our conceptual system, and that is through metaphors. Or rather, we might be able to better understand the conceptual system by looking at the language we use. For instance, when we are sad, we typically lower our shoulders, our eyebrows drop, our mouth corners droop, and our head hangs. But when we are happy, we erect our posture, lift the corners of our mouth, and raise our eyebrows. Happiness seems to go with an upward state and sadness with a downward state. That physical state is also found in metaphors.

> I am in high spirits. I am feeling up. That boosted my spirits. My spirits rose. I am in the clouds. Thinking about her lifts me up. But sometimes I am feeling down. I am feeling depressed. I am really low. I fall into a depression. My spirits sank.

Or to take another example: if you add something to a pile, the level goes up. This physical state of more is up and less is down can also be found in metaphorical expressions, embodied in language.

The number of subscriptions being sold keep going up. The chances of him winning are high. His income rose last year. The prices hit a historical peak. Prices went through the roof. That is a very high number. Or the activity went down last year. The number of errors is low. His income fell. He is underage. You may turn the heat down a little.

Metaphors nicely demonstrate that the mind is a body,[27] and that our conceptual system is embodied, an idea that has been tossed around, re-shaped, exchanged, or torn apart, an idea that was considered sweet by some, bland by others, and yet others needed to chew on it a bit more. In short, there are many examples in metaphor showing how what is very abstract and linguistic can be very concrete and embodied indeed. We keep metaphorical words in mind through grounding.

AFFORDANCES

The idea in embodied cognition is that we activate modality-specific infor-mation from language. We basically look at the affordances in the meaning of a word, the things we can do with the meaning of the word in the real world. Imagine you are on a camping trip and you forget your pillow.[28] One simple solution for this rather inconvenient problem is to fill up an old sweater with clothes and rest your head on the sweater. That seems to be an easy solution. In the absence of clothes, you could also consider filling up the sweater with leaves as a makeshift pillow to get you through the night. But if somebody suggested to you to fill the sweater with water, you would be surprised, to say the least. Filling a sweater with water would result in a wet sweater without any water in a matter of seconds. Basically, it's not a good idea to fill your sweater with water as a substitute for your forgotten pillow. Participants have no problem with the clothing solution, hardly any problem with the leaves solution, but raised major concerns with the water solution. Computational models are presumably unable to solve this. Because com-puters do not have human minds and bodies that allow them to consider the affordances of objects.[29]

And what happens when we read a sentence? According to an embod-ied cognition account, the answer to that question is not too difficult. We transform words and syntax into an action-based meaning. For each word we read, we activate the perceptual experiences we have with that word or link the word to its referent in the outside world. We activate the affordances of the word. Under the guidance of the syntax of the sentence, meshing of the affordances takes place, after which we can understand the sentence.[30] So if we read a sentence like "Edison stood on the chair to change the lightbulb," we activate the perceptual simulations and affordances of the words *Edison*, *standing*, *chair*, and *lightbulb*. The syntax of the sentence helps us to mesh these many affordances into a coherent mental representation; in this case, one of the affordances of a lightbulb (it can be held in the hand) is meshed with one of the affordances of the chair (it can be stood on to raise the body). Language is for action.[31]

EMBODIED REVOLUTION?

If one looks at the number of scientific papers on embodied cognition, one could argue that the cognitive revolution in the late 1950s—the excitement that artificial minds can be built that are similar to human minds—was followed by an embodied cognition revolution in the late 1990s. An avalanche of primarily experimental studies showed evidence for the claim that cognition is embodied. I will not discuss the findings of these individual studies, even though we can raise questions for many.[32]

One issue may be worth mentioning: Scientists generally measure whether two conditions are statistically significant, that is, whether the statistical findings of a study can be attributed to chance or whether they are real effects. It is obviously important to know whether two findings are statistically significant. After all, if I conclude that participants did one thing faster than the other as a consequence of the manipulation of my experiment, I want to have excluded the possibility that they would have done so anyway. But equally important, and some would argue even more important,[33] is the magnitude of the difference. Not so much whether there is a difference—no matter how small or large—but whether the difference is large enough.

Some have argued that the magnitude of the findings in embodied cognition studies is small.[34] The results may seem to be interesting from a statistical significance point of view, but the magnitude of the differences is so small that they are hardly worth reporting. We did a large analysis on any embodied cognition paper we could get our hands on and computed the effect size, the magnitude of the difference being reported. The conclusion was simple: Embodied cognition studies should not be dismissed. The magnitude of the differences being reported is large enough to take them very seriously.[35]

Perhaps the embodied revolution has been a paradigm shift in the cognitive sciences. Most cognitive scientists prior to that revolution must have had it all wrong, as many had not realized that language requires perceptual simulations and grounding. It seems obvious. We have a mind's eye. For the language we read or listen to, we automatically create mental images. We must, because only when words are linked to perceptual information do they become meaningful.

So imagine how hard it must be to have a life without imagery.[36] There are people who seem to be unable to create images the way most of us can. When being told to count some sheep to fall to sleep, they are unable to do that. And when they think of their loved one, all they remember is some features of the person, similar to the features discussed in the previous chapter. The only thing they have inside their head is an internal monologue.[37] This condition of living a life without imagery has been called *aphantasia*. It is a condition involving a lack of sensory imagery, but not a lack of metacognition, and is likely to have a neurological cause. We must worry about those who are reported to have aphantasia. Their language must obviously be very impaired. They must struggle with speaking, they must have problems with understanding language, and they will certainly stay away from book stores. That does not at all turn out to be the case. Those being reported to have aphantasia are like everybody else. They read books; they live their lives like any one of us. And that must be puzzling if perceptual simulation is essential for language processing.

Also, if we activate all the affordances we can when reading about zipping zippers, hitting the keys on a piano, flushing toilets, unlocking cylinder locks, flying helicopters, and operating sewing machines, we must have a pretty good sense (not an abstract, amodal, and arbitrary sense!) of zippers, piano keys, toilets, cylinder locks, helicopters, and sewing machines.[38] That does not quite turn out to be the case. We tend to be overconfident in our understanding of how things work (and perhaps think we mesh more affordances than we actually do). For example, imagine we read the sentence "The cyclist stood up from his saddle, stood on his pedals, accelerated the chain, and won the Tour de France." From this chapter you may conclude that we can only understand this sentence by simulating a bike, activating affordances of *saddle*, *pedal*, *chain*, and *wheels*. We must have a master's degree in cycology, if not a PhD!

Some elegant experiments in a paper with an equally elegant title—"The Science of Cycology"—shows something different. Participants were asked to draw the frame, pedal, and chain of a bike on a minimalistic drawing of the bike. Participants made considerable errors in their drawings. The pedals were placed on the front wheel or attached to the frame but completely detached from the chain, or attached to the chain but fully detached from the frame. In many cases the drawings placed the pedal in a position that a cyclist sitting on the saddle would not be able to reach (or the opposite with pedals placed such that cyclists would have the imprints of their knees in their neck). So much for affordances. Meanwhile the frame was drawn in a construction that would collapse with anybody sitting on the bike. So much for embodiment. Or the frame connected front wheel and back wheel, making steering a challenge. So much for perceptual simulations.

When participants were simply doing the experiment, about 40 percent made errors. When they were told that the quality of their drawings did not matter, but that the drawings were supposed to represent how bicycles worked—what the pedals and the chain of the bike do, why the frame of the bike is a particular shape, how to steer a bike—the errors increased to 60 percent! When cycling experts were asked the same question, the error rate dropped, but still lingered at around 10 percent. We may think that we master the perceptual simulations that come with bikes and cycling, but apparently we are not expert embodied cycologists. Some may think we perceptually simulate and embody concepts all we want, but we apparently cut some corners.

I started out this chapter with the Chinese room argument and said that the argument was to show not that computers cannot think but that symbol manipulation was simply not enough for thinking. The same question can be raised for the embodied cognition argument made in this chapter. Are perceptual simulations enough for cognition? Can perceptual simulations explain language processing? Is it really the case that for every word we read or hear, we activate all the perceptual simulations possible, all its affordances, keep those affordances in mind, and mesh them with other affordances until all words (or rather perceptual simulations) are understood? Undoubtedly it is true that we can generate pictures, sounds, feelings, tastes, and smells when reading or listening to a word. But the question is whether we always must and will.[39]

Let me give an example. I hope you have been able to read this book at least this far. I also hope you have been able to understand most of what I have written. Following the embodied cognition agenda, we then have to conclude that what you have done is activate the perceptual experiences for all the words you have read. And that process is so essential for comprehension that it should not be too difficult to backtrack and take a word and imagine what perceptual simulations you have created in understanding that word. The many experiments have shown that we do this all the time, for nouns like *eagle* and *nail*, for verbs like *push* and *pull*, for *kick*, *lick*, and *pick*, and for a variety of metaphors.

So here is the challenge. Open this book (or any other book you would like) to any page, and randomly point at a sentence on that page. And now explain to me what perceptual simulations you have created, or could have created, when comprehending the sentence. I bet that this turns out to be much harder than the experiments described in this chapter may suggest. In other words, with enough mental effort, we might be able to ground some abstract, amodal, and arbitrary words to perceptual experiences, but it may certainly not be the entire story as to how we keep those words in mind. And that brings us to the same conclusion for this chapter that is also drawn in chapters 4 ("Training"), 5 ("Instinct"), and 6 ("Network"): that grounding too is an incomplete explanation for keeping those words in mind.

But there is another problem. It is one thing for each of the four individual explanations to not sketch a complete picture. It is yet another to conclude that even the four explanations together do not paint a complete picture of how we keep those words in mind! And that is exactly the argument this book will try to make. There is more to keeping those words in mind than training, instinct, network, and grounding. The reason is that each of the four explanations discussed so far make an assumption about our cognitive system that needs to be scrutinized, as the next chapter will explain.

· 8 ·

Shortcut

But all of this depth, richness and endless scope for exploration is utterly fake. There is no inner world. Our flow of momentary conscious experience is not the sparkling surface of a vast sea of thought—it is all there is.

—Nick Chater[1]

You may still be glowing with pride. And rightly so. Already at a very young age, you have demonstrated mastering language production and comprehension. You are able to capture well over sixty thousand words in some 10 sextillion sentences, and within a quarter of a second of reading a word, you access its sound, its word structure, its meaning, and its relations to other words. You have been able to do it, and you are able to do it fast. You effortlessly hop, skip, and jump from one word to another one (and not necessarily the next one). And you have been doing this here for already seven chapters.

There is, however, an important caveat in the story I have covered so far. In the previous chapters I discussed language training, a language instinct, a neural network, and grounded cognition as an explanation for how we keep those words in mind. Without being reinforced by our environment, we are unable to train our language skills. Without a knack for language, it will be challenging to spin our linguistic webs. Without an infrastructure that provides a distributed representation of information, our linguistic sandcastle collapses. Without grounding words to perceptual information, we are stuck in a symbolic merry-go-round without meaning. There are few, if anyone, who would argue that without reinforcing language skills through the environment, without the ability of extracting rules from language input, without some kind of neural network, or without the ability of linking words to information in the outside world, we would be able to keep those words in mind.

It is not all or nothing. It is far more likely each of these explanations for how we keep those words in mind is a contributory explanation, whereby they all form concurrent complementary causes for our language skills.

In the discussion of these four explanations, however, there is one major problem: These explanations work well under the assumption that our mind has enormous mental depths, that our perceptual skills are attuned to activating all the affordances a concept can have, that our mental machinery continuously works at full speed in perception, action, and cognition. But these mental depths are the fly in the ointment. Our mental depths are not that deep. In fact, they are rather shallow. We'd rather go for the quick and dirty solution than for the slower and accurate solution. We'd rather go with little energy for imperfect solutions to a cognitive problem than full-blown ideal solutions to a cognitive problem that will cost us more energy. We'd rather go for a principle of least effort than spend mental effort on our cognitive tasks. We'd rather take cognitive shortcuts. Essentially, we are cognitively lazy. The pride you started this chapter out with may have dampened somewhat with the insult of being cognitively lazy. Let me try to get you out of your cognitively lazy chair and convince you of going for the path of least cognitive resistance, the path of shortcuts, with examples from perception, memory, cognition, and language.

PERCEPTION

Let's cut to the chase. Have a look at the lady on the left and the gentleman on the right. Nothing unusual so far, unless of course you may have taken some cognitive shortcuts.

Source: Getty Images.

Before you accuse me of presenting R-rated materials in a book that could (and should!) be opened by anyone, let me reemphasize that it is not these two pictures that are the source of some raised eyebrows. Not at all. There is nothing unusual about these pictures, other than that some aspects of the pictures happen to be blackened out. No, *you* are the source of the raised eyebrows. It is *you* taking cognitive shortcuts that may perceive the picture as an R-rated example, not the picture itself. It seems your mind is simply unwilling to get the picture straight. On this page, you will see the exact same pictures but now without the Swiss cheese effect and banner.

The effect you experience here, you have often experienced without paying (as) much attention to when watching the sunset. When the sun goes down, it may seem to be suddenly cut in half, but as we know, the next morning, the sun is as complete and glorious behind the horizon as the lady in the bikini is behind the Swiss cheese effect, and the gentleman is behind the banner that happened to hide his swimsuit.

Source: **Getty Images.**

Indeed, we are just cognitively lazy when it comes to pictures. In 1980, a professor of psychology at the University of York, Peter Thompson, presented participants with a picture of Margaret Thatcher, the prime minister of the United Kingdom at the time.[2] Or rather, he presented participants with two pictures. In the picture we see the face of the prime minister—but the effect can be repeated with anybody really—upside down. There is nothing unusual to notice, other than that the portrait is 180 degrees turned. The upside-down picture of Thatcher looks fine, except for the fact that it is upside down. However, when the portrait is flipped 180 degrees, a monstrous portrait emerges. It turns out that the eyes and mouth were placed in the correct form, while the face was flipped. When the face was flipped back in the original position, only then the uncomfortable reversal of features became obvious. But only then.

I will not repeat the experiment with Margaret Thatcher, but with myself. Below you will find a picture that may look a little odd, but nothing seems seriously wrong, other than that my face is hanging upside down. Particularly the eyes and the mouth look off (at least I hope these are the only features that look alien to you, as only these two features have been modified). Now turn the picture around. You find a portrait that looks scary, at least scarier than when it was presented upside down.

If your perceptual simulation skills are so astonishing that your mind reenacts the information presented in a sentence, as we have seen earlier, then at the very least those same perceptual simulation skills should perceptually simulate bikinis and swim trunks, or revert a picture and attend to facial features. But these perceptual simulation skills let you down. Any artificial neural network would have easily predicted bikinis and swim trunks, and identified reverted eyes and mouth in a picture upside down or not, with very little computational effort. So why has your human neural network not been able to complete this simple task?

You might only get a little comfort out of the fact that monkeys and chimpanzees are not very good at recognizing inverted pictures either. When images of chimps were presented, some with the eyes and mouth inverted 180 degrees, the chimpanzee participants selected inverted faces that matched or did not match a sample chimp face. Even though they clearly noticed the difference between the face being upside down or not, they could not distinguish whether the chimp face had inverted eyes and mouth[3]—just like the humans could not for the human faces. They too had taken cognitive shortcuts.

No matter how much training you get, no matter how much you rely on your nonshortcut instincts, no matter how well your neural network functions, and no matter how many perceptual simulations you activate, your cognitive laziness prevails, which is surprising. Because these explanations are the explanations for language processing, why would they not work for something as straightforward as pictures?

"Fair enough, there may be some cognitive laziness, but it is not that bad," you may argue. It is merely a matter of keeping multiple visual representations in mind, which makes it difficult to deal with these examples. Keeping a reverted picture in mind together while also taking into account the facial features that are reverted is difficult. And keeping two versions of a picture (particularly this picture) with or without a Swiss cheese effect and without or without a banner in mind is also cognitively quite taxing. Indeed, the examples I have given so far are cognitively taxing. But so is language processing. Keeping those sixty thousand words in mind, and accessing their phonology, morphology, syntax, semantics, and pragmatics while making predictions about the words to come, is cognitively very taxing indeed.

Lazy Conformity

Imagine the people around you are each presented with a card with a two-inch line drawn on it. The card is then taken away, and everybody, including you, is asked which of the lines on a different card are most similar to the line drawn on the original one, a line of one, two, or three inches. To you it is obvious. Of course the line that is two inches long, that one looks most like the original line. But the seven members of your group are not convinced. In fact, they all agree that it is not the two-inch line, but the three-inch line. If you are like most people, you are willing to adjust to what you really think is true.

In the 1950s, Solomon Asch conducted experiments like this.[4] Eight people were seated around a table and were presented with the cards with lines of different length. However, the eight people were not all participants. Only one was. The others were carefully instructed by the experimenter to sometimes give the answer everybody would agree on. But in some of the other trials, there would be a clear discrepancy. Rather than fighting for what the actual participant thought was right, she went along with the crowd at least in some of the cases. In a post-interview, participants explained they knew the others were wrong, but just conformed to the majority. Pretty lazy, cognitively speaking.[5]

Recall the experiments I mentioned in chapter 3 ("Guess"). In these experiments, eye gaze was recorded during reading, but the text being displayed was adjusted while participants were reading a text. That is, when they fixed on one word, the letters of all the other words in the text were replaced by x's. If the characters four letter spaces to the left of the word and fifteen letters to the right of the fixation were x-ed out, participants were not at all hampered in their reading process. In other words, participants would not notice if 80 percent of a single line in this book were crossed out, as long as the crossing out moved with their fixations on a word. That is a rather shocking conclusion. You think you see letters on this page, but if somebody magically were to cross out the characters while you were reading, you would have no idea! While you are reading these words from the page, you think you can see what is just left, right, above, and beneath the word you read, but you don't. You think you are seeing a page in front of you, but you cannot be certain.[6]

To make matters worse, if you think about it, we just make a lot of shortcut assumptions. For instance, while you are reading, you assume that the environment just behind you is still there, but this can only be an assumption (don't look over your shoulder now!). Perhaps some film crew just removed the environment behind you and replaced this with something completely different. You would not know, unless you got out of your cognitively lazy chair and looked around (and even then we have just seen you cannot rely on your senses). So we assume things we cannot see, and if we can see them, our mind has taken shortcuts to the assumption.

This is also shocking for the conclusions we have drawn so far. Any artificial neural network would easily be able to identify x's in a text, whether or not they are moving with reading speed, but a human neural network is unable to do so. Perceptual simulations should have been able to help us out, but they don't. And even with training, we'd rather take the shortcut.

If making assumptions about the world around us without really knowing starts to feel like another episode of the *Twilight Zone*, I am sorry to tell you that this is not at all science fiction. In a series of experiments, psychologist Daniel Simons has shown our ability to make shortcuts when it comes to change blindness—not seeing a change that is so obvious in hindsight. You may know the example from a gorilla dancing in the back of a screen, while you are counting how many passes a team of basketball players makes. In another experiment, Simons asked a confederate to stand behind a counter.

A customer participant approached the counter and asked for a package. The confederate kneeled down to pick up the package, but another confederate stood up and continued the conversation. The far majority of the customer participants had no clue somebody else was standing in front of them.[7] For them, making some convenient cognitive shortcuts seemed easier.

MEMORY

Not only do we not excel on perception tasks, but we also do not excel on memory tasks either. Perhaps even worse, chimps outperform us on memory tasks. When it comes to memory, we take shortcuts. For instance, when remembering phone numbers—though I have been getting worse at it with all the numbers safely stored in my smartphone—we use memory shortcuts to keep those numbers in mind by chunking a large sequence of numbers into smaller chunks.[8] For instance, if we try to remember the number 3 1 3 4 6 6 3 8 5 2, we take the shortcut of chunking the sequence into 3 1 3—4 6 6—3 8—5 2. It saves cognitive resources.

Now imagine the following task. On a computer monitor I present you nine numbers, 1, 2, 3, 4, 5, 6, 7, 8, and 9, as presented in the picture on the left, below. Your task is to press with your index finger on each number in ascending order, as quickly as possible. But you are pressured for time. After pressing 1 on the touch screen, you will have to press the number 2, and then equally fast number 3.

Now let's repeat that task, but let's make things a little more complex. After you press the number 1, within 650 milliseconds all the other numbers maintain their position, but are masked, as in the picture on the right, below. You are, however, still involved in the same task, pressing the numbers in their ascending order, and doing this as fast as you did this before. Undoubtedly, you will fail after the first numbers. I certainly do.

If you feel that 650 milliseconds is way too much time to remember the position of the nine numbers on the screen, let's try a third of that time, 210 milliseconds, about the time you are reading each word in this sentence (and all the others you have read so far). We will reduce the number of items from nine to only five, but you only have 210 milliseconds to glance over the screen and store the five numbers before recalling their order. I wouldn't come further than perhaps two numbers at best.

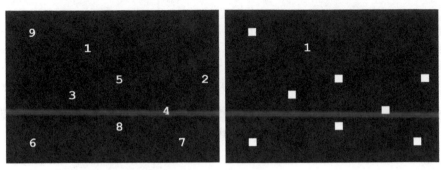

Source: **Kawai and Matsuzawa (2000).**

Now let's take Ayumu, a chimp trained on this task at Kyoto University.[9] Ayumu got 80 percent correct when recalling the order of numerals when they were flashed for 650 milliseconds, similar actually to human performance. But human performance decreased to less than 40 percent when the numbers were shown for 210 milliseconds. Ayumu's performance didn't. It stayed at 80 percent. Ayumu the chimp beat human college students on this memory task both in accuracy and in speed. And not by a small margin.

Whether human performance is so bad because of cognitive inability or cognitive shortcuts, I do not know. But the finding of chimps outperforming us on this task is at least remarkable given the explanations discussed so far on how we keep those words in mind. Granted, the chimps received a peanut for any successful task, but no matter how much training is provided, no matter how many rewards and how much positive reinforcement other than peanuts are given, it is unlikely you will be able to beat Ayumu. No matter how much brainpower we put into the task, how well our neural network is trained, or how many perceptual simulations we make, chimps beat us.[10]

Your memory is fallible not just to new information. When it comes to information you are very familiar with, you struggle as much. You should be quite familiar with a one-dollar bill. There are some 11.7 billion dollar bills in circulation, with each one-dollar bill lasting about 5.8 years. It is estimated that each dollar bill that is ever printed is used for at least two payments a week, so you should have seen them many, many times over and over again. So let me ask you, who is the president featured on the one-dollar bill? Does the face of the president of the United States look to the left or the right? And is the U.S. treasury seal placed on the left or the right of the bill? How many times do you see the number 1 on the bill? Once, twice, trice, perhaps even four times? Even some hesitation constitutes evidence for your cognitive laziness. Something that is so familiar, you are unable to recognize instantly.

Not only are we taking cognitive shortcuts when remembering information we have stored from a while back, but we also take shortcuts when relying on immediate memories. Putting your hand in water of 57°–59°F (14°–15°C) for, say, one minute is not pleasant. In one experiment,[11] participants were asked to put their hand in 57°F/14°C water for one minute. In the second trial, participants put their other hand in 57°F/14°C water for sixty seconds, but were asked to keep it underwater for an additional thirty seconds, during which the temperature raised to 59°F/15°C. Participants were then asked to choose which trial they would not mind repeating. You would expect the answer to be totally obvious. Of course, if you can choose between being exposed to an unpleasant situation for sixty seconds and one lasting ninety seconds, you would choose the sixty-second option in a heartbeat. But participants remembered disliking the ninety-second trial less than the sixty-second one, because at least the temperature was slightly higher—but only for the last thirty seconds, which participants apparently took too much cognitive effort to remember.

So perhaps your memory is not outstanding on number sequences or pain experiences, but undoubtedly your memory for geographical locations is impeccable. Let's check your geographical knowledge. I am going to assume that you know the location of some of the larger places in the United States and Canada, places like San Francisco, Seattle, Vancouver, or Montreal. What lies further north, Washington, DC, or Chicago? Not too difficult to answer, it seems. Obviously, Chicago lies further north, although only some 200 miles latitude difference. Here is another one. What lies further north, Toronto at Lake Ontario in Canada or Seattle, some 2.5 hours south of Vancouver? That seems to be an equally easy question. Canada lies north of the United States, so Toronto lies north of Seattle latitudinally. But here you are wrong. In all of our cognitive laziness, we assume that the border between Canada and the United States is a straight line, but it is not. In fact, it curves, so much so that Minneapolis and Seattle lie north of Toronto.

Here is an opportunity to compensate for this trick question. What lies further west, Reno, some 3.5 hours northwest of San Francisco, or Long Beach, just west of Los Angeles, overlooking the Pacific Ocean. Not too difficult either. You may have argued that your latitude estimates were a bit off, and indeed, this is the opportunity to redeem yourself longitudinally. But you are wrong again. In all of your cognitive laziness, you likely placed Long Beach west of Reno. After all, something land-inward is east of something at the west coast ocean line. But as with the northern border of the United States, the western border is not straight. Reno really lies west of Long Beach, and west of Los Angeles if one considers their longitudes.[12]

Incorrect estimates don't stop at geographical locations. Our estimates of city population sizes also show all the signs of cognitive laziness. Largest city in the United States? New York. You got that right. Some 9 million people in New York City. Now, what is the largest city in the Americas? New York? Wrong. Mexico City perhaps? You are right that Mexico City is larger than New York, but only by some half million people. The answer is Sao Paolo in Brazil with 12 million people. Okay, estimating numbers is tough. Let's make comparisons. Which is larger: New York or Istanbul, Turkey? The Big Apple? Wrong! Istanbul, with 5 million people more than New York. An easy one then: Karachi, Pakistan, or New York? Well, it is easy because Karachi has double the population of New York. In fact, the largest city in the world has a population almost three times higher than New York!

When it comes to estimates, we are off all the time. Let me illustrate with a range of questions and their answers, taken from Duffy's 2018 *Perils of Perception*, and let's compare the numbers. Below you will find some questions. When you read the question, try to come up with an answer yourself, and only then look to the right. The numbers on the right show the average guesses your fellow countrymen make, followed by the actual numbers in reality. Your estimates are likely very similar to those of your fellow countrymen, and when compared to the number to the right, very wrong.

		Actual (estimates from others)
1.	What proportion of the population of your country is aged 65 or over?	36% (14%)
2.	How many people aged 20 or over in your country are overweight or obese?	50% (66%)
3.	When asked in a survey, what percentage of people do you think said they were happy or very happy?	49% (90%)
4.	What percentage of women and girls aged 15-19 in your country do you think give birth each year?	24% (2.1%)
5.	Out of every 100 young adults aged 25-34, about how many do you think live with their parents?	34% (12%)
6.	What is the proportion of immigrants among your country's population?	33% (14%)
7.	Out of every 100 people in your country, how many are Muslim?	17% (1%)
8.	What percentage of the population in your country will be Muslim in four years' time?	23% (1.1%)
9.	Out of every 100 people in your country, how many do you think are unemployed and looking for work?	32% (6%)
10.	Do you think the murder rate in your country was higher / lower or about the same in your country?	47% higher (11% lower)

Source: Duffy (2018).

As you can see, the differences between what others had guessed and the actual difference is large, as much as 20–40 percent! I bet the estimates from your fellow countrymen were very much in line with your own estimates. We don't rely on the facts; we'd rather rely on our pessimistic cognitive shortcuts.

And it is not even with known information that your memory lets you down. The same can be said for new information you try to remember. For instance, have a look at the following list of words, and try to keep them in mind.

sour	candy	sugar	bitter	good	taste	tooth	nice
honey	soda	chocolate	heart	cake	tart	pie	

Now put this book away and write down (or think of) all the items you can recall. This was actually an experiment in the mid-1990s.[13] Participants were asked to remember a word list like this and were then exposed to a recognition test. Nothing challenging, as you remembered the words, and all you need to do is list which words you recognize: *elephant, mouth, candy, honey, tooth, sweet, pie*. Undoubtedly, you rejected having seen *elephant*, hesitated on *mouth*, and recognized all the others as being part of the list. And you were wrong. Even though all items are related to sweetness, the word *sweet* never appeared in the list. Your memory produced false recollections. You thought you had seen something that you had never seen.

COGNITION

We have now seen a number of examples from perception and memory demonstrating our cognitive laziness. There are many more of these examples that painfully remind us how lazy we are in our thinking. In fact, in many respects our cognitive skills do not beat those of our fellow primates, the chimpanzees.

It seems so simple. Humans have a relative brain size three times bigger than primates of the same body size. Humans have a cerebral cortex that is more developed than that of other primates. And it would therefore be no surprise that these bigger brains allow us humans to perform all kinds of cognitive tasks better than other species: greater memory, faster learning, faster perceptual processing, more robust inferences, better planning, better symbolic processing. A group of researchers from Germany, Spain, and the United States tested whether this is true, by comparing a battery of tasks to our closest ancestor, the chimpanzee.[14] And they came to a different conclusion than what seemed to be obvious before you started reading this chapter.

They asked human children and chimpanzees to perform a number of tasks, ranging from locating a reward to using a stick in order to retrieve a reward that was out of reach. On many cognitive tasks, humans, at least 105 human children in Germany of about 2.5 years of age, did not do better than chimpanzees, at least 106 chimpanzees that lived in Uganda or the Republic of Congo. On locating a reward, on tracking the reward after it got rotated, and on discriminating quantities and adding numbers, the chimps did as well as the humans.

You may argue that the cognitive performance of a 2.5-year-old is on par with that of a chimpanzee of a similar age, but that we rapidly grow to superior cognitive performance when we get older. That is true, but our cognitive brilliance is often off. Or rather, we'd rather go for cognitive shortcuts than for logic, as Amos Tversky and Daniel Kahneman have shown in a series of experiments. Perhaps the most famous experiment is the one with bank teller Linda. Three groups participated in the study: a group of undergraduate students naïve to statistics, probability, and decision theory; an informed group of first-year graduate students in psychology, education, and medicine; and a sophisticated group of PhD candidates in decision science with advanced studies in statistics, probability, and decision theory. All three groups of participants were presented with the following text:

> Linda is 31 years old, single, outspoken, and very bright. She majored in philosophy. As a student, she was deeply concerned with issues of discrimination and social justice, and also participated in anti-nuclear demonstrations. Which is more probable?
>
> 1. Linda is a bank teller.
> 2. Linda is a bank teller and is active in the feminist movement.

Some 89 percent of the participants in the naïve group, 90 percent in the informed group, and 85 percent in the sophisticated group answered option 2. This was repeated in a second experiment, when—again—the vast majority of the participants opted for the second option. Would you belong to the majority group or the minority of 10–15 percent of the participants?

It does not take much logical thinking to know that the second option is far less likely than the first one. To make an analogy: it is more likely that you are a reader of this book, than that you are a female reader of this book (or a male reader). Similarly, it is far more likely that you are a bank teller than that you are a feminist bank teller. And yet, a cognitive shortcut likely (with some 85 percent probability) pushed you toward a conjunction fallacy.

Now you may object that you read the text differently. Really, you had read it as if you had two options: "Linda is *only* a bank teller and not a feminist" *or* that "she is a bank teller and also active in a feminist movement." That's not quite how people generally respond to examples like these, but perhaps you are the not-so-cognitively-lazy exception. To be certain that 85 percent of the participants do not belong to this exception either, one could present them with the arguments behind the conjunction fallacy, basically confronting them with the error and asking them which argument they would choose.[15]

Argument 1
Linda is more likely to be a bank teller than she is to be a feminist bank teller, because every feminist bank teller is a bank teller, but some women bank tellers are not feminists, and Linda could be one of them.

Argument 2
Linda is more likely to be a feminist bank teller than she is likely to be a bank teller, because she resembles an active feminist more than she resembles a bank teller.

When confronted with the argument, the probability of getting it wrong decreased from the previous 85 percent, but still 65 percent of the participants chose the second option. They still did not want to get out of their lazy chair.

But taking cognitive shortcuts does not stop with bank tellers and feminist movements. It continues with sharks. Sharks, don't you hate them? Just the thought of it. You are swimming along the beach, and there is yet another shark attack. Remember that one at Miramar Beach in Florida a while back? The other one at the beach close to San Diego in California? Nobody wants to swim in the ocean anymore, because before you know it another Great White has started nibbling at your feet. So let me raise some silly questions. What is more likely: that you die from a shark attack or from an accidental gun discharge? That you die from a shark attack or choking on food? That you die from a shark attack or a champagne cork?

There is every reason to be concerned about the shark attack. There is a chance of one in 264.1 million you too will be killed by a shark. It might, however, be useful to place this number in perspective a bit. Are you concerned about dying from sunstroke? Probably not, or at least not as much as dying from that shark attack. Yet it is three thousand times more likely you will die from a sunstroke than from a shark attack. By the way, it is equally likely that you will die from an accidental gun discharge, which is also three thousand times more likely than that shark attack. In fact, if you are concerned about sharks, I'd be more concerned about choking on food. Each year the National Safety Council releases the lifetime odds of death for selected causes. Below, you will find the findings for 2017. Many of your fears will be placed in perspective, demonstrating that you are cognitively lazy in what you fear.

Cause of Death	Odds of Dying
Heart Disease	1 in 6
Cancer	1 in 7
Chronic Lower Respiratory Disease	1 in 27
Suicide	1 in 88
Opioid overdose	1 in 96
Motor Vehicle Crash	1 in 103
Fall	1 in 114
Gun Assault	1 in 285
Pedestrian Incident	1 in 556
Motorcyclist	1 in 858
Drowning	1 in 1,117
Fire or Smoke	1 in 1,474
Choking on Food	1 in 2,696
Bicyclist	1 in 4,047
Accidental Gun Discharge	1 in 8,527
Sunstroke	1 in 8,912
Electrocution, Radiation, Extreme Temperatures and Pressure	1 in 15,638
Sharp objects	1 in 28,000
Cataclysmic Storm	1 in 31,394
Hot surfaces and substances	1 in 46,045
Hornet, wasp and bee stings	1 in 46,562
Dog attack	1 in 115,111
Passenger on an airplane	1 in 188,364
Lightning	1 in 218,106
Railway passenger	1 in 243,765

Source: National Safety Council estimates based on data from National Center for Health Statistics—Mortality Data.

In fact, rather than dying from a shark attack, it is far more likely to die from contracting an infection in a hospital, an excessive cold, or a sand-hole collapse. And it is far more likely to die from a champagne cork. A champagne cork? Yes, that's right: approximately two dozen people are killed by champagne corks each year, with weddings the most common place this happens. There are only sixteen people killed by shark attacks each year. That is sixteen too many, but you probably never feared a champagne cork in your life and now realize you should.

Imagine out of nostalgia you are interested in that one Prince album. You search on eBay, and somewhat to your surprise, somebody sells the item for $22.67. You need to place a bid. What would your bid be? Perhaps $22.80? Perhaps $23? Now you have already gotten the hang of it, and you were also looking for that other Prince album. That one too is available online, for only $20.00. What would your bid be? Most likely you would place a bid for $25 or so. Now, this is funny. Your bid is determined by the original price. Of course, it shouldn't be. Assuming that you would value the two albums similar in price (and I have not even told you which albums they were, so it seems to be a reasonable assumption they are similar in price), you would place different bids not on their value, but on the price given to you. Moreover, your bid is likely to occur in small increments in the case of the one album (after all, the decimals trigger you to do exactly that), but in larger increments of the other album (even though the original price was lower). What has gotten into you?

Basically, you anchor your estimates. Kahneman and Tversky noted initial values given to people affected their estimates.[16] For instance, one group of participants were given five seconds to estimate the total of the following mathematical equation.

$$1 \times 2 \times 3 \times 4 \times 5 \times 6 \times 7 \times 8$$

Another group saw the same equation, but now in reverse:

$$8 \times 7 \times 6 \times 5 \times 4 \times 3 \times 2 \times 1$$

The estimate given by the first group was approximately 512, but that of the second group was over four times higher at 2,250. Now both groups of participants were well off, with the correct outcome being 40,320. Basically, participants were demonstrating what Kahneman and Tversky called anchoring and adjustment heuristic. In a similar study, Kahneman and Tversky rigged a wheel of fortune so it would always land on either 10 or 65. Participants were asked, "Was the percentage of African countries in the United Nations higher or lower than the number from the wheel of fortune?" followed by the question "What percentage of African countries are in the United Nations?"

Those participants presented with the number 10 had an average guess of 25 percent, but those presented with the number 65 had an average guess of 45 percent.[17] The point is that the estimates changed because of the spinning of a rigged wheel of fortune. Our cognitive laziness lets us rely more on a rigged wheel of fortune than our memory. The idea of anchoring and adjustment is rather powerful, and can also be found in impression formation.

Do we like the person we talk to at that party? Do we dislike him or her? And why? Below you see an excerpt from a text. I am not asking you to carefully read the text, but to skim through it, say for just a few seconds. How much do you like Miss Johnson on a scale of one to ten?

> Miss Johnson had a fine person, many brilliant attainments. She advocated a high tone of sentiment. But her mind was poor, her heart barren by nature; nothing bloomed spontaneously on that soil; no unforced natural fruit delighted by its freshness. She was very showy, but she was not genuine. She was not good; she was not original; she used to repeat sounding phrases from books; she never offered, nor had, an opinion of her own, but she did not know the sensations of sympathy and pity; tenderness and truth were not in her. She was a mark beneath jealousy: she was too inferior to excite feeling. Pardon the seeming paradox; I mean what I say.

Now let me ask you to do the same for the following text, again spending only a few seconds skimming through it, but now determining how much you like Miss Pederson.

> Miss Pederson was a mark beneath jealousy: she was too inferior to excite feeling. Pardon the seeming paradox; I mean what I say. She was very showy, but she was not genuine; she had a fine person, many brilliant attainments, but her mind was poor, her heart barren by nature; nothing bloomed spontaneously on that soil; no unforced natural fruit delighted by its freshness. She was not good; she was not original; she used to repeat sounding phrases from books; she never offered, nor had, an opinion of her own. She advocated a high tone of sentiment, but she did not know the sensations of sympathy and pity; tenderness and truth were not in her.

Which text character did you rate as nicer, Miss Johnson or Miss Pederson?[18] Most likely Miss Johnson won from Miss Pederson. That would be funny, because the descriptions are identical. The order of the descriptions differed, however. In the first excerpt, positive features were presented first, in the second, positive features were immediately countered by negative features. However, our cognitive laziness lets us determine somebody by first impressions. If our first impressions are good, then it is hard to make them bad. If our first impressions are bad, it is hard to compensate with good impressions. We basically let our first impressions govern all impressions, knowing that first looks are deceiving. We take a cognitive shortcut!

In 1948 psychology professor Bertram Forer wondered whether he could describe the personality of his students on the basis of their test results. For each of his thirty-nine students, he wrote a brief personal personality sketch and asked each of the students to what extent the personality sketch applied to them. One example of such a sketch looked like this:

> You have a great need for other people to like and admire you. You have a tendency to be critical of yourself. You have a great deal of unused capacity which you have not turned to your advantage. While you have some personality weaknesses, you are generally able to compensate for them. Your sexual adjustment has presented problems for you. Disciplined and self-controlled outside, you tend to be worrisome and insecure inside. At times you have serious doubts as to whether you have made the right decision or done the right thing. You prefer a certain amount of change and variety and become dissatisfied when hemmed in by restrictions and limitations. You pride yourself as an independent thinker and do not accept others' statements without satisfactory proof. You have found it unwise to be too frank in revealing yourself to others. At times you are extroverted, affable, sociable, while at other times you are introverted, wary, reserved. Some of your aspirations tend to be pretty unrealistic. Security is one of your major goals in life.[19]

Each of the students was asked to rate how the sketch applied to them on a scale of zero to five. If the sketch was an absolutely perfect match, a student scored a 5; if the match was more like a mismatch, a score of 0 was given. Forer's efforts paid off. Students gave an average accuracy of 4.3 for the sketch that Forer had made especially for them, except that everybody received the same sketch! Either all thirty-nine students were exactly the same—a rather unlikely conclusion—or the students applied cognitive shortcuts and found patterns that applied to them. And particularly with positive words being spoken, we love those patterns.

LANGUAGE

Our linguistic skills are remarkable. In this chapter, we have seen that our perceptual simulation skills, our memory skills, as well as our computations are not as impressive as we may have thought. One could argue that it is therefore questionable whether they are the best explanation for us being a language genius. But even when we consider our remarkable language skills, there is reason for concern. After all, we are able to parse complex sentences in a variety of syntactic structures, but we hardly apply this skill. Even though we are able to generate complex sentences, that have aspects of recursion—so that a sentence is embedded in another sentence, which may be embedded in another sentence, whose subordinate clause can be embedded in yet another

sentence, and so forth—we hardly see these sentences. If our language instinct is an explanation of language processing, why don't we produce such
long sentences? Or why do we struggle with these sentences? Sentences like
this one:

> Just exactly like Father if Father had known as much about it the night
> before I went out there as he did the day after I came back thinking Mad
> impotent old man who realized at last that there must be some limit even
> to the capabilities of a demon for doing harm, who must have seen his
> situation as that of the show girl, the pony, who realizes that the principal
> tune she prances to comes not from horn and fiddle and drum but from
> a clock and calendar, must have seen himself as the old wornout cannon
> which realizes that it can deliver just one more fierce shot and crumble to
> dust in its own furious blast and recoil, who looked about upon the scene
> which was still within his scope and compass and saw son gone, vanished,
> more insuperable to him now than if the son were dead since now (if
> the son still lived) his name would be different and those to call him by
> it strangers and whatever dragon's outcropping of Sutpen blood the son
> might sow on the body of whatever strange woman would therefore carry
> on the tradition, accomplish the hereditary evil and harm under another
> name and upon and among people who will never have heard the right
> one.[20]

These are the first 217 words of a 1288-word sentence. Granted, the
entire sentence is the longest sentence in literature, from William Faulkner's
Absalom! Absalom!, but we do not quite appreciate its length and syntactic
structure. Our language instinct is perfectly able to understand the grammatical structure, but we'd rather go for the shortcut, as it takes too much
cognitive effort and we are cognitively lazy. And *effort* and *shortcut* do not go
together well. As I showed in chapter 3, we sometimes experience garden-
path sentences, sentences that lead us astray on the syntactic path we chose
when starting out the sentence. Sentences such as the following[21]:

- The complex houses married and single soldiers and their families.
- Sam ate the hot dog and the vegetables went untouched.
- The government plans to raise taxes were defeated.
- The investigation revealed the error resulted from gross negligence.

These are perfectly grammatical sentences, but we stumble over them.
Our energetic language instinct should have no difficulty with them—and
indeed, we are able to parse them—but we choke. We reread, and try again,
until we have found a syntactic structure that works. As we have seen in chapter 3, these garden-path sentences get you to walk on one syntactic structure

path, and when you realize you are stuck, you need to decide on another path. The evidence of our cognitive laziness is the fact that garden-path sentences do not occur very frequently outside the research labs in which they are tested. How often have you tripped over the grammatical structure of a sentence? It hardly ever happens, because the writer or speaker has provided you with enough context to make the right predictions and the right cognitive short-cut. When garden-path sentences do occur, as in newspaper headlines, they often lead to rather humorous interpretations:

- Chinese Cooking Fat Heads for Holland
- Miners Refuse to Work after Death
- Dr. Ruth to Talk about Sex with Newspaper Editors
- Lung Cancer in Women Mushrooms
- Teacher Strikes Idle Kids
- Enraged Cow Injures Farmer with Axe
- Squad Helps Dog Bite Victim
- Juvenile Court Tries Shooting Defendant
- Killer Sentenced to Die for Second Time in 10 Years
- Dealers Will Hear Car Talk at Noon

These headlines are funny not because the sentences are funny, but because our cognitive laziness makes them funny. We apply a syntactic structure to a sentence and then realize that generates some undesirable interpretations. These undesirable interpretations are sometimes not so much driven by the syntax as they are by other aspects of our cognitive laziness, like stereotypes, as in the example below.

> The CEO fired the secretary after a long stretch of arguments about the handling of the emails. He packed up his belongings, put them in a carton box, and left the building.

As soon as you read the second sentence, your cognitively lazy mind probably wondered why the CEO left the building. It was the secretary who was fired, so why should the CEO box his belongings in a box? But if you think about this a bit longer, you should also ask why the masculine personal pronoun *he* refers to the CEO. Why would *he* not refer to the secretary? You accepted CEOs being male and their secretaries being female. In the olden days perhaps, but it is time to get out of your cognitively lazy chair.

Speaking of the olden days, I will assume you know some of the stories in the Bible. I would like you to think carefully and give me the answer to a very simple question: How many of each animal did Moses take on his Ark? That would be an easy question, regardless of your background. Two, right?

Two animals of each kind were taken on the Ark when the flood arrived. If you proudly think you got the right answer, I need to disappoint you again. Your memory let you down, as it was not Moses who took any animals on any Ark. It was Noah who did that. In a series of experiments in the early 1980s, psychologists asked participants questions like these.[22] In the majority of the cases, participants had no clue they were wrong in their answers.

Perhaps we take cognitive shortcuts with syntactic constructions, but at least our mind is brilliant when it comes to activating perceptual simulations. Let's put that possibility to the test with the following example:

> Two guards were on duty outside a barracks. One faced up the road to watch for anyone approaching from the north. The other looked down the road to see if anyone approached from the south. Suddenly one of them said to the other, "Why are you smiling?"

So how did one guard know his companion was smiling? A simple story and a simple question. Try all your grounding of the words of the story, all the meshing of all the affordances of the words in the sentences, all the perceptual simulations that come to mind, and it is likely you will still be puzzled finding an answer to this simple question. Because we have now pretty much established that you and I are cognitively lazy, let me help you out: the two guards were facing each other. Not enough perceptual simulations for you? Let me ask the following question:

> If you are running and pass the guy in second place, what place are you in?

Not a very difficult question. In fact, rather simple. What place are you in? You think deeply, embody the situation, and generate the answer. First, right? You pass the guy in the second place, so now you are first. Perceptual simulation likely lets you down again. Cognitive shortcuts took over. If you pass the guy in second place, obviously you are now in second place. Not first.

You might argue that recognizing the order of digits on a computer screen might simply be explained by visual attention, that the previous examples can be explained by perceptual simulation, that the other examples say more about training, network, and grounding than instinct. The garden-path sentences I just presented show that cognitive shortcuts in those cases also wreak havoc. But when it comes to language processing, there are more examples of shortcuts we take. Let's do the easiest language-processing task possible, and just count the number of times the letter *f* is used in the following snippet of text. Things cannot get simpler than that, can they?

The Federal Bureau of Investigation (FBI) concluded that the impressive results came from years of scientific research combined with the experience of years that were put in.

If you counted at least two *f*'s, there is good news. You are awake. Did you count three? Even better, because it is clear you can count. But obviously, you didn't see more than three. Or did you? Perhaps even four? And if you counted four, you may have seen five, or perhaps as many as six? And if you are now scratching your head, being baffled that some others might count more than three *f*'s, you are not alone. Most people have little difficulty identifying three. But very few eventually get to six. And yet, there indeed are six *f*'s in the snippet above. Undoubtedly you spotted the *f*'s in *Federal* and *FBI*, you probably got *scientific*, but you missed the three prepositions that are so obviously stated that you can't miss them (anymore). So even when relying on your own reading processes, even simply counting a character in a text, you took cognitive shortcuts. You could have counted six *f*'s, but you didn't. So things seem to be rather clear. When it comes to perception, when it comes to memory, when it comes to language, and in fact, when it comes to a whole slew of cognitive tasks, it is surprising how poorly we often perform on these tasks.

COGNITIVE SHORTCUTS

Mankind has reached enormous achievements, and yet, you may ask, we take cognitive shortcuts and are cognitively lazy? We have climbed the highest mountains on earth, created incredible pieces of art, stepped foot on the moon, dove to the deepest places in the ocean, invented calculus, created computers and the internet, developed medications and vaccines and so on. Cognitively lazy, taking the path of least cognitive resistance, taking cognitive shortcuts, really?

Indeed, let's not end this chapter on a pessimistic note. When you see a Swiss cheese picture of a woman in a bikini or a picture with a banner of a guy in swim trunks, when you experience the Thatcher illusion, when you think about the memory and cognition examples given here, you become aware of the mistakes you made. After reading practically all the examples used in this chapter, you probably said to yourself, "Of course! Why didn't I think about this earlier?" If you practiced on the tasks presented in this chapter, you would do better, much better. So ultimately we are able to cognitively manage things—or at least are aware of them—but we generally don't want to put too much effort into a task.

Over the last fifteen years or so, more and more researchers have come to the conclusion that rather than viewing the human mind as the most powerful computer, viewing human cognition superior to any other cognition—nonhuman or artificial—we may have to reconsider the human mind as a device that goes to great mental depths. Daniel Kahneman in *Thinking, Fast and Slow*[23] makes a distinction between the good-enough and perfection system, two cognitive systems running side by side. One system is satisfied with good enough; the other is only satisfied with perfection. One system is fast, instinctive, and emotional, operating on the principle of "what you see is all there is," on autopilot, jumping to conclusions on the basis of associative memories. That system often draws the wrong conclusions, including many of the ones we have seen in this chapter. The other system is a slower, more deliberative, and more logical counterpart. That system is the one that makes it hard to multitask. When that system is active, there is not much else you can do. The system aiming for good enough is not only prone to mistakes, but also forgiving. It will get us by. And that system we rely on most.

Good enough is what Gerd Gigerenzer calls gut feelings.[24] Think about your first date. Did you carefully think about the advantages and disadvantages of this person? Most likely you didn't. You liked the person and went out on a date. When buying a house, you didn't carefully consider all the drawbacks. Sure, you contemplated the mortgage and some of the renovations, but you had already fallen in love. You went for your gut feeling. Gigerenzer argues that reflection and reason are overrated. Cognitive, emotional, and social mindsets we generally call intuition are what commonly drive us. These gut feelings are more often than not simply right. And I would not dispute that.

Most recently, Nick Chater has argued even more forcefully that the mind is flat.[25] Where we often think we have hidden mental depths, most often we simply make rule-of-thumb decisions. Those cases where we *think* that we are involved in deep thoughts and careful decision making, we are basically doing not much more than making our minds up: justifying the gut feeling decisions we have already made. We are making things up as we go. We can now look back at that important decision we made and come up with tons of smart reasons why we made that decision, but really, when we were confronted with making that decision, we just chose a go-with-the-flow attitude. The path of least cognitive resistance.

And being cognitively lazy is not at all a bad thing. In fact, one could even argue that the title of this chapter is just wrong. It suggests we are a Homer Simpson sacked out on the couch, unwilling to be even a little bit rational. There is a reason for us not to do so well on some cognitive tasks. Relying on our gut feeling, on heuristics, is a good thing. It helps to take cognitive shortcuts.

Perhaps the most illustrative example is that of the traveling salesman. Imagine you are a salesman traveling through the United States visiting some of the larger cities in the country. On your list of cities to visit are thirteen locations: Atlanta, GA; Boston, MA; Chicago, IL; Dallas, TX; Houston, TX; Los Angeles, CA; Miami, FL; New York, NY; Philadelphia, PA; Phoenix, AZ; San Francisco, CA; Seattle, WA; and Washington, DC.

The question is how to plan your visits wisely. You are allowed to only visit a city once, and you are required to take the shortest route (after all, you are working for a sustainable company, and you want to reduce your carbon footprint). Let's simplify the problem for now. If there were only five cities you needed to visit, there are twelve possible routes to evaluate, namely $(5-1)!/2 = 12$. For six cities, that number increases to sixty, for seven cities to 360 possible routes, and for the thirteen cities listed above, there are 239,500,800 combinations. Contrary to the origin of the traveling salesman problem in 1832, and the popularity of the scientific problem in the 1950s and 1960s, today's computers can handle the traveling salesman problem (at least when considering thirteen cities) in seconds. But a fast desktop computer will need to make some 240 million calculations. We don't. Perhaps we could, but our cognitive laziness provides us with a cognitive shortcut yielding a solution that may not be perfect, but is certainly good enough.

Or let's take another example. Imagine a baseball player catching a ball.[26] There are at least two ways to catch the ball. One is that we consider acceleration, velocity, displacement, time of flight, maximum height of profile, the relation between horizontal range and maximum height, the maximum distance of the projectile, the angle of reach, and air resistance. By determining the initial velocity in meters per second, the acceleration due to gravity, the identification of the launch angle, the drag coefficient due to the spherical projectile, the radius and mass of the projectile, the air density in kilograms per cubic meter, as well as the cross-sectional area of the projectile in squared meters, it is possible to determine exactly where the baseball will land—assuming that it is thrown from a static point, which is hardly ever the case when baseball players throw a ball. Another way to catch a ball is to keep your eye on the ball and hold up your baseball glove. It may not be perfectly accurate, but most of the time it is. It is certainly good enough.

ELEPHANTS

In Dutch they are called "elephant paths," in French "donkey paths," and in German "trample paths." In English they are "desire paths," but I like the Dutch phrase the best. You see them everywhere, particularly in parks. Rather than taking the path that others hope one would take, for instance around the grass, pedestrians often decide differently. As elephants (or donkeys), they trample over the grass and create their own path. It is the path of least resistance. It takes less effort crossing the field than going around the field. It makes our lives easier and more efficient. Elephant paths emerge from choosing a path of least resistance frequently. The shortcuts people take are formed by a wisdom of the crowd. Let me explain that a bit more.

Imagine I present you with a bowl of jelly beans and ask you to estimate how many beans are in the bowl. That seems to be an almost impossible task. A hundred? A thousand? A million? The more people you ask to make an estimate, the better you can estimate the exact number.[27] People guess taking cognitive shortcuts. For a bowl of 4,510 jelly beans, some might say 450, and some might say fifty thousand, but the majority converges on the exact estimate. In fact, when you ask a large number of people to give their best estimate, the average answer of all answers given turns out to come close to the exact number of jelly beans. What this shows is that by using the same shortcut repetitively, a pattern starts to form that comes close to the ideal situation. Perhaps language comprehension is a Dutch elephant path, a French donkey path, an English desire path. Perhaps language is the wisdom of the crowd, with frequent shortcuts forming the path of least cognitive resistance.

Relying on cognitive shortcuts or cognitive laziness may in fact be beneficial. Even though this chapter could be interpreted as me arguing that our mind lacks rationality, that's not quite what I argued. A review of the excellent popular science book *The Knowledge Illusion* in the *New York Times* starts out stating that the authors, "cognitive scientists Steven Sloman and Philip Fernbach, hammer another nail into the coffin of the rational individual."[28] Illustrated with a picture of a Greek philosopher with the word *vacant* in its eyes, the message is clear: We lack all rationality. I don't think this is quite what Sloman and Fernbach conclude, and not what the reviewer emphasizes, but it is true that the superiority of human cognition has been questioned more than once before.

I have not tried to argue that human cognition lacks rationality. Instead what I have tried to show is that human cognition is not superior. It is not superior to animal cognition (or rather, nonhuman animal cognition), and it is not superior to artificial intelligence (or rather, computer models). And if toward the end of this chapter you would agree that human cognition is fallible and not perfect, we are left with a conclusion and with a question. If human perception, memory, and cognition are not always outstanding, it may be too easy to attribute our amazing language capabilities to training, instinct, network, or grounding. If our cognitive skills were simply outstanding, I would be quite willing to make that attribution. If our cognitive skills were far superior to that of nonhumans, I would understand why we have the language system that we have and other species don't. But if our cognitive superiority is not that obvious, there is a problem. How is it that we take cognitive shortcuts all the time, that we tend to be cognitively lazy, and yet we can keep well over sixty thousand words in mind and process them so rapidly? I'll try to come to an answer in the next chapter, not dismissing the four explanations from the four previous chapters—again, I think they all form pieces of the language puzzle—but introducing a complementary explanation.

· 9 ·

Patterns

> We are pattern seekers, believers in a coherent world, in which regularities . . . appear not by accident but as a result of mechanical causality or of someone´s intention. We do not expect to see regularity produced by a random process, and when we detect what appears to be a rule, we quickly reject the idea that the process is truly random.
>
> —Daniel Kahneman[1]

*R*emember the dollar bill from the previous chapter? Do you happen to have one in your wallet? In the age of electronic payment, you might not have one readily available. You may want to get one quickly, for it has some very important revelations. Have a look in that piggy bank and see whether you can fetch one. The information the one-dollar bill reveals simply is astonishing.

On the front side, you see a face of one of the presidents of the United States. On the back side you'll find some important historical clues. Here you can see the two faces of the Great Seal of the United States, a pyramid on the left, an eagle on the right. Let's start with the pyramid. Let's count the steps of the pyramid. As you will see there are exactly thirteen. That number turns out to be interesting. At the base of the pyramid you'll see the date 1776 in Roman numerals. The latter two numbers nicely add up to 13. The motto above the pyramid reads *Annuit coeptis*, exactly thirteen letters ("favors our undertakings"). The bald eagle on the right has equally important clues as the pyramid. The eagle has a ribbon in its beak that bears the motto *E pluribus unum* (which means "one out of many"). That Latin motto too has exactly thirteen letters. Over the eagle's head are stars. The total number of stars is, you guessed it, thirteen. The eagle also holds a shield. If you count the number of stripes on the shield, there are exactly thirteen. And the appearances of *thirteen* do not end there. The eagle's left claw holds war arrows. If you count them, there are thirteen. In its other claw it holds an olive branch of peace. The branch has leaves. Not surprisingly anymore, exactly thirteen of them.

The one-dollar bill was first issued in 1862, under the presidency of Abraham Lincoln. Lincoln, the sixteenth president of the United States, was assassinated, and perhaps the one-dollar bill that so much highlighted the unlucky number thirteen was a forewarning. If you add 1 + 3, you end up with the number 4; if you add up 1862, the issuing date of the one-dollar bill, you end up with the number 17. Subtract 4, and you then have the number 13. And 1 + 3 brings you to the number 4, which is the total of the *1*'s presented in the corners of the dollar bill. In fact, the dollar bill reads two times 1 and 1. November is the eleventh month. 11 + 11 = 22. On the 22nd of November, another president was assassinated. The first letter of that president's last name started with the eleventh letter of the alphabet, *K*ennedy. In a place, *Dallas, Texas*, whose letters add up to the number 11. The frequently occurring number 13 and the number 11 also come back when we link Kennedy to the dollar bill. 13 − 11 = 2, the sum of the two ones of the dollar bill, and if we read 13 as 1 + 3 and 1 + 1, and subtract their sums, we again end up with the number 2. The bad luck of the number 13 represented in the one-dollar bill that applies to both Abraham Lincoln and John F. Kennedy reveals an interesting pattern. And that pattern does not stop with the one-dollar bill!

Lincoln was elected president in 1860, and in 1960, exactly one hundred years later, Kennedy was elected. Both Lincoln and Kennedy were concerned with civil rights. The number of letters in the names of both presidents is the same: seven letters each. Kennedy had a secretary named Lincoln. Both Kennedy and Lincoln had vice presidents with the last name, Johnson, and both vice presidents were southerners. Andrew Johnson was born in 1808 and Lyndon B. Johnson exactly one hundred years later in 1908. Abraham Lincoln was elected to Congress in 1846, and John F. Kennedy was elected to Congress exactly one hundred years later in 1946. Both Abraham Lincoln and John F. Kennedy were assassinated. Both assassins (John Wilkes Booth and Lee Harvey Oswald) had three names, and these names added up to the same number of letters, fifteen in total. Both assassins were southerners. Lincoln was killed in Ford's Theater. Kennedy died while riding in a Lincoln convertible made by Ford Motor Company. Both were shot in the back of the head and sitting next to their wives. Both presidents were shot on a Friday. Both assassinators were assassinated themselves before their trials.[2]

So many patterns simply cannot be coincidences! After all, what are the chances? The issuing of the one-dollar bill during Lincoln's presidency with the unlucky number 13 printed all over the place must have been a forewarning, for both Abraham Lincoln and John F. Kennedy.

EXPECTATION BIAS

The similarities in the patterns I pointed out are astonishing. But in looking for similarities, we tend to forget the dissimilarities. The fact that *one dollar* printed on the one-dollar bill contains nine characters, *in God we trust*, also printed on the one-dollar bill, contains twelve characters, and *the United States of America* twenty-four characters, we quickly want to forget. After all, it doesn't fit the pattern.

We are also readily willing to ignore that Lincoln was born in 1809 and Kennedy was born in 1917, 108 years apart, that Lincoln died in 1865 and Kennedy died in 1963, 98 years apart. That the number of letters in Abraham Lincoln and John F. Kennedy have little in common, fourteen versus twelve. That Lincoln was fifty-six years old at the time of his death, while Kennedy was forty-six. Lincoln was killed in April and Kennedy in November, the fourth month of the year and the eleventh month—Lincoln on the fifteenth, Kennedy on the twenty-second. Lincoln and Kennedy didn't belong to the same party, didn't come from the same state, didn't come from the same part of the country, didn't have the same first names, didn't have the same initials, and didn't have the same upbringing, with Lincoln coming from a poor family and not going to college, and Kennedy coming from a rich family and going to Harvard. Both looked very different, one bearded the other one not, and dressed very differently. Lincoln was elected to a second term; Kennedy didn't finish his first. Lincoln was inside when shot; Kennedy was outside. Lincoln's assassin was twenty-six years old, Kennedy's assassin was twenty-four. Both assassins were born in different months and different years (the latter has conveniently been ignored). Both assassins had different backgrounds, different professions, and killed for different reasons.

I can go on and list a lot of differences, many more differences—far more than there are similarities among one-dollar bills, Abraham Lincoln, and John F. Kennedy. And yet what will stick in your mind are the patterns I just pointed out. We are prone to an expectation bias.[3] Once we start to see patterns, we see them everywhere. But at least at the next party conversation, you will be talking about the astonishing patterns between dollar bills and presidents.

PATTERN-MATCHING SKILLS

Humans are magnificent pattern matchers. We cannot deal well with chaos, and we readily bring order in disorder. Moreover, we are stubborn pattern seekers. We persistently stick to a pattern once we think we have found one, and we will not let go. It is as if we sniff for patterns in the environment around us, and once we smell a trace of a pattern, we will continue sniffing along, finding every single bit of evidence that confirms our predictions. Anything that does not match our initial evidence we readily dismiss; anything that could match our evidence we wholeheartedly embrace[4] and readily add to the initially fragile evidence for the pattern, until we are convinced that the pattern we thought was there seems to be there. Whether or not the pattern *is* actually there, we find less important.

We seek patterns. Even when the visual chaos is complete, we will not let go. Let's consider some visual pandemonium, as in yet another image, presented below. You see a bunch of seemingly random stripes. If I asked what you see on the picture below, with a conscious mind you could tell me that you see chaos. But it is likely that you will not come to that conclusion. It is more likely you will tell me that you see four zebras standing next to one another. And despite the fact that a zebra answer is odd, because there is not one single zebra out of the four visible, you make up zebras from the patterns you see. If you think you see a zebra, you will not let go of the zebra.

Source: **Getty Images.**

We seek patterns. Even when the visual chaos is complete, we will not let go. You can try this out yourself. On a sunny day when there are clouds high up in the sky basking in the sun, have a look at those clouds. See whether you find anything familiar in the configuration of clouds. I bet you do. And moreover, I bet when you do, you will not let go. When, for instance, you see a human face, an animal, or some monster in those clouds, you pick up a pattern in the visual pandemonium and will not let go. Once a pattern, always a pattern.

What these examples show is that the sum is often different than its parts. In our pattern seeking, we place everything that looks the same in one group and everything that looks different in another. This is a good thing, for it otherwise becomes impossible to distinguish one team from the other in a football match. The colors of the same team look the same and thus belong to the same group. Similarly, anything that is closer to something else we place in the same group. That too is a good thing, as it helps you in identifying zebras in visual chaos. That's a good thing too, as you would otherwise live in a fragmented world.

For auditory information, things are not much different. We seek familiar patterns. Let's consider a party on Friday night. The DJ plays the latest beats, and the dance floor is filled. The beats, bass, and the loud noise around you make it hard to follow your conversational partner. You are trying to make up the words that are coming out of her mouth. You are desperately forming patterns out of the information that does reach you through the loud noise. Or imagine a quieter party, a cocktail party, where you can hear your conversational partner. You carefully listen to what she is saying, not hearing what the people next to you are talking about (after all, all your attention is focused on your conversational partner). And yet, as soon as the people standing next to you mention your name, you do pick it up.[5] You search for the patterns that are frequent and thus familiar to you.

When I was younger, I often listened to a radio show that included a radio game. Listeners of the show could call in and participate in the game, which consisted of recognizing the two songs played simultaneously. The task of the contestant was to disentangle the music they heard and name the two songs. It required some serious pattern matching. Contestants had to listen through the two beats playing at the same time, the lyrics—which had become one big cacophony—and the other instruments—which sounded confused. Disentangling two patterns of songs based on similarities and proximities in sound within a song was quite a challenge, and only few contestants managed to win the prize: five albums of your choice sent to you. At my age, it sounded like winning the Powerball lottery!

Even though recognizing two songs played at the same time often turns out to be hard, once you recognized the patterns in the song, you would have no difficulty singing the remainder of a song. Think about it. As soon as that song of the past plays, you recall knowing it, but cannot yet find the pattern you have been looking for. But once you find it, you happily sing along as if it had never been out of your mind. But without finding the initial patterns in melody or lyrics, you would be lost.

How often have you been singing the lyrics of a song, only to later find out that these lyrics were not quite right? You didn't quite hear the words but formed combinations of sounds that seemed to make sense. "Saving his life from this warm sausage tea" (rather than "spare him his life from this monstrosity" in Queen's "Bohemian Rhapsody") or "See that girl, watch her scream, kicking the dancing queen" (rather than "see that girl, watch that scene, dig in the dancing queen" in ABBA's "Dancing Queen") or "Here we are now, in containers" (rather than "here we are now, entertain us" in Nirvana's "Smells Like Teen Spirit"). We are stuck to patterns. And once you have found a pattern, it never gets out of your head again.

Finding patterns in olfaction or gustation is very similar. If I present you with a glass of good wine—but for not-so-good wine, it is no different—and ask you what you smell and taste, you might respond with "cherry and other red fruits," "with a hint of oak," "a pinch of cinnamon." Basically, it requires you to identify patterns in the smells and flavors you experience and labeling these patterns. And once you have experienced some smells or flavors, it will become easier to pattern match the smell and flavor again later.

Humans are great pattern seekers. Still not buying it? Let's place some bets! Heads or tails? I flip the coin, and it lands on its head. I flip the coin again, and it lands on its head again. I flip it again, and it is heads again. You start to become suspicious. Three times in a row heads must mean something sneaky is going on. If I now ask you again to choose heads or tails, you likely choose heads. For most of us, we see a pattern emerging after the coin landing on heads three times. And when we see a pattern coming, we won't let go. Yet chances of obtaining heads are as high as obtaining tails, assuming of course the coin allows for an equal chance of landing on its head or tail in the first place and that you are not an expert at flipping coins, having mastered the skill of determining the outcome. Chances of obtaining heads the first time you flip a coin is 1/2, and the second time it is $1/2 \times 1/2$. Three times in a row makes it 1/8, or 12.5 percent. Basically, the number of outcomes of the coin flipping is n^r, where n is the number of options you have at each coin flip (heads or tails) and r is the number of times you flip the coin. So there are eight possible outcomes, where heads three times is one of them. A heads-heads-heads outcome is as likely as a tails-tails-tails outcome, and as likely as a heads-tails-heads outcome.

Our pattern matching takes extreme forms that can even lead to superstition. You sit on the couch and think of your best friend. You should call her, because it has been a while since you two hung out. And then the phone rings. On the other end of the line is the familiar voice of your best friend. This cannot be a coincidence! Out of all the people that could have called you, your best friend calls—the one you just thought about, out of all the people you could have thought about. This is a clear case of telepathy. Your friend must have sensed you were thinking of her while she reached for the phone. Or while she reached for the phone, you must have started to think of her! But if you think a little further, of all the people who would call you, your friend is the most likely person to call. And of all the people you could think about, that same friend is most likely who you would think about. Moreover, if there is a reason for you to think about that friend, chances are that friend has a similar reason to think about you and call you. Where you may have been convinced of a pattern, there is not much more than coincidence. Telepathy has not beaten science. Instead, your pattern-matching skills ignored science.

Let's return to the number 13 that I started out this chapter with. Imagine it is Friday the thirteenth. Soon one is coming up again. And as any paraskavedekatriaphobic—those who have a fear of Friday the thirteenth, in case the word was not yet registered in your mental lexicon—knows, that is bad news. If you are a triskaidekaphobic—those who have a fear for the number 13, another word for your mental lexicon—things are not much better.

You had set your alarm for 7 a.m., but it does not go off. Luckily you wake up not too late, get dressed, rush downstairs, and find you are out of coffee. You get into your car, and even though there hardly ever is a traffic jam, now—especially on this day—there is an accident on the road to work that puts you in the middle of the traffic jam. This can hardly be surprising. We see a pattern emerging, and we won't let go.

There is, in fact, no reason to be concerned on Friday the thirteenth. There are fewer cars on the road, and people tend to be more cautious. But as a paraskavedekatriaphobic and triskaidekaphobic, you might find that evidence as evidence for your fear: see, the number of accidents would have been higher had there been more cars on the road—clear evidence for the bad luck on that unlucky Friday! It is as if the pattern, albeit a pattern you heard of but never actually experienced, proves you right, even when you are wrong. Because if your alarm had failed any other day, and you had run out of coffee (as happens every so often), and you were stuck in the traffic jam (as you so often are), you would not even have thought about blaming Thursday the twelfth. You noticed a pattern and found evidence for it.

Examples like these show you excel in pattern-seeking abilities. Not only are you an avid language user, who is able to keep more than sixty thousand words in mind and process them with lightning speed, but you also have another ability to be proud of, that of detecting patterns in sequences and making predictions. For instance, when seeing *2, 4, 6, 8, 10*, you are able to continue with *12, 14, 16*, and *18*. And even when it gets a bit harder, as in *1, 3, 6, 10, 15, 21*, you are able to continue with *28, 36, 45*, and *55*. The more numbers you have, the easier it gets to detect the pattern (anchoring and adjustment). Pattern-matching skills go much further. Very few people would choose *1, 2, 3, 4, 5, 6* as the numbers on their lottery form, despite the fact that the chances of winning the jackpot on this number are as high (or actually as low) as winning the jackpot on the following number sequence: *91, 34, 65, 19, 23, 87*. As another example, try to come up with six numbers that are not part of a sequence. It turns out to be a difficult task. Before you know it, you produce *62, 52, 42, 32*, and you are stuck in a pattern. Bored of numbers? Let's take a look at your horoscope for today.

> Right now you should allow yourself to think with your heart instead of your cold gray matter. Today, communicating your feelings should be your top priority. Go for low-maintenance entertainment. Your everyday routine will seem very stale today, and you're going to be in desperate need of some high energy to bring a bit of freshness to the same old same old. Do your best to maintain a controlled, calm demeanor when someone says something shocking to you today. This is no time to feel embarrassed or reluctant to be vulnerable, especially with people who love you for who you are. Call up some of your famous flexibility, because you are going to need it today! You woke up this morning pretty sure of which choice you would make, but as this day continues to unfold, you will learn a few things that might sway your opinion. Be active early in the day. The morning is a good time to resolve a recent misunderstanding. This day's events could create a lot of uncertainty in your near future, but don't worry—it's the type of uncertainty that stimulates your curiosity and drives your creativity. Being cheerful, staying positive, and having fun are extremely important undertakings for you today—in fact, fun is vital if you want to keep good energy levels.

Looks like a perfect horoscope. You should start feeling with your heart, your everyday routine does need some freshness, you need to become a bit more flexible, and the uncertainty you are facing today would help you with your curiosity, concluding with the best advice: Fun is vital for your life. The problem, however, is that I do not know your zodiac sign, and I cannot know what day, month, or year you are reading your horoscope. Instead, the horoscope presented above is a collection of sentences from all twelve horoscopes the moment I am writing this. For one horoscope, I took the first sentence, from another the second, the next one the third, and so on. The horoscope presented above thus does not exist, or rather, it is a mashup of all horoscopes. Undoubtedly you recognized yourself in the horoscope above. That recognition is not a surprise because of the ambiguity of the horoscope, but more importantly, because of the patterns you recognize between you and what is stated.

MORE FALLACIES

Let me present you with some easy multiple-choice questions, the ones so familiar to you from high school and college—simple and basic questions you undoubtedly readily have the answer to. All I am asking is to circle the right answer for each of these six questions. Go for it.

1. What is a gnu?
   a. a kind of snake
   b. a kind of bird
   c. a kind of antelope
   d. a kind of fish
2. Who was the first man on the moon?
   a. Louis Armstrong
   b. Elon Musk
   c. Neil Armstrong
   d. John Young
3. How long should you boil a hard-boiled egg?
   a. 2 minutes
   b. 6 minutes
   c. 12 minutes
   d. 40 minutes
4. How many people live in Kenya?
   a. 12.5 million
   b. 37.5 million
   c. 52.5 million
   d. 72.5 million
5. What does a barometer measure?
   a. Solar activity
   b. Humidity
   c. Atmospheric pressure
   d. Dew
6. Which is the largest of these four cities?
   a. Shanghai
   b. Sao Paulo
   c. Delhi
   d. Mumbai

The questions were not too difficult, I suppose. And with some guess-work, you probably got them all correct. But I guess you started to hesitate on question 4. And with question 6, you also hesitated. Even though this multiple-choice test, like any other multiple-choice test, could have the third choice as the right answer six times in a row, you were probably reluctant to fall for that pattern. You basically fell victim to what researchers have called the gambler's fallacy. You wondered whether four times the same answer would be possible with presumably randomized answers. And when all an-swers were linked to the same letter, you started to feel uncomfortable. That cannot be right. There must be another answer coming up now that breaks the pattern. The name gambler's fallacy comes from gamblers at the roulette table. After a series of reds on the roulette table, the gambler's expectation of another red decreases. You see a number of reds in a row—or multiple-choice answer options—and you think—against all logic—that the occurrence of black will result in a more common sequence than the occurrence of an ad-ditional red.

Gambler's fallacy is ironic. Because if the shooter of your favorite bas-ketball team were scoring time after time, you would start thinking not about gambler's fallacy but about him having a hot hand. You would think all the luck was with him, and the fact that he scored earlier increases your expecta-tion that he will score again. If your favorite player scored from behind the three-point line three times in a row, you would just count for it to happen the fourth, fifth, and sixth time. Because you have the illusion of control in the basketball example (after all, that lucky shirt you wear every match must have made the difference!), you fall prone to the hot hand fallacy. Knowing that you don't have the (illusion of) control with the multiple-choice test, you want to avoid falling for the gambler's fallacy, for the pattern you see in front of you.

PRINCIPLES OF STRUCTURE

In the early part of the twentieth century, a group of psychologists defined specific principles we use to form patterns in the information we perceive.[6] They even called these principles "laws." For instance, we see four groups of three circles in the picture on the left.

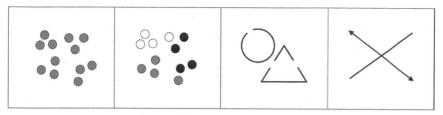

Laws of Proximity, Similarity, Closure, Continuation

That is odd, because there are just twelve circles, but we group them, and we group them on the basis of their proximity. Those circles that are closer to one another are perceived as belonging to the same group. Another principle suggests that if objects look similar, we tend to cluster them together, as in the second picture from the left. We cluster the white circles, cluster the grey circles, and cluster the black ones (unless you cluster by their proximity and ignore their similarity in color). And in the third picture from the left, we use the principle of closing something that is not closed, as in the circle. Or rather than identifying a massive caret on top of three lines that are attached, we simply view a triangle. And to the far right, we tend to see continued lines rather than two arrow lines, each one with a 90-degrees angle in it. We don't like interruptions; we go for completeness, totality, closure, and continuation.

The principles defined for the perception of shapes and color also seem to apply to language. For instance, while you are reading the words of these pages, you are relying on the proximity to keep the words apart. The proximity of the characters helps you identify the words in a sentence. And you do the same thing with paragraphs. When glancing over this page, the paragraph breaks are nicely marked by space. Or reversely, what is not separated by space apparently belongs to the same unit. And this is no different for sounds. Even though somebody's speech stream may sound uninterrupted, tiny little pauses—if not already really small ones between words—can be found between sentences. It helps to organize pieces of information on the basis of how close these pieces are in relation to one another.

And for grouping on the basis of similarity, things are not much different. At the most basic level, you assume that words that look or sound similar belong to the same group. The Law of Similarity and the Law of Proximity must belong to the group of laws because they look (or sound) the same. But we can take things a step further. We could even state that the words that tend to be short tend to be more grammatical in nature, whereas the words that tend to be longer tend to be more meaningful. And indeed, short words such as *for, the, of, are, not, much, at, the, that,* and *and,* all tend to be grammatical glue rather than meaningful items. On the other hand, words like *similarity, things, different, basic, level,* and *assume,* are words that look longer, and we could cluster longer words to the group of being more meaningful than shorter words. Does that sound like a stretch? Maybe, but in any case, it is worth noting that short words tend to be grammatical in nature, whereas longer words tend to be lexical in nature. It would then be awkward for us, the pattern seekers, not to pick up on this grouping. And if the lexical and grammatical item groupings sounded like a stretch, let me stretch things a bit further. Let's consider a grouping by meaning. Let me mention a man and a woman; he is seventy-five, and she is seventy-four. He likes gardening, and she loves designing. They both enjoy a quiet life together. On the basis of similarities in meaning (*man—he; woman—she; man and woman—they*), you have clustered the words in groupings.

We also saw that if there is a break in an object we perceive, we tend to perceive the object as a whole, as was the case in the "broken" circles and triangles. This principle can also be applied to language. You may experience this at the end of a page. You are reading the sentence, and while you are reading its words you suddenly—. Indeed, you suddenly have reached the end of the page, or the sentence in this example. And without the closure of a sentence, it simply does not feel right. You need closure. And continuation. I can start a sentence, interrupted by another one, but continue the original sentence. In spoken language, the power of the continuation is even stronger. When somebody talks to you, and halfway through the sentence, they are interrupted by a cough, the cough does not interrupt the sentence. You consider a continuation of the sentence despite the cough.

Many of these examples were already presented in chapter 3 ("Guess"), when language processing was described as making educated guesses. We can now add "educated guesses based on perceived patterns."

HUMANS AND OTHER ANIMALS

Humans are pattern seekers. What about other species? Don't they excel in finding patterns? Clearly they do. It is certainly not only humans who follow the organization principles presented so far. Animals do too—perhaps not so much organizational principles for language, but certainly organizational principles for perceptual information. For instance, cats were shown videos in which four Pac-Man sectored discs rotated (see the next page); one of the frames looked like the one on the left.[7]

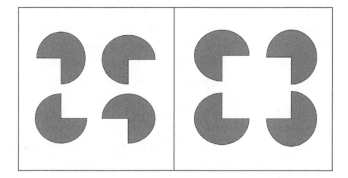

The discs rotated, but once in a while they configured to an illusionary square, as in the picture on the right above. The moment the illusionary square emerged, the cats received food. It took these cats very little time to figure out the pattern. Apparently, they had learned the subjective contour of a square, and this mastered the organizational principle. The square was not really there, but the contours could be made up from the shapes. Barn owls also showed their subjective contours skills when shapes—triangles and squares—were presented against a grated background.[8] The owls had little difficulty detecting the shapes and pecked one of two keys and were given rewards delivered by an automated feeder. And before you start noticing a pattern and draw the conclusion that the principles of perceptual organization apply to nocturnal predators only, macaque monkeys also passed the test.[9]

There is a large and growing body of literature that demonstrates that animals are good at finding patterns and making predictions. Since the 1980s, the field of animal cognition[10] has shown us that the question of whether we are smart enough to know how smart animals are,[11] to cite the title of primatologist and ethologist Frans de Waal, is fully justified. De Waal reports chimpanzees saying goodbye to their loved ones, thus being aware of the future separation, or chimps holding their breath awaiting being tickled, or chimps escaping their cage, running through the hallways in the middle of the night, but upon returning from their escapade, carefully closing the door behind them so nobody would find out—except that they had forgotten to remove their droppings from the hallway.

Or take another example de Waal gives, that of Lisala, a bonobo living in a jungle sanctuary near Kinshasa in the Democratic Republic of the Congo. Lisala—with her baby clinging to her lower back—carried a heavy fifteen-pound rock on her shoulders. She walked with the heavy burden on her shoulders for half a mile. Then she stopped, took the rock, and used it as a sledgehammer on some very tough nuts that were lying around in a slab of rock. After having cracked the nuts she needed, she left the rock behind and returned with her baby. These and other examples all provide evidence for planned social strategies in chimps, evidence for cooperation, altruism, deception, conflict resolution, and empathy. These examples all show that animals are smart, think in patterns, and think about the future—just like humans.

But animal responses to patterns show some interesting differences between humans and nonhumans. Let's have a look by taking another example of your ability to identify patterns and make predictions. Let me ask you to look at a sequence of green and red lights flashing up in front of you, one after the other, here depicted in greyscale, the darker grey being red and the lighter grey being green. At the end of the sequence, I will ask you what color most likely will follow next. Here we go.

That does not seem to be too difficult. Green and red lights alternate in this sequence, so after every green light you can expect a red light, and after every red light, well, a green one. So light grey is the answer. Your pattern-matching skills have not let you down. Now let's try another sequence.

What color would you choose at the end of this sequence? Red or green? Chances are you chose red, or the darker grey depicted here. That is both good news and bad news. The good news is that you are not an animal. Most animals—such as chimps, pigeons, and rats—will go for green. It must be comforting to know that you are not a chimp, a pigeon, or a rat. And in case you were already aware of that, it must be comforting to know you do not behave like one. You chose a color that most of your fellow human beings would choose too. However, if you selected red, the bad news is that you are wrong. Almost 80 percent of the lights that were flashed to you were green, so it would be a safer bet to choose green over red. Apparently, animals are smarter, for they go for frequency rather than pattern.[12] What makes matters worse is that while you were going for patterns and thought you found one, the data does not present a pattern. A sequence of random numbers made you think you found a pattern—after so many green lights, there must be a red light coming up—yet there was not one. We want to see patterns even in randomized stimuli, and make predictions on the basis of these perceived patterns.[13]

Let's look at this finding in a little more detail, because it reveals something interesting about our pattern-matching abilities. The psychologist Randy Gallistel trained rats to run a T-shaped maze.[14] They ran into the maze, and at the end they could take a left or a right. On both sides of the top of the T-shape, feeders were placed, sometimes with and sometimes without food. In 75 percent of the cases, the food came out of the left feeder; in the other 25 percent, the food came out of the right feeder. So the rat had an easy task. The chances of getting food were three times higher when a rat chose the left feeder, and so the rats optimized their performance (and minimized their hunger) by choosing the left feeder. Simple.

Now above the feeder, out of the rat's eyesight, lights were placed. These lights turned on when the feeder contained food, 75 percent of the time for the left feeder, 25 percent for the right feeder, but switching between left and right feeder randomly. Undergraduate students at Yale University were allowed to see the rats running through the maze and were allowed to see the lights turning on before, so they could anticipate whether the rat chose the right path even before it got the food. After a series of trials, the students were asked to predict where the food would come from next.

The rats always chose the left feeder, but the students didn't. Instead, they matched the relative frequency of their choices to the relative frequencies of the feeders releasing food, and thus chose the left feeder 75 percent of the time. That is odd, because apparently the student did not go for the optimal solution. Here is why. The chance of getting food by using the maximizing approach the rat took is 75 percent, namely, the percentage of time that they chose the left feeder times the percentage of time the left feeder was releasing food ($1.0 \times 0.75 + 0 \times 0.25 = 0.75$). The nonrats (the humans, as we call them), however, went for a probability-matching approach, which only gave them a success rate of 62.5 percent ($0.75 \times 0.75 + 0.25 \times 0.25 = 0.625$). Therefore, not so much with perceptual organization, the principles I defined earlier, but with regards to patterns, we find a difference between animal behavior and human behavior, rats typically going for a choice that optimizes their success, and humans going for a solution that yields inferior performance but matches the probability. Humans were sniffing for patterns, rats for food. And not only did rats beat humans in their performance, but pigeons did also.[15]

LEFT AND RIGHT HEMISPHERES

A large part of the impressive academic career of Michael Gazzaniga, a professor of neuroscience, is dedicated to studying split-brain patients.[16] In these patients, the corpus callosum, the band of fibers that connects the left and right hemispheres, has been removed. These patients, for instance, suffered from epileptic seizures, and by removing the communication channel between the left and right hemisphere, the neural chaos that started in one hemisphere could be constrained to that one hemisphere and not spread over the entire brain, including both hemispheres.

The split-brain patients allowed Gazzaniga and his team to investigate the role of the two hemispheres. Whereas for us, non-split-brain patients, our brain knows what our body is doing. When we snap our fingers with our left hand, we know, and when we do this with our right hand, we know. For split-brain patients, this is not the case. Because of the cross-wiring of our body and our brain—movement with our left arm and leg activates our right hemisphere and vice versa, and activation in our right hemisphere moves our left arm and leg (and in fact, our entire left side of our body) and vice versa. What would happen to a split-brain patient if information is presented to one and not the other hemisphere?

When Gazzaniga and his team investigated this question with a group of split-brain patients, they presented one of them with two pictures[17]: A picture of a chicken claw was presented to the right visual field, thus processed by the left hemisphere. A picture of a snow scene was presented to the left visual field and was processed by the right hemisphere. Next the patient was presented with a set of pictures in front of him that could be seen by both visual fields and thus processed by both hemispheres. The left hand pointed to the shovel, not surprisingly, given that the right hemisphere had processed the snow scene. The right hand pointed at the chicken, not surprising either given that the left hemisphere had seen the chicken claw. When the patient was asked why he had chosen these items, the response, generated by the language centers in the left hemisphere, was: "Oh, that's simple. The chicken claw goes with the chicken." Then, looking at his right hand pointing at the shovel, he said: "And you need a shovel to clean out the chicken shed." The left hemisphere had apparently interpreted the situation, providing post hoc an answer that fit the circumstances. The left-hemispheric brain had found a pattern, made sense out of senseless information, and stuck to it.

This post-hoc making-sense activity, the left-brain *interpreter* as Gazzaniga called it, was demonstrated in several studies. Another patient was presented with the word *bell* to the left visual field (the right hemisphere) and the word *music* to the right visual field (the left hemisphere). A series of pictures was then presented, and the patient picked among four pictures with musical instruments the one with a bell tower depicted on it.[18] When he was asked why he picked the bell, he answered that he must have heard a bell ringing on his way over. Once more, his left-brain interpreter made up a story. Or when the words *red* and *banana* were presented to a patient, *red* to the left hemisphere, *banana* to the right, the patient picked up a red pen among a number of colored pens and drew the banana.[19] When he was asked why he had chosen the red pen and was drawing with his left hand, he interpreted the situation and argued that it was easier to pull down with his left hand. Again, it seemed as if the left hemisphere tried to make sense out of an environment that the brain considered to be unstable.

If the left hemisphere has an interpreter, what about the right hemisphere? In a series of experiments, Gazzaniga and his team found that the right hemisphere was better than the left hemisphere at rejecting pictures and words that were similar but not the same as the presented materials.[20] Compared to the left hemisphere, the right hemisphere showed superior memory performance for line drawings and pictures of faces, as well as test words. For instance, when a split-brain patient in a memory task was presented with a list of words that included *apple* and *peach* (but not *plum*), the left hemisphere was more likely than the right hemisphere to incorrectly state that *plum* had been presented. It seems that the right hemisphere created an accurate record of the past, whereas the left hemisphere confabulated and guessed. The left hemisphere seems to make sense of the linguistic and cognitive world, while a right-hemisphere interpreter is making sense of the visuospatial world. It seems the right hemisphere is visually more intelligent than the left. It is good at what is called veridical perception, perceiving the world accurately, correctly seeing and remembering stimuli. The left hemisphere is better at making sense of the cognitive and linguistic world.[21] It does not so much have to be accurate, as long as it makes sense for a cognitive shortcut.

STABLE AND UNSTABLE ENVIRONMENTS

So let's recap. Humans are great pattern seekers. They seem to use different principles in organizing the information they are exposed to, and these principles may also apply to reading and hearing language. But humans are not necessarily better at finding patterns in data. When other animals are tested on their pattern-finding abilities, they show a somewhat similar performance. In fact, they too are good at predicting the future, at least bonobos, chimpanzees, Western scrub jays, crows, and dolphins do. Cats and barn owls do well when it comes to the law of closure or the law of continuity.[22]

But humans very much differ from animals when it comes to finding meaning in sequences of information. Whereas animals go for the better maximizing approach, humans go for pattern matching. Moreover, the pattern-matching ability—resulting in suboptimal performance—lies in the left hemisphere, whereas the ability to maximize seems more prominent in the right hemisphere. However, humans only pattern match when the environment is unstable. When the environment is stable, they are happy to take the maximizing approach. Finally, pattern matching rather than optimizing—left hemisphere for pattern matching, right hemisphere for maximizing—and pattern matching in an unstable environment but maximizing for a stable environment can be found in humans, but particularly in humans older than four years of age. We are good at guessing, confabulating, making inferences, fantasizing, and solving problems. And we are particularly good at doing that with our left hemisphere.

THE PATTERN SO FAR

As we reach the end of this chapter, you might be looking for a pattern not only in this chapter but also in this book. Let me play the interpreter in your left hemisphere and help you establish that pattern. Language provides a rather unstable environment; when children are about four years old they become fluent in language; animals do not seem to have a language system as complex (or rather unstable) as ours. And of the two hemispheres, language is primarily processed in the left hemisphere. Like the dollar bill, Abraham Lincoln, and John F. Kennedy we started the chapter out with, these associations between pattern-matching and language skills may be a coincidence. But I don't think they are.

We started out this book with the observation that humans are able to keep over sixty thousand words in mind. The quest for the answer on how we are able to keep those words in mind, then, put us on a journey to four explanations, each addressed in four chapters. We started the journey with the training as an answer, with reinforcement guiding us to use language. The journey continued with a language instinct being an answer to keeping those words in mind, with the argument that we have a knack for language because we have the instinct for it. We looked at a neural network that brings input and output together, learns over time, and explains the speed of processing. And we considered grounding as an explanation for keeping those words in mind with meaning arising out of perceptual simulations. Obviously, none of these answers should be entirely dismissed, as training, instinct, network, and grounding are somehow needed in language processing. Similarly, none of these answers should be considered mutually exclusive. It is far more likely that a combination of these explanations form an answer to language acquisition and language processing.

But the problem is that whenever we encounter a cognitive task, we first take a cognitive shortcut to the answer. This means we commonly get the answer wrong and get outperformed by pigeons and chimpanzees. And that poses a problem to the explanation of any answers to how we are able to keep those words in mind. If we are unable or unwilling to even rotate a simple picture, to accurately count the number of characters in a sentence, to draw some logical conclusions, or to estimate the probability in a simple sequence, or otherwise take the easiest way out as to not waste any cognitive energy, then we should scratch our head again and wonder about the discrepancy behind taking cognitive shortcuts (with far-from-impressive results on a range of cognitive tasks, including language tasks) and the four explanations we have discussed so far. So how can we then explain the discrepancy between the miserable failure on so many cognitive tasks and the incredible success on the linguistic cognitive task of language processing?

In this chapter we have seen that humans, compared to other species, are proficient in pattern matching. Humans are able to detect patterns easily, and we are able to do this even when the pattern is noisy (or even when no pattern is present!). If I were to flip a coin and it landed on heads three times in a row, you would soon start accusing me of manipulating the coin. So why are you so proficient at detecting a pattern in the flipping of the coin?

One explanation for detecting a manipulated coin is that you are triggered by the environment. You were once taught that coins landing on heads three times in a row are problematic coins. Each time you notice that the coin lands on heads is a confirmation of a pattern, starting with the second time the coin lands on heads. You receive a confirmation, a positive reinforcement, that you are on the right track. These environmental cues are the explanation for your pattern-matching ability.

You may, however, argue that the reinforcement for finding a pattern is hardly sufficient. In fact, you don't really receive a reward or a punishment for finding a pattern, merely a confirmation of being on the right track. Moreover, the three-times-in-a-row pattern does not provide one with the richness one needs for detecting patterns in the coin flipping. Because of this poverty of the stimulus, there needs to be an alternative explanation. That explanation might lie in a pattern-acquisition device or instinct. Patterns are processed in the left hemisphere, and humans have a neurological device that is reserved for pattern recognition. It is as if we have an instinct to detect patterns.

The problem with the argument of a pattern instinct is that we do not quite know where the pattern-acquisition device is located in the human brain. Perhaps the explanation does not so much lie in an innate device or instinct, but in the general computational architecture of the brain, a neural network. We rapidly compute the probability of heads five times in a row, conclude that the chances of this happening are 12.5 percent, and thus find a pattern. We have trained our network with input matching to output in order to compute the correct probabilities.

But if the computational architecture is an explanation for you recognizing a pattern in me flipping the coin, why are you so bad at estimating probabilities in most cognitive tasks? Even in the coin-flipping task itself, had the coin landed on its head twice, you may have already suspected a pattern. Instead, perhaps your ability for recognizing a pattern in the coin flipping does not come from computations, but rather from a reenactment of the coin flipping. You view the falling of the coin as you falling down yourself, and because the likelihood of you falling flat twice in a row is already very unlikely, falling flat on your face three times makes you detect a pattern, regardless of the mathematical probabilities behind it.

As with explaining our ability of language processing, these explanations assume that the cause of detecting the pattern of flipping the coin lies in environment, brain, computation, memory, or a combination of those. None of these explanations are wrong. Yet perhaps the explanation for finding a pattern in the coin flipping lies not so much in training, instinct, network, or grounding, but in the pattern itself. The pattern of three heads in a row affords recognizing the pattern. This would mean that the pattern affords being discovered by training, instinct, network, and grounding.

There are many arguments why detecting a pattern in coin flips is an oversimplification of detecting patterns in language. For instance, the flips of a coin and the pattern of those flips are universal, whereas there are thousands of different languages across the world (albeit perhaps with different levels of universality). Moreover, languages have evolved over time and serve as a tool of communication. You may argue that flipping a coin may be a tool for placing bets, but it is hard to make the argument that coin flipping has evolved over time. So, if you (falsely) accused me of manipulating a coin—after all, 12.5 percent is a small probability, but certainly an acceptable probability— you can readily and accurately accuse me of simplifying the problem of how you can keep those words in mind. But the coin flipping is only an illustration to make my point.

My point is that when we are considering coin flips, you would not argue that detecting a pattern of three heads in a row comes from training, instinct, network, or grounding. Instead, you attribute your skill to detecting the pattern not to these external factors but simply to the coin itself, the coin landing on its head three times. The same argument I would like to pose for language processing. Instead of arguing that language processing solely comes from the four explanations covered so far, we could argue that language processing comes from the language system itself.

The argument that we keep those words in mind because of the language system is built on one major assumption: that language consists of patterns that allow for language users to extract meaning. And that is quite a big assumption, because so much in language argues so strongly against that assumption. Any linguistics textbook states that one of the central features of the language system is that language is arbitrary: there is no intrinsic relation between the sound of the word and its meaning.[23] Those same textbooks argue that a rule-system acts on a language when it comes to phonology, morphology, and syntax. We can form some 10 sextillion sentences, but combinations are only allowed that follow a careful system of grammatical rules. The *form* of language—the sound of the word, the word structure, the sequence of words or sentences, and their interrelations—does not predict its meaning. Presumably.

· *10* ·

Sound

No one disputes the fact that linguistic signs are arbitrary. But it is often easier to discover a truth than to assign it to its correct place.

—Ferdinand de Saussure[1]

Some 2,300 years ago, the Greek philosopher Plato presented a dialogue between Socrates, Cratylus, and Hermogenes. Socrates asks the other two whether names have an intrinsic relation to the things they signify, and are therefore natural, or whether they are—as de Saussure argued two millennia later—arbitrary.

> Hermogenes: I have often talked over this matter, both with Cratylus and others, and cannot convince myself that there is any principle of correctness in names other than convention and agreement; any name which you give, in my opinion, is the right one, and if you change that and give another, the new name is as correct as the old—we frequently change the names of our slaves, and the newly-imposed name is as good as the old: for there is no name given to anything by nature; all is convention and habit of the users;—such is my view. But if I am mistaken I shall be happy to hear and learn of Cratylus, or of any one else.
>
> Socrates: I dare say that you may be right, Hermogenes: let us see;—Your meaning is, that the name of each thing is only that which anybody agrees to call it?
>
> Hermogenes: That is my notion.
>
> Socrates: Whether the giver of the name be an individual or a city?
>
> Hermogenes: Yes.

[. . .]

Socrates: Do you admit a name to be the representation of a thing?

Cratylus: Yes, I do.

Socrates: But do you not allow that some nouns are primitive, and some derived?

Cratylus: Yes, I do.

Socrates: Then if you admit that primitive or first nouns are representations of things, is there any better way of framing representations than by assimilating them to the objects as much as you can; or do you prefer the notion of Hermogenes and of many others, who say that names are conventional, and have a meaning to those who have agreed about them, and who have previous knowledge of the things intended by them, and that convention is the only principle; and whether you abide by our present convention, or make a new and opposite one, according to which you call small great and great small—that, they would say, makes no difference, if you are only agreed. Which of these two notions do you prefer?

Cratylus: Representation by likeness, Socrates, is infinitely better than representation by any chance sign.[2]

For Hermogenes, a horse is called a horse, because the language community agrees calling a four-legged animal that neighs and that you can ride on a horse. There is no relationship between the sound of the word and its meaning. Cratylus on the other hand is not so sure about arbitrariness. Some 1,700 years after the fictional dialogue between Hermogenes, Cratylus, and Socrates took place, the same question on whether the sound of a word tells us something about its meaning can be found in Shakespeare's *Romeo and Juliet*. Similar to Hermogenes, Juliet asks herself:

> What's in a name? That which we call a rose
> by any other name would smell as sweet.[3]

Just like Hermogenes, Juliet argues that a rose is a rose regardless of its name.[4] And like Hermogenes, Juliet is right: *asukume* (Zulu) and *ya tashi* (Hausa) smell just as sweet as *rose* does. As with *horse* and *rose*, what we call a dog we could have called *crwth* or *cwm*, except that these words have already been reserved for a traditional Welsh stringed musical instrument and a valley head created by glacial erosion. We could have called a dog a *doll, god, log, bog, dig, dag*, or any other combination of sounds.

THE SIGN IS ARBITRARY

If there were a Billboard hit chart for the most-quoted phrases in linguistics, "*le signe est arbitraire*" would make it high up in the charts. If your French is a bit rusty, the phrase translates to "the sign is arbitrary." The quote can be found in the collected works of Ferdinand de Saussure,[5] a Swiss linguist and semiotician considered to be one of the founders of twentieth-century linguistics. According to de Saussure, there is no intrinsic relationship between the sound of a word and its meaning. A dog in English is a *hond* in Dutch, a *koira* in Finnish, an *ilio, 'iilio* in Hawaiian, a *kelev* in Hebrew, a *kutta* in Hindi, a *sobaka* in Russian, a *kutya* in Hungarian, a *hundur* in Icelandic, an *inu* in Japanese, a *pies* in Polish, a *kukur* in Nepalese, a *cane* in Italian, and a *gae* in Korean. Different sounds for the same animal. Apparently, there is nothing in the meaning of the concept that dictates the sound of the word.

Now you could perhaps argue that the concept of a dog in the Netherlands, Finland, Hawaii, Israel, India, Hungary, Iceland, Japan, Poland, Nepal, Italy, and Korea may not be the same across cultures. But even in countries with two languages, like Belgium and Canada, where the concept of the four-legged barking animal must be the same, a dog is called a different word in each of the languages spoken in the country. A dog in Belgium is called a *chien* in the French-speaking part of the country or a *hond* in the Flemish-speaking part; in Canada that same dog is called *chien* in the French-speaking part or *dog* in the English-speaking part. Very different sounds for very much the same meaning. We have different words for the same meaning, and the word is totally arbitrary.

Perhaps most concepts have arbitrary words affiliated with them, but there is at least one category where one can argue that the relation is fixed: the category of words called onomatopoeia. Onomatopoeias are words that sound the same as their meaning. Animal sounds are perhaps the best example of onomatopoeias. *Woof woof* simply means what it sounds like, the barking of a dog. At least onomatopoeias are not arbitrary. Take that, Ferdinand de Saussure!

But if we take a closer look at animal sounds, we see that they too differ across languages. For instance, dogs bark presumably identically across all canines, but the way the identical barking is represented in language differs. English dogs bark *woof woof*, Dutch dogs *waf waf*, Finnish dogs *jape jape*, Hawaiian dogs *kū maʻa*, Israelian dogs *hav hav*, Indian dogs *bow bow*, Russian dogs *gav gav*, Hungarian dogs *vau vau*, Icelandic dogs *voff voff*, Japanese dogs *wan wan*, Polish dogs *hau hau*, Nepalese dogs *vūpha vūpha*, Italian dogs *bau bau*, and Korean dogs *meong meong*.

If the sign is really arbitrary, this would be a rather disheartening conclusion, at least for the relationship between the sound of a word and its meaning, for we then have to conclude that there are no patterns. It would mean this chapter would become the shortest chapter in this book.

ICONICITY

But is it really the case that the sign is arbitrary? If we look closer at the language system, there is randomness, but there may also be patterns. And these patterns might provide the clue to the puzzle how we keep those words in mind. These patterns in language might provide cues for the meaning of the words. All that is needed then is some training that reinforces us in the configuration in which these words should be expressed and comprehended, an instinct that helps us pick up these patterns, some network architecture that allows us to train these patterns, and grounding in a perceptual experience when such grounding is needed.[6] To make a long story short, we may not always see the linguistic pattern of the forest through the chaos of the linguistic trees.

Let's revisit the claim "the sign is arbitrary" by turning back the clock some 5,500 years.[7] Obviously, there are no records of the languages spoken at the time, but fortunately there are some written records. In an area where the Euphrates and the Tigris rivers join and empty in the Persian sea, then called Mesopotamia (literally "Land between the Rivers"), now called Iraq, Sumeria was found. Sumeria was one of the first civilizations in the world. Along the valleys of the Tigris and Euphrates, Sumerian farmers grew grain and other crops, and over time urban settlements emerged.

Clay tablets made by the Sumerians have been found around sites along the riverbeds of the Euphrates and the Tigris. These tablets provide the earliest examples of writing we have discovered thus far. When considering these tablets, an interesting evolution can be observed. The earliest tablets are pictographic in nature. From the pictograms on the tablets, we can guess what the meaning of the writing is. A pictogram of a fish means "fish," and that of grain unsurprisingly means "grain." Pictograms were mixed with ideograms. In ideograms the link between the writing and what the writing meant has become less obvious. For instance, the ideogram of a bowl means "to eat," that of a foot "to stand." The early Sumerian script was a combination of pictograms and ideograms, the direct relation between the sign and what it means, and a more indirect relation of the sign and what it means.

Now from the earliest Sumerian writings 5,500 to 5,200 years ago, in a time span of about three hundred years, a change can be observed. One can scratch a beautiful drawing in clay, but to repeat this process often enough to distribute the information, one needs to find shortcuts. The shortcuts were found in the cuneiform method of writing. In cuneiform writing the pictograms and ideograms were not scratched in clay anymore, but a stylus was used, most likely because of the speed of the writing process. The stylus was pressed into the soft clay, and short straight strokes emerged, thicker at the top and to the left as a consequence of the pressure being placed in the direction of writing. In cuneiform writing, few pictographs or ideographs can be found. The writing has become pretty much abstract, except that it now includes phonological information. Whereas the pictograms and ideograms were nonphonological, the cuneiforms were phonological in nature, just like the present-day writing system.

It seems as if Sumerian writing showed a fixed, nonarbitrary relation between the sign and its meaning initially, with pictograms representing the meaning. Ideograms were similar, except that a level of abstraction can be found between the sign and its meaning. Ideograms would require some level of convention. The user could guess the meaning from the sign, but the meaning is not obvious. As a consequence of rapid distribution of the writing system—more urban settlement, more tablets—it seems as if the writing system took a cognitive shortcut. The relation between the sign and its meaning became pretty much arbitrary, with the meaning of a symbol only being determined on the basis of convention. The next page shows a series of examples from David Diringer's impressive description of the evolution of writing systems.[8]

On the left you see the original pictograph, on the right its meaning. With very little imagination, the pictograph gives cues about its meaning. In the fourth column, the classic Assyrian script is presented, in which the relation between form and meaning is lacking. The script is arbitrary. Early cuneiform, preceding the classic Assyrian script, presented in the third column, has pictographic elements that link form to its meaning as well as arbitrary elements that transition to the classic Assyrian script. The second column is a copy of the first column. It presents the pictograph but rotates in such a way that it makes the link with the early cuneiform clearer.

"That was then, and this is now," you might say. But when it comes to the evolution of language, we have little else to work from. Tablets that stood the test of time are all we have to reconstruct how (written) language evolved, unless we can observe languages within a lifetime. One such language is Israeli Sign Language (ISL), which emerged only eighty years ago. It has some ten thousand signers, and because of the history of ISL, it has become possible to investigate how the language evolved over time. Fifteen native ISL signers were divided into three age groups—young, middle, and older—and they were asked to tell a short life story. The first generation signed only with

Original pictograph	Cuneiform position	Early cuneiform	Classic Assyrian	Meaning
				heaven, god
				earth
				man
				woman
				mountain
				mountain woman
				head
				mouth to speak
				food
				to eat
				water in
				to drink
				to go, to stand
				bird
				fish
				ox
				cow
				grain
				sun, day
				to plow

Source: Diringer (1962).

their dominant hand. As the community of signers grew larger, the language started to become more complex, with facial expressions and torso, and ultimately the nondominant hand was used to provide more nuances. Moreover, whereas the first generation of signers signed about 104 signs per minute, the latest generation has become far more efficient with 153.2 signs per minute.[9] The language became more nuanced and more efficient over time. A cognitive shortcut emerged.

If we don't want to wait eighty years to see how a language evolves, we might simulate language evolution. A team of researchers at the University of Edinburgh came up with a very clever idea to recreate language evolution in the lab,[10] not having to rely on clay tablets, and not even having to rely on a sign language that evolved albeit in only eighty years. They simulated generations of language users by doing the game you might have played when you were younger: the Telephone Game, in which you whisper something to the person next to you, who whispers what she heard to the person next to her, who whispers what she heard to the person next to her, and so on. The end result is always funny, as very little of the original message actually stands the test of (whispering) time. Simon Kirby and his team did something similar, asking participants to whisper an utterance to the next person, who would whisper the utterance to the next person. The researchers also recorded a video of a participant pantomiming a concept and showed the recording to another participant, who would then pantomime the concept to another participant—for instance, the pantomiming of the word *photographer*. In the first generation a participant would pantomime holding a camera, clicking the button on top of the camera with her right index finger, holding up her hand to stop the imagined person, then circling her hand as if to point the imagined person to turn around, and clicking the imagined button with her index finger again. A pantomime of a model shoot. In the fifth generation the pantomime looked very different. There you see somebody pointing at himself, and making three consecutive clicking movements with his index finger. That's it. It is harder to get the meaning out of the pantomime because it is much shorter and far less complex. It seems to be a cognitive shortcut.

Whenever I think of the evolution of Sumerian, the changes across generations in Israeli Sign Language, and the experiments that simulate language evolution in the lab, I get reminded of my economics teacher in high school explaining to me the evolution of money. The story is similar to the evolution of language. In the early days, people traded their goods. If I had a cow, I had milk. If you had grain, you had bread. And so we could trade my milk and your bread. The value of the products was about the same, and that value could be directly linked back to the product we traded. Over time, however, things became a little cumbersome. If you didn't need milk, I still had to make sure I would trade it before it became spoiled. And with a larger community of traders, that made sense: I could trade my milk to somebody else who may have had some meat, which could be traded in for bread. But with a community growing larger and larger, it seemed easier to replace the actual product with specific value (bread, milk, meat) for something a little more abstract, like gold or silver. My milk could now be traded in for some silver, with the same value. The advantage was that I could trade more efficiently and would still be certain my products would retain their value. Over time, however, as the trading community developed trust in the principle of a concept keeping its value, the gold or silver could be replaced with something even more abstract, for instance, a piece of paper. As long as everybody agreed the piece of paper meant the value we agreed on, that piece of (actually worthless) paper would be worth the value of my milk.

The comparison between money and language may seem farfetched, but it illustrates some interesting similarities. Whereas the relation between the sign and its meaning was initially based on similarity, over time it became more abstract, with some similarity between the sign and its meaning, to ultimately being fully abstract. The process of abstraction can be explained by a growing community of people buying into the absence of a relation between the sign and what it means. As long as the community agreed, the sign system worked. It also provided a convenient cognitive shortcut, so it was no longer necessary to keep in mind all forms and meanings.

SOUNDS AND MEANING

Let's assume a language neither one of us knows. The language has words we do not know the meaning of, but luckily for us, two words and their meanings are known. The words are *kiki* and *bouba*. The meanings of the two words are a spiky pointy shape and the other a bubbly round shape. But unfortunate for us foreign language learners, the labels of the two shapes have actually been mixed up, so we do not really know which shape is called *kiki* and which one *bouba*. Is the spiky one *bouba* or *kiki*? And what about the bubbly one? Which one would you choose?

In the early part of the twentieth century, German psychologist Wolfgang Köhler asked participants to give names to different forms.[11] Participants were presented with a star shape and a spilled-ink shape and were asked which one would be most likely called *takete* or *buluba*. Participants overwhelmingly choose *takete* for the shape with the sharp edges, and *baluba* for the more round shape. In later experiments, *takete* was replaced with

kiki, and *buluba* with *maluma* and *bouba*, but the outcomes were the same. Participants assigned the word requiring a rounder shape of the mouth to the rounder shapes, and the word with a more angular mouth shape to the more angular shape.

But the *kiki-bouba* effect is not limited to consonants that start with a *k* or *b* or to spiky and round shapes. The effect can also be found for vowels. Let's go back again to the made-up language that we do not speak. New words have been discovered in our made-up language, and again we are lucky because we are informed what the words mean. They refer to smaller and larger greebles, blueish little monsters that can take the size of a dog, deer, cow, elephant, or dino, concepts with words like *tikiti, tebibi, kekomo, wutoli*, and *gobudu*.[12] As with *bouba* and *kiki*, the labels for these words are mixed up again. We simply do not know whether the smallest greeble is *gobudu* or *tikiti*. For most of us, we guess very homogeneously. We reserve the /i/ and /e/ vowels for small greebles and /u/ and /o/ for the largest greebles. *Tikiti, tebibi, kekomo, wutoli*, and *gobudu* are nicely ordered according to size according to our, and the participants', intuition. And the greebles agree.[13]

Perhaps we guessed smaller greebles to be *tikiti* or *tebibi*, and larger greebles to be *wutoli* and *gobudu*, because of the associations with words that we do know: smaller words such as *little, tiny, mini, bit, dinky, micro, slim*, and *lesser*; and larger words such as *large, tall, bold, ample, bulky, grand, macro, massive, monstrous, super*, and *voluminous*. Of course, that is interesting in itself. Perhaps as English language users we follow the patterns of our language and apply them to the language we do not know. But it may tell us more about the language that we do know than the language that we do not. Moreover, the decision between small and large seems rather binary. The word we do not know is either larger or smaller. That's it. What if we asked people for the meaning of these words on multiple features, beyond large and small?

In another clever study,[14] two dozen nonexisting words were given to participants, such as *ackie, ambous, axittic, bomburg, cougzer, gricker, flissil, keex, heonia, cruckwic, horgous*, and *boodoma*. With enough of these nonexisting words, we can build an entirely new language! Participants were asked whether each of these words was best described as being dominant, small, large, spiky, feminine, intelligent, round, submissive, unintelligent, or masculine. They could choose one to four features describing the nonexisting words. But they were not done yet.

Next, they were asked to draw a creature that looked like the nonexisting word. For instance, what would a *horgous* look like? What is cool—in a nerdy sense—is that we now know three things: the word (*horgous*), the features (e.g., that it is large and masculine), and an interpretation of what a *horgous* looks like. What is even cooler—in an even nerdier sense—is that we can now ask another group of participants to give the name of the creature somebody else drew (is it a *horgous*, a *bomburg*, or a *fissil*) and the features that go with the drawing (is it dominant, small, large, spiky, feminine, intelligent, round, submissive, unintelligent, or masculine?). And what is coolest—in the nerdiest sense—is that the results were fully consistent. The picture of a *horgous* was considered by participants to be large and round, fully in line with the features other participants gave to the word *horgous*. A picture of a *keex* was considered to be small and spiky, just like the features given to the word *keex* by other participants. *Heonia* was considered feminine, according to the features given to the picture and the features given to the word, by two different groups of participants. And when participants got confused, and did not get the word *horgous* right for the large masculine drawing of a monster, they were more likely to confuse it with a *bomburg* than with a *keex*. How cool is that?

Of course, we could argue that these sound–meaning effects are found as a consequence of learned mapping between a nonsense word and a selected feature. By repeatedly showing the word and a selected meaning, it becomes easy to link specific nonsense words to specific features. Moreover, participants had the opportunity to go into a careful deliberation with themselves to find out which word feature best fits which meaning feature. That's what you may think. And that is not actually the case. The mapping between rounded sounds and rounded objects and spiky sounds with spiky objects is found not only in adults but also in children as young as 2.5 years old.[15] And what about the careful deliberation before you link *shick* to the spiky object and *dom* to the rounded object? Brain-imaging studies show that this mapping happens as early as 140–180 milliseconds after you see the picture of the spiky or rounded object.[16] Not enough at all for any deliberation, but fast enough for a cognitive shortcut.

These examples show that there are cues in the sound of the word that may give away aspects of its meaning. If we look at actual language samples, there are quite a few examples that demonstrate that the presumed arbitrary relation between the sound of a word and its meaning should not be so readily dismissed as the beginning of this chapter suggested. For instance:

- *clank, clash, clap, clack, cling, click, cluck, clamp, clip, clod, clog, clam, clinch, clutch, clasp, clump, clench, claw, clay,* and *cloy* suggest a clang;
- *float, flush, flee, flail, flop, flap, fleet, flit, flag, flex, fling, flare, flash, flip, flick, flat, flaunt, fluster, fleck, flirt, flinch,* and *flake* suggest a flow;
- *glint, gloss, glare, glaze, glee, glad, glimpse, glance, gloom, gloat, glum, glide, globe,* and *glove* suggest a glow;
- *skid, skip, skate, skimp, scud, scour, skirt, scope, skin, sketch, skew, scat, scoff, scare,* and *skull* suggest skimming;
- *stick, stump, stanch, steep, stall, stuff, stir, stamp, sting, stomp, stash* suggest stiffness;
- *stripe, strip, stretch, streak, strait, string, strap, stream, stride, strive, strut, strum, strength, strain, stroll, strife, strange, strew, stress* suggest something being straight;
- *swish, swoop, swipe, sweep, swirl, swat, swoon, switch, swag, swap, swell, swill,* and *swim* suggest something swinging;
- *creep, crack, crick, cramp, crutch, creak, crouch, cross, cringe, crane, croak, crimp, crag, crow, crash, crawl, crunch, crush, crib, crate, crump, crab, crumb* suggest something being crooked;
- *drift, droop, drape, drawl, drown, dregs, drug, drain, droll, drench, drool, drip, dry, drum, dram* all drag on;
- *grunt, groan, gruff, grim, grouse, grudge, grasp, grope, grab, grip, graft* all growl;
- *slip, slope, slant, slick, slink, sleek, slime, sleet, sludge, slosh, slop, slouch, slough, slash, slow, sling, slack, slam, slay, slit, sloth, slap, slog, slave, slang* all slide along;
- *sniff, snort, sneeze, snore, snuff, snarl, sneer, snoop, snub, snob, snack, snap, sneak, snatch, snag, snip* all have something to do with a snout;
- *squash, squirt, squirm, squelch, squeal, squeak, squawk, squid, squall, squander* squeeze each other out.[17]

The sounds at the beginning of these words give away features of their meaning. If I presented you with the word *glim*, you may have absolutely no idea what this archaic seventeenth-century word means, but you would not be very surprised to hear it means something that furnishes light (like a lantern or candle), or that a *slugabed*, another seventeenth-century archaic word, is a couch potato, a person who stays in bed for too long.

And you are right, these are carefully cherry-picked words that prove my point. The problem with these examples is that they are just that: examples. For each category there are twenty to thirty words that fit the category, while there are many words starting with a *cl-*, *cr-*, or *sl-* sound—*clown, cradle,* and *slot*—that do not quite fit the bill. And if for the sixty thousand words we know, there are some twenty words that fit each category—though this seems to be rather unlikely, as the list presented above should then have been considerably longer—we would still have to remember two thousand categories. Moreover, they are carefully selected words from carefully selected categories. How do they generalize across a language?

Corpus linguistic studies may come to the rescue. Large numbers of words can be analyzed on their sounds, and the relationship between the number of words that have these sounds and a particular word category can be mapped out. For instance, we could take a large number of words and see how the sounds of these words allow for distinguishing whether we are dealing with nouns or verbs. Extensive studies have shown that it is possible with over 90 percent accuracy to predict whether a word is a noun or a verb, solely on the basis of its sound (and not its morphology).[18] That means that knowing whether a word is an activity[19] or not can be established only on the basis of its sound, not just for English, but also for Dutch, German, and Japanese, and not for a few words, but for thousands of words! This means that language users can use the sound of the word to identify whether they are dealing with a noun or a verb, which means not only that they can make estimates about whether they are dealing with an activity (verb) or a concept (noun), but also that they can make estimates about the structure of the sentence—not only on the syntactic rules or the meaning of the word but also on the basis of the sound of the word. These are not corpus linguistic or computational linguistic observations. Language users use this information in online sentence processing. Take for instance the two sentences below[20]:

Chris and Ben are glad that the bird perches seem easy to install.
Chris and Ben are glad that the bird perches comfortably in the cage.

The two sentences both include the word *perches*, a word that is a homonym. It can mean a perch a bird can rest on, a branch or horizontal bar, or the process of perching, the resting on the branch. The word can thus be a noun or a verb, a concept or an activity. Based on the word itself, there is nothing that tells us whether it is one or the other. An extensive analysis of the sound of the word, however, showed that on the basis of the sound, *perch* is noun-like than more verb-like.

And when participants were asked to read sentences like these, they read the first sentence until the word *perches* faster—even though they had not yet seen the rest of the sentence. A word like *needs* also has two meanings: the state of requiring help, the necessity, *or* the process of requiring help, as below—noun or verb, concept or activity.

The teacher told the principal that the student needs were not being met.

The teacher told the principal that the student needs to be more focused.

A corpus linguistic analysis found that *needs* is more a verb than a noun. When participants read these sentences, they were considerably faster in the second than in the first sentence. So even though it may seem that the sounds of words have an arbitrary relationship with their meaning, there are exceptions with words that fit a clanging, flowing, sticking, swinging, and drifting tendency. Though these words may be carefully chosen, the pattern holds up for nonsense words that relate to the size of greebles or the nature of a horgous. And for language at large, it seems that the sound of a word can distinguish reliably (but not perfectly) whether the word is a noun or a verb, or whether it is more positive or negative in valence. Reading and response time studies confirm that language users employ these patterns in their reading and comprehension processes.

In another cool study—there are many of them—participants were asked to first rate words on their iconicity.[21] They got an instruction like the following:

> Some English words sound like what they mean. For example, SLURP sounds like the noise made when you perform this kind of drinking action. An example that does not relate to the sound of an action is TEENY, which sounds like something very small (compared to HUGE which sounds big). These words are iconic. You might be able to guess these words' meanings even if you did not know English. Words can also sound like the opposite of what they mean. For example, MICROORGANISM is a large word that means something very small. And WHALE is a small word that means something very large. And finally, many words are not iconic or opposite at all. For example there is nothing canine or feline sounding about the words DOG or CAT. These words are arbitrary. If you did not know English, you would not be able to guess the meanings of these words.[22]

The researchers were then able to have iconicity ratings for some three thousand words. Participants felt that the words *humming*, *click*, and *hissing* were very iconic. The sound of the word gave away its meaning. But words like *dandelion*, *silent*, and *would* did not, according to the participants. In addition to onomatopoeias, verbs, adjectives, and adverbs were overall considered iconic, but nouns were not so much. The words were also split up by the modality they were describing. Visual words like *murky*, *tiny*, and *quick*; gustatory words like *juicy*, *suck*, and *chewy*; and olfactory words like *sniff* and *whiff* were iconic. And tactile words like *mushy*, *crash*, and *crisp*; and auditory words like *hissing, buzzing,* and *clank* were also iconic. Overall, however, the iconicity scores for visual, gustatory, and olfactory words were lower than those for auditory and tactile words. So across some three thousand words, iconicity was found, but the level of iconicity by syntactic category or the modality the words could be linked to varied.

In my own lab, we investigated the question of whether we could identify sounds that might cue language users on the meaning of a word.[23] We took thousands of words that participants had already rated as being more positive or more negative. Words like *torture, murder,* and *morgue* excelled in negative valence and *birthday, vacation,* and *happiness* in positive valence. For all these thousands of words, we identified all the phonemes, the sounds of a word. We then computed whether the word started with a plosive (like *t, k, p* or *d, g, b*) or whether the plosive occurred somewhere in the middle of the word, and how often. We computed the number of vowels and where they occurred in the word, as we did with nasals (like *n* and *m*). Some twenty sounds characteristics were coded, not just for the English language, but also for Dutch and German. And in our efforts, we added Chinese. Our task was to determine the smallest number of phonemes that would maximally distinguish between positive and negative valence.[24] And for all four languages we looked at, one phoneme made the difference. If a word started with a nasal, it told us a little bit about the valence of a word. Not a lot, but just enough.

Even more interesting, the nasal at the beginning of a word told us that the word was more negative in meaning for English, Dutch, and German, but when a word started with a nasal in Chinese, it was considered more positive in meaning. And this allowed us to conduct several experiments. In the first experiment we presented Dutch words with neutral valence to Dutch participants and Chinese words with neutral valence to Chinese participants, words such as *lipstick, speculation, reaction,* and *noun, notification,* and *north.* These words were neither positive nor negative in meaning, and only half began with a nasal sound. The Dutch participants responded that the neutral-valence words were more negative when they started with a nasal; the Chinese participants did just the opposite. We then divided the Chinese words that started with a nasal and those that did not and presented the Dutch participants who did not speak a word of Chinese with the Chinese words and the Chinese participants who did not speak a word of Dutch with the Dutch words. Dutch participants felt that the foreign words they did not know sounded more negative when they started with a nasal than when they did not. For the Chinese participants, Dutch words sounded more positive when they started with a nasal. We presented the words on a screen, and we presented the words through headphones, and the results were the same.

In the case of valence, the sound of a word—the nasal in the first position of the word—gives us some cues on whether the word is more likely to be positive or negative in meaning. It does this not with a perfect accuracy, but its patterns allow for a 55–60 percent classification in the right category, just above chance and—for participants—apparently just enough to recognize a pattern—one that would provide a cognitive shortcut to the language user.

Another study[25] took the opposite approach. Rather than looking at a large number of words in a small number of languages, this study looked at a small number of words across a large number of languages. In fact, the study looked at a very large number of languages, 4,298 languages across the world! The systematicity in the sounds of forty words were compared across those thousands of languages. Thirty of these words, or 75 percent, showed a sound–meaning association bias. For instance, the meaning of "small" was associated with a high /i/ sound, as in the French *petit*, Finnish *pieni*, Hausa *karami*, or Hungarian *kicsi*. The meaning of "round" was associated with the r sound across a large number of languages, such as French (*ronde*), Finnish (*pyöristää*), Hausa (*da'ira*), or Hungarian (*kerek*). The meaning of "tongue" was linked to an /l/ sound, "nose" with an /n/ sound, and "breasts" with an /m/ sound. The similarities here between sound and meaning could not be attributed to a language coming from the same language family. For instance, English comes closest to Frisian, Dutch, and German in terms of language family relations, so it may be no surprise that there are commonalities across these languages. But finding similarities between French, Finnish, Hausa, and Hungarian is not that easy to explain. And extend that to thousands of languages that share the same sounds for forty words that can be found across these languages!

A number of studies show that we cannot conclude that the relationship between the sound of the word and its meaning is fixed, but that there is systematicity in capturing aspects of the meaning of a word by its sound alone. The discussion between Hermogenes and Cratylus that Plato started some 2,300 years ago continues. With de Saussure's adage—which supports the Hermogenes camp—reigning for almost a century, there is an increasing number of researchers who bring some convincing Cratylus arguments to the table, an argument that might help us in understanding how we keep those words in mind, with sound–meaning patterns providing a convenient cognitive shortcut.

WHY SO ARBITRARY?

If there is evidence of a sound–meaning relationship in language, why then is it the case that for most words and most categories, there is no such direct relationship? Early Sumerian pictographs help us identify their meaning. Why, then, did the writing system change from cuneiforms, in which the relationship between form and meaning is less clear, to classic Assyrian script, in which the relationship between form and meaning is absent? Why did the relationship between form and meaning become arbitrary? Even if computational and psychological research find more and more pieces of the sound-meaning puzzle, with more and more categories being explained by the sound of the word, then it is still the case that words with different sounds in different languages mean the same thing. What went wrong in the evolution of language?

Imagine a world in which every word has a direct relation to its meaning, for instance the Sumerian world. Every sign on the clay tablet had a direct relationship with the meaning of that sign. Or let's consider the early generations of those using Israeli Sign Language: each sign nicely represented what it meant. The fixed relation between the sign and what it means makes it quite easy to understand a sign, even for somebody unfamiliar with the sign language. Learning would be quite easy, and memory would not be too complex. Indeed, the direct relationship between the form and its meaning would work quite well for a relatively small number of signs, as presented in the picture on the far left.[26] Let's plot the perfect relationship between the word and its meaning on a horizontal and vertical axis. The position on the form-axis perfectly correlates to the same position on the meaning-axis. The pictograph of a head on a position on the form-axis directly links to the meaning of "head" on the meaning-axis, and the same is true for *ox, cow, fish,* and *grain* on the Sumerian clay tablets. Or take a modern English example of onomatopoeias like *meow, woof, neigh, baa,* and *moo* on the form-axis and their respective position for the animal sound on the meaning-axis.

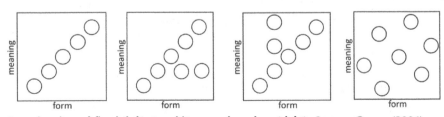

From iconic and fixed (left), to arbitrary and random (right). *Source*: Gasser (2004).

But now let's increase the number of word forms, keeping the cognitive space the same, as in the second picture from the left. More different word forms—because of the different circles on the form-axis—mean the same thing. Synonymy enters the system. The word forms *gaze, see, glance, watch, survey, study, seek, search for, peek, peep, glimpse, stare, contemplate, examine, gape, ogle, scrutinize, inspect, leer, behold, observe, view, witness, perceive, spy, sight, discover, notice, recognize, peer, eye, gawk, peruse,* and *explore,* to name a few, all try to stay in the form-axis to relate to the meaning "look" (many circles on the form-axis all with the same position on the meaning-axis).

In the third picture from the left, the opposite happens. Ambiguity enters the system. One word form on the horizontal axis, say *break*, fights on the meaning-axis for space with meanings like "flight," "pause," "breakup," "interval," "diminish," "injure," "damage," "quit," "give up," "habit," and others (many circles distributed on the meaning-axis, all sharing the same unique position on the form-axis).

The more words we would like to express and the more meaning we have, the more the system becomes arbitrary, as in the picture on the far right. The downside of the arbitrary system is that it is harder to learn the language. After all, one word form has a totally different meaning than another word form. We cannot predict the meaning on the basis of the word form, and it is thus much harder to remember the signs and their meanings. However, there is good news. Once you have learned the language, the lexicon and meanings can grow without a problem.[27] The schematization allows us to make some predictions. If a word is frequent, it can be arbitrary in its sound–meaning relationship, because the language user will experience the word so often that the pattern does not need to come from the sound–meaning relation.[28] For an infrequent word, however, such a sound–meaning relation would provide a convenient cognitive shortcut.

The examples given here are simplifications. First of all, I really did not want to draw sixty thousand circles on the horizontal form-axis. Secondly, I certainly did not really want to draw 240,000 circles on the vertical meaning-axis. Thirdly, and more importantly, the examples above are simplifications because of the two-dimensional space in which they are drawn. Words don't operate on a one-dimensional meaning scale. A word can be positive or negative, while being strong or weak, while being active or passive.[29]

Take, for instance, the words from the valence study in which the sound of the word predicted whether a word was positive or negative. Now take the other study in which the sound of the word marked whether the word was a noun (a passive meaning) or a verb (an active meaning). But these same words may also operate on the dimension of strong-weak (or concrete-abstract). The word-form patterns that may help direct the meaning of the word on the valence scale (e.g., the presence of a nasal) may only show an arbitrary relationship on the active-passive scale.

Early vocabulary development—*early* in terms of both *early languages*, as the Sumerian clay tablets, the first generation of Israeli Sign Language, as well as language evolution in the lab, and *early language acquisition* in children—benefits from a direct relationship between the sound of a word and its meaning. But as vocabulary grows, the advantage at the individual word level vanishes, but systematicity between sounds and categories of words remains.[30] That is, adding individual circles to the figure confuses the language system with synonymity and ambiguity, but rather than making the entire system fully arbitrary, providing clusters of circles—systematicity in the sound and categories of words—helps the language user.

The claim that the relationship between word form and word meaning is strictly arbitrary needs to be softened. There are patterns in the sound of the word that give clues on the meaning of the word. But there is another reason why the plotting of word circles on the form-axis and the meaning-axis is an oversimplification: the meaning of the word is determined not only by the word itself but also by its context. Even if there were no systematicity whatsoever in the sound of the word and its meaning, we can in fact find systematicity in language as long as we abandon the idea that words pretty much operate in isolation. We need to broaden the picture and look at not only words in isolation but also combinations of words, the way they typically operate in language. And that's where we find more patterns that provide language users with more cognitive shortcuts.

· *11* ·

Order

Our interest . . . stemmed from a desire to test the degree to which linguistic constraints on conjunct ordering are mirrored by constraints on the human processing of information in other types of behavior; opening up the possibility that the linguistic constraints observed here are special cases of more general constraints on human information processing.

—William E. Cooper and John Robert Ross[1]

*W*hat came first, the chicken or the egg? You might wonder what this question has to do with the question of how we are able to keep those words in mind. A lot, as it turns out. In the previous chapter, we looked at whether the sounds of words give cues on their meaning. There is an increasing amount of evidence that there are sound patterns that reveal aspects on semantic dimensions like valence and activity. With a large vocabulary, however, it is beneficial that there is an overall arbitrary relationship between the word form and its meaning, interlaced with systematic relationships. However, whereas the evidence I presented in the previous chapter focused on words in isolation, we already concluded chapters ago that words do not operate in isolation. They operate in sentences and even more so in text and discourse.

Let's first look at the direct neighborhood of a word and investigate the question of whether the word order of two-word combinations also gives cues away on their meaning, just like the sounds of the words show biases toward their meaning. And I don't mean word combinations such as *Batman* and *Robin*, *Scooby* and *Shaggy*, *Waldorf* and *Statler*, *Bert* and *Ernie*, *Calvin* and *Hobbes*, *Homer* and *Marge*, *Thelma* and *Louise*, *Ben* and *Jerry*, *Tweety* and *Sylvester*, *Jekyll* and *Hyde*, *Wallace* and *Gromit*, or *Fred* and *Barney*. Instead, I mean common word combinations we use on a regular basis. Let me illustrate.

Take any two concepts and observe their order, for instance the words *table* and *chair*. I am as free to use a sentence such as "I see the chair stand next to the table" as I am to use the sentence "I see the table stand next to the chair." There is absolutely no reason to wonder why the word *chair* preceding the word *table* is more common than the word *table* preceding the word *chair*. The word order in these combinations is absolutely arbitrary. Or take the words *positive* and *negative*. As a language user, I have full flexibility to use these concepts in any order, and so do you. We can have the order *positive* preceding the word *negative*, as in the sentence "I was considering both the positive and negative sides of the decision." But I can also use the order *negative* preceding *positive*, as in the sentence "I considered the negative before the positive side regarding the decision ahead of me." No phonetic, phonological, morphological, syntactic, semantic, or pragmatic rules prevent me from using one order more than the other. We are free to use any order we would like, and we should—no pattern; any random order will do.

HIGH IS HIGH

A while back I wondered whether it is really the case that word pairs are used in any random order. The reason for me wondering was an experiment that demonstrated that we use perceptual simulation in language processing, as discussed in chapter 7 ("Grounding"). In one experiment, participants were presented with word pairs that referred to concepts high in the perceptual world around us, and word pairs lower in the perceptual world around us—for instance, words such as *attic* and *basement*. In this experiment either the word *attic* was presented above the word *basement*, or the word *basement* was presented above the word *attic*. What the researchers who conducted this experiment found is that when *attic* was presented above *basement*, participants were faster processing the word pairs than when *basement* was presented above *attic*. They argued that this finding is no surprise, for when we process the words *attic* and *basement*, we activate perceptual information that attics are high and basements are low. Consequently, presenting *attic* above *basement* is easier to process than *basement* above *attic*. Makes sense.

But I wondered whether what is true in the perceptual world might also be true in the linguistic world. Might it be the case that the word order *attic-basement* would also be more frequent than the order *basement-attic*?[2] That would be pretty interesting! After all, if this was the case, one could argue that language encodes the perceptual world around us. Or more precisely, that language encodes our interpretation of the perceptual world around us. That would be rather cool, because it would mean that we can make predictions about the perceptual world on the basis of the linguistic world.

To test this possibility, I took a large corpus of electronic texts, or rather, the largest corpus of texts I could get my hands on, a collection of 1,024,908,267,229 words from all the English language that Google has to its availability. And that's a lot of language! I then computed the frequency in which two words appear in a particular order in a five-word window. That is, I counted the number of times that *attic* appeared before *basement* with none, one, two, or three words in between. And I did the same for *attic* following *basement*. So how often do we find the word *attic* and another word (perhaps another word [perhaps yet another word]) followed by *basement*? The frequencies were quite obvious. The word order for the higher concept preceding the lower concept was considerably larger than the other way around. Let me illustrate this with actual high and low words.

high - low	10,889,873	low – high	8,837,003
up - down	7,880,470	down – up	1,325,239
above - under	172,570	under - above	218,694
top - bottom	7,880,470	bottom - top	1,325,239
head - toe	3,315,925	toe – head	424,015
arm - leg	376,344	leg – arm	5,332
eyes - nose	321,889	nose - eyes	60,772
nose - mouth	190,325	mouth - nose	79,038
head - neck	175,756	neck - head	115,502
head - shoulders	1,320,016	shoulders - head	84,008
shoulders - feet	330,734	feet - shoulders	15,571
heaven - earth	6,445	earth - heaven	6,024
sky - ground	1,013,818	ground - sky	137,504
ceiling - floor	2,795	floor - ceiling	4,959
north - south	127,655	south - north	390,190

For these word combinations, the frequencies speak for themselves. There are exceptions such as *above–under*, *sky–ground*, and *ceiling–floor*, but overall the pattern is pretty consistent. As you can see, in the large majority of the cases, the concept that is above the other in the perceptual world comes first linguistically, and the concept that is below the other perceptually comes second linguistically. If you don't quite believe me, you can try it out yourself and take any two concepts for which we know that one appears above the other. Even though we language users have full flexibility over the order, there is a high-low order that outperforms a low-high order. Not because some language rule ledger tells us that the higher concepts go first, but simply because the language system has apparently evolved in such a way that language users prefer mentioning higher concepts first and lower concepts second. The perceptual world order seems encoded in the linguistic word order.

It's one thing to determine whether language has encoded these high-low patterns. It is another to determine whether language users utilize these patterns in their processing. I conducted an experiment to find out. Participants saw the high-low word pairs in different orders—higher concept above the lower concept or vice versa—and responded as quickly as possible whether the words were semantically related. Obviously, to not make it too easy for the participants, word pairs were added that had very little semantic relationship. And indeed, participants responded faster to the high-low order than the low-high order. The knowledge people have about the perceptual world around them gets translated into a linguistic structure. And that's easier for the speaker or writer producing the word order. It is also easier for the hearer or reader who perceives the word order. For them a translation takes place from linguistic structure to the knowledge about the perceptual world. Killing two birds with one stone. Or to put it less violently and more psychologically, helping two minds with one pattern.

Our interpretation of the perceptual world gets translated in linguistic structures, at least when it comes to word order. And when the linguistic word order matches the perceptual world order, language gets processed faster. But if you put on your Sherlock Holmes deerstalker hat, tweed suit, and traveling cloak, and light up a calabash pipe, you might comment that we need to investigate this case a bit further. After all, if the linguistic world is represented in the perceptual world, how do we know that language users actually take advantage of the linguistic world rather than perceptually simulating the perceptual world? Does linguistic order trump perceptual order, or does perceptual order trump linguistic order? That question is difficult to answer, because the two are mapped onto each other.

There is, however, a small number of word pairs that do not obey that mapping, such as the ones I showed in the examples above: *above–under, sky–ground*, and *ceiling–floor*. If word orders like these are processed faster in their most frequent linguistic order (*under–above, ground–sky, floor–ceiling*) than in their perceptual order (*above–under, sky–ground*, and *ceiling–floor*), we can conclude language users rely on the linguistic order more than a perceptual simulation order. Conversely, language users rely on the perceptual simulation order more than a linguistic order, when the frequencies matter less than the perceptual patterns. For the small number of word pairs found, the linguistic frequencies reigned supreme. So the linguistic order maps onto the perceptual order, but the linguistic order won in processing these word pairs. The pattern in language served as a cognitive shortcut to the user.

POWER RULES

Being up comes first; being down comes second. Being up is also more frequent than being down. So there are advantages to being high up in terms of frequency and order. But there are more advantages. Taller people are more likely to win presidential elections; they are more likely to be in high-status positions, earn higher salaries, are considered more persuasive, and are considered more attractive.[3] And it also works the other way around. If you are in a position of power, you judge yourself as being taller.[4] As there are advantages of being high up, there are advantages of being powerful, also linguistically. Power really goes to your head, so much so that it affects word order. Take any two words, one being powerful and the other being less powerful, and the pattern in language is clear about the order. Power precedes powerless, as you can see below.

Teachers and students as well as conductors and orchestras do not quite follow the expected pattern of powerful preceding powerless, likely because there are *orchestra conductors* and *student teachers*, but overall the pattern is as clear as higher concepts preceding lower concepts: powerful concepts precede the less powerful. Even though the word order of a more powerful and less powerful concept seems arbitrary, it is not. Far more often the word order maps onto a world order, with more powerful concepts preceding less powerful concepts. And regardless of what we may think of power and authority, linguistically this order has an advantage both for the production and for the comprehension of language. We can use a cognitive shortcut and rely on the pattern in language to guess which word refers to a more or less powerful concept.

powerful-powerless	7,162	powerless-powerful	1,297
employer-employee	553,799	employee-employer	295,964
teacher-student	958,332	student-teacher	1,255,594
master-slave	401,888	slave-master	78,941
rich-poor	1,091,623	poor-rich	160,819
parent-child	1,278,229	child-parent	444,181
king-servant	19,627	servant-king	13,024
conductor-orchestra	55,794	orchestra-conductor	112,025
trainer-trainee	5,142	trainee-trainer	2,843
judge-defendant	12,854	defendant-judge	4,567
attorney-client	534,652	client-attorney	36,915
father-son	1,704,100	son-father	331,337
mother-daughter	1,448,942	daughter-mother	252,741
strong-weak	182,659	weak-strong	141,281

SUNNY SIDE UP

Are there even more advantages to being on top? Absolutely! Being high up makes you happier, at least linguistically. I just mentioned an experiment in which high-low concept order was processed faster than low-high concept order. Another experiment we conducted explored why we can be in high spirits, but sometimes feel down in the dumps. That is, happy seems to be "up" and sad seems to be "down." If you look at metaphorical language, there are various examples that suggest that *happy* is affiliated with high and *sad* is affiliated with low, as we have seen in chapter 7 ("Grounding"). We cheer her up because she got the job, she was in high spirits, she was on cloud nine, and she was in seventh heaven. But when she lost the job, she was feeling down, she was very depressed, and she fell into a depression, because her spirits sank. And indeed, when participants were presented with happy words above sad words, they processed each word pair faster than when sad words were presented above happy words. The explanation may come from the perceptual world in which people who are happy smile and perk up while people who are sad droop. Some researchers have argued exactly that: we perceptually simulate happy as being up and sad as being down, and that's why people process *happy* above *sad* faster than *sad* above *happy*.[5] But as with the attic–basement effect, the explanation may also come from the world of language.

positive - negative	1,971,449	negative - positive	395,008
plus - minus	659,969	minus - plus	46,344
good - bad	4,899,144	bad - good	712,751
smile - frown	33,454	frown - smile	4,387
celebrate - mourn	1,647	mourn - celebrate	1,177
right - wrong	1,748,646	wrong - right	218,322
happy - sad	163,140	sad - happy	37,715
heaven - hell	561,333	hell - heaven	63,938
laugh - cry	194,680	cry - laugh	24,660
optimistic - pessimistic	21,754	pessimistic - optimistic	5,755
pass - fail	428,065	fail – pass	37,763
win - lose	383,916	lose - win	37,165
manic - depressed	2,321	depressed - manic	2,300
winners - losers	332,881	losers - winners	17,781

As you can see, happy words go first, before the sad words, more so than the other way around. As before, we put this to the test in an experiment ourselves[6] and did not settle on whether the happy concept placed above the sad concept was processed faster than when the sad concept was placed above the happy concept, but we wanted to find out whether the processing could be explained by the word-order frequency. And as with the high-low concepts, processing times were nicely explained by word order. Happy comes first in language. Happy comes first in our minds.

From all this happiness and sadness, you may have ended up with mixed emotions. Well, mixed emotions do not go so well in language. My graduate student and I took 252 emotion words that were used in another study.[7] We compared the emotions words with each other, yielding some 63,252 combinations. Some of these combinations had matching emotions, for instance both being happy words, while some others had mismatching emotions, for instance one being a happy word and the other being a sad word. The frequency of matching emotion words was considerably higher than that of mismatching emotions. Apparently we want to stay in the same mood, linguistically speaking.

We then took a subset of adjectives and paired them with nouns, so that participants saw sentences like "birthdays can be delightful," "birthdays can be depressing," "separation can be delightful," and "separation can be depressing." Language statistics explained the difference between same-emotion and different-emotion sentences, but also explained emotion shifts. Feelings are apparently encoded in language, just like up-down relations, powerful-powerless relations, and happy-sad relations. In word order too, there turns out to be less randomness than we seem to have to our availability. And that pattern provides a useful cognitive shortcut for language processing.

LADIES FIRST?

Higher concepts come first, powerful concepts come first, and happy concepts come first. And they are perceived higher in the perceptual world. Perhaps less excitingly, at least from the perspective of political correctness, is that language is sexist. Extremely sexist. Take any two words for which one denotes a male concept and the other a female concept, and compute the frequency in language. Contrary to the common saying that ladies go first, language does not let itself be driven by etiquette. For language, it is males who go first, followed by females.

You may immediately object that *ladies and gentlemen* is far more likely than *gentlemen and ladies*. And you are right. As with the other examples, there are always exceptions to rules, but overall the pattern holds. We could argue that the order of *ladies* preceding *gentlemen* is conventionalized, and this linguistic order has grown to be frequent in the noncommon order. For now, let's just assume that there are exceptions to the sexist pattern. The system

men - women	15,780,713	women - men	7,507,961
husband - wife	1,232,105	wife - husband	353,317
boy - girl	1,540,940	girl – boy	552,527
father - mother	1,135,407	mother - father	924,564
male - female	5,975,986	female - male	2,546,964
brother - sister	2,532,189	sister - brother	649,858
uncle - aunt	91,785	aunt - uncle	207,134
gays - lesbians	446,708	lesbians - gays	120,924
king - queen	941,561	queen - king	298,065
prince - princess	204,495	princess - prince	49,960
actor - actress	344,454	actress - actor	31,885
rooster - chicken	6,919	chicken - rooster	6,835

is not waterproof, as *uncle–aunt* also shows, but in the majority of the cases, a male–female order is more frequent than the reverse order. *Women* follow *men*, linguistically. Language is a bit dated when it comes to word order, but it sure helps language users in their language production and comprehension, providing a useful pattern that can serve as a cognitive shortcut.[8]

VENI, VIDI, VICI

Metaphorical language uses embodiment for valence, but also for time. We look back on the past but look forward to the future. It is as if we are standing in the present literally facing the future, while the past is behind our back. Embodiment in action. But this order we can also find in language, it seems. Julius Caesar once spoke the famous words "*veni, vidi, vici*," which translates to "*I came, I saw, I conquered*." Caesar used the phrase in a letter to the Roman

Senate to refer to a swift, conclusive victory. After he arrived, he saw what was going on and conquered Pharnaces II of Pontus at the Battle of Zela. He first came to the location, then saw what was going on, and then conquered. The linguistic order matches the turn of events. A common joke among linguists is that Caesar used the phrase "*vidi, vici, veni*" in other locations under other circumstances. I leave it aside whether the joke is funny, but my point is that the order of words also affects meaning of time.

We find temporal order in verbs by the tense of the verb being used. Imagine I am on a whale-watching tour and say, "I see a whale, and I saw a dolphin." You would immediately know what I saw first. If I said, "I see a whale, and I see a dolphin," or "I see a dolphin and I see a whale," it is also clear what I saw first. What we find for verbs is no different for nouns or adverbs. Recall that as a language user, we have all the freedom in the world to use any order, yet an obvious pattern emerges, in the footsteps of Caesar's pattern: what came first precedes what comes later.

morning – afternoon	1,198,022	afternoon – morning	3.20
afternoon – evening	981,755	evening – afternoon	2.64
evening – night	146,982	night – evening	18.27
sooner – later	1,255,890	later – sooner	1.28
yesterday – today	444,235	today – yesterday	70.77
today – tomorrow	1,156,505	tomorrow – today	39,594
old – new	3,998,519	new – old	26,660
previous – next	42,037,518	next – previous	32,859
then – now	1,402,085	now - then	16,273
preceding – succeeding	9,620	succeeding - preceding	1,075,495
before – after	5,551,742	after - before	297,163
then – now	1,402,085	now - then	2,290,712
past – present	2,946,713	present - past	5,189,904
present – future	1,904,665	future - present	2,403,471
earlier – later	221,587	later - earlier	738
start – finish	1,319,991	finish - start	494,496

As you can see, the majority of the words follow an order matching the temporal order. There are exceptions, such as *today–yesterday*, but overall the pattern is pretty clear. That is, in language, it is far more likely to find an early–late order than a late–early order, even though nobody dictates such a pattern. We are free to use any order, but we somehow prefer using one order over the other.

You might object that this may be another nice example showing temporal order, but one that is redundant. In the *veni, vidi, vici* case, we already demonstrated that temporal order is reflected in word order. Or you might argue that these words show a nice example, but they are carefully selected words. We can easily extend it to days of the week and months of the year. And for presidents in both the United States and the former Soviet Union. In one study[9] we took the names of all forty-four presidents of the United States. One problem was that there are a number of presidents with the same name (Adams, Bush, Harrison, Johnson, and Roosevelt), and we removed those from the analysis, only using the president that occurred first. We did the same with the names of the eight leaders of the former Soviet Union— Lenin, Stalin, Malenkov, Khrushchev, Brezhnev, Andropov, Chernenko, and Gorbachev. For both the presidents of the United States and the leaders of the Soviet Union, the order of word pairs with the former president being mentioned before the later president was more frequent than the reverse pair. History textbooks can teach us history, but word order in general language can provide us with a cheat sheet—a cheat sheet that we earlier called a cognitive shortcut.

HOMER SIMPSON

If there were a competition for the first place in word orders, the category "Here" wins over "There," "Now" over "Then," "Adults" over "Children," "Male" over "Female," "Positive" over "Negative," "Singular" over "Plural," "Living" over "Nonliving," "Friendly" over "Unfriendly," "Solid" over "Fluid," "Agent" over "Patient," "Powerful" over "Weak," and "High" over "Low." It was what Cooper and Ross call the "Archie Bunker effect,"[10] after the fictional self-centric, chauvinistic, and misanthropic character from the 1970s American television sitcom *All in the Family*. If the 1970s is well before your time, consider Archie Bunker the archetype of Homer Simpson. The Archie Bunker effect (or Homer Simpson effect) is a nice analogy, but it is hardly an explanation. At least, I hope there is no little homunculus in my brain that tells me what order I should use when putting the valence, singularity, animacy, solidity, and egocentrism in the ordering of my words.

And if there were such a homunculus—so far no evidence has been found for one—I certainly hope it is not one that has all the characteristics of Homer Simpson.

For an answer, let's look at how humans produce language. We observe the world around us, create ideas from the world around us, and express them in language. We have eyes in our head not in our feet, we look forward not backward, we stand upright and don't lie down (at least in most of the speaking situations), and we tend to be happy (or prefer to be happy), rather than sad.[11] Perhaps, then, it is no surprise then that when we form sentences, we structure our language according to the environment we perceive most directly. Language encodes the perceptual world around us the way we perceive that world.

If that's the case, it offers a number of cognitive advantages. First, the speaker does not have to restructure sentences in her utterances. She can basically map the world onto linguistic structures. Second, the comprehender has the advantage that very little is needed to bring the linguistic utterances back to the ideas in the world. And there is another advantage. The words that come first are also most frequent in language. Higher-concept words are more frequent than lower-concept words, happy words are more frequent than sad words, powerful words more frequent than powerless words, and male words more frequent than female words. Another pattern advantage that language offers us in understanding the world around us is a mapping of the perceptual world onto the linguistic world, and frequency guides us in this mapping.

As we saw in chapter 5 ("Instinct"), where we discussed a language instinct as an explanation for how we keep those words in mind, language users extract a rule system from language that we call grammar. It is immediately clear to a beginning language user whether a sentence is grammatical or not. Besides, ungrammatical sentences will ultimately raise some eyebrows. But when it comes to word order in the sense that we have discussed it in this chapter, we are not bound by what is grammatical or not, or acceptable or not. The order is arbitrary. In line with the adage *le signe est arbitraire*, I could imagine de Saussure saying *l'ordre est arbitraire* from the previous chapter ("Sound"): the order in which concept words are presented is arbitrary. But that is not the case. We live in a free linguistic society. In this linguistic society there are some rules, but they do not apply to word order of concept words. And yet, in our linguistic society we map linguistically what we perceive in the world around us. Language encodes the perceptual world. It provides a pattern and thus a cognitive shortcut.

SNARC

Snarc is not a misspelled elasmobranch fish that is characterized by a car-
tilaginous skeleton, gill slits on the sides of its head, and pectoral fins not
fused to its head, commonly known as *shark*. A snarc is not a nonsense word
used in nerdy language experiments either. But *snarc* is very much related to
experiments. *Snarc* (or rather SNARC) is an effect known to many cognitive
scientists.[12] The SNARC effect stands for "spatial numerical association of
response codes." It is a pretty interesting finding, I think.

Imagine sitting in front of a computer screen with digits being flashed
at you. The only thing you need to do is respond whether the digit is an even
or an odd number. You see *3* flashed in front of you, and you respond "odd";
you see *6*, and you respond "even." The way you respond is by pressing one of
two buttons. For instance, you answer "odd" with your left hand, and "even"
with your right hand, but you can also reverse this for a different group of participants. The SNARC effect reveals something about the hand with which
you answer, regardless of whether you answer "odd" or "even." If the digit is
relatively low—as is the case with *1*, *2*, *3*, and *4*—you are responding faster
with your left hand than your right hand. But when the digit is high—as is
the case with *6*, *7*, *8*, and *9*—you are responding faster with your right hand
than your left hand. Lower numbers are faster to your left, and larger numbers
are faster to your right, regardless of handedness. The argument that most
researchers have advocated is that participants have a mental number line in
their minds, with the lower numbers on the left and the higher numbers on
the right. When processing digits, we activate the mental number line.

Sterling Hutchinson and I thought the SNARC effect was strange. If
words referring to high concepts and words referring to low concepts could
be explained by the perceptual world, but could actually better be explained
by language, this might also be the case for the famous SNARC effect. First,
we wanted to establish whether magnitude is encoded in language, just like
spatiality, valence, authority, gender, and time, as I discussed earlier. We
found that the higher the magnitude of a single number word, the lower its
frequency, with the opposite for lower-magnitude words. *One* is more frequent than *two*, which is more frequent than *three*, and so on. *Nine* is least
frequent, followed by *eight*, and so on.

We then computed the frequency of word pairs denoting numbers.
We created word pairs like *three-four*, *four-three*, *one-nine*, *eight-six*, and so
on. We found that word pairs that start with the lower magnitude followed
by the higher magnitude are more frequent than the other way around.[13]
So the frequency of the word gave information about the magnitude of the
number the word represented, and for word pairs, low-magnitude followed

by high-magnitude numbers were more frequent than the other way around, both neat patterns in language that language users may utilize as a cognitive shortcut. Neither of these findings were a SNARC effect per se, but they were interesting nevertheless because they opened the door for a linguistic explanation of the SNARC effect.

In an experiment with participants, we were able to replicate the SNARC effect. Dozens of other studies had already done this. But we were wondering whether language (word frequency) or magnitude (meaning of the number words) explained the findings. The answer was that both did. That opened the door for a SNARC effect even further. The SNARC findings could either indicate a mental number line or a language pattern.

In the second experiment, we tried to disentangle the two explanations. We used not the number words but the digits. Importantly, we also added the number *zero*. *Zero* (or rather *0*) made two opposite predictions. On the one hand, the digit *0* is lower in magnitude, resulting in a prediction that participants would respond fastest to it with the left hand (just like *1*, *2*, *3*, and *4*). On the other hand, the digit *0* is less frequent in language than *1* and *2*, which resulted in the prediction that participants would respond to it faster with the right hand (just like the *6*, *7*, *8*, and *9*). This allowed us to pitch a SNARC magnitude explanation against a language explanation. Word frequency won. Language and magnitude both explained the findings equally well, but *zero* was a tie breaker, in favor of the language explanation.

In these two experiments, we also found something else, something that could not be explained by SNARC. We looked at the response times when participants first saw the word or digit representing the lower magnitude (for instance *2*) and then a word with a higher magnitude (for instance *9*) and vice versa. We found that participants were considerably faster in the low–high magnitude order than the high–low magnitude order, matching the frequencies we found in our computations of word pairs. This order effect was never part of the SNARC effect, and could not be explained by SNARC, but it could be explained by language patterns and cognitive shortcuts.

If language better predicts the SNARC effect than magnitude does, why would it then be the case that higher-frequency words are processed faster with the left hand than the right hand, and the other way around for lower-frequency words? Well, one clue might come from the other findings presented so far in this chapter: the word that comes first is more frequent than the word that comes second, as we have seen for *high–low, happy–sad, teacher–student, man–woman*. To test this, we moved SNARC away from magnitude and only tested word frequency. We created two sets of words, one set related to animate words and the other to inanimate words. We now asked participants to not make an even-odd judgment, but an animate-inanimate judgment with their left and right hand (and changed this for another group of participants). No SNARC effect possible. The findings, however, did demonstrate a SNARC effect. High-frequency words tended to be processed faster with the left hand, whereas low-frequency words tended to be processed faster with the right hand.

We have all the linguistic freedom to say *six-nine* or *nine-six* in language. I can move the words around in linguistic context any way I'd like. And yet, the order turns out not to be randomly distributed. There is a clear preference we have for lower-magnitude words to go first in language and higher-magnitude words to go second. And those lower-magnitude words are also more frequent than higher-magnitude words. Language encodes magnitude, language also explains the SNARC effect commonly only attributed to something inside the mind of the language user rather than outside in language itself. Moreover, experimental findings explain a range of effects in SNARC-like experiments that cannot be explained by SNARC. Magnitude too is structured in word order, providing language users with a cognitive shortcut for keeping those words in mind.

SHALLOW AND DEEP

In a number of examples presented here, I have shown that language encodes the perceptual world and language users take advantage of these encodings. The linguistic word order explains language processing as well, and often better than perceptual world order does. But finding patterns in language and showing some language-processing effects is one thing, and demonstrating that participants use these patterns for their cognitive shortcuts is another.

Together with Patrick Jeuniaux I ran a series of experiments.[14] Some of these were particularly memorable experiments, and I often tell my students about them in my classes (and caution PhD candidates about them). These concerned four experiments in a large study. We collected participants, ran the four response-time experiments, and were eager to analyze the data. Everything had gone well, and we were ready to see whether our hypotheses were confirmed or had to be falsified. Running the experiments had taken weeks, but we then reached the point in time where our curiosity got its satisfaction.

To me, as a researcher, this is often the most exciting time of a study. You do your literature review, you reason through what others have done, and you try to understand what needs to be done to stand on the shoulders of these giants and help our understanding of how we keep those words in mind further along. You then design your experiment, make sure that everything works, and start running your study. You arrange time slots, deal with participants who had to cancel an appointment at the last minute, and run the study.

Patrick and I looked at the data, and we found *nothing*. I mean, we really did not find anything in the data. Because there was no data. We ran a long and tedious study, and there was no data. All the response times, some 7,690 data points we looked at, showed a response time of 0 milliseconds. Response times for making judgments on a word can be fast, but 0 milliseconds is about 250 milliseconds per word too fast. Something must have gone wrong. And it had gone wrong. In the response-time computer program we used at the time, various settings had to be selected for information to be recorded. In programming the experiment, one of those items was "response times recorded." In our programming trials, we had conveniently not selected this option. We had wasted 7,680 valuable data points that would have answered our research questions had we checked things more carefully. Our disappointment was huge. The next morning, we met again in our favorite coffee place. Were we willing to go through the tedious process again? Strengthened by the caffeine, we flexed our muscles and got back to work.

In the experiments, we wondered whether what I had earlier found for words would also apply for pictures. Take, for instance, a monitor and a keyboard. When the word *monitor* is presented above the word *keyboard*, participants were faster in responding whether the two words were related in meaning than when *keyboard* was presented above the word *monitor*. As I mentioned earlier, I had found that the word order that matched the perceptual world was responded to faster than the word order that did not match the perceptual world.[15] And I had found that this effect could be attributed to the word order more than the perceptual order. But perhaps this was no surprise. In a way, we biased participants to go for the linguistic explanation, because the experiment was linguistic in nature. I had presented words, so no wonder word order better explained the finding than the perceptual order of what those words referred to. Comparing the word-pair findings to picture-pair findings would help us answer whether this was correct.

Another point that was concerning us had to do with the cognitive task. In previous experiments, participants were asked to judge whether the two words presented to them were related in meaning. Participants were asked to make a semantic judgment that activated perceptual information in the real world. What would happen if the cognitive task were not so much a linguistic judgment of the similarity in meaning, but judging whether these two concepts had this order relationship in the real world? Not asking participants to make a semantic judgment and assuming they make a perceptual simulation, but directly asking them to make that perceptual simulation!

Now in order to decide whether two concepts have an actual order in the real world—say, ceiling is always above floor—you need to at least know the words *ceiling* and *floor* and their semantic relationship. But for their semantic relationship, you don't necessarily need to know whether they have a specific order in the outside world. In other words, the task of judging whether two concepts appeared one above the other in the outside world implied the semantic judgment task, but not the other way around. Therefore, we argued the cognitive task of judging the order of concepts in the outside world was deeper than the semantic judgment task.

We first conducted a rating experiment and asked participants to evaluate to what extent two concept pairs were above one another. Indeed, *bumper–headlights* got lower ratings than *ceiling–floor*. With the frequencies and the ratings of the word pairs in our back pockets, we ran four experiments. The first experiment was identical to the one I had run previously. Participants saw two word pairs and were asked to evaluate whether the two were similar in meaning. To avoid that participants would only see words that had a perceptual order (actual or reversed), we also included filler items like *scissors* and *pencil*. The second experiment was identical, except that we then asked participants whether the two concepts the words referred to appeared in that order in the outside world: the deeper cognitive task. *Ceiling–floor* should be responded to negatively, as should *scissors–pencil*. The third and fourth experiments replicated the first two experiments, except that we used pictures instead of words. Drawings were used to push participants toward perceptual representations rather than linguistic representations.

This time we had carefully selected the "response times recorded" option, as well as "save participant's answer." In the first experiment, the semantic judgment task with the words, we looked at whether the word-pair frequency and the concept-pair ratings explained the response times. The linguistic frequencies indeed explained the response times, as we had found before. But the perceptual ratings did not. The linguistic explanation trumped the perceptual explanation.

But that may be no surprise. The cognitive task was perfectly suitable for a linguistic explanation, and the words were, well, more linguistic than perceptual in nature. In the second experiment, we asked participants whether the two concepts appeared above one another in the perceptual world. And the response times showed an interesting change compared to what we had found with the semantic judgment task. The frequencies of the word pairs again explained the response times, but did this as well as the perceptual ratings of the word pairs did. If you ask participants to be more perceptual, they become more perceptual. But the linguistic frequencies play an equally important role.

When these experiments were repeated with pictures rather than words, the findings showed that perceptual ratings best explained the response times when participants had to judge whether the pictures were similar in meaning, as well as when participants had to judge whether the two concept pairs appeared above one another in the outside world. In fact, these perceptual ratings explained the response times the very best for pictures being judged perceptually. But linguistic frequencies still played a role—less so for the semanticity judgment, but definitely for the perceptual order.

If this all sounds too scientific, let me apologize and slide down on the slides of my stuffy ivory tower and explain. If the cognitive task is shallow, then language users rely more on language patterns than on grounding. If the cognitive task is deep, they then rely more on grounding than on language patterns. And not surprisingly, when language users see words, they rely more on language patterns than on grounding, but when they see pictures, they rely more on grounding than on language patterns. Language provides a cognitive shortcut to the perceptual world particularly in shallow cognitive tasks.

In another experiment, Louise Connell and I zoomed further in on the cognitive task, this time not manipulating the task but monitoring how fast participants performed a task.[16] We split the response times into three groups—fast response times, slow response times, and medium response times—and then put the linguistic frequencies and the perceptual ratings in the mix. The linguistic frequencies best explained the fast response times, but not so much the slow response times. The perceptual ratings best explained the slow response times, but not so much the fast response times. And both linguistic frequencies and perceptual ratings explained the group in the middle, which was neither fast nor slow. If the cognitive task or the time to make a judgment calls for cognitive shortcuts, we rely on language patterns.

The question that remains, of course, is what the default is: shallow and quick, or deep and slow? If quickly extracting meaning from language is what language processing is about, and if language statistics best explain this, I am tempted to go for shallow and quick as the default in language processing. And if you read chapter 8 ("Shortcut"), you would probably agree with me. But if language patterns explain shallow and quick processing, can we also find evidence in the brain?

You may recall from chapter 5 ("Instinct") that language is processed in the temporal lobe of the left hemisphere in the brain—not exclusively, for the entire brain lights up in activation when our eyes read language or our ears hear speech—but the temporal cortical areas, more specifically Broca's and Wernicke's areas, show activation. When it comes to seeing information, the visual cortex lights up, the area in the occipital lobe at the very back of our brain. What we can do is compare the relative extent to which the visual cortex is active or the temporal cortex is active during language processing. Obviously, when we read a word, the visual cortex must be active. But is it more active than the language cortex? And at what stage during processing?

Sterling Hutchinson and I ran an EEG study to find out.[17] As before, participants evaluated word pairs in a semantic-judgment (shallow) task or a perceptual-simulation (deep) task, while we monitored the activation in different parts of their brain. We were not so much interested in whether a specific receptor lit up, or whether a particular brain area was active. Instead, we compared the relative activation of the visual cortex and the language cortex over time. When we compared the receptors in the language cortex and the visual cortex, we found that there was more activation in the visual than in the language cortex when we asked participants to make perceptual simulation judgments. And there was more activation in the language cortex than the visual cortex when we asked participants to make semantic judgments. But most interestingly, we found that the language cortex received more activation early on in the task, and the visual cortex received relatively more activation than the language cortex at the end of the task. It seemed as if language patterns provide early, quick, and shallow shortcuts, while grounding is later, slower, and deeper—which seems spot-on for a language user who aims to save cognitive resources. Word order maps onto world order. When processing is quick and shallow, language users rely more on word order. If processing is slow and deep, they rely more on world order. In the brain of the language user, we find something similar, with relatively more activation in linguistic cortical areas early and relatively more activation in perceptual cortical areas later.

ICONICITY IS NOT ARBITRARY

To what extent can we conclude that the examples given in this chapter represent evidence that language is not arbitrary? The fact that word order matches perceptual order seems clear evidence to me that there is no random, arbitrary relation, but rather an iconic, nonarbitrary relation. It reminds me of a quote by Talmy Givón, an eminent professor of linguistics and cognitive science at the University of Oregon. Throughout his work, Givón has advocated an evolutionary approach to language and communication. On arbitrariness in language, Givón once said: "All other things being equal, a coded experience is easier to store, retrieve and communicate if the code is maximally isomorphic to the experience."[18] In other words, a representation of experience in language is easier to use if the language is maximally similar to the experience.

And that's exactly what high-low, positive-negative, power-powerless, male-female, early-late, and low-high-magnitude word patterns show.

But the iconic relation between form and meaning can be taken further, if we look a little further. First of all, we can make a theoretical argument. We can argue that language must be nonarbitrary in nature because language is an adaptively motivated system. If we agree that language evolves over time to be a convenient tool for the language user, we will probably have to agree that there is some naturalness to language—in its sounds, in its word order, but also in its grammar.[19] Givón's view of the mapping of a language and experience being easier for language use has a number of consequences. It means that the more language maps onto experience, the more predictable it is. It also means that if language is more predictable, less coding material is needed. And as a consequence of this, less mental effort is needed.[20]

Think about it. If elements in language are predictable, they are regular, and if they are regular, they are patterns. These patterns become easiest to process if they can be mapped onto our experience, and they are therefore nonarbitrary in nature. Although we need to be careful with the circularity of this reasoning—language patterns are iconic because they are processed faster because they are iconic—it opens exciting avenues on how we keep those words in mind. Those avenues at least allow us to look for patterns of iconicity, rather than have us take a detour because the avenue has a no-entry sign.

Givón gives several principles of grammatical organization arguing for nonarbitrariness in grammar. Let me try to interpret them. One of the principles is that in speech, less predictable information receives more stress in intonation. We often see this in dialogue. If I respond to something you are saying, I take some old information from what you said and add something new to it. ("I was at that coffee place at the corner yesterday." "The coffee place on *Highland and Poplar*?") The old information is predictable, while the new information is not (well, otherwise it would have not been so new, I guess). The new information is stressed, to force attention to it.[21] Here is another example: If we talk about setting up a meeting and we discuss Monday or Tuesday as options, you may ask, "You mean Monday or Tuesday *this* week or *next* week?" Less predictable information is emphasized more, because more attention needs to be given to it.

For some other principles of iconicity in grammar, let me try out my literary skills by presenting a little story.

> Once upon a time, far far away, there lived a large purple ogre. The ogre lived all by himself and had very few friends. One day he received a letter from the king and queen to come to their castle. The ogre packed his belongings and followed the path to the castle. The following day he arrived. In the castle, the ogre was welcomed by the royal couple and was told to

set out on a journey to save the princess from a dragon. The ogre killed the dragon in a dramatic fight and saved the princess. After having returned to the castle, the king offered a bag of golden coins to the ogre for his help.

It is obvious I need a little more practice before my literary novel on the purple ogre can even be considered for publishing. But that is not quite the point of the story. This story is to show the principle of temporal order being mirrored in linguistic order. That is, the events that are described in language follow a temporal order unless they are marked otherwise. *The following day* marks that something has changed in the temporal order. That is, in general we follow the *veni, vidi, vici* patterns I referred to earlier. If we don't, additional information is needed—and additional mental effort is required—to highlight a break of what could have been predicted otherwise.

And this is true not only for temporal order but also for spatial continuity. The reader may assume that events take place in the same place, unless they do not. So when we read a text like the literary-novel-in-the-making on the purple ogre, we assume the setting of each sentence to be in the same place, unless there is a discontinuity in the location. *In the palace* marks such discontinuity.

If information is predictable, it does not need to be expressed. If there is continuity in time or place, no additional information is needed. It is odd to say "once upon a time, far far away, there lived a large purple ogre. Once upon a time, far far away, the ogre lived all by himself and had very few friends. One day once upon a time, far far away, he received a letter from the king and queen to come to their castle."

And the same is true for descriptions of the ogre. At first, the reader does not know who the character of the story is, and the new information needs to be expressed: *a large purple ogre*. But once we know, we don't need to refer to the large purple ogre again. We can summarize with *the ogre*. And once it is clear that we are really only talking about the ogre, we can shorten things even more and just refer to him with a pronoun. If we start talking about a variety of other things—say, the dragon and the princess—the ogre becomes less predictable information, and may need to be referred to as *the ogre* or *the large purple ogre*.

When we look at a sentence, including the large purple ogre sentences above, we typically start with the concept that did something, followed by the concept that was undergoing that something, followed by a person who benefits from the concept undergone that something done by the other concept. Let me make that more concrete: "The ogre killed the dragon." In 75 percent of the world's languages, the subject precedes the object. In English, Chinese, French, and Russian, we say, "The ogre killed the dragon." In Urdu, Hindi, Japanese, and Korean, we say, "The ogre the dragon killed." In Arabic and

Irish, we say, "Killed the ogre the dragon." In languages that emerge from the simplifying and mixing of different languages into a new one, this is also the most common order.[22]

For some languages, the subject does not precede the object. In Austronesian, a language family spoken in Southeast Asia and Madagascar, "killed the dragon ogre" is the standard order, in Cariban languages Apalaí and Hixkaryana, "the dragon killed the ogre" is standard, and in Warao, a native language spoken in northern Venezuela, "the dragon the ogre killed" is the standard order. But the order in which the object precedes the subject in a sentence, like in Austronesian, Apalaí, Hixkaryana, and Warao, is rather uncommon. So why is it then that the subject precedes the object more often than the other way around?

The grammatical subject is more often than not the agent of the sentence, the person or thing doing something. The grammatical object is more often than not the patient of the sentence, the person or thing undergoing something. That is not always the case, of course. In "the dragon was killed by the ogre," the patient has suddenly become the grammatical subject. However, passive sentences are used only about 20 percent of the time, particularly in those cases when the patient needs to be emphasized or the agent plays a rather unimportant role.[23] That is interesting. So the meaning of the concept determines the order in the sentence. Sounds like a language pattern to me. Sounds like a useful cognitive shortcut to me, one that helps to keep those words in mind.

To illustrate this further, let's assume my large purple ogre novel became such a success that its rights got sold for a motion picture. In one scene the ogre killed the dragon in a dramatic fight and saved the princess. What would that scene look like? Most likely, you would pay most attention to the ogre fighting the dragon. Apparently, you find the ogre more important than the dragon, the agent more important than the patient. And this is indeed what eye-tracking research in participants watching films demonstrates. When people view visual depictions of actions, we place special attention to the agent.[24] And what is more important is placed first, and what is placed first is more frequent, and what is more frequent is processed faster.

TODAY'S LANGUAGE IS
YESTERDAY'S PERCEPTUAL EXPERIENCE

We started out this chapter with the question, *What came first, the chicken or the egg?* I promised that question would play a central role in this chapter. And it did. First of all, *chicken* comes before *egg*, in terms of word order. Just like higher concepts precede lower concepts, powerful concepts precede less powerful concepts, happy concepts precede sad concepts, male concepts precede female concepts, and early concepts precede later concepts, more than the other way around; *chicken* precedes *egg*. And with the knowledge that word order is mapped into world order, the age-old question finds an answer.

But the issue of whether the chicken or the egg came first has also shown to be important for another reason. We can argue that the more frequent concept is presented first, or what is less coded comes first (and what is less coded is more frequent). It also happens to be the case that what is less coded is processed faster, or that what is more frequent is processed faster. But here the chicken and the egg question emerges again. Is what is less coded easier to process, or is what is easier to process less coded? Most of the current research suggests that language has been shaped to fit the human brain rather than vice versa.[25]

Talmy Givón once argued that "today's morphology is yesterday's syntax,"[26] with syntactic constructions like *going to* and *being the cause of* being combined later to fixed expressions like *gonna* and *because*.[27] Givón has also been credited with the phrase "today's syntax is yesterday's discourse."[28] We have seen examples in the previous chapter, when I discussed Sumerian writing of 5,500 to 5,200 years ago, where writing was pictographic but later became conventionalized and abstract; or Israeli Sign Language, which started to be more iconic in nature, but became more complex and efficient; or language evolution in the Telephone Game, where very iconic gestures become shorter and faster and more abstract. What we experience in the world around us gets encoded in language.

In this chapter, I discussed several iconicity principles. I left one out, not because it is less important—on the contrary!—but because I wanted to spend a bit more time on it. That iconicity principle concerns the distance with which pieces of information are presented together and their relevance. Concepts that belong together in meaning are also presented together in language and speech. That is, words that have close spatial proximity in language or temporal proximity in speech belong together in meaning. This iconicity principle extends the idea of nonarbitrariness we started out with in the previous chapter. And it extends it so much that we will devote an entire chapter to it—the next one.

· _12_ ·

Company

The restrictions on relative occurrence of each element are described most simply by a network of interrelated statements, certain of them being put in terms of the results of certain others, rather than by a simple measurement of the total restriction on each element separately.

—Zellig Harris[1]

_I_ had a scary moment yesterday morning. Just like every other morning, I drove to work. Traffic was pretty bad, but in the end, I made it on time. I parked my car on campus, got out, and grabbed my laptop bag. When I walked toward the department building, I heard some noise behind me. I turned around, as the noise was getting worse, and noticed a frurp running toward me. At first, I thought the frurp was randomly running around like a headless chicken, but then I realized that the frurp was in fact chasing me. I ran, but the frurp was so fast it almost caught up with me. Not that I am scared of frurps in general, but I am not a big fan of them either. I walked faster, started to run, and hoped the frurp would not be able to get me. In the end, I was glad I was able to outrun the frurp and make it safely into the building, away from the frurp.

John Rupert Firth, better known as J. R. Firth, was a well-known linguist. Firth knew a thing or two about frurps. Or rather, he knew nothing about frurps, but knew a lot about giving meaning to words based on their context. And consequently he knew a lot about frurps. Firth posed the famous adage: "You shall know a word by the company it keeps."[2] The meaning of a word can be estimated by the linguistic context of that word. Firth's adage is powerful with regards to the ability of keeping those words in mind, as knowing the meaning of one word allows us to know the meaning of accompanying

227

words. And with all the words we use on a regular basis from the more than sixty thousand different words that are in our mental lexicon, we have many opportunities to know a word by the company it keeps. In fact, each time we hear, read, speak, or write a word we know, we strengthen our knowledge of the accompanying words and strengthen the knowledge of those accompanying words because of the company they keep with yet other words. Let's investigate Firth's adage a little more.

First of all, you do not need to worry. To the best of my knowledge, frurps do not exist. You shall never encounter a frurp, let alone be chased by a frurp. Because the word *frurp* does not exist. Not in your mental dictionary, not in mine, not in anybody's. I double-checked both my Oxford English and my Merriam-Webster dictionaries, and the word *frurp* is not one of the 470,000 entries. And yet you have been able to get a pretty good sense of what a frurp may be. Based on the context of the word *frurp*, you have been able to deduct aspects of the meaning of *frurp*. For instance, without knowing what a frurp is, you have been able to conclude it is unlikely to be a paperclip (for paperclips do not move), it is unlikely to be a dinosaur (for dinosaurs do not roam around on campus), and it is not an ant either (for ants tend to not chase people). Despite not knowing the meaning of the word *frurp*, because nobody has ever explained the word to you, it is likely you infer some creature that can have the intention of chasing people and can potentially outrun them. That would suggest that extracting the meaning of a word based on its context may not allow us to get to the exact meaning, but we will be able to make a decent approximation of its semantics, a shortcut. We do not know whether frurps tend to be black, brown, beige, green, or purple. Neither do we know whether they bark, meow, growl, roar, or chirp, but we can form a very general mental representation of the nature of a frurp.

In a way the previous chapter has already demonstrated that you shall know a word by the company it keeps. Even with very little context, it becomes possible to deduct aspects of the meaning of a word based on its limited (word order) company. From the fact that the word pair *happy and sad* appears more frequently in language than *sad and happy*, we can conclude two things. One is that happy words go first and sad words go second, but we can conclude something else as well: apparently *happy* and *sad* have something in common, in this case, valence. If you happen to encounter the word pair *kvelling and sad* several times, it is more likely that *kvelling* has something to do with valence, either being a synonym or an antonym, than it has to do with a paperclip, dinosaur, ant, or frurp.[3] Not necessarily so, but likely so. Context, even very limited context that is not much more than one word, already gives clues about the meaning of the word based on the company it keeps.

KEEPING THEM COMPANY

Let's dig a bit deeper into Firth's adage "You shall know a word by the company it keeps." It reminds us of one of Talmy Givón's principles of iconicity, introduced in the previous chapter. If a word is in the near-spatial (for language) or -temporal (for speech) proximity of another word, it is likely the word has something in common conceptually. So knowing a word by the company it keeps is an iconicity principle, at least according to Givón, and I wholeheartedly agree with him. It demonstrates a nonarbitrariness component of language.

So if we need to determine the similarity in meaning between the words *dog* and *cat*, all we need to do is determine the likelihood that the word *dog* is used in the same sentence as the word *cat*. We need to find out whether *dog* is a neighbor of *cat*. If they are used in each other's proximity, it is likely they have something in common conceptually. But what do you do if you cannot find sentences in which the two words appear together? One answer is to collect more language until you find the two together, but that may be cumbersome when comparing words that simply hardly ever appear in the same sentence.

There is a way out. In the sentence "A dog and a cat lived in the house," we can argue that you shall know the meaning of the word *dog* on the basis of the company the word *dog* keeps (i.e., "and a cat lived in the house"). For the same reason, we can argue that there is a semantic relationship between *dog* and *cat*, because they co-occur in the same sentence.

Now imagine we do not find any sentence in which *dog* and *cat* co-occur. That would be rather strange, but just bear with me. In the language we encounter, we do happen to read the sentences "A dog walked in the park" and "A cat walked in the park." As with the sentence in which *dog* and *cat* appear together, we can argue that *dog* and *cat* must have something in common semantically, because they share the same context ("walked in the park").

Now imagine again that there are no words surrounding the word *dog* that ever surround the word *cat*. That is, the neighbors of the word *dog* are never the same as the neighbors of the word *cat*, like in the sentence "The man walked the dog in the park" and "A lady had a cat in her house." That is all the language we have, and there is no overlap in neighbors. But imagine there is another sentence like "The man and the woman lived in a house close to the park." Even though *dog* and *cat* have nothing in common because they do not share any neighbors, the neighbors of the neighbors do have something in common: they appear in the same sentence, as is the case for *man*, *woman*, *house*, and *park*. And we can go on. Even though *dog* and *cat* may not share the same lexical neighbors, the neighbors of the neighbors of the neighbors of the neighbors of the neighbors (and so on) may have something in common, and therefore, at higher-order co-occurrences, *dog* and *cat* ultimately may have something in common.

It is as if we have a language matrix in our mind consisting of words and their context—for instance, paragraphs, as they nicely place words in context. Imagine an enormous matrix with more than sixty thousand rows—for all the words that we have in our mental lexicon—and fifty thousand columns—for all the contexts, say, all the paragraphs we have ever read. This matrix is enormous, some 3 billion cells. In each of these cells, we mentally count how many times a word appears in a paragraph. So far, in the current paragraph you are reading, the word *matrix* would have a score of 4, but the word *spaghetti* would have a score of 0, because it has never occurred in this paragraph. It is likely when the paragraph concerns Italian food, the cells for the columns for the Italian food paragraph in the matrix will have frequencies higher than zero. At the same time, the columns for that paragraph will likely have frequencies of zero for words related to dogs and cats. The matrix will thus have scattered frequencies, blocks with lots of zeros (for *matrix*, *cats*, and *dogs* in the Italian food paragraphs), and with frequencies higher than zero (for *spaghetti* and *pizza* in the Italian food paragraphs). Some parts of the matrix will be dense; others will be sparse.

Now imagine that we would like to compute from the matrix whether the words *dog* and *cat* are similar in meaning. Based on the current way we have represented the matrix, we would have to scroll through all the paragraphs to consider whether *dog* and *cat* share lower or higher frequencies in the same row. But as we have seen before, it is not only whether they appear in the same row; it might also be the case that *dog* appears with a word in a row (say, *bark*) and cat appears with a word in a row (say, *meow*) but *dog* and *cat* never both have frequencies higher than zero in the same row. For *bark* and *meow*, however, this may be the case. And getting to the neighbors of the neighbors is computationally expensive. In conclusion, computing the first-order co-occurrences is easy (comparing the frequencies of two words in the same row), but computing the higher-order frequencies is difficult.

But there is a solution in matrix algebra you may remember from high school. We can split up a matrix into smaller matrices. One of those matrices gives a concise version of the massive word x paragraph matrix we started out with. And that concise matrix is not too sparse and not too dense. In fact, that concise matrix offers an interesting take on the meaning of words. Each word in the matrix has a row with the summarized frequencies. These frequencies can be seen as values that point to a direction in a multidimensional space. Each word points into a dimension.

Interestingly, we can compute the distance between the dimensions in space. One word may point into one dimension, another word into another dimension. The meaning of the words have become word vectors, and if the distance between the vectors is small, the words apparently share a part of the semantic space, and if the distance between dimensions is large, words are very dissimilar. The cosine match between the words gives a good estimate on how similar words are in meaning in a 300-dimensional space—a space with several dimensions that mathematically makes sense but cognitively is incomprehensible. We can now ask the space, the "long-term memory" of the language we have trained the space on, to what extent two words have the same meaning. The cosine value of the two words gives the semantic similarity. Mathematically speaking, the cosine can be −1 to 1; practically speaking the cosine is 0 for no relation in meaning and 1 for a perfect relationship in meaning.

If this all becomes too mathematical,[4] let me try to illustrate. Let's take the titles of the first seven chapters of this book, the words *words*, *language*, *guess*, *training*, *instinct*, *network*, and *grounding*. We can compute the frequencies with which these words appear in the same sentence, as we did in the previous chapter. The matrix of frequencies looks like this.

	words	language	guess	training	instinct	network	grounding
words	1,635,208	78,532	9,969	1,916	80	3,111	0
language	211,035	2,239,419	2,492	57,783	292	30,514	3,712
guess	5,923	2,213	81,530	926	354	542	0
training	9,371	437,193	305	3,299,629	1,049	344,417	223
instinct	152	23,204	196	360	8,872	0	0
network	16,821	61,669	1,083	204,419	0	5,160,320	557
grounding	56	750	0	78	0	155	6,903

It seems that it is most likely the same word occurs with itself in the same context, as the diagonal of the matrix has the highest frequencies. It also shows that some combinations never appear in the same context, word combinations like *guess-grounding*, *instinct-network*, and *instinct-grounding*. We could perhaps say that *words* and *language* have a lot in common because they have the highest frequencies, but overall it is difficult to make these comparisons, and we cannot say anything about the null frequencies.

Now let's create a semantic space on a large corpus of English texts and create a matrix of the words and paragraphs in that text, apply matrix algebra, and obtain a concise version of the matrix. Let's again query the semantic space with the title words of the first seven chapters of this book and compute the similarity in meaning between the words. The result is presented below. As you can see the diagonal of the matrix has the value of 1. This is not surprising as the semantic similarity between a word and itself is perfect. What you also see is that the matrix is symmetrical. The same value can be found for *words–language* and *language–words*. Now when we look at the word *words*, it has a strong similarity in meaning with *language* (0.5) and also with *mind* (0.3), but with words like *training, instinct, network,* and *grounding*, it has little in common in meaning.

	words	language	guess	training	instinct	network	grounding
words	1	.5	.18	.07	.04	0	0
language	.5	1	.08	.09	.06	.05	.03
guess	.18	.08	1	.03	.08	.02	0
training	.07	.09	.03	1	.09	.06	.09
instinct	.04	.06	.08	.09	1	.02	0
network	0	.05	.02	.06	.02	1	.08
grounding	0	.03	0	.09	0	.08	1

The idea is simple and powerful: Based on large amounts of language, a "long-term memory" gets created that is organized efficiently to avoid sparsity and density. To compute the similarity in meaning, we consult the long-term memory, which determines the distance between the two linguistic items, a distance that represents the meaning between the two items. Even though the amount of language that is needed to train the "long-term memory" is large—some one hundred thousand words in forty thousand paragraphs is ideal—it is considerably less language we need than what is needed for finding enough cases of two words appearing in the same sentence, some forty thousand times less. And that's a lot less.

To illustrate how much less, let me try to make it more concrete by taking the two largest books I know: the *Bible* and Proust's *Remembrance of Things Past*. If we were to compute the similarity between two words—say, *dog* and *cat*—we need about 15 percent of the *Bible* to compute the similarities in the concise-matrix solution, but about five times the entire *Bible* if we were to aim for the same similarities coming out of words appearing in the same sentence. Or if we take *Remembrance of Things Past*, only 8 percent is needed for the concise-matrix solution, but four times the novel is needed for finding the words in the same sentence.

And there is another advantage of computing similarities in meaning using these higher-order co-occurrences. The linguistic items that are compared can be words, but they can also be sentences, paragraphs, or even entire texts.[5] Computational tools like these have been quite useful. In one study, the TOEFL test—the Teaching of English as a Foreign Language test that any student from abroad needs to pass to study at a U.S. university—was used as a test case. The computer was asked to estimate the right multiple-choice answer, and the estimates allowed the algorithm to pass the test. I have taken three sample questions from the Educational Testing Service (ETS) website and computed the cosine values.[6]

1. It is difficult to get young people to plan for their old age, which seems very *distant* to them.
a. impossible	.57
b. far away	.62
c. observable	.18
d. fearful	.38

2. Receptors for the sense of smell are located at the *top* of the nasal cavity.
a. upper end	.44
b. inner edge	.35
c. mouth	.33
d. division	.19

3. It is not possible for people to recall everything that they have thought, felt, or done.
   a. remember   .63
   b. appreciate   .22
   c. repeat   .22
   d. discuss   .41

Apparently language is organized in such a way that very simple techniques (computing how often a word appears in the company of another word) and other relatively simple techniques (computing the likelihood of a word appearing in the company of another word if the language space were large enough) allow for estimating the meaning of words—or, better yet, estimating the similarities in meaning between words, sentences, paragraphs, or texts. That means entire novels can be compared on their semantic content.[7]

But let's return to words to do justice to the title of this book. Let me take some tree words like *pine, maple, oak, birch*, some bird words like *robin, canary, sparrow, penguin*, and some wild animal words like *tiger, lion, zebra, giraffe*. As we did before with the two words combinations, we could take the same large collection of texts, of some trillion words, and count the number of times two words appear together in a five-word chunk of text. So we compute the frequency that *maple* occurs with *lion, tiger, zebra, canary*, and the other words, and we do the same thing for penguin co-occurring with *lion, tiger, zebra, canary*, and the other words. The result of these twelve words and their accompanying words is a matrix of 12 × 12 = 144 cells. By looking at these frequencies of a word accompanying another word—and following Firth, we know the meaning of a word by the company it keeps—we can estimate similarities in meaning. The matrix has a similar structure as the one I showed earlier: *canary* has most in common in meaning with *robin* and *penguin*, least with *maple*.

All these matrices might be dazzling. Moreover, it is hard to capture an overview of the relations with so many numbers. Thanks to a simple statistical technique[8] that places the items with high values together and lower values further apart, we can create a map, in the current example a road map of the biological world. Two words that more frequently accompany each other are placed near each other on the map; if they do not frequently accompany each other, they are placed far apart from each other. As the figure below shows, language helps us to organize the world, in this case into trees, birds, and mammals (I have added circles to outline the groupings). You shall know the meaning of *tiger* by the company it keeps with other words, such as *lion, giraffe*, and *zebra*. For now, it does not matter what the dimensions mean; all that matters is that a map of trees, birds, and wild animals can be formed based not on any biology or encyclopedia, but solely based on the company the words keep.

	pine	maple	oak	birch	robin	canary	sparrow	penguin	tiger	lion	zebra	giraffe
pine	1	.8	.82	.64	.14	.01	.11	.05	.11	.12	.22	.23
maple	.8	1	.81	.64	.14	0	.11	.05	.03	.01	.15	.18
oak	.82	.81	1	.63	.16	.06	.16	.09	.15	.13	.19	.21
birch	.64	.64	.63	1	.06	-.02	.03	-.02	.08	.08	.09	.11
robin	.14	.14	.16	.06	1	.19	.23	.3	.16	.11	.14	.09
canary	.01	0	.06	-.02	.19	1	.09	.19	.14	.16	.09	.07
sparrow	.11	.11	.16	.03	.23	.09	1	.26	.07	.05	.09	.03
penguin	.05	.05	.09	-.02	.3	.19	.26	1	.09	.02	.08	.18
tiger	.11	.03	.15	.08	.16	.14	.07	.09	1	.68	.42	.35
lion	.12	.01	.13	.08	.11	.16	.05	.02	.68	1	.46	.33
zebra	.22	.15	.19	.09	.14	.09	.09	.08	.42	.46	1	.68
giraffe	.23	.18	.21	.11	.09	.07	.03	.18	.35	.33	.68	1

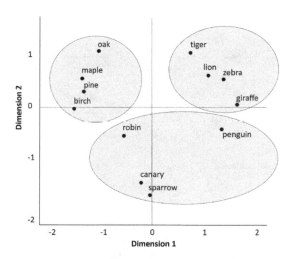

As you can see from the figure, tree words cluster well, wild animal words cluster well, and bird words seem to cluster well.[9] The one exception is the word *penguin*, which in language is less considered to be a bird than *robins*, *canaries*, and *sparrows* and more a wild animal, though on the map above, it is flirting with the birds. Similarly, *robin* is closer to the tree words than *sparrow* and *canary* are. Based on these tree words, bird words, and wild animal words, we can see that language has apparently carved out the natural world for us solely based on words co-occurring in the same language context. You shall know the meaning of a word by the company it keeps! Even though language users have all the freedom to use words in any context they would like, language users apparently do not. Instead, they choose those words that are similar in meaning in similar contexts.

Remember chapter 6 ("Network"), where we looked at how the attributes and actions of concepts can be obtained from training a neural network? And how the network learns which features are important and which ones are not, thereby generating attributes and actions? It turns out we can also query the language system for these relations; we find that for language there are flowers, trees, and plants, as there are birds, fish, and animals (the latter being alive, moving around, and having skin).

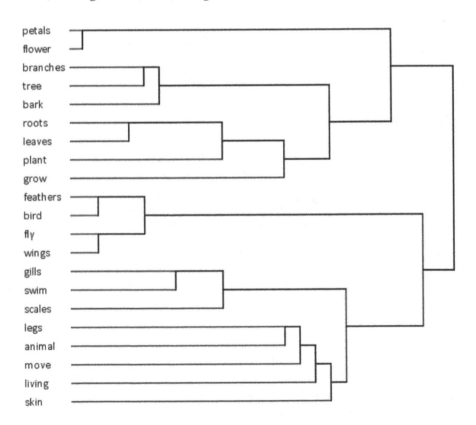

If the language system allows for queries on the meaning between concepts, language has encoded these patterns, providing a convenient cognitive shortcut to the language user. And because the language user produces and comprehends language, these patterns get trained over and over again.

And the meaningful relations are not restricted to flora and fauna; they also apply to abstract words. We can repeat this exercise with words other than those for trees, birds, and wild animals, by for instance looking at emotion words. Again, we can compute the frequency of six emotion words appearing together in the same context, resulting in a 6 × 6 matrix of frequencies. According to the language system, *surprise* has more in common with *disgust* and *joy* than with *sadness* and *anger*.

	surprise	disgust	joy	sadness	anger	fear
surprise	1	.42	.46	.35	.35	.36
disgust	.42	1	.36	.34	.43	.44
joy	.46	.36	1	.56	.43	.49
sadness	.35	.34	.56	1	.66	.63
anger	.35	.43	.43	.66	1	.76
fear	.36	.44	.49	.63	.76	1

This matrix can then again be visualized on a two-dimensional plane, such as in the figure below.

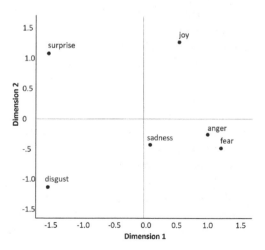

The two dimensions can be viewed as perspectives on meaning. On dimension 2, the vertical axis, you see that more positive emotions are presented away from more negative emotions, with *surprise* and *joy* clustering together on one dimension, and *disgust, sadness, anger,* and *fear* clustering on the other dimensions. Dimension can thus be interpreted as a positive versus negative meaning of emotion words. Dimension 1, the horizontal axis, distinguishes *surprise* and *disgust* from *joy, sadness, anger, fear*. Dimension 2 is less clear but may represent a sudden response, a startled surprise, a sudden experience of disgust, versus emotions that develop more over time.

I can give many more of these examples, and later I will. For now, it suffices to say that what seemed to be semantic chaos earlier, with language users having full flexibility of using any word in any context, turns out to be semantic patterning. We do not talk about random things; we talk about things that belong to each other semantically. Consequently, we can estimate the meaning of a word by the company it keeps. And that is quite convenient. Language users can use a cognitive shortcut for the pattern—the linguistic company it keeps—to estimate its meaning.

KNOWING THE LOCATION OF A CITY NAME
BY THE COMPANY IT KEEPS

Imagine that you land in a foreign country—the same or a different one as in chapter 7 ("Grounding")—and you are lost again because you don't speak or understand the foreign language in that country, and nobody in the country speaks any language other than the foreign language you don't speak. This seems a recipe for linguistic disaster. You are on an assignment in that country and need to travel from the city you arrived in to the three largest cities in the country, not the smaller ones. And the order in which you visit these cities needs to be determined as efficiently as possible. That is, you don't want to travel to a city in the northeast, then to a city in the southwest, and then to a city in the northeast.

The assignment was loud and clear, the only problem is that you left the specifics of the assignment at home, as well as your chargers, cell phone, laptop, GPS, and other mobile devices. Quite an inconvenience! All you know are the cities in the country and which ones are the largest ones in that country. More problematically perhaps, you do not have a map. You have no idea what the country looks like; you have no clue what the cities are like, except that there are three of the largest cities somewhere in the country that you need to visit. And the success of your important assignment depends on you. The only thing you happen to have is a year's worth of newspapers from that country written in the foreign language of that country. Newspaper articles often start with the city and date at the very top of the article, and that may be of help, because you now know which words are city names and which ones are not. But you don't have a map, and you don't speak the language, so you are basically lost.

A couple of years ago, Rolf Zwaan and I wondered whether we could predict the location of cities based on how these cities were mentioned in newspapers,[10] a rather absurd question.[11] Would it be possible to estimate the longitude and latitude of cities based on how city names were mentioned in text? On the one hand, this seemed to be ridiculous. After all, if anybody asked where geographical information comes from, my answer would have been simple. That information comes from the maps you studied in school, or the maps you found on the internet. The information may have come from your own travels in a country or through the world. Or the information may have come from strict descriptions of geographical information, such as "take a left on Martin Luther King Boulevard, and then go straight ahead, and you'll find your destination on your right," or "Memphis is located some six hours north of New Orleans, some six hours west of Atlanta, some eight hours south of Chicago, and some eight hours east of Dallas." Clear geographical descriptions based on geographical texts.

On the other hand, if it is possible to know the meaning of a word by the context it keeps, if it is possible to categorize the animal kingdom on the basis of animal names in language, why would it then not be possible to categorize cities on the basis of city names in language? Rolf and I argued that cities that are located together are talked about together. We predicted that the meaning of the geographical location of a city name could be known by the context of city names that city name keeps. In our enthusiasm, we also thought we might be able to predict the population size of a city based on the frequency with which the city name was mentioned in text.

We identified fifty of the largest cities in the United States and retrieved their population size as well as their longitude and latitude. All the large cities you can think of in the United States were thus included, from New York to Chicago, from Los Angeles to San Diego. And we took over two years of newspaper articles from three newspapers, the *New York Times*, the *Wall Street Journal*, and the *Los Angeles Times*. For each of these newspapers, we trained a semantic space, whereby the words and their context are placed in word vectors. As you may recall, a large matrix of words and paragraphs gets transformed into a smaller matrix so that the word vectors ultimately point to somewhere in the 300-dimensional space, and the similarities of the directions of the word vectors are an estimate of the similarity between the words. These three spaces from the three newspapers we then queried on the similarities between city names. To make a long story short, we estimated the meaning of a city name by the context it keeps with other city names. Based on this, we got a large matrix of fifty cities by fifty cities, with the similarity scores in each of the 2,500 cells. And we then extracted a two-dimensional solution from this matrix. In other words, we computed the score a city had on a horizontal and a vertical axis, just like the position of a city on a map.

There is every reason to believe the crazy idea of estimating the latitude and longitude of cities based on how the city names appear in text would fail. Take, for instance, the similarity in meaning of the city names. One would expect that *New York* and *New Orleans* would be very similar in meaning—and thus in latitude and longitude—because of the word *new* they shared. This would perhaps benefit *San Francisco* and *San Diego* but would harm *New York* and *New Orleans*. At the same time, *New York*, *New Orleans*, and anything "new" would be confused; *Virginia Beach* would be considered to be very sandy; *Washington* would be a city, a state, and a president; and *Phoenix* would rise from its ashes. For the semantic context of these words, things would not be much better. Music would bring Detroit, Memphis, Nashville, and New Orleans together too close for geographical comfort.

We first looked at whether language would be able to help us predict the population size of the fifty cities by looking at the frequency with which the city was mentioned in each of the three newspapers. We found a strong relation between population size and frequency size, so strong that frequency of a city name seemed to be a good proxy for the number of people living in a city. In fact, when we asked participants to estimate the population size of each of the fifty cities, they did not do as well as our simple frequency counts did. So if you are ever lost in estimating how many people live in a city, just open a year's worth of newspapers, and count the number of times a city name is mentioned. It gives you a decent relative estimate of the population size.

Let's go back to the geographical location of the cities. When we computed the estimated position on the horizontal and vertical axis and compared this with the actual latitude and longitude of each city, we found, to our surprise and excitement, that there was a relation between the two. The relative position that we had estimated based on the city name being mentioned in text was very similar to the relative longitude and latitude of the city on an actual map. And not just for one newspaper, but for the *New York Times*, for the *Wall Street Journal*, and for the *Los Angeles Times*. We were pleasantly surprised.

We also asked several participants to estimate the city location. This was useful because it showed that the participant estimates were comparable to the computational estimates. The linguistic estimates consisted of mistakes. One of the major mistakes was Honolulu. According to the linguistic estimates, the city of Honolulu was estimated just off the coast of California. Interestingly, our participants made exactly the same mistake. Our participants too had ignored the fact that Honolulu is a six-hour flight from Los Angeles—or, if you'd rather peddle, some 2,500 miles of physical exercise.

When we submitted the paper, one of the reviewers made an important point. It seemed rather cumbersome to take a text, rip it apart into three hundred dimensions, reduce these dimensions into two dimensions, and then see whether these two dimensions correlated with the longitude and latitude of the cities. I realized it not only was cumbersome but also undermined the argument that geographical locations are encoded in language, that there are geographical patterns that language users can use as a cognitive shortcut. Perhaps the argument should have been that geographical locations can be extracted from sophisticated computer models. That would still have been interesting from a scientific—or rather, computer scientific—point of view, but not so much from a psychology of language point of view. And it would have generated a very different book than the one you are reading now.[12]

So rather than using language to train a computer model, and looking at the outcomes of the computer model, we looked at language itself. We computed the frequencies with which two city names occurred together in a sentence. We needed a considerably larger corpus than the newspapers that we used, but when we looked at the frequencies, we found similar results. The magic did not lie in the computational algorithm; it lies in language.

So we were able to rule out the possibility that the magic of predicting the longitude and latitude of cities on the basis of the linguistic company they keep actually came from the computer program we used. If we translated the city names to word vectors using matrix algebra, we got the same results as if we had used a considerably larger corpus and simply tagged the number of times two city names appeared in the same sentence. But that corpus had to be much, much larger than the corpus that matrix algebra could deal with. It was as if the burden of language were released by the mathematical function.

But just like any other scientific discovery, I wanted to rule out any other options. After all, it was possible that the finding could be attributed to the specific map of the United States. If the frequency of city names correlates with the population size of a city, and given that the larger cities in the United States lie in the West and on the East coast, it might be the case that the fact that we were able to map the linguistic findings on the geographical locations was a function of the specific map of the United States. Another potential reason we got the results we did was that perhaps the results came from language, but only the English language. It may be the case that English relies on distributional semantics, but other languages do not.

So together with some colleagues, I conducted another study,[13] one we affectionately called the Chinese route argument, a tongue-in-cheek reference to the Chinese room argument I mentioned in chapter 7 ("Grounding"). If no meaning can be extracted from arbitrary symbols, then it should not be possible to extract a map of China from a collection of Chinese words. We took a large body of Chinese texts and created a matrix of Chinese city names, and after plotting the linguistic map of city names and comparing it with the actual map of China, we obtained results very similar to the map of the United States and the city names from English. The longitude and latitude of cities in China could be predicted based on how Chinese city names were mentioned in Chinese language.

We were a step closer to generalizing our findings beyond the United States and the English language. Building on our excitement, we extended the work to the Arabic language to predict the longitude and latitude of cities in a multitude of countries. So we took Arabic texts from various sources and repeated the same procedure that we used before, trying to predict the longitude and latitude for cities in the Middle East. Again we were able to predict the longitude and latitude of the largest cities in the Middle East, including Egypt, Iraq, Jordan, Kuwait, Lebanon, Oman, Syria, United Arab Emirates, and Yemen.[14] It seemed like if you wanted to know the geographical location of a city, all you needed to do was look at the linguistic context that city name keeps, because language encodes geographical locations—a pattern that provides a wonderful cognitive shortcut when you are lost in a foreign country and forgot to take your chargers, cell phone, laptop, GPS system, and other mobile devices.

KNOWING THE ARCHEOLOGICAL SITE
BY THE COMPANY IT KEEPS

Gabriel Recchia and I wondered whether we could push the envelope a little.[15] Being able to predict the longitude and latitude of cities on the basis of the company these city names have in the language of newspapers was cool. Being able to predict the longitude and latitude for cities in the United States on the basis of English texts, for cities in China on the basis of Chinese texts, and for cities in the Middle East on the basis of Arabic texts was even cooler. But how could these findings be used? One option we considered was in a field less familiar to us cognitive scientists, that of archeology.

In the previous chapter, I mentioned Sumerian script when discussing arbitrariness in language. The Sumerian cuneiform script had an ancestor script, likely the same ancestor script as the Indus Valley Script. The Indus

Valley civilization was a civilization in what is now northwest India that lasted from 3300 BCE to 1300 BCE. As with the Sumerian civilization flourishing in the basins of the Euphrates and the Tigris, the Indus Valley civilization flourished in the basins of the Indus River. Because the Indus Valley civilization can be considered one of the most ancient urban cultures of mankind, the Indus script is important. The Indus script has, however, not yet been deciphered. We don't really know what the various signs mean. We don't even know whether it is a language or a writing system! What we do know is that more than 4,700 inscriptions in the Indus script have been excavated on stamp seals, sealings, pottery, miniature tablets, copper tablets, and copper tools.

The script consisted of a little over four hundred signs that look a bit like the pictographs and early cuneiform of the Sumerian script. But we don't know what the signs mean. The signs, typically about five next to one another, appear on sealings. These inscriptions are quite short. It is therefore not likely that inscriptions would contain multiple place names, as with the newspapers. However, if the signs that tend to be used vary from location to location, then it seems likely that objects from nearby excavation sites will contain similar symbols. If some sign (⊕⅏) is particularly common on sealings stamped at Harappa in the north, and sealings from Harappa were commonly transported to Kalibangan due to its geographical proximity, then we may expect (⊕⅏) to be common on sealings found at Kalibangan. Given that sealings likely accompanied shipments of goods from city to city on a regular basis, whereas stamp seals themselves were probably not objects of trade, interactions among nearby places would more likely be reflected in sealing distributions, and less likely in seal distributions.

So Gabe and I used the 417 signs in almost two thousand inscriptions on seals and 723 inscriptions on sealings. This created a matrix similar to that of city names in the United States and paragraphs in newspapers. As before, we created a matrix from which a more concise matrix was computed. We ultimately calculated the longitude and latitude of the five excavation sites that are known from archeological research and determined whether our computational estimates matched the archeological estimates. They did, at least for the sealings. For the seals, as expected, we were not able to predict the excavation sites. Of course our algorithm made mistakes, but overall it provided some useful shortcuts to the excavation sites.

Apparently, we were able to estimate the excavation sites of the sealings. However, we were able to do that for *known* excavation sites and test it on *known* excavation sites. Might we also be able to put our algorithm to the rescue for archeologists? Four sealings have an unknown geographic origin. The computational analysis we conducted couldn't predict the excavation site

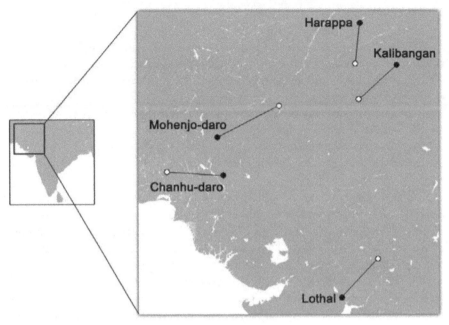

Source: **Recchia and Louwerse (2015).**

for one, but for the most readable sealing, we were able to predict that the origin was most likely Harappa, for another Harappa or Kalibangan (but not Mohenjo-dara or Lothal), and for yet another sealing Harappa or Lothal (but not Mohen-dara or Kalibangan).

You might wonder what the relevance is of sealings that you don't know or geographical origins that you do not know. What Gabe and I showed was that we were able to use computational linguistics tools for excavation sites, and to put computational linguistic tools to the rescue for archeologists. Not because the tool was so powerful, but simply because the Indus script signs—whether they were representing a language or not—functioned based on the idea that their meaning was determined by the company they kept. It provided a convenient cognitive shortcut for archeologists.

LINGUISTIC MAPS

Now that we have established that geographical locations are somehow encoded in language, we need to know whether language users in fact extract this information for their geographical estimates. And answering this question is rather difficult. If I asked you where to find New York on a map, it would be very complex to disentangle all the information you could have gotten from all your different sources. It might have come from your visit to New York, from watching a documentary on New York, from studying a map of the United States, as well as from language. But how would it be possible to single out language from all the other sources of information? Every time I would find a way to single out language as a source, it may have been contaminated by other sources of information, including real-world experiences.

Whenever scientists, at least those of the cognitive psychology type, want to be able to control the situation, they manipulate the variables. We might want to create a world that participants do not recognize, and have two participant groups, one being exposed to a text that mentions made-up city names and the other exposed to a map that lists made-up city names. The two groups we place in separate rooms and have them study the text or the map, except that this new text requires many hours of reading, so we might have to put the participant groups in a locked room for several days. And to avoid contamination from other sources, we would not give the participants access to any information other than the text or the map. Now, one could try to submit such an experiment to an ethical review board committee, but chances are they would not approve such an experiment; indeed, it would be a rather barbaric one.

So we are stuck—unless we rely on a fictional world, and use one participant group that studies an actual map of that fictional world, and the other we wouldn't have read a large text but would select those participants on the basis of already having read an existing text. The fictional world is called Middle Earth, and the text is called *Lord of the Rings*. Together with a graduate student, I started on a journey through Middle Earth.[16]

The problem with *Lord of the Rings* is that the text is rather small for any serious computational linguistic analysis. So what do you do as a scientist if there is not enough data? You collect more data. Writing a friendly letter asking J. R. R. Tolkien for more books would not be a good idea, so we had to work with what we had. We took both *The Hobbit* and *The Fellowship of the Ring* trilogy and computed the word frequencies in each paragraph as we had done before. Based on this, we were able to create the word vectors and compute the distance between the word vectors to estimate the semantic similarity between the city names that occurred in Tolkien's work. Compared to the actual maps of Middle Earth, the result was not fantastic but was comparable to our earlier results. And given that we simply didn't have enough language to work with, we were in fact quite happy with the result.

We then conducted two experiments. In one experiment, we asked people if they had read *The Hobbit* and *The Fellowship of the Ring* trilogy. If they had not, we included them in the experiment and presented them with a map of Middle Earth and the location names. They studied the city names and the location for about half an hour, after which they were tested on their memory for the location names and their locations in Middle Earth. We gave them a blank piece of paper with a vertical and horizontal axis and asked them to point to the locations on the blank map. Participants did well. Studying the location names and the map gave them enough information to replicate the map. They made mistakes, but the mistakes were minor.

Another group who had read *The Hobbit* and *The Fellowship of the Ring* trilogy participated in another experiment. They did not get the opportunity to study the location names and the map but received the blank map and were asked to draw the city names on the blank map. Having read *The Hobbit* and *The Fellowship of the Ring* must have helped them, because this group of participants performed quite well too. They made slightly more errors than the group who had not read Tolkien's work, but the findings were comparable.

So we had four data sources:

1. the longitude and latitude of location names in Middle Earth;
2. the computational estimates of the longitude and latitude of location names in Middle Earth;
3. the group who had studied the map but had not read the Tolkien texts; and
4. the group who had read the Tolkien texts but had not studied the map.

The question we were most interested in was whether the map estimates from the group who had not read the texts better matched the map than the text estimates, and whether the map estimates from the group who had read the texts better matched the computational estimates than the map estimates. And that was indeed the case. Readers better matched the text estimates; nonreaders better matched the map estimates.

Whenever I give talks and tell my audience about the Tolkien findings, members of the audience always interrupt me. Somebody impatiently wiggles in their chair, looks at me with raised eyebrows, first hesitates, but then sticks their hand in the air and interrupts, "Wait a minute, the Middle Earth map is printed in the Tolkien books! What you are telling us about the readers may have come from that map, more than from the language!" I always appreciate it when people ask questions, as it keeps me reconsidering my findings. In this case, we already took care of the answer. We looked at the maps of Middle Earth that are printed in the Tolkien books. Across eleven editions we could get our hands on, less than a third of the places were displayed on these maps. But we also tested whether the readers had prior map knowledge.

We asked them how often they had consulted the maps but found no difference in performance between those who frequently consulted the maps and those who didn't.

Undoubtedly, you now have the other question in mind that audience members often ask. Usually a different person has been wiggling in their chair and raises her hand. "You can talk about studying maps and reading texts, but there is a *Lord of the Rings* movie that readers and nonreaders alike could have gotten all their information from!" That question we also accounted for. It was a tedious task, but by carefully watching the *Lord of the Rings* movies, we found only eight out of the thirty-two locations were mentioned in dialogue, and a map of Middle Earth with location names was presented only three times in total, each time for less than thirty seconds. And when a map was shown, only nine cities could be distinguished.

What this study illustrates is not that the readers do not use visual representations but that readers might use language to *form* visual representations. That is, I would like to be the first to argue that we can represent a visual map in our mind from looking at a map. But likewise, I would like to be the first to argue that we can represent a visual map in our mind from language. Language patterns allow us to do so and help us to keep those words in mind.

KNOWING YOUR FRIENDS BY THE COMPANY THEIR NAMES KEEP

What works for geographical maps may also work for social maps. Imagine you want to plot your social network, all of the friends you have on LinkedIn, Twitter, Facebook, or Instagram. One way to do this is to draw connections. If Emma has a connection with Olivia, James, and Isabella, and Sophia has a connection with Olivia but not with Emma, while Noah has a connection with James, William, and Oliver, and Oliver not with James or William but with Sophia, we can create a spider web of social connections. This is the way that LinkedIn, Twitter, Facebook, or Instagram can make friend requests. If three people know each other, but you only know one of the three, it makes sense that the other two might be candidates for becoming a friend. This is typically the way social-network mapping works. But there is another way, nicely provided by language, by knowing the person by the linguistic company she keeps.

In one study, we investigated whether we could build a network of social relations on the basis of language itself, rather than by connections between the individuals.[17] We took the *Harry Potter* books and identified all the characters in the book. As with the example given above, we then created a matrix of semantic distances between the character names and plotted this matrix on a two-dimensional plane. We then did the same with the *Song of Ice and Fire* (perhaps now better known as *Game of Thrones*). Now the problem was that we needed to compare the language findings with actual findings. And that's tricky, because nobody wants to go through the painstaking exercise of creating a social network of all the characters. We identified sixty-five characters in the *Harry Potter* books, so that would mean there are some 4,225 potential connections that needed to be drawn. And for the five *Song of Ice and Fire* books, 1,385 characters accumulated 2 million potential connections!

Two decades ago, a group of journalists started a website with interactive maps of a person's network of influence. These maps are relevant to get a sense of the political or economic landscape of individuals of influence: who is connected to whom, and might that connection explain why this person is also in touch with another person? Sadly, the website closed down two years ago. The good news for us is that the website was up and running when we conducted our research, and—even better—the painstaking work that the journalists had done was not limited to politics and economics, but had extended to *Harry Potter* and the *Song of Ice and Fire*. Not all character names were plotted, and some character names were difficult to use because they were the same, but when we compared our linguistic estimates of where characters stood in the social network of Hogwarts School of Witchcraft and Wizardry (*Harry Potter*) and Westeros and Essos (*Song of Ice and Fire*) with the social network that the journalists had created, we found a surprisingly good map. Apparently, language has encoded the social relations between people, providing a socially convenient cognitive shortcut. And when we tested the knowledge of participants on these social relations, we found that human estimates were on par with computational estimates.

PLATO'S PROBLEM

It is easy to highlight the arbitrary relation between sound and meaning, but it is remarkable that there are quite a few nonarbitrary mappings between sound and meaning—not for one category of words, but for many, and not for one language, but for many. Calling the relation between sound and meaning arbitrary is too strong a claim, for there are many systematic patterns between sound and meaning.

Similarly, it may be easy to argue that two concepts can be placed in any order, because the order of concepts seems random too, but it is quite amazing how many word pairs follow clear meaningful patterns. Even though it is perfectly feasible for language users to switch word order without affecting the meaning they try to convey, they typically don't. These patterns are not coincidental. They are mapped onto our perceptual experiences.

Patterns in language, whether in the sound of words or in the order of words, are demonstrated in the previous two chapters. The current chapter also demonstrates this by looking at words in context. We could estimate the meaning of a word by calculating the direct linguistic context of a word, the immediately linguistic company a word keeps, but we can also calculate the indirect linguistic context of a word, by looking at the context shared by the context shared by the context of a word. These patterns turn out to be quite powerful in estimating the meaning of a word, so powerful that we can build semantic networks and are even able to predict the longitude and latitude of cities based on the linguistic context of the city names, or the social network of people based on the linguistic context of the characters.

You may recall the reasons why humans must have some language instinct, the argument discussed in chapter 5 ("Instinct"). One of these reasons was the poverty of the stimulus: the observation that the environment does not provide us with enough linguistic information to learn language. Language users have more knowledge than our limited experience provides. How can this discrepancy be explained?[18]

Chomsky called this dilemma Plato's problem. Plato struggled with the same question twenty-four centuries ago and provided a solution, the same solution that Chomsky provided: if the environment does not provide us with as much as we know, we must have innate ideas that pave the way for knowledge that we get through experience. In chapter 5, we saw that the stimuli may not be as poor as portrayed. But the current chapter shows the stimuli can be quite poor. The interrelations between stimuli that may be weak *prima facie* may in fact become very strong through the weak interrelations they have with other stimuli. But Chomsky applied Plato's problem not to semantic cognition but to *syntactic* cognition. He asked how we could learn syntax if the linguistic environment did not provide us with the right information. Semantics had nothing to do with that question, according to Chomsky, at least.

The solution outlined above, whereby we look at the linguistic context of words, is a solution of distributional linguistics: words have weak interrelations between one another, a network that together forms meaning. In a way, we have measured how often a word appears in the context of another word, and if the two words appear together frequently, they have semantic information in common. Words that tend to have a large number of distributional regularities in common with other words tend to have similar meanings.

A slight twist of this idea, but only a slight one, is the following idea: words of the same syntactic category tend to have a large number of distributional regularities in common. The beginning of this chapter gave the example of two sentences: "A dog walked in the park" and "A cat walked in the park." Because the words *dog* and *cat* have the same linguistic context, they are similar in meaning. But we could also say that if the words *dog* and *cat* have the same linguistic context, they form the same syntactic category. This idea is not new either. Chomsky's mentor, Zellig Harris, proposed such a distributional hypothesis,[19] and when it gets applied, the results are remarkable.

Using computational linguistics, some clever cognitive scientists put the hypothesis to the test.[20] Syntactic categories of words could be predicted with about 70 percent accuracy simply by working with the context in which the words occur, not on the basis of some language instinct—unless computers do have a language instinct after all! Pronouns, auxiliary verbs, adjectives and adverbs, and particularly nouns were all classified into the right syntactic category, not because of some preexisting or learned syntactic rules, but solely on the basis of knowing the syntactic category of a word by the linguistic company it keeps.

One could object that it is not so surprising that an algorithm can extract syntactic information from large amounts of linguistic data; that is the entire point of the poverty-of-the-stimulus argument: the linguistic stimuli a language-learning child is exposed to is extremely poor. Had the data been rich, perhaps then it would be possible for a child to extract syntax from data, but all the child hears is child-directed speech that is simply not representative of the rich language we adults are exposed to, so the argument goes. But that is exactly what made the computational linguistic predictions so interesting: they were not based on large amounts of well-formed linguistic data. Instead, they were based on the data the child is exposed to, a large corpus of parent–child interactions. The stimuli used for the algorithm were as "poor" as any child is exposed to!

Now if a simple algorithm is able to do a simple substitution test, and finds that if one word can be substituted for another word then that word belongs to the same syntactic category, we can surely expect that a champion in pattern matching, the *homo sapiens*, is able to do this. And that may be at least one piece of a larger puzzle of how we are able to acquire syntax in language: through distributional semantics, through the company words keep.

For syntax and semantics alike, by picking up on patterns in language, we can build a network of interdependencies that allow us to extract meaning. And if these weak patterns are mapped onto perceptual experiences, we can take a convenient shortcut in language comprehension and production. What we need is an instinct to pick up on these linguistic patterns, a network that distributes these patterns so that interrelations emerge, some grounding of the patterns when needed, and training so that these patterns become reinforced. Through training, instinct, network, grounding, and perhaps above all through the sound, order, and context relations between words and their meaning that are encoded in language itself, we keep those words in mind.

· *13* ·

Bootstrapping

Everything is related to everything else, but near things are more
related than distant things.

—Waldo Tobler[1]

$\mathcal{B}$aron Munchausen was a remarkable character. He was a calm and rational
man. His many adventures, however, were anything but quiet and reasonable.
They were simply amazing. Take, for instance, this one: Baron Munchausen
was a notable horseman. One day he visited Lithuania and tamed an unruly
horse everybody was afraid of. To demonstrate his excellent horse-riding
skills, he then pranced his horse around on a dining table without breaking
any of the tableware!

   In another adventure, he threw his silver hatchet a bit further than he
had actually intended, after which it landed on the moon. The baron did
not waste any time and climbed to the moon using a rope, got the hatchet,
and then climbed back down. Unfortunately though, the rope was not long
enough, but the brilliant Baron Munchausen had a solution. While climbing
down, he cut off the rope above him, tied it to the end he was still holding,
slid down further, and repeated these steps until he made it safely back to
the ground. If you think this all sounds rather unbelievable, you are just plain
wrong. According to the baron, these adventures are absolutely true. And if
anybody could know, it is the baron himself. After all, he was the main character featured in all of his adventures.[2]

   In one of his other adventures, the baron, always dressed impeccably
with his uniform and his bicorn on his head, rode his horse proudly through
the fields. Unexpectedly, he got caught in a swamp. With no help around, the
situation looked rather grim. There was no way the baron could have gotten
himself and his horse out of this dire situation. But the baron would not be

251

Baron Munchausen had he not come up with an idea, a great idea it turned out. While holding his horse firmly between his knees, he grabbed his pigtail and lifted himself and his horse up by his pigtail out of the swamp. An ingenious solution! Rumors say there is another version of this true adventure in which the baron did not grab his pigtail, but his bootstraps, and lifted himself and his horse to safety by pulling himself up by his bootstraps.[3]

The baron's adventure of pigtail pulling, or bootstrapping, may remind you of the symbol grounding problem and the Chinese room argument from chapter 7 ("Grounding"), where a person is stuck in a Chinese room, not speaking a word of Chinese, and receiving Chinese characters that he translates into other Chinese characters. Others have made the analogy of somebody landing in a foreign country where she doesn't speak the language. She is lost and is certainly lost for words. All she has is a dictionary that describes the word of the foreign language she does not speak in the foreign words of the language she does not speak.

In the previous chapter, I offered a solution to this symbolic merry-go-round and argued that all one needs is enough language spoken in that country—for instance, a year's worth of newspapers written in the foreign language. All you need to do is count how often city names are mentioned together in the foreign language texts, and you would be able to make an estimate of the longitude and latitude of the cities in the foreign country. I illustrated this solution for different countries—at least the United States, China, the Middle East, and the fictional Middle Earth—for different languages and scripts—including English, Chinese, Arabic, and the Indus script. Basically, I offered a convenient computational linguistic GPS system to help you whenever you were lost in a foreign country with a foreign language you do not speak. With the frequency with which city names appear together in the newspaper corpus, you would be able to create a map of the country you do not know on the basis of the language you do not know!

But when you look at this solution a bit more, my computational linguistic GPS solution is no different than the Baron Munchausen bootstrapping (or pigtailing) solution. The solution I presented to get us out of the linguistic swamp is using the meaning of a city name by the meaning of other city names, which got their meaning from that city name. That is pretty much the way Baron Munchausen got himself out of the swamp! He pulled himself out of the swamp using his own bootstraps, just like I determined the geographical location of cities on the basis of the cities I tried to get the geographical locations from. That indeed is a symbolic merry-go-round! And it will make you dizzy!

What I have really shown in estimating the geographical locations of cities on the basis of city names is that we can predict the *relative* distances between cities on the basis of language. But we are unable to tell what north, south, west, and east are. Like Baron Munchausen, what we need is some solid ground under our feet, some grounding. So let's go back to those geographical estimates from the previous chapter. As before, let's compute the semantic similarities between cities like New York, Philadelphia, Chicago, Orlando, Seattle, and San Francisco. After having obtained a matrix of similarity measures between the city names, we can draw a map of the United States, like the one below.

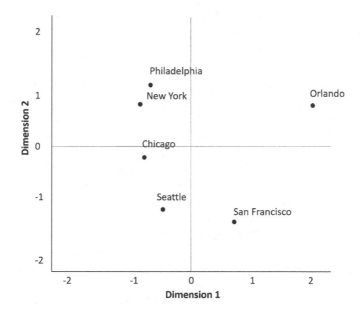

These are the relative positions between the cities in the United States. If you were to compute the distances between the city names presented on this map and the actual distances between the city names in the United States, you would find an almost-perfect correlation between the real distances and the similarity-based estimated distances.[4] But as you can also see from this figure, this is hardly a map of the United States. Contrary to an actual map, New York and Philadelphia are located in the northwest, Orlando in the northeast, and Seattle in the southwest. Any high school student placing the cities on a map like this would fail the geography test, and would fail it badly. There is no real map of the United States, one might conclude. There is no "longitude" and "latitude," and there is thus no geographical meaning coming from distributional semantics. What is needed to get out of the symbolic spaghetti is the grounding of the city names to their actual geographical locations.

This is an important point, because what is true for the meaning of geographical locations based on language I would argue is true for the meaning of all words in language. I have argued that we may be cognitively lazy, but we excel at finding patterns in data. Because language has encoded perceptual experiences, all comprehenders need to then do is extract meaning out of those patterns—patterns provided by the sound of a word, the order of word combinations, as well as the linguistic company a word keeps. But what is missing in my argument is an anchoring of each word in something in the outside world, some form of grounding. Something that gets it out of the Chinese Room, something that grounds symbols, something that gives us firm ground to get us out of the swamp. Only then we can speak of meaning rather than relative semantic relationships.

Let's have another look at the geographical map of the United States on the previous page. It may be true that the exact location of the cities may be unclear from the map. But the real question is whether *all* six cities need to be grounded in order to become geographically meaningful. Are all the words we keep in mind linked to their referents, or can we get away with a linguistic shortcut? Might it be the case that by knowing the longitude and latitude of some of the cities, we may be able to bootstrap all of them? Let's say that of the six cities presented in the map above, we only added extra information about one city and one city only. Let's say we happen to know the geographical location of Orlando, a city we know is located in the southeast of the United States. This minimal added information allows for the actual location of all the other cities to fall into place. After all, we now know we need to turn the map above 90 degrees, so that Orlando is positioned in the bottom right corner (the southeast), and suddenly it becomes clear that New York lies in the northeast, close to Philadelphia, and Seattle and San Francisco lie on the west coast. We bootstrap the geographical meaning of the six cities based on the grounding of one city to its actual location outside the world of language!

This offers an interesting insight in how we keep those words in mind. Even though the words become meaningful by referring to information outside the world of language, in the external world, it seems to be equally true that meaning comes from the linguistic company the words have. The adventure of Baron Munchausen pulling himself out of the swamp—and the analogy with a solution to bootstrapping the location of cities based on their linguistic company—may have seemed absurd initially, but perhaps it is not that ludicrous. Perhaps when we are lost in words, bootstrapping may in fact

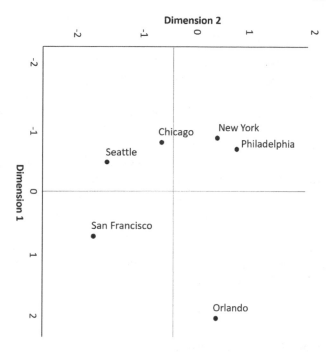

be part of the solution for the problem of how we keep the meaning of those words in mind. We can bootstrap the meaning of a maximum number of words through the grounding of a minimal number of words.

In the previous chapter, I referred to the famous adage by J. R. Firth: "You shall know a word by the company it keeps." I explained this adage the way Firth intended it: "You shall know the meaning of a word by the linguistic company it keeps." On the basis of the linguistic context of a word, we pretty much know what the word means. But by advocating Firth's adage, I have also exposed myself to criticism of being a Baron Munchausen. If the meaning of a word comes from the words in the context of that word, whose meaning comes from the context, there is an immediate need for symbol grounding. So for reasons of completeness, I would argue that Firth's adage may have to be clarified a little. You shall know the meaning of a word by the linguistic and perceptual company it keeps, not only by linguistic company, as was suggested in chapter 7 ("Grounding"), but also by some (and perhaps minimal) perceptual company.[5] Let me explain by introducing you to the world of semiotics and, specifically, to the world of the American philosopher Charles Sanders Peirce.

SIGNS

Signs and sign-using behavior are studied by the field of semiotics. The term *semiotics* comes from the word *semeion* (or rather σημεῖον in ancient Greek) and means "sign." The study of sign-using behavior, because that's what communication ultimately is, can be traced back to Aristotle and Plato. At the start of chapter 10 ("Sound"), I already introduced you to semiotics in the *Cratylus* dialogue between Hermogenes and Socrates, on the relationship between names and their meaning. Do names have an intrinsic relationship with their meaning, or are they arbitrarily determined? This discussion has turned out to be one of the most fundamental questions in semiotics, and is related to the fundamental question in this book on how we keep those words in mind.

In the early part of the nineteenth century, semiotics became increasingly popular, with philosophers like John Locke and David Hume considering how the human mind uses signs to convey meaning to others.[6] Toward the end of that century, two other philosophers worked on theories of the sign, each one at a different side of the Big Pond—one in France and the other in the United States. Their names were Ferdinand de Saussure and Charles Sanders Peirce. They both turned out to play a pivotal role in semiotics, as well as in linguistics, philosophy, anthropology, and in fact all fields affiliated to the cognitive sciences.

On one side of the ocean, Ferdinand de Saussure, the linguist whom we already met in chapter 10, proposed that a sign consists of two parts: the signifier and the signified, or the (spoken) word and the actual object (the signified) that the signifier refers to.[7] For de Saussure the sign consisted of a dyadic relationship between the signifier and the signified, and that relationship—as we have seen—is arbitrary in nature. There is nothing in the signifier that reveals the nature of the signified, other than an arbitrary relationship built by convention.

Around the same time, Charles Sanders Peirce, on the other side of the ocean, proposed his own semiotic theory in the United States. The *Collected Papers of Charles Sanders Peirce* now encompasses eight heavy volumes, with over 5,500 pages of writings.[8] Let me focus on some of the most important distinctions made by Peirce and not dive into eight-volume discussions.[9]

Contrary to de Saussure, for Peirce the sign was not the smallest unit of meaning. Instead Peirce viewed any thing or phenomenon, regardless of its complexity, as a sign from the moment it entered into a process of being attributed meaning. And contrary to de Saussure, for Peirce, the sign consists not of two parts, but of three parts. Peirce distinguished the way of representing, what the sign stands for, and the sense made of the sign.[10] Put differently, the difference between de Saussure's dyadic theory of the sign and Peirce's triadic theory of the sign is the difference between what is outside the mind of the comprehender and inside the mind of the comprehender.

Peirce is most well-known for the differences in relation between the sign and what it represents. That relation, according to Peirce, can be based on similarity, on contiguity, and on convention, on an iconic, indexical, and symbolic relation. They make signs icons, indices, and symbols. This distinction helps us appreciate the relation between the word, the mental representation, and the referent in the outside world, but also how we understand the meaning of a word by the linguistic company and perceptual company it keeps.

An icon stands for something else because of the similarity between the sign and the representation. A picture of my wife represents my wife. There is no doubt that what you see is her. Similarly, a self-portrait of Van Gogh represents Van Gogh. Here, too, there is no doubt what the sign represents, because the similarity determines the iconic relationship between the picture and who is in the picture. But there are also signs that have a different way of denoting their object. Take, for instance, my footprint. The footprint does not look like my foot, or anybody else's foot. But there is an indirect relationship between my foot and my footprint. This relationship is indexical, and footprints are an example of an index. An index stands for something else not because of its similarity but because of the spatiotemporal relationship the sign has with what it represents. A footprint does not look like my foot, but because of the contiguity between my foot and the footprint, the footprint has an indexical relation with my foot.

Similarly, smoke is an index of fire. Smoke does not look like fire, but if there is smoke, there is likely fire. Not always—there could be a smoke machine creating smoke on the dance floor of your favorite club. And the print may have come from something other than my foot. But if smoke and fire (or footprint and foot) are shared in time and space, they become related, indexically.

In addition to icon and index, Peirce introduced symbols. Symbolic relationships exist not on the basis of resemblance or on the basis of contiguity, but on the basis of convention. As a society, we have agreed on a symbolic relationship. Take, for instance, a wedding ring. A wedding ring does not look like marriage. It does not have a contiguity relationship with marriage. Instead, as a society we have agreed that wearing a ring symbolizes marriage. The symbol of marriage could have been a lot of other things—a beard on husbands, as in the Amish community, or a cosmetic powder on the forehead on Hindu wives. In fact, we find many symbols in religion. We consider something holy because we as a (religious) group have agreed that something is holy.

A distinction similar to Peirce's between icons, indices, and symbols can already be found in British philosopher David Hume's *Treatise of Human Nature* (1739–1740). In *Book 1, On Understanding*, Hume distinguishes three principles of association, one of *resemblance*,[11] one of *contiguity*, and one of *cause and effect*. In the principle of resemblance, the picture of my wife would lead me to think of my wife because of the obvious similarity, just like in Peirce's icons. In the principle of contiguity, the picture of my wife would lead me to think of my son and daughter because of the spatiotemporal relationship they have, just like Peirce's index. And in cause and effect, the thought of the scar on my leg leads me to think of the motorcycle accident I had a while back.[12]

We can also find Peirce's distinction between icons, indices, and symbols in language. Onomatopoeias like *woof-woof* and *cock-a-doodle-doo* sound like what they represent, the actual sound of a dog or rooster. There is little confusion when you hear *woof-woof* that it represents the sound of a dog—I guess otherwise it would not qualify as an onomatopoeia, for English at least. The sound of the onomatopoeia sounds like the sound of the animal. There may be differences across languages, as we have seen earlier, but overall no comprehender would confuse the word *cock-a-doodle-doo* with the sound of a dog, or *woof-woof* with the sound of a rooster, whereas the word *dog* can mean different things in one language, say English, and *rooster* can mean different things in different languages.[13]

Language also has indices, the signs that get meaning depending on their spatiotemporal context. Personal pronouns are one such example. When my son yells to my daughter, "You did it!" and she yells, "No, you did it!" they refer to different references depending on the spatiotemporal context. For my son, *you* is my daughter, and for my daughter, *you* is my son (to which I often jokingly shout back, "No, *you* did it!"). And when I am addressing you in this book, *I* and *you* represent "me" or "you," depending who says it. *You* can be you, but *you* can also be me. It just depends on the spatiotemporal context in which the pronoun is used. Yet another example of an index are terms like *here* and *there*, *now* and *then*, and *this* and *that*. It just depends what these words mean. What is *here* for me *now* is *there* for you *then*. Indeed, language seems to be heavily dependent on the spatiotemporal context in which it is used.

And in addition to the icons and indices in language, language also has Peirce's third category of a sign: symbols. Language has many symbols. Language is generally considered to be the prime example of symbolic communication. Think about any word that has an arbitrary relation between the sound of the word and its meaning.

Icons, indices, and symbols—that typology was not too bad. So we have a sign that consists of a signifier, a reference, and a mental representation, and the meaning of the sign can be based on similarity, contiguity, or convention. We can find many examples of signs—from pictures to footprints to wedding rings—also in the linguistic world—from onomatopoeia to pronouns to most lexical and grammatical items.

IT'S ALL RELATIVE

In practice, however, the distinction between icon, index, and symbol turns out to be not so clear-cut at all. It may be the case that a picture of my wife refers to my wife because the person depicted in the picture simply looks like my wife. But what do we do with the self-portrait of Picasso? Perhaps in the early self-portraits—those of 1896 and 1900—I would be able to recognize Picasso himself because of the similarities in the portrait and the actual person. But for the primitive aesthetic and the quirky Cubist style self-portraits of 1972, there is no similarity between the portrait and Picasso. We can just make sense of a human, but it is simply because we have agreed that the portrait of Picasso is Picasso himself that we can call it a self-portrait. So really it seems a symbolic relation between the 1972 self-portrait and the painter.

For the temporospatial relationship that constitutes an index, things are not much different. Imagine a time when there were no smoke machines. Imagine we lived 1 million years ago as the Homo erectus.[14] We had just invented fire. We are still 1 million years away from smoke machines, and we have never seen anything remotely looking like smoke (there is no mist; there is no breath vapor), until we discovered fire. Now, in our world, each time we see smoke there is fire. Smoke without fire does not exist. Would the indexical relationship between smoke and fire now not be an iconic relationship? Smoke now resembles fire?

For symbols, things are not too easy either. Let's look at a twenty-dollar bill. The twenty-dollar bill symbolizes the value of twenty dollars' worth. The twenty-dollar bill itself is only worth 10.5 cents if you consider the entire production process, but in our society we have agreed that it is worth more. It's simply convention that a twenty-dollar bill represents twenty dollars in value. Now let's consider the early days of money, when a golden coin held its actual value in gold.[15] Does that mean that money has become more symbolic, despite the fact that both their values have been agreed to be the same? Should we then consider careful analysis before we can call a symbol symbolic?

In other words, the questions about the extent to which the relation between sign and object are iconic, indexical, or symbolic can even be projected on icons, indices, and symbols themselves. An image of a chair is typically classified as having an iconic relationship with the object it represents. The icon shows physical similarities with its object. But the same picture can also be more of an index, for instance, when it derives its meaning from being combined with a table. And finally, the picture can become more symbolic, as in the case of a picture of an artful interpretation of the concept of chair. I am not arguing here that pictures are indices or symbols, but that the degree of iconic, indexical, and symbolic relationships within a sign can vary, in nonlinguistic signs as well as linguistic ones.

Similarly, nonverbal communication devices such as gestures can be iconic, indexical, and symbolic in nature.[16] Gestures can be very iconic when they physically resemble the object, such as when the tips of two index fingers touch together to depict the roof of a house. They can also be indexical, as is the case with a pointing gesture using an index finger, where the deictic gesture can only be understood in context (the spatial and temporal contiguity with what it refers to). Finally, gestures can be symbolic, as with thumbs up, which commonly signifies a job well done, but also signifies to fellow divers "I am going up," for Germans and Hungarians the number 1, and for Japanese the number 5.

For verbal communication, things are not much different. Words are often classified as symbolic, because of their conventional relationship between form and meaning. But onomatopoeias tend to show a close physical similarity between the sound and what it means. Deictic words are not so much symbolic, but indexical and should be considered in their spatiotemporal context to be meaningful. Words become meaningful through indexical relations (temporal or spatial contiguity), with their statistical regularity determining the extent to which a symbol is conventional or becomes habitual. And that turns out to be important for keeping words in mind.

SIGN INTERDEPENDENCY

Imagine a toddler who is exploring the world around her. She has just learned how to stand on her feet and tries to understand her surroundings. There are so many things to see and learn. How would she be able to understand what her surroundings mean? How would she know to be careful touching a white stove, whereas a white refrigerator would be no cause for harm? How would she make sense of the world?

If there is one thing I, her *father*, would recommend, it is just to wait and see how the process of understanding the world automatically evolves over time. Really, nothing needs to be done. Every child has the remarkable skill to adapt to their environment and to be able to learn. If there is one thing I, the *scientist*, would recommend for her to do, it would be to read up on David Hume's *Treatise of Human Nature,* specifically *Book 1, On Understanding.* Hume's Principle of Contiguity would help the young child with understanding the world around her.

But given that two-year-olds are unable to read yet, and certainly do not want to be read Hume as a bedtime story, I would recommend that the toddler follow Waldo Tobler's formulation of Hume's Principle of Contiguity: "Everything is related to everything else, but near things are more related than distant things" (the quote from the start of this chapter). And that might remind you of Firth's adage in the previous chapter. Paraphrasing Firth: you shall know the meaning of the persons, things, and events around you from the company they keep. Advising a child to follow up on a principle proposed by Hume may sound bizarre, and I would agree. But Hume's Principle of Contiguity, Firth's adage, and Peirce's notion of indexical relationships turn out to be very informative in understanding how we keep track of the world around us. Let me try to explain.

Imagine the world of the toddler consists of only four objects: what we know as a dog, a cow, a pig, and a cat.[17] How would a toddler make sense of the fact that in the four objects she sees dogs and cats cluster, and cows and pigs cluster? The answer lies in the Principle of Contiguity: everything is related to everything else, but near things are more related than distant things. It is more likely the toddler sees a dog and cat nearer to one another, or in one another's company, than that they see the dog with the cow, or the pig with the cat. It is certainly possible that the toddler sees a cat with a cow, but more likely that she sees a cat with a dog. And if you were to find the clustering on the basis of the objects themselves too simplistic, the Principle of Contiguity can also be applied to the features of each of these animals. The features of dogs—being small, living in a house, and being accompanied by people, to name only a few—have more in common with the features of cats than with the features of cows—the latter being large, living on a farm, and being accompanied by more from the same species, to name only a few. This is similar to what I discussed in chapter 6 ("Network"). So all the objects the toddler sees are related, but the toddler is able to make stronger associations between some objects on the basis of the spatiotemporal relationships: contiguity, as Hume would call it, or indexical relationships between icons, as Peirce would call them.

Let's consider how the toddler—now about twelve months old—learns how to use language. How would she learn that she is dealing with the words *cat, dog, cow,* and *pig*? One answer to this question is simple: Any parent recalls a situation during which they told their toddler what the word for a particular animal was. Imagine the parent and child visiting a petting zoo. The parent tells the young toddler pointing to a pig, "This is a piggy." The word the child hears is directly grounded to the animal in front of her. This seems to be the most straightforward way of learning the meaning of a word: the pointing at a referent in the real world with the vocalization of the name of that referent. Chapter 7 ("Grounding") plays out when the grounding of the word to an object in the world is a fact.

And the learning will really take off when the child not only is shown the relation between the word and its referent but also carefully starts to show signs she has mastered the relationship. When she utters the word *piggy* herself in the petting zoo, the parents are overwhelmed with joy, so the connection between the word and the meaning strengthens through the positive reinforcement of the vocalization. It is chapter 4 ("Training") that plays out in front of the parent and child right there in the petting zoo.

In the relationship between the word and the referent, or the grounding of the name of the animal to the animal itself, the Principle of Contiguity actually plays a role. It is far less likely that the words *dog* and *cat* are expressed in the vicinity of the pig (or cow) than the word *cow* (or *pig*) is. The four words are all related to the four objects, but the words expressed in the vicinity of objects are more related to these objects than distant objects.

Now even though linking the word to the animal in the presence of a child seems to be a straightforward way of understanding how children learn the meaning of words, it is too simplistic, as Paul Bloom explains from the very start in his book *How Children Learn the Meaning of Words*.[18] In fact, there are several challenges with this way of learning the meaning of a word. First of all, how many times does the parent need to point at the piggy and say "this is a piggy" in order for the child to remember the mapping of the word and the animal? Just once? Now undoubtedly the child is eager to learn the meaning of the word *piggy*, but if I point out to you that a *raphus cucullatus* is the name for a dodo, a *sus scrofa domesticus* the name for a domestic pig, and a *gallus gallus domesticus* the name for a chicken, would you instantly remember the name for a dodo, pig, and chicken? One-shot learning is difficult for an adult, let alone for a young toddler who does not have word learning as the first item on her bucket list. And it requires quite some cognitive effort. One needs to carefully pay attention to the word and to the object. Making the wrong connection could easily make a "pig" a dog, cat, or cow. Word learning on the basis of literally pointing at a word's meaning is rather expensive: each word needs to be matched with each object the word refers to, preferably with some reinforcement that makes it clear that the matching has been established ("Good job! That's a piggy!"), like the gavagai in chapter 1 ("Words").

However, studies have shown that we don't need continuous feedback to still learn. In a word-learning experiment, Patrick Jeuniaux, Rick Dale, and I presented participants with a two-word utterance like "pima sogi" and four objects that differed in shape (circle or star), size (small, medium, or large), and color (white, grey, or black).[19] It was the participants' task to point out which of the objects was "pima sogi." Participants were supposed to learn the meaning of six words. They got over a hundred trials with combinations of objects being presented to them.

In one condition participants received feedback on the choice they made, being told whether they were correct or not. But we also used a no-feedback condition. So all participants saw was a nonsense word combination and a bunch of shapes that differed in size and color, and they were asked which object combination represented the nonsense word combination. Perhaps not very surprisingly, just like the toddler learning the word *pig*, participants learned the word "pima sogi" when told what the word referred to, at a rate almost five times higher than when just randomly choosing the object. But when participants were not told what the words—such as "pima sogi"— meant, they only needed to be presented with the words and objects several times to establish the link. With no feedback, they may have done worse than with feedback, but they did perform twice as well as the success rate using only chance. Just being exposed to these objects and names multiple times was enough to make the connection![20]

So how were participants able to map the meaning (shape and color) to a word without getting feedback? Imagine you were a participant in our experiment. What you do is identify the differences between the shapes. You see a white circle. But that circle could indicate you need to focus on a circular object (rather than a star-shaped object), or the color white (rather than grey or black), or the medium size (rather than the smaller or larger size). However, the only way to find out what to focus on is to see the white circle in context. Only then does it become clear what the object is really about. Basically, you need to realize that everything is related to everything else, but near things are more related than distant things, and you have not quite figured out what things are near and what things are distant, until you have actually encountered them—the Principle of Contiguity.

Our "pima sogi" experiment shows that we are making associations and learn the meaning of an object through multiple exposures, in spite of the uncertainty about the meaning of a word on each individual exposure. On each exposure, we don't know which meaning is the right one, but by encountering a word in a number of different situations, the number of possible meanings over time is reduced. The advantage of this way of learning is that the right mapping does not have to be pointed out (as in the case of linking the word *piggy* to its referent), and the learning of the word's meaning does not happen in a single exposure but happens over time, with the mapping being less cognitively demanding—and humans like less cognitively demanding, as we have seen. They like going for shortcuts.

This type of learning, in which the mapping between word and object evolves over time, has been called "cross-situational learning."[21] By keeping track of the frequency of the various possible mappings between a word and objects across situations, the language learner is able to map words to their references. Let me explain.

Imagine a toddler hears the word *dog* and sees the objects of—what we will ultimately learn to be—a dog, a cow, and a cat, as in the figure below. Initially, the toddler could identify the dog, the cow, and the cat as a *dog*. There are three candidates. However, upon hearing the word *dog* a second time, now being exposed to a dog, cat, and pig, the toddler can eliminate cow as a candidate. And because pig was not present in the first exposure, the pig is not a candidate, leaving two possibilities—a dog and a cat—as the meaning for *dog*. By now being presented with a dog, cow, and rooster, we can also eliminate the cat as a candidate, making the link between *dog* and the dog.[22]

The process of finding the link between word and object seems to be one of elimination. It is considerably cheaper than the one-shot learning. In the figure above there are only three exposures, but imagine a multitude of exposures. Slowly but surely the right referent emerges, as if chapter 6 ("Network") is playing out right in front of us, like a neural network. Now, statistical learning across situations is error prone. Perhaps *dog* means something entirely different. But this cross-situational learning provides you with a good

Word : "dog"

Target:

Exposure	Context			Candidates		
1						
2						
3						

heuristic, a useful rule-of-thumb, to get you in the ballpark of meaning. How does it do that? The answer is no longer surprising: on the basis of the adage that everything is related to everything else, but near things are more related than distant things—on the basis of the Principle of Contiguity.

Now we have established associations made between referents on the basis of their contiguity, a grounding of words to their referent, as well as cross-situational learning where different relations between words and referents are made, reducing cognitive load and emphasizing distributional semantics. And that leaves us with one piece of the puzzle missing, the piece that was central to the last chapter. Remember Firth's "You know the meaning of the word by the company it keeps"? In the previous chapter, we saw that words also get meaning through the relationships they have with themselves. There are semantic relations between *dog*, *cat*, *cow*, and *pig*; some of them we may consider to be stronger than others. If we plot the semantic relations between the words *dog*, *cat*, *cow*, and *pig* in the same way we did in the previous chapter, the relations between *dog* and *cat* (and between *cow* and *pig*) are considerably stronger than the relations between *dog* and *cow* (or between *cat* and *pig*). All words are related to all other words, but those words that are placed near to one another are more related than words that are further apart—chapter 12 ("Company") in action.

What we have seen so far is that based on the Principle of Contiguity, we can cluster objects in the real world, because these objects are likely near to one another in the real world. We have also seen that words can be grounded to the real world, because when words are expressed, they are likely to be expressed in the vicinity of the objects. And we have seen that in the case of multiple objects being a candidate for a word, the word being presented in a different situation disambiguates the meaning of the word. And finally we have seen that words in the contiguity of other words more likely have a relationship in meaning. Now this system of dependency relations between words and objects has a number of advantages. If a word is not expressed in the vicinity of the object, its meaning might rely more on the relationships with other words than on the relationships with other objects. At the same time, if a word is mentioned out of context, the grounding of the word in the external world allows for the word to become meaningful nonetheless. The interdependency of the linguistic symbols thus has distributed meaning.

Remember the example at the start of chapter 12 ("Company") of me being chased by a frurp on my way to campus? Just like the word *pig* was unknown to the child, the word *frurp* is unknown to you (or at least it was until I told you the story of being chased by a frurp). The frurp becomes meaningful by linking the word to its object in the external world. By grounding it. But without explicitly pointing out how to ground a word, we can make

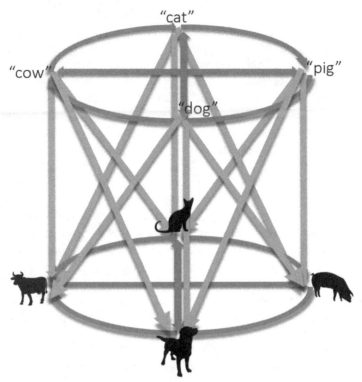

Cross-situational learning between words, concepts, and words and concepts.

estimated guesses on the number of times you see a frurp associated with other objects—both the object frurp with other objects, as well as the word *frurp* with other words, words that can be grounded themselves. Moreover, the grounding can take place through linking the words to their referents, as well as through elimination: seeing the frurp in certain contexts but not in others helps you to fine-tune the meaning of *frurp*.

This system of interdependencies turns out to be quite powerful. We, language users, do not have to depend on one strategy—linking the word to the object, associating words, associating objects, and linking words to other objects—but rely on emerging meanings through all strategies available to us. And all available strategies have one thing in common: the Principle of Contiguity.

But the example of frurps—as with the example of dogs and pigs—assumes that words are the same and that, through using different strategies, we can bootstrap their meaning. Now remember the conclusion we drew earlier that words have different degrees of iconic, indexical, or symbolic relationship with their referents? In explaining the distinction between icons, indices, and symbols, we singled out onomatopoeias for icons, pronouns for indices, and most other words for symbols because of their arbitrary relationship with their referents. But I concluded it is a matter of degree.

If we now look at the language system at large, an interesting picture unfolds. In chapter 10 ("Sound"), we saw that most words are arbitrary. The evidence is that they differ across languages, despite the fact that their meaning is the same. But we also saw that some words share systematicity in meaning. Their similarities in sound help us identify whether they are nouns or verbs or whether their meaning is more positive or negative. And we saw examples of sound symbolism, such as *bang*, *clang*, and *slide*. If all words were the same in nature, we would have strategies to extract their meaning, through different associations. But the words themselves help us in this process. The *bang*s, *clang*s, and *slide*s help us ground; the systematicity in the sound of the word, as for nounness and verbness and for valence, helps us determine relationships between words, and the arbitrary relationships between words help us to rely on grounding of objects and linking to other words. And they do not do this exclusively.

We keep those words in mind by linking the word to its referent in the outside world or the perceptual simulation of that referent in our minds, but we can also extract its meaning from the linguistic context. We know the meaning of a word by the linguistic and perceptual company it keeps. The extent to which we rely on the linguistic or the perceptual company varies depending on the stimulus, the cognitive task, and the speed. For instance, it depends on whether we read or hear words or see pictures. If we extract meaning out of words, then we seem to rely more on the linguistic context, but not entirely, as we also rely somewhat on perceptual information. Similarly, when we see a picture, we tend to rely more on perceptual information, but not entirely, as we also rely somewhat on linguistic information.[23]

Whether we rely more on the linguistic or perceptual company a word keeps also depends on whether we can get away with a good-enough understanding, or whether we need to go in further detail. When we are rushed, we tend to rely on linguistic company more than perceptual company. But when we have the time, or when we are asked to think hard about the meaning of a word, we rely more on perceptual context than on linguistic context. In keeping those words in mind, it seems to be a trade-off between thinking fast and slow.[24]

CAROUSEL OF INTERDEPENDENCIES

What is described above is a carousel of relations of words and referents that are all interrelated. Words are mutually dependent on one another, as the previous chapter has shown; they are mutually dependent on their referents, as symbol grounding and generating of affordances has shown; and the referents are dependent on one another, as the example of situational learning has shown. The carousel of interdependencies presented here is based on knowing the meaning of words by the linguistic and perceptual company they keep. The relations of this carousel are all indexical relations, based on contiguity. This carousel of relations between words and their referents offers a new perspective on the four explanations of how we keep those words in mind, discussed in the early chapters of this book.

In *The Symbolic Species*, Terrence Deacon points out that the explanation for our ability to learn language should not be sought in the mind of the speaker—as chapter 5 ("Instinct") described—or in the mind of parents or teachers—as chapter 4 ("Training") described—but outside the mind of the language user, parents, or teachers, in the language system itself. That idea is a powerful one, but it becomes even more powerful if the language system is built onto the perceptual system. That is, if we consider words and word combinations not as symbols, as Peirce argued—with arbitrary relations between words and meaning, and with no interdependencies between the words themselves—but as a language system that has evolved over time to encode the perceptual information out there in the world. This language system has weak associations between the sound of a word and its meaning, weak associations between the order in which words are presented and their meanings, and weak associations between the linguistic contexts in which these words operate and their meanings. Deacon highlights the associations between words, between referents, and between words and referents. But if language were to create meaning because of a mapping of the language system onto the perceptual system, the patterns Deacon observes become stronger, and the shortcut language users can take easier.

So let's revisit the explanations given in chapters 4 ("Training"), 5 ("Instinct"), 6 ("Network"), and 7 ("Grounding") in reverse order. Let's first return to symbol grounding (chapter 7). When processing language, grounding is essential. When we read (or listen to) words, we can generate pictures, as well as auditory, olfactory, gustatory, and tactile experiences we have with the referents of the words we process. Cognition is, to a large extent, embodied. It is unlikely the linguistic system is completely isolated from a perceptual system. Frankly, I do not know any researcher who would argue that the systems are fully separated, even though my enthusiasm about the opportunities of a computational model of mind may have given the wrong impression. I do know many researchers, however, who wonder whether every word in every circumstance always needs to be grounded. The carousel of interdependencies suggests that words *can* be grounded but do not always and continuously *have to be* grounded, as they can also rely on the contiguity of other words. With very little grounding, the carousel of interdependencies can bootstrap the meaning of words through the interdependencies these words have with each other.

The advantage of the language system is that it is mapped onto the perceptual system. When I formulate an utterance as a speaker, I can translate prelinguistic conceptual knowledge into linguistic conceptualizations. I translate perceptual experiences into language.[25] As a function of language use, perceptual information becomes encoded in language. Just as in producing language, in comprehending language I get reminded of the language structures and the link to perceptual information. The associations between words, between perceptual representations, and between words and perceptual representations get strengthened the more they are used.

And the idea that if words, perceptions, and words and perceptions are fired together, then they are wired together[26] brings us to chapter 6 ("Network"). The carousel of interdependencies requires some kind of network—ideally, a network that does justice to the many interdependencies in the carousel, a network where meaning is distributed over multiple links rather than fixed, a network in which meaning can spread between words, between referents, and between words and their referents. Something like an artificial neural network, a network in which interdependencies are weak, but the sum of weak interdependencies makes the network robust and powerful. If the linguistic context does not provide the interdependencies that are needed, language users can more rely on the perceptual information. But if shortcuts need to be made, language users can stick to the linguistic interdependencies.

In the experiments described in chapter 12 ("Company"), we saw that linguistic interdependencies, the language statistics, play a role in processing both words and pictures, just like perceptual simulations play a role in processing words and pictures. So whether the linguistic or perceptual interdependencies that dominate are fixed depends on the strength of the relations that have been formed in the network, and because information is distributed, it depends how "the water flows through the network," to use the metaphor I used earlier.

I hesitate to use the words "linguistic and perceptual systems." Many giants whose shoulders I try to balance on have similar hesitations about the introduction of "systems" and introduce them but only metaphorically speaking.[27] "Linguistic and perceptual systems" suggests that there is a module in the human brain that is linguistic and that there is a module that is perceptual (or perhaps even one that is reserved for individual modalities).

No such modules exist. Instead, there is a network of relations where there are stronger activation patterns in some parts than others under particular circumstances. It is more likely there is a continuity of mind, with a continuous mental flow between fuzzy interdependencies.[28] The mind is more like a spiral wishing-well coin collector that you sometimes see in shopping malls and zoos. You place a coin on its side, and it starts to spiral, first in large circles slowly, and then in smaller circles, first slow, then faster and faster, as if it gets attracted to a point in space—the hole at the bottom of the spiral. Now, individual coins hardly ever follow the exact trajectory. They move to a situation where, from a distance, they settle at the end of the spiral, not static but dynamic, not specific but approximate. They are patterns of activation.

In artificial neural networks, patterns of activation are learned from data, no matter how arbitrary the data is. Artificial networks are as good at training noisy data as they are at structured data. Whether the input is 101011000 or 10101001 does not matter to them, and neither do they care whether the output is 101 or 010. Intuitively, however, one would expect that if there were something nonarbitrary in the configuration of input units, the network would learn more efficiently, faster and better. It would be easier to form pathways in the network if there were structure in the input data than when the network needs to form pathways on input units that lack structure. Recent findings in the research on artificial neural networks show that these networks tend to prioritize learning simple patterns first. Structured data thus has benefits over unstructured data.[29] It is fortunate for the language user that the input from language system to the output of meaning is not an arbitrary configuration but has patterns at the sound, word-order, and context levels!

Learning patterns in data requires at least two components. One is a knack for identifying these patterns. If there is no mechanism that allows for discovering the patterns in data, there is no learning of the patterns in the data. A second component is the presence of actual patterns in the data. That may seem obvious, but whereas the first component is readily assumed, the second is not. Let's first look at the knack for finding patterns. We also know that humans are unique in their pattern-seeking skills, as described in chapter 9 ("Patterns"). We also know that humans are unique in their (human) language capabilities, as described in chapter 5 ("Instinct"). Maybe, just maybe, the two are related. Perhaps we are such good pattern sniffers because we are continuously confronted with (linguistic) data that includes patterns, and we are so good at language because we are so good at finding patterns. There are a lot of regularities in language and an instinct picks up on those regularities.[30] If you have heard about *one dog and two dogs* and *one cat and two cats*, it is not too difficult to get from *one wug* to *two wugs*,[31] or to get from *today I talk* and *yesterday I talked* to *today I fralk* and *yesterday I fralked*.

But what about all that is irregular in language? How would we learn the determiners, the prepositions, the auxiliary verbs, the conjunctions, the pronouns, and the adverbs that are so irregular? These grammatical items are the glue that keep those other words in line! Well, I have mentioned that there are patterns in data, but I have not mentioned one of the biggest regularities in language, because it does not directly apply to the meaning of words, only indirectly. This regularity has been found across all languages across the world. It seems universal. It's the law. And it was popularized by George Kingsley Zipf, who the law was named after. Zipf's Law states that the most frequent word will occur approximately twice as often as the second most frequent word, three times as often as the third most frequent word, and so on.

Following from Zipf's Law, we also learn that 20 percent of the words in a language determine 80 percent of the language use. So if you want to learn a language, all you need to do is learn the words that make up the 20 percent most frequently used, and you pretty much sound like an avid language user, for 80 percent of it. If we look at English, the most frequently used words are *the, be, to, of, and, a, in, that, have, I, it, for, not, on, with, he,* and *as*—no meaningful words in sight, all grammatical items. For children (as well as for those learning English as a second language) these words also turn out to be the hardest to learn.

But language structure comes to the rescue! The irregular words, such as the grammatical items, can maintain their irregularity, because their irregularity is compensated for by their frequency. If we look at nouns (the first one we find is the fifty-fifth most frequently used word), then we find *time, person, year, way, day, thing, man, world,* and *life*—all pretty meaningless concepts. I mean, it is hard to describe what time is, or what a person is, or what a year is. It's not that difficult to describe what a dog or a cat is. But the fact that the words themselves are rather meaningless is compensated for by the fact that they occur very frequently. Those frequently used words can bootstrap their meaning from the other less frequently used words that are more meaningful.

Zipf's Law postulates something else, something that is important when considering how we keep those words in mind. The relative frequency of a word is also related to the number of links the word has.[32] If a word has many links to other words, there is again an interdependency. "Meaning" of the frequently used word can be borrowed from the many less frequently used words it is connected to, whereas the less frequently used words are structured by the very frequently used word. Its high frequency secures the pattern. We also see this in the language-learning child. Initially, the child relies heavily on iconic words that have a strong sound-meaning connection, and hears and uses these words frequently. Over time, the support coming from iconicity is less needed, and more arbitrariness seeps into the system.[33]

So frequency matters. That brings us to chapter 4 ("Training"), where the explanation for how we keep those words in mind is *training*. Our pattern-seeking ability gets better and better the more linguistic data we are confronted with. Once we have identified patterns, we can use these patterns, as well as variations on the patterns. And as long as there are interdependencies between words, between referents, and between words and their referents, we can be quite creative in our variations. The more structured data we are exposed to, the better we are able to identify the patterns in the data (and the interdependencies in the carousel). Learning to find these patterns requires training. The more practice, the better the performance. And the more frequent the patterns, the more recent the patterns, and the more similar the context, the better the learning.[34]

THUS

Let's return to the very question asked in the book: how do we keep those words in mind? How can we explain the fact that humans have no problem keeping more than sixty thousand words in mind and don't struggle with some 10 sextillion sentences they may read or hear? How do humans so rapidly assign meaning to sequences of sounds or letters? Well, we need some grounding so those meaningless sequences of sounds and letters make sense. We need to make references between words and the outside world, escaping from a symbolic merry-go-round. We also need some network architecture that provides distributed representations—distributed pieces of words and distributed pieces of the outside world and particularly the connection between them, preferably distributed connections so that if no perfect connection can be made, the network can happily reconstruct a full picture from the fragments. We need a brain, preferably specialized parts of the brain that are equipped to deal with linguistic systems, a neurological machinery that allows for learning language quickly and efficiently, and some training so that the linguistic units and their referents flow through the network repetitively and the connections in the network become stronger and stronger over time. These are four of the explanations for how we keep those words in mind.

But these four explanations do not immediately take into account the fact that our mind is flat. We commonly do not process information deeply, but we instead go for shallow solutions. Rather than full-fledged, complete processing, we go for quick-and-dirty processing. If it is good enough, it is good enough for us.[35] The consequence is that we often do not excel in deep solutions to cognitive tasks. We come up with quick solutions that do the job—not much more and not much less. We are convinced that we are deep thinkers, that our perception is almost flawless, that we have magnificent memory skills, and that we are able to process information better than any other species is able to. The past few decades of research in animal cognition have shown that we have another quality: hubris. In many tasks, we do not perform better than other species; in fact, sometimes we do not perform well at all.

So how then do we keep those words in mind? Is it training, instinct, network, or grounding? The answer also needs to be sought outside the training, instinct, network, and grounding of the language user, in language itself. We keep those words in mind by using language. With the examples from predicting meaning based on a word's sound, based on word order, and based on the company words keep, I have tried to show that language is not some disorganized stuff that language-learning children happen to cram into their minds. On the contrary, language has evolved over time into a convenient communicative tool. And as it goes with evolution, the fittest linguistic elements adapted and survived. The language system evolved in a mapping onto the perceptual world around us. These patterns provide ideal cognitive shortcuts for language users, when acquiring language, when producing language, and when comprehending language. The answer to the question of how we keep those words in mind is provided in the subtitle of this book: *language creates meaning.*

And that brings us back to the start of this book, where in chapter 1 ("Words") I referred to Terrence Deacon's *Symbolic Species* and in the prologue I described the parable of the ants on the beach in Herb Simon's *The Sciences of the Artificial.* At the end of this chapter, I will again refer to Deacon and Simon, to keep their words in mind while paraphrasing them.

> In addition to training, instinct, network, and grounding, there is another possibility that has been almost overlooked. Training, instinct, network, and grounding offer an answer that inverts cause and effect. These explanations assert that the support for language acquisition must originate from *inside* the brain, on the unstated assumption that there is no other possible source. But there is another alternative: the extra support for language learning is vested neither in the brain of the child nor in the brains of the parents or teacher, but *outside* brains in language itself, in the patterns in language that language users use as a cognitive shortcut.[36]

> A human, viewed as a language-using system, is quite simple. The apparent complexity of his language skills is essentially a reflection of the complexity of the language system in which humans find themselves.[37]

• 14 •

Avenues

Most of the fundamental ideas of science are essentially simple, and may, as a rule, be expressed in a language comprehensible to everyone.

—Albert Einstein and Leopold Infeld[1]

"So what?" Whenever I am at a party and somebody politely asks me what I do for a living, I excitedly tell them that I am scientist. Throughout the years, I have learned that following up that answer with a lecture about my research does not result in me being the popular guy at parties, so often I leave it at that succinct answer. When the follow-up question comes—"What do you teach?"—and I answer, "Cognitive psychology and artificial intelligence," it often yields humorous suppositions that I am likely able to read the mind of my conversational partner or at least rebuild his or her brain in a computer. If my conversational partner would like to know more, I enthusiastically tell them about my work (trying to keep it to a thirty-second elevator pitch out of fear this may be the last party I will ever be invited to). Often I sense a frown, a desperate attempt of my conversational partner to look interested, and a sense of "so what?" I don't know whether the "so what?" impression is my imagination or not, but the feeling does not escape that one wonders what the relevance is of the research I conduct.

Even if that feeling is only my imagination, scientists should keep trying to climb down from their ivory tower and explain in layman's terms what they are doing, why they are doing it, what the relevance of their research is, and how society can benefit from it. And climbing down from the ivory tower often turns out not to be that easy. Indeed, I often find it much easier to hide my message in scientific jargon than to explain what the societal impact of my research might be.

Explaining the relevance of scientific research has become more important than ever. Today we read or hear more and more often the view that science is just a matter of opinion.[2] The difference between writing something on Twitter or in a LinkedIn blog, according to that view, is pretty much the same as what is written in an academic journal, except for the unreadable academic jargon. Unless all other opinions are also based on empirical evidence and careful statistical analyses, and are painstakingly fact-checked, there may be pieces of truth in that view. But most opinions I know are not based on empirical evidence and are not scrutinized before they are expressed.

It may be worthwhile to explain the scrutinizing scientific process to demonstrate that science is *not* just a matter of opinion. Whenever an academic paper gets written and rewritten, after several versions the researcher might be courageous enough to submit the paper to a journal. The editor of the journal may flat-out reject the paper, often arguing that the paper is undoubtedly interesting but does not quite fit the scope of the journal. But if you are lucky, the paper you spent so much blood, sweat, and tears on might get sent out to reviewers, typically three of them. These experts in that field of research write extensive reviews in which they readily point out all the weaknesses you had not considered when you initially wrote the paper. In addition to their extensive reviews, the reviewers cast their vote. And you are happy if the outcome you receive in an action letter is a "Reject and Resubmit." It means that the paper needs to undergo a major revision, but then, if you are lucky, it might get published in the end. You carefully follow all the reviewers' suggestions in a revision of the paper, and resubmit, after which it gets sent out to the same or different reviewers. The outcome of that process may be a simple "Reject," and you are back to square one. Thanks, but no thanks. But the outcome may also ultimately lead to the process of the paper being accepted, after another round of revisions. Meanwhile, my Tweets and LinkedIn blogs—never scrutinized by my peers—have already gotten old and forgotten.

SOMETHING BASIC

When I conduct an experiment, build a computational model, or run a simulation, it is electrifying when the results come in—not always gratifying, but always electrifying. Basic research, also called *fundamental* or *pure* research, is important. Not led by the flavor of the day or the hype of tomorrow, dedicated scientists work on a problem for years, hoping to find a breakthrough to further expand the knowledge in a particular area. The solution of the problem may not have an immediate use or application.

Much of the work I do can be classified under basic research. It aims at improving scientific theories. Much of it does not generate findings that have immediate applications on a practical level. For instance, if I show that words starting with an *n* or *m* tend to be associated with a negative valence in English but not in Chinese,[3] or that concepts high in the perceptual world linguistically precede those lower in the perceptual world,[4] that language statistics explain conceptual processing,[5] or that the map of Middle Earth can be created using the language of the *Lord of the Rings* trilogy,[6] it does not have an impact on society, one could argue.

However, I would argue that basic research *does* have societal impact in the long run. For me, the only difference between basic research and applied research is time. I have to admit that I generally do not know how much time, but many scientific discoveries result in the theories, methods, algorithms, and results that are used for further research and will ultimately be applied to a societal problem sometime. The same is true for the research that formed the foundation for this book, from the relation between the sound of the word and its meaning, to the order of words, to knowing the meaning of the word by the company it keeps.

Understanding how we keep those words in mind, how language creates meaning, may be categorized under basic research. That training, instinct, networks, and grounding are some but not all explanations for how we keep those words in mind is knowledge for knowledge's sake. That patterns in language are built onto perceptual information and provide useful cognitive shortcuts to language users may also be knowledge for knowledge's sake. There is no immediate application of answering how we keep those words in mind.

There is nothing wrong with knowledge for knowledge's sake. Our educational system is built on it. Many concepts, facts, and formulas we learn at school have no immediate application. And the same is true for many scientific findings. But I would argue that these scientists should try to climb down from their ivory tower and explain what the *potential* societal impact of their research could be. However, if I make that argument, I should at the very least climb down myself and explain what the societal impact of the current basic research is. I, at the very least, ought to put my money where my mouth is. What, then, are the societal impacts of language creating meaning?

UNDERSTANDING THE MIND

An easy answer to the question "What is the relevance of the research underlying this book?" is the insight in how the human mind works. That answer in itself would do for me, but perhaps it is still too much "ivory tower" for others. Let's dig a little deeper.

If we have a better understanding of how people acquire and process language, have an understanding of in which parts of the brain activation can be expected, it would help in understanding the consequences of a stroke and the rehabilitation of people who suffered a stroke.[7] If we have a better understanding of which words go together semantically, we might be able to identify specific problems in the semantic memory of patients. Others have shown how artificial neural networks can show neurogenerative diseases,[8] but with an understanding of how we keep those words in mind, and by being able to measure the semantic relations between words, we might be able to measure developments in the disease through the language spoken by the patients over time.

For instance, understanding how we keep those words in mind can lead to opportunities to understand how to read our minds. Imagine if computers were able to predict what you are thinking! If we know the semantic relationships between words, we might be able to do exactly that. Marcel Just and his team have shown that, using brain-imaging techniques, it is now possible to predict whether you think of one concept or the other, whether the concept is a spoon or a house, or whether an emotion is disgust, anger, or envy.[9] Consider the practical clinical psychology solutions these techniques provide. Indeed, it is now possible to spot suicidal thoughts using these brain scans.[10] Suicidal and nonsuicidal participants were asked to think about the concepts to which stimulus words like *death* and *overdose* referred. A computer algorithm was able to accurately distinguish the two groups of participants based on their thoughts. Now estimating which words go together in language allows us to map out clusters of meaning. So if we can predict the "location" of one word in the brain, we can predict the location of many others.

That provides many exciting opportunities for understanding neurological disorders, predicting neurological disorders, and helping rehabilitate those who suffer from these neurological disorders.

COMPUTATIONAL MODELS

The work discussed in this book of course touches on the field of computational linguistics. And the applications of the work presented here are endless. Speech recognition systems[11] that computationally try to extract what has been said from how it has been said may be better able to estimate what the speaker is talking about by linking sound to meaning and by zooming into a target word by having established the context of what is being talked about.

Rather than only trying to get the maximum recognition, these systems can benefit from sound-meaning relations, word-order effect, and interrelations between words. In the context of a bakery, *flour* is a better candidate than *flower*, but for a florist, the opposite applies.

Using the context in which words operate also allows us to build better search engines.[12] Chapter 12 ("Company") described how we can estimate the meaning of a word with other words, sentences, paragraphs, and texts. If I need to find a specific article on a topic, all I need to do is find the article that has the highest cosine value with the word I used for my search. And as everybody who uses Google knows, the more search terms (the more context) you give, the more accurate the search results will be.

Let's take the idea of semantic relations further. Imagine you work in a company and have a massive amount of documents, say, a law firm. Somehow, you would like to organize these documents in a comprehensive system, but you do not have the manpower to do so, and you don't really know where to start. After all, the documents that are piling up can be categorized in so many different ways. By date or by author is doable, but what if you would also like to be able to categorize them by content? The techniques presented in the previous chapter can be used for mapping documents based on their topics, computationally, based on semantic similarities between the documents. The algorithm searches through the documents, determines the company the words keep, which documents share semantic content, and out comes a series of topics and the documents that fit these topics.

These techniques can also be used in measuring language. Together with a team at the University of Memphis, I worked on a coherence evaluation system.[13] We wanted to find out whether we could improve the standard readability formulas that consider the number of words in a sentence. We felt that textbooks written for third and fourth graders chose the right words, and perhaps even the right sentence length, but lacked coherence. Sentences jumped from one to the other, without the coherence in meaning. But how do you measure the coherence in text? That requires somebody understanding the meaning of the text! With techniques discussed in the previous chapter, we were able to build a tool that evaluated the quality of text in terms of the coherence between sentences, paragraphs, and chapters. That benefited the authors of the textbooks, as they now had a quality evaluator. It helped teachers, as they were then able to better find textbooks that matched their students. And it helped the students themselves!

An understanding of how we keep those words in mind helps develop many computational linguistic models that can be used for a variety of applications, including speech recognition, picture labeling, machine translation, text summarization, and a range of other applications.[14]

VIEWS

If language encodes perceptual information, we could argue that differences found in different language must be linked to differences in perceptual information. Just like Ferdinand de Saussure's "the sign is arbitrary" was taken as (linguistic) gospel for about a century, the idea that the way language users perceive and conceptualize the world could never be influenced by the language spoken by those users was also taken as (linguistic) gospel.

The hypothesis that language influences thought is known as the Sapir-Whorf Hypothesis, named after Benjamin Lee Whorf and his advisor, Edward Sapir.[15] Whorf argues that we cut nature up and organize it in concepts, and this organization is codified in the patterns of our language. Whorf illustrates this using examples from Hopi, an Amerindian language spoken by the Native American Hopi tribe in Northeastern Arizona. In Hopi, there is one word for everything that flies, except birds, the word *masay'taka*. Whorf argues that if language users have only one word for insects, airplanes, and pilots, they must have a different concept for flying objects than English speakers have, who cut nature up and codify different words for flying things. Conversely, English speakers have one word for snow, whereas Eskimo languages have a range of different words. And even though we can as English speakers distinguish icy snow and slushy snow, the fact that we need an adjective to describe these differences rather than only one word suggests that we carved out nature in a different way than Eskimos have.

The dismissal of the Sapir-Whorf hypothesis can probably be explained by the strong conviction that language is universal. Language structures are the same, and therefore our thinking must be the same. Recently, however, more and more studies show there are differences between languages, and these differences can explain differences in views.[16] The problem with the Sapir-Whorf hypothesis is whether language influences (perceptual) thought, whether (perceptual) thought is encoded in language, or both. But you can imagine that the interdependencies for Hopi Native Americans for the *masay'taka* are very different than for us, native speakers of English both in linguistic and perceptual context.

The point is that we can look at differences in views across cultures by looking at the language itself. We could also investigate these different perceptions within cultures, by for instance mapping out how the difference between mentioning *men and women* and *women and men* has evolved over time. Language demonstrates emancipation. Whereas *men and women* was ninety times more frequent than *women and men* in 1960, it was sixty times more frequent in 1970, fifteen times in 1980, and only five times more frequent in 1990, a pattern that has remained the same until now. We are far from being emancipated, but progress has been made. By using the research that formed the foundation of this book, we have created a thermometer for differences across societies, as well as for developments within our own society.

LEARNING A LANGUAGE

When I learned my foreign languages in school, I vividly recall the long word lists I had to memorize. No pictures like the ones Bill Lowery from chapter 1 ("Words") used for learning the medical devices, but simply translations of the words. That was a long time ago, but my son is learning similar word lists (and enjoys it as little as I did at the time). Just like I kept those foreign words in mind, my son tries to keep them in mind. A while back he asked me why he needed to know what *snake charmer* was in French. Like every other father, I answered that in school it is important to learn how to learn, and learning how to learn includes learning item lists. I answered that a diploma was important for later and that learning a foreign language was important. But I really wondered why he had to learn a word like *snake charmer* and why he had to learn it by linking the foreign word to its translation in the native language. After all, *snake charmer* is not in the 20 percent of the most frequently used words, not in English and not in French. And we know that 20 percent of the words in a language can get you through 80 percent of the language use. Rather than learning the translation of *snake charmer*, it would be more important to learn the 20 percent, a conclusion that comes out of the research described in this book.

Similarly, if the answer to how we keep these words in mind comes from the grounding of the word in the environment as well as from the company the word keeps in context, then one way *not* to teach children a new language is to have them associate *charmeur de serpent* with *snake charmer*. Instead, either have the French word be accompanied by all the modalities that go with it (pictures and sounds at least), or place the French word in French linguistic context, and preferably do both. (Some free advice based on the research underlying this book. . . .)

Perhaps learning language would help with an understanding of the mathematics of language, of the patterns that any language seems to conceal. By understanding these patterns, and understanding how these patterns are similar (and sometimes different) across languages, learning a (second) language may become less like cramming unrelated words and more like acknowledging how language creates meaning.

RECREATING PAST AND PRESENT

Chapter 12 ("Company") showed how geographical maps can be extracted from language. Maps of the United States can be created from the language in the *New York Times*, maps of China and the Middle East can be created from Chinese and Arabic texts, and a map of Middle Earth can be created from the *Lord of the Rings* trilogy. The application of this ivory tower research lies right around the corner. The corner of the past.

To get a better understanding of the past, we can read books about the past written by historians who have interpreted the information from the past. But using the techniques discussed in the book, we might be able to look at the past through the eyes of who lived in the past. Let me explain. Imagine we would like to get a better sense of the Middle Ages. We can read medieval books; we can look at artifacts from the Middle Ages to get a sense of medieval society. But if perceptual information is encoded in language, and the perceptual information obviously comes from those who lived during those times, we should be able to extract aspects of the medieval society from medieval language.

For instance, we should be able to create a map of medieval places not only based on the medieval maps themselves but also based on the medieval language in the texts that stood the test of time. We can generate geographical maps drawn linguistically by medieval authors and look at the perceptual world of the Middle Ages through the eyes of those who lived during those times, or rather through the medieval language mapped onto the medieval world. And the same is true for the social networks discussed in chapter 12 ("Company"). We can get a better understanding of the social networks that include the relations between individuals mentioned in text by using the adage that we know the name of a person by the linguistic company the name keeps. And what is true for the Middle Ages is true for the Roman Empire is true for Ancient Greece and is true for the Indus Valley Civilization.

If we can interpret maps and social networks biased by those who encoded the language, there is relevance not only in recreating the past but also in understanding the present. By using the language in social media, we should be able to recreate the perceptual information from its users. An unexpected application of the work outlined in this book emerges. We should be able to view the world through the eyes of terrorists and get an insight into the spatial maps and social networks based on the language they use. Forensic linguistics at work.

VIRTUAL HUMANS

When I worked at the University of Memphis, I had the great fortune of working with Art Graesser. When I joined the university, we worked on the intelligent tutoring system, AutoTutor.[17] AutoTutor was a computational tutor that allowed students to learn a variety of topics, from conceptual physics to computer literacy, by having a dialogue with the system. AutoTutor asked a general question, and when the student answered, it extracted the meaning from the answer, made sure it followed up with a natural conversational response, and adjusted its pedagogical strategies based on how the student was proceeding through the lesson. The experiments we conducted demonstrated that talking to AutoTutor increased student scores on a test. The system was never biased, never got tired, was always available, and yet provided a natural conversation.

How did AutoTutor keep those words in its artificial mind? Well, by using the linguistic company these words kept. AutoTutor estimated the meaning of the words of a student's utterance by using similar algorithms as I introduced in chapter 12. For instance, when a student answered a question, AutoTutor measured the answer by comparing it with a perfectly good answer and a perfectly bad answer, and gave the right feedback and triggered the student with additional questions.

At the time, AutoTutor was fantastic in its dialogue management. AutoTutor, however, did not look very human. With today's technology, we can use photogrammetry and scan somebody in, making a virtual version of herself. And with today's technology, we can build a dialogue-management system that learns from past conversations, pretty much like an artificial neural network. In several recent projects, we have taken advantage of today's technology in getting meaning out of words computationally.

For instance, in a current project, my team and I are building conversational systems for healthcare. Working together with hospitals, we are building conversational systems that do not replace the expert knowledge of medical doctors, but can help patients with their immediate questions and concerns.[18] Using the many computational linguistic techniques outlined in this book, we are building a system that can predict the intention of the speaker, that can predict what the speaker tries to convey, and that can participate in a conversation that is hardly distinguishable from a human–human conversation.

In another project, we are currently collaborating with SpaceBuzz, a non-profit organization spearheaded by European Space Agency astronaut André Kuipers, who spent four hundred days in space on two space missions. In the SpaceBuzz project, we create ambassadors of planet Earth.[19] In an innovative educational program aimed at introducing primary school education, we teach children subjects like science and technology in the context of sustainability, in a playful and easy-to-learn way. The program has been developed in line with the career path of a real astronaut. It comprises a preflight astronaut training and a variety of activities and lessons in the classroom that prepare children for their journey through space. Children first need to pass the preflight astronaut training. (They all will, but do not pass that on!) A fifteen-meter-long rocket ship then arrives at their school to virtually launch children into space. When children sit down in the rocket and put virtual reality headsets on, their chairs move hydraulically, and the rocket is launched into space under the guidance of a virtual reality embodiment of an actual astronaut. We are currently working on the astronaut scan, voice, and importantly dialogue management.

Some ten thousand children have already experienced SpaceBuzz in schools. With a visit to NASA's Lyndon B. Johnson Space Center in Houston and a presence at the International Astronautical Congress in Washington, the SpaceBuzz rocket ship has been experienced by some sixty astronauts and some two thousand international visitors. Iranian-American astronaut Anousheh Ansari could not have said it better: "I think it should be something that every human being, young and old, gets to see. Of course children will really enjoy it and will take this experience to heart, but I think we should take it to the UN and make all the world leaders do the same thing."[20] If soon we are able to use the sound of a word to improve speech recognition, use word order and word context to build a better conversational system, and use the techniques to keep those words in artificial minds to provide children across the world with high-quality education accessible for all, I would call that societal impact!

SOCIETAL PUZZLES

These are some of the many examples that demonstrate the societal relevance of basic research in cognitive science, linguistics, psychology, neuroscience, education, anthropology, and artificial intelligence. Examples that are pieces of the puzzle to understand the human mind and the complexities of language. Pieces of the puzzle to understand the human brain in order to help when things go wrong. Pieces of the puzzle to how to build better natural language technology tools that make our linguistic lives easier. Pieces of the puzzle to better understand the past, present, and future. Pieces of the puzzle to improve (second) language teaching and learning. To build artificial minds for healthcare and education. These are all examples of societally relevant puzzles whose pieces come from another puzzle: a seemingly more basic research puzzle that tries to figure out how we keep those words in mind and how language creates meaning.

Notes

PREFACE

1. The parable of the ant is taken from Herb Simon's *The Sciences of the Artificial* (Cambridge: MIT Press, 1969), in which Simon explains how simple ideas can be applied to complex situations to come up with a great result. Terrence Deacon's *The Symbolic Species* (New York: W. W. Norton, 1997) builds on a similar argument by explaining how humans are symbolic species not by their environment, their brains, or the brains of their parents, but—outside the environment and brains—by language itself.

CHAPTER 1: WORDS

1. William James, *The Principles of Psychology*, 2 vols. (New York: H. Holt, 1902), chapter 2, p. 29.

2. "Wordplay" is part of the second episode of the first season (1985–1986) of the television series *The Twilight Zone*. "Wordplay" was written by Rockne S. O'Bannon and directed by Wes Craven, first broadcasted October 4, 1985.

3. Raymond S. Nickerson, "Confirmation Bias: A Ubiquitous Phenomenon in Many Guises," *Review of General Psychology* 2, no. 2 (1998): 175–220.

4. Max Louwerse, "Bits and Pieces: Toward an Interactive Classification of Folktales," *Journal of Folklore Research* (1997): 245–49; Max Louwerse and Willie Van Peer, *Thematics: Interdisciplinary Studies*, vol. 3 (Amsterdam: Benjamins, 2002).

5. Vladimir I. A. Propp, *Morphology of the Folktale*, International Journal of American Linguistics (Bloomington: Research Center, Indiana University, 1958); Teun Adrianus Van Dijk, *Some Aspects of Text Grammars. A Study in Theoretical Linguistics and Poetics*, Janua Linguarum Series Maior (The Hague: Mouton, 1972).

6. Max Louwerse, "An Analytic and Cognitive Parametrization of Coherence Relations," *Cognitive Linguistics* 12, no. 3 (2001): 291–316.

7. Arthur C. Graesser, Shulan L. Lu, Tanner G. Jackson, Heather H. Mitchell, Andrew Olney, and Max M. Louwerse, "AutoTutor: A Tutor with Dialogue in Natural Language," *Behavior Research Methods Instruments & Computers* 36, no. 2 (2004): 180–92.

8. SRF Kultur, "«Gavagai»—the Philosophical Thought Experiment," YouTube, April 13, 2018, video, 2:06, www.youtube.com/watch?v=0YY4qxkqm3o.

9. Willard V. Quine, *Word and Object*, Studies in Communication (Cambridge: Technology Press of the Massachusetts Institute of Technology, 1960).

10. See Paul Bloom, *How Children Learn the Meanings of Words* (Cambridge: MIT Press, 2000).

11. Trevor A. Harley, *The Psychology of Language: From Data to Theory*, 3rd ed. (New York: Psychology Press, 2008).

12. Terrence William Deacon, *The Symbolic Species: The Co-Evolution of Language and the Brain*, 1st ed. (New York: W. W. Norton, 1997), 105.

13. For a similar argument, see Morten H. Christiansen and Nick Chater, "Language as Shaped by the Brain," *Behavioral and Brain Sciences* 31, no. 5 (2008): 489–509.

CHAPTER 2: LANGUAGE

1. George Kingsley Zipf, *The Psycho-Biology of Language; an Introduction to Dynamic Philology* (Boston: Houghton Mifflin, 1935), 20.

2. William Shakespeare and Theobald, *The Works of Shakespeare: In Seven Volumes. Collated with the Oldest Copies, and Corrected*, 1st AMS ed., 7 vols. (New York: AMS Press, 1968).

3. Bradley Efron and Ronald Thisted, "Estimating the Number of Unseen Species: How Many Words Did Shakespeare Know?" *Biometrika* 63, no. 3 (1976): 435–47.

4. J. R. R. Tolkien, *The Lord of the Rings*, 3 vols. (London: Allen & Unwin, 1954).

5. Efron and Thisted, "Estimating the Number of Unseen Species."

6. William E. Nagy and Richard C. Anderson, "How Many Words Are There in Printed School English?" *Reading Research Quarterly* (1984): 304–30.

7. Marc Brysbaert, Michaël Stevens, Paweł Mandera, and Emmanuel Keuleers, "How Many Words Do We Know? Practical Estimates of Vocabulary Size Dependent on Word Definition, the Degree of Language Input and the Participant's Age," *Frontiers in Psychology* 7 (2016): 1116.

8. This estimate can be found in several studies, including Jean Aitchinson, *Words in the Mind: An Introduction to the Mental Lexicon* (Oxford, UK; New York: Blackwell, 1987), George A. Miller, *The Science of Words* (New York: Scientific American Library, 1991), and William E. Nagy and Patricia A. Herman, "Breadth and Depth of Vocabulary Knowledge: Implications for Acquisition and Instruction," *The Nature of Vocabulary Acquisition* 19 (1987): 35.

9. If you feel that the estimate of 120,000 × 120,000 is a bit too high, because recognizing sixty thousand words does not mean knowing the meanings of those words, the numbers can be adjusted easily. Let's assume we truly know the word and its meanings in only half of the sixty thousand cases; the estimate of total word-meaning relations would drop to "only" 3.6 billion!

10. Dan Jurafsky and James H. Martin, *Speech and Language Processing: An Introduction to Natural Language Processing, Computational Linguistics, and Speech Recognition*, Prentice Hall Series in Artificial Intelligence (Upper Saddle River, NJ: Prentice Hall, 2000), 4.

11. Jurafsky and Martin, *Speech and Language Processing*.

12. John Langshaw Austin, *How to Do Things with Words*, vol. 88 (Oxford: Oxford University Press, 1975); Herbert P. Grice, "Logic and Conversation," in *Syntax and Semantics 3: Speech Acts*, ed. Peter Cole and Jerry L. Morgan, 41–58 (New York: Academic Press, 1975).

13. These are the percentages for conversations. For academic discourse, the percentages are different (e.g., 31 percent noun, 16 percent verb, 3 percent adverb, 10 percent adjective, 4 percent pronoun, and 15 percent preposition). But I'll try not to sound too academic, so let's focus on the percentages for conversation.

14. Christopher J. Conselice, Aaron Wilkinson, Kenneth Duncan, and Alice Mortlock, "The Evolution of Galaxy Number Density at Z< 8 and Its Implications," *The Astrophysical Journal* 830, no. 2 (2016): 83.

15. BBC Earth Unplugged, "How Many Grains of Sand Are in the Sahara?" YouTube, December 3, 2014, video, 4:12, www.youtube.com/watch?v=jQ41Gk80djs.

CHAPTER 3: GUESS

1. Ludwig Wittgenstein, *Philosophical Investigations* (New York: Macmillan, 1953), 64.

2. Trevor A. Harley, *The Psychology of Language: From Data to Theory*, 3rd ed. (New York: Psychology Press, 2008).

3. James McKeen Cattell, "The Time It Takes to See and Name Objects," *Mind* 11, no. 41 (1886): 63–65.

4. Gerald M. Reicher, "Perceptual Recognition as a Function of Meaningfulness of Stimulus Material," *Journal of Experimental Psychology* 81, no. 2 (1969): 275; Daniel D. Wheeler, "Processes in Word Recognition," *Cognitive Psychology* 1, no. 1 (1970): 59–85.

5. Keith Rayner, Alexander Pollatsek, Jane Ashby, and Charles Clifton Jr., *Psychology of Reading* (New York: Psychology Press, 2012).

6. Kenneth S. Goodman, "Reading: A Psycholinguistic Guessing Game," *Literacy Research and Instruction* 6, no. 4 (1967): 126.

7. Michael W. Eysenck and Mark T. Keane, *Cognitive Psychology: A Student's Handbook*, 5th ed. (Hove, UK; New York: Psychology Press, 2005).

8. David J. Townsend and Thomas G. Bever, *Sentence Comprehension: The Integration of Rules and Habits* (Cambridge: MIT Press, 2001). For a similar analogy when driving to a friend's house, see Talmy Givón, "Coherence in Text vs. Coherence in Mind," in *Coherence in Spontaneous Text*, ed. Morton Ann Gernsbacher and Talmy Givón, 59–115 (Amsterdam: Benjamins, 1995).

9. See chapter 6 in Brian Christian and Tom Griffiths, *Algorithms to Live By: The Computer Science of Human Decisions*, 1st U.S. ed. (New York: Henry Holt, 2016).

10. J. Ridley Stroop, "Studies of Interference in Serial Verbal Reactions," *Journal of Experimental Psychology* 18, no. 6 (1935): 643.

11. Erich Rudolf Jaensch and Wilhelm Neuhaus, *Grundformen Menschlichen Seins* (Berlin: Otto Elsner, 1929).

12. George Kingsley Zipf, *The Psycho-Biology of Language; an Introduction to Dynamic Philology* (Boston: Houghton Mifflin, 1935); George Kingsley Zipf, *Human Behavior and the Principle of Least Effort; an Introduction to Human Ecology* (Cambridge: Addison-Wesley Press, 1949).

13. James H. Neely, "Semantic Priming Effects in Visual Word Recognition: A Selective Review of Current Findings and Theories," *Basic Processes in Reading: Visual Word Recognition* 11, no. 1 (1991): 264–336; Timothy P. McNamara, *Semantic Priming: Perspectives from Memory and Word Recognition* (New York: Psychology Press, 2005).

14. David E. Meyer and Roger W. Schvaneveldt, "Facilitation in Recognizing Pairs of Words: Evidence of a Dependence between Retrieval Operations," *Journal of Experimental Psychology* 90, no. 2 (1971): 227–34.

15. Judith F. Kroll and Gretchen Sunderman, "Cognitive Processes in Second Language Learners and Bilinguals: The Development of Lexical and Conceptual Representations," in *The Handbook of Second Language Acquisition*, ed. Catherine J. Doughty and Michael H. Long, 104–129 (Oxford: Blackwell, 2003).

16. Admittedly, the motor response takes time, but for illustrative purposes, I will leave this aside for now.

17. Harley, *The Psychology of Language*.

18. Ralph Norman Haber and Maurice Hershenson, *The Psychology of Visual Perception*, 2nd ed. (New York: Holt, Rinehart and Winston, 1980).

19. Keith Rayner and Alexander Pollatsek, *The Psychology of Reading* (Englewood Cliffs, NJ: Prentice Hall, 1989).

20. Keith Rayner and George W. McConkie, "Perceptual Processes in Reading: The Perceptual Spans," in *Toward a Psychology of Reading*, ed. Arthur S. Reber and City University, 104–23 (Hillsdale, NJ: Erlbaum, 1977).

21. Alexander Pollatsek, Shmuel Bolozky, Arnold D. Well, and Keith Rayner, "Asymmetries in the Perceptual Span for Israeli Readers," *Brain and Language* 14, no. 1 (1981): 174–80.

22. Mitsuo Ikeda and Shinya Saida, "Span of Recognition in Reading," *Vision Research* 18, no. 1 (1978): 83–88; Naoyuki Osaka and Koichi Oda, "Effective Visual Field Size Necessary for Vertical Reading during Japanese Text Processing," *Bulletin of the Psychonomic Society* 29, no. 4 (1991): 345–47; A. W. Inhoff and W. M. Liu, "The Perceptual Span and Oculomotor Activity During the Reading of Chinese

Sentences," *Journal of Experimental Psychology: Human Perception and Performance* 24, no. 1 (1998): 20–34.

23. George A. Miller and Jennifer A. Selfridge, "Verbal Context and the Recall of Meaningful Material," *The American Journal of Psychology* 63, no. 2 (1950): 176–85.

24. Harley, *The Psychology of Language*; Townsend and Bever, *Sentence Comprehension*.

25. Fang Yang, Lun Mo, and Max Louwerse, "Effects of Local and Global Context on Processing Sentences with Subject and Object Relative Clauses," *Journal of Psycholinguistic Research* 42, no. 3 (June 2013): 227–37.

26. Eric Wanner, *On Remembering, Forgetting, and Understanding Sentences* (The Hague: Mouton, 1974).

27. Wanner, *On Remembering*.

28. Samuel Fillenbaum, "Memory for Gist: Some Relevant Variables," *Language and Speech* 9, no. 4 (1966): 217–27.

29. Walter Kintsch, David Welsch, Franz Schmalhofer, and Susan Zimny, "Sentence Memory: A Theoretical Analysis," *Journal of Memory and Language* 29, no. 2 (1990): 133–59.

30. Roger C. Schank and Robert P. Abelson, *Scripts, Plans, Goals, and Understanding: An Inquiry into Human Knowledge Structures*, The Artificial Intelligence Series (Hillsdale, NJ; New York: L. Erlbaum Associates, 1977).

31. Reading is a guessing game according to Goodman, "Reading."

32. Philip Rubin, Michael T. Turvey, and Peter Van Gelder, "Initial Phonemes Are Detected Faster in Spoken Words Than in Spoken Nonwords," *Perception & Psychophysics* 19, no. 5 (1976): 394–98.

33. Paul D. Allopenna, James S. Magnuson, and Michael K. Tanenhaus, "Tracking the Time Course of Spoken Word Recognition Using Eye Movements: Evidence for Continuous Mapping Models," *Journal of Memory and Language* 38, no. 4 (1998): 419–39.

34. Eiling Yee and Judie C. Sedivy, "Eye Movements to Pictures Reveal Transient Semantic Activation During Spoken Word Recognition," *Journal of Experimental Psychology: Learning, Memory, and Cognition* 32, no. 1 (2006): 1–14.

35. Richard M. Warren, "Perceptual Restoration of Missing Speech Sounds," *Science* 167, no. 3917 (1970): 392–93.

36. Janice M. Keenan, Brian MacWhinney, and Deborah Mayhew, "Pragmatics in Memory: A Study of Natural Conversation," *Journal of Verbal Learning and Verbal Behavior* 16, no. 5 (1977): 549–60.

CHAPTER 4: TRAINING

1. B. F. Skinner, *Verbal Behavior*, The Century Psychology Series (New York: Appleton-Century-Crofts, 1957), 148–49.

2. R. Allen Gardner and Beatrice T. Gardner, "Teaching Sign Language to a Chimpanzee," *Science* 165, no. 3894 (1969): 664–72; R. Allen Gardner, Beatrix T.

Gardner, and Thomas E. Van Cantfort, *Teaching Sign Language to Chimpanzees* (Albany: SUNY Press, 1989).

3. Keith J. Hayes and Catherine H. Nissen, "Higher Mental Functions of a Home-Raised Chimpanzee," in *Behavior of Nonhuman Primates*, ed. Allan M. Schrier, Harry F. Harlow, and Fred Stollnitz, 59–115 (New York: Academic Press, 1971).

4. Herbert S. Terrace, Laura Ann Petitto, Richard Jay Sanders, and Thomas G. Bever, "Can an Ape Create a Sentence?" *Science* 206, no. 4421 (1979): 891–902.

5. *Project Nim*, directed by James Marsh (Santa Monica, CA: Lionsgate, 2011).

6. William A. Haviland, Harald E. L. Prins, Bunny McBride, and Dana Walrath, *Cultural Anthropology: The Human Challenge* (Boston: Cengage Learning, 2013), 76.

7. Stefaan Blancke, "Lord Monboddo's Ourang-Outang and the Origin and Progress of Language," in *The Evolution of Social Communication in Primates*, 31–44 (Cham, Switzerland: Springer, 2014).

8. Irene M. Pepperberg, *The Alex Studies: Cognitive and Communicative Abilities of Grey Parrots* (Cambridge: Harvard University Press, 2009).

9. Nova Science Now, "Irene Pepperberg & Alex," YouTube, November 13, 2011, Video, 11:55, www.youtube.com/watch?v=cO6XuVlcEO4.

10. Michael S. Gazzaniga, Todd F. Heatherton, and Diane F. Halpern, *Psychological Science* (New York: W. W. Norton, 2010).

11. Steven J. Haggbloom, Renee Warnick, Jason E. Warnick, Vinessa K. Jones, Gary L. Yarbrough, Tenea M. Russell, Chris M. Borecky, et al., "The 100 Most Eminent Psychologists of the 20th Century," *Review of General Psychology* 6, no. 2 (2002): 139–52.

12. "But to treat Skinner's unreasonable theories as representative of the centuries-old tradition of empiricist thought is a travesty. So far as I know, Skinner was never much read outside of the USA. To expect the world at large to believe in innate knowledge, because some half-forgotten American psychology professor did not believe in minds at all, is surely a bit rich" (Geoffrey Sampson, *The "Language Instinct" Debate*, Rev. ed. [London; New York: Continuum, 2005], 54).

13. John O. Cooper, Timothy E. Heron, and William L. Heward, *Applied Behavior Analysis*, 3rd ed. (Hoboken, NJ: Pearson, 2019).

14. Cooper et al., *Applied Behavior Analysis*.

15. Skinner, *Verbal Behavior*, 335.

16. Skinner, *Verbal Behavior*, 336.

17. Irene M. Pepperberg, "Evolution of Communication from an Avian Perspective," in *Evolution of Communication Systems: A Comparative Approach*, ed. D. Kimbrough Oller and Ulrike Griebel, 171–92 (Cambridge: MIT Press, 2004).

18. Pierre Swiggers, "How Chomsky Skinned Quine, or What 'Verbal Behavior' Can Do," *Language Sciences* 17, no. 1 (1995): 1–18; Dagmar Divjak, *Frequency in Language: Memory, Attention and Learning* (New York: Cambridge University Press, 2019).

19. Herbert H. Clark, *Using Language* (Cambridge, UK; New York: Cambridge University Press, 1996), 153.

20. This is a generalization; see Divjak, *Frequency in Language*.

21. Charles Egerton Osgood, "Verbal Behavior, by BF Skinner," *Contemporary Psychology* 3 (1958): 209–12; D. E. Broadbent, "Review of Verbal Behavior," *British Journal of Psychology* 50 (1959): 371–73.

22. It has been suggested that Skinner's name is well-known because of Chomsky's review. That doesn't seem to be true. When looking at the frequency of Skinner and Chomsky being mentioned, and Skinner's work and Chomsky's work being mentioned, Skinner well outperforms Chomsky. In the list of most eminent psychologists of the twentieth century, Chomsky is number 38, Skinner number 1. In similar lists of those most cited, Skinner is listed high (at worst in the top 10), and Chomsky is not listed at all (Haggbloom et al., "The 100 Most Eminent Psychologists of the 20th Century").

23. Kenneth MacCorquodale, "On Chomsky's Review of Skinner's Verbal Behavior," *Journal of the Experimental Analysis of Behavior* 13, no. 1 (1970): 83.

24. Geoffrey B. West, *Scale: The Universal Laws of Growth, Innovation, Sustainability, and the Pace of Life in Organisms, Cities, Economies, and Companies* (New York: Penguin, 2017), 218.

25. There are 297 rules, but 91 rules are related to the game.

26. Martin D. S. Braine, "On Two Types of Models of the Internalization of Grammars," *The Ontogenesis of Grammar* (1971): 161.

27. D. Kimbrough Oller, "Underpinnings for a Theory of Communicative Evolution," in *Evolution of Communication Systems: A Comparative Approach*, ed. D. Kimbrough Oller and Ulrike Griebel, 49–65 (Cambridge: MIT Press, 2004).

28. Betty Hart and Todd R. Risley, *Meaningful Differences in the Everyday Experience of Young American Children* (Baltimore: Paul H. Brookes, 1995).

CHAPTER 5: INSTINCT

1. Noam Chomsky, *Aspects of the Theory of Syntax*, Massachusetts Institute of Technology Research Laboratory of Electronics Special Technical Report (Cambridge: MIT Press, 1965), 200–201.

2. Steven Pinker, *The Language Instinct*, 1st ed. (New York: W. Morrow, 1994), 18.

3. Noam Chomsky, *The Architecture of Language* (New Delhi: Oxford University Press, 2000), 50.

4. Joel Dick, "Time Magazine's All-TIME 100 Nonfiction Books," List Challenges, www.listchallenges.com/time-magazines-all-time-100-nonfiction-books. John Collins, *Chomsky: A Guide for the Perplexed* (London; New York: Continuum, 2008), 9.

5. Chomsky himself commonly refers to Claude Elwood Shannon and Warren Weaver, *The Mathematical Theory of Communication* (Urbana: University of Illinois Press, 1949).

6. Miles Shang, "Javascript/Canvas Linguistics Syntax Tree Generator," 2011, https://github.com/mshang/syntree.

7. George A. Miller, "The Cognitive Revolution: A Historical Perspective," *Trends in Cognitive Science* 7, no. 3 (2003): 141–44.

8. Artificial intelligence is now one of the disciplines in cognitive science, in addition to linguistics, psychology, philosophy, neuroscience, education, anthropology, and economics.

9. Harald Hammarström, "Linguistic Diversity and Language Evolution," *Journal of Language Evolution* 1, no. 1 (2016): 19–29.

10. Noam Chomsky, *Current Issues in Linguistic Theory (Janua Linguarum 38)* (The Hague: Mouton, 1964).

11. Pinker, *The Language Instinct*, 135.

12. Anne Fernald, "Four-Month-Old Infants Prefer to Listen to Motherese," *Infant Behavior and Development* 8, no. 2 (1985): 181–95.

13. Jacqueline S. Johnson and Elissa L. Newport, "Critical Period Effects in Second Language Learning: The Influence of Maturational State on the Acquisition of English as a Second Language," *Cognitive Psychology* 21, no. 1 (1989): 60–99.

14. Susan Curtiss, *Genie: A Psycholinguistic Study of a Modern-Day "Wild Child,"* Perspectives in Neurolinguistics and Psycholinguistics (New York: Academic Press, 1977), 180.

15. Susan Curtiss, "The Case of Chelsea: The Effects of Late Age at Exposure to Language on Language Performance and Evidence for the Modularity of Language and Mind," in *Connectedness: Papers by and for Sarah Vanwagenen*, ed. T. Carson and Linnaea Stockall Schütze, 115–46 (UCLA Working Papers in Linguistics, 2014).

16. Cecilia S. L. Lai, Simon E. Fisher, Jane A. Hurst, Faraneh Vargha-Khadem, and Anthony P. Monaco, "A Forkhead-Domain Gene Is Mutated in a Severe Speech and Language Disorder," *Nature* 413, no. 6855 (2001): 519–23; Eva M. Fernández and Helen Smith Cairns, *Fundamentals of Psycholinguistics*, Fundamentals of Linguistics (Chichester, UK; Malden, MA: Wiley-Blackwell, 2011).

17. Gary F. Marcus and Simon E. Fisher, "FOXP2 in Focus: What Can Genes Tell Us About Speech and Language?" *Trends in Cognitive Sciences* 7, no. 6 (2003): 257–62.

18. Johan J. Bolhuis and Martin Everaert, *Birdsong, Speech, and Language: Exploring the Evolution of Mind and Brain* (Cambridge: MIT Press, 2013).

19. Harold Goodglass, "Agrammatism," in *Studies in Neurolinguistics*, ed. Haiganoosh Whitaker and Harry A. Whitaker (New York: Academic Press, 1976), 238.

20. Harold Goodglass and Norman Geschwind, "Language Disorders (Aphasia)," in *Handbook of Perception*, ed. Edward C. Carterette and Morton P. Friedman (New York: Academic Press, 1976), 410.

21. Sean B. Carroll, "Genetics and the Making of Homo Sapiens," *Nature* 422, no. 6934 (2003): 849–57.

22. Ghislaine Dehaene-Lambertz, Stanislas Dehaene, and Lucie Hertz-Pannier, "Functional Neuroimaging of Speech Perception in Infants," *Science* 298, no. 5600 (December 6, 2002): 2013–15.

23. Mariacristina Musso, Andrea Moro, Volkmar Glauche, Michel Rijntjes, Jürgen Reichenbach, Christian Buchel, and Cornelius Weiller, "Broca's Area and the Language Instinct," *Nature Neuroscience* 6, no. 7 (2003): 774–81.

24. Noam Chomsky, *Language and Problems of Knowledge: The Managua Lectures*, vol. 16 (Cambridge: MIT Press, 1988), 62.

25. Michael Tomasello, "What Kind of Evidence Could Refute the UG Hypothesis?: Commentary on Wunderlich," *Studies in Language* 28, no. 3 (2004): 642–45; Michael Tomasello, *Constructing a Language: A Usage-Based Theory of Language Acquisition* (Cambridge: Harvard University Press, 2003), 284–85; Mark C. Baker, *The Atoms of Language*, 1st ed. (New York: Basic Books, 2001); Noam Chomsky, "Three Factors in Language Design: Background and Prospects," paper presented at the invited address at the 78th annual meeting of the Linguistic Society of America, Boston, MA, 2004; Stephen Crain and Diane C. Lillo-Martin, *An Introduction to Linguistic Theory and Language Acquisition* (Malden, MA: Blackwell, 1999); Janet Dean Fodor and William Gregory Sakas, "Evaluating Models of Parameter Setting," paper presented at the Proceedings of the 28th Annual Boston University Conference on Language Development, Boston, MA, 2004; Martin Haspelmath, "Optimality and Diachronic Adaptation," *Zeitschrift für Sprachwissenschaft* 18, no. 2 (1999): 180–205; Marc D. Hauser, Noam Chomsky, and W. Tecumseh Fitch, "The Faculty of Language: What Is It, Who Has It, and How Did It Evolve?" *Science* 298, no. 5598 (2002): 1569–79; Ray Jackendoff, *Foundations of Language: Brain, Meaning, Grammar, Evolution* (New York: Oxford University Press, 2002); William O'Grady, Michael Dobrovolsky, and Francis Katamba, *Contemporary Linguistics* (New York: St. Martin's, 1997); Dieter Wunderlich, "Why Assume UG," in *What Counts as Evidence in Linguistics: The Case of Innateness*, ed. Martina Penke and Anette Rosenbach, 147–74 (Amsterdam: John Benjamins, 2007).

26. David Lightfoot, *The Development of Language: Acquisition, Change, and Evolution*, Blackwell/Maryland Lectures in Language and Cognition (Malden, MA: Blackwell, 1999), 63.

27. Elissa L. Newport, "Maturational Constraints on Language Learning," *Cognitive Science* 14, no. 1 (1990): 11–28.

28. Christine Moon, Hugo Lagercrantz, and Patricia K. Kuhl, "Language Experienced in Utero Affects Vowel Perception after Birth: A Two-Country Study," *Acta Paediatrica* 102, no. 2 (2013): 156–60.

29. Walking on two legs—so-called bipedalism—is found by only a few living species. Only humans, gibbons, and large birds walk by lifting one foot at a time (compared to kangaroos, for instance, who can stand on two feet, but hop rather than walk).

30. Victoria Fromkin, Stephen Krashen, Susan Curtiss, David Rigler, and Marilyn Rigler, "The Development of Language in Genie: A Case of Language Acquisition Beyond the 'Critical Period.'" *Brain and Language* 1, no. 1 (1974): 81–107.

31. Susan Curtiss, "Abnormal Language Acquisition and the Modularity of Language," *Linguistics: The Cambridge Survey* 2 (1989): 112.

32. Pinker, *The Language Instinct*, 236.

33. Michael C. Corballis, "The Uniqueness of Human Recursive Thinking: The Ability to Think About Thinking May Be the Critical Attribute That Distinguishes Us from All Other Species," *American Scientist* 95, no. 3 (2007): 240–48. Recent research has shown that monkeys too seem to have recursive thinking skills: Stephen

Ferrigno, Samuel J. Cheyette, Steven T. Piantadosi, and Jessica F. Cantlon, "Recursive Sequence Generation in Monkeys, Children, US Adults, and Native Amazonians," *Science Advances* 6, no. 26 (2020): eaaz1002.

34. Herbert S. Terrace, *Why Chimpanzees Can't Learn Language and Only Humans Can* (New York: Columbia University Press, 2019).

35. And with similarities being made between human syntax and phonological syntax in birds—both birdsong and human language are hierarchically organized in a syntactic format—birds also prefer the left-side dominance for their phonological syntactic utterances. If there are similarities between syntax in birds and humans and given that birdsong does not have semantics or words, this may lead us to a language organ.

36. Richard H. Bauer, "Lateralization of Neural Control for Vocalization by the Frog (Rana Pipiens)," *Psychobiology* 21, no. 3 (1993): 243–48.

37. Patrick J. Gannon, Ralph L. Holloway, Douglas C. Broadfield, and Allen R. Braun, "Asymmetry of Chimpanzee Planum Temporale: Humanlike Pattern of Wernicke's Brain Language Area Homolog," *Science* 279, no. 5348 (1998): 220–22; Muhammad A. Spocter, William D. Hopkins, Amy R. Garrison, Amy L. Bauernfeind, Cheryl D. Stimpson, Patrick R. Hof, and Chet C. Sherwood, "Wernicke's Area Homologue in Chimpanzees (Pan Troglodytes) and Its Relation to the Appearance of Modern Human Language," *Proceedings of the Royal Society B: Biological Sciences* 277, no. 1691 (2010): 2165–74.

38. Wolfgang Enard, Sabine Gehre, Kurt Hammerschmidt, Sabine M. Hölter, Torsten Blass, Mehmet Somel, Martina K. Brückner, et al., "A Humanized Version of Foxp2 Affects Cortico-Basal Ganglia Circuits in Mice," *Cell* 137, no. 5 (2009): 961–71.

CHAPTER 6: NETWORK

1. James L. McClelland, David E. Rumelhart, and Geoffrey E. Hinton, "The Appeal of Parallel Distributed Processing," in *Parallel Distributed Processing. Explorations in the Microstructure of Cognition.*, ed. James L. McClelland, David E. Rumelhart, and PDP Research Group, 3–44 (Cambridge: MIT Press, 1986), 10.

2. Allan M. Collins and M. Ross Quillian, "Retrieval Time from Semantic Memory," *Journal of Verbal Learning and Verbal Behavior* 8, no. 2 (1969): 240–47.

3. Thomas K. Landauer and Jonathan L. Freedman, "Information Retrieval from Long-Term Memory: Category Size and Recognition Time," *Journal of Verbal Learning and Verbal Behavior* 7, no. 2 (1968): 291–95; Benson Schaeffer and Richard Wallace, "Semantic Similarity and the Comparison of Word Meanings," *Journal of Experimental Psychology* 82, no. 2 (1969): 3.

4. These views of semantic networks either base themselves on the prototype, and are called prototype theories, or instances of a category; you already guessed it, they are called instance or exemplar theories. Lloyd K. Komatsu, "Recent Views of Conceptual Structure," *Psychological Bulletin* 112, no. 3 (1992): 500–26; Eleanor Rosch,

"Principles of Categorization," in *Cognition and Categorization*, ed. E. Rosch and B. B. Lloyd (Hillsdale, NJ: Erlbaum, 1978).

5. Gregory L. Murphy and Douglas L. Medin, "The Role of Theories in Conceptual Coherence," *Psychological Review* 92, no. 3 (1985): 289–316.

6. Allan M. Collins and Elizabeth F. Loftus, "A Spreading-Activation Theory of Semantic Processing," *Psychological Review* 82, no. 6 (1975): 407.

7. George A. Miller, *WordNet: An Electronic Lexical Database* (Cambridge: MIT Press, 1998).

8. Actually, the chain goes further. Object is a Physical Entity is an Entity.

9. Walter Kintsch and Teun A. van Dijk, "Toward a Model of Text Comprehension and Production," *Psychological Review* 85, no. 5 (1978): 363–94.

10. Collin F. Baker, Charles J. Fillmore, and John B. Lowe, "The Berkeley FrameNet Project," paper presented at the 36th Annual Meeting of the Association for Computational Linguistics and 17th International Conference on Computational Linguistics, volume 1, 1998.

11. Karin Kipper Schuler, "Verbnet: A Broad-Coverage, Comprehensive Verb Lexicon," PhD dissertation, University of Pennsylvania, 2005, https://repository.upenn.edu/dissertations/AAI3179808.

12. Douglas B. Lenat "Cyc: A Large-Scale Investment in Knowledge Infrastructure," *Communications of the ACM* 38, no. 11 (1995): 33–38.

13. Doug Lenat, "What AI Can Learn from Romeo & Juliet," *Forbes*, July 3, 2019, www.forbes.com/sites/cognitiveworld/2019/07/03/what-ai-can-learn-from-romeo--juliet/?sh=7bec33861bd0.

14. Charles G. Gross, "Genealogy of the 'Grandmother Cell,'" *The Neuroscientist* 8, no. 5 (2002): 512–18; R. Q. Quiroga, L. Reddy, G. Kreiman, C. Koch, and I. Fried, "Invariant Visual Representation by Single Neurons in the Human Brain," *Nature* 435, no. 7045 (2005): 1102–7.

15. Anderson, James A. *An Introduction to Neural Networks.* Cambridge: MIT Press, 1995.

16. This might be a reminder of all the horror stories that the end of the world is near due to artificial intelligence. Whenever somebody reminds me that the end is near, I optimistically respond that the beginning is closer.

17. Ian Goodfellow, Yoshua Bengio, and Aaron Courville, *Deep Learning*, Adaptive Computation and Machine Learning (Cambridge: The MIT Press, 2016).

18. Beth A. Ober and Gregory K. Shenaut, "Semantic Memory," in *Handbook of Psycholinguistics*, ed. Matthew J. Traxler and Morton Ann Gernsbacher, 403–53 (Amsterdam; Boston: Elsevier, 2006); M. Ross Quillian, "Word Concepts: A Theory and Simulation of Some Basic Semantic Capabilities," *Behavioral Science* 12, no. 5 (1967): 410–30.

19. Timothy T. Rogers and James L. McClelland, *Semantic Cognition: A Parallel Distributed Processing Approach* (Cambridge: MIT Press, 2004).

20. Until somewhat later (Jean M. Mandler, Patricia J. Bauer, and Laraine McDonough, "Separating the Sheep from the Goats: Differentiating Global Categories," *Cognitive Psychology* 23, no. 2 [1991]: 263–98; Sabina Pauen, "Evidence for

Knowledge-Based Category Discrimination in Infancy," *Child Development* 73, no. 4 [2002]: 1016–33).

21. Larissa K. Samuelson and Linda B. Smith, "Children's Attention to Rigid and Deformable Shape in Naming and Non-Naming Tasks," *Child Development* 71, no. 6 (2000): 1555–70.

22. Goodfellow et al., *Deep Learning*.

23. Allegedly the quote comes from Indiana poet James Whitcomb Riley (1849–1916).

CHAPTER 7: GROUNDING

1. Alan M. Turing, "Computing Machinery and Intelligence," *Mind* 59, no. 236 (1950): 460.

2. John R. Searle, "Minds, Brains, and Programs," *Behavioral and Brain Sciences* 3 (1980): 417–57.

3. Of course, the Chinese Room could have been called equally well the "English Room" in which a speaker of Chinese who does not speak English uses a ledger in English.

4. Searle, "Minds, Brains, and Programs."

5. John R. Searle, "Twenty-One Years in the Chinese Room," in *Views into the Chinese Room: New Essays on Searle and Artificial Intelligence*, ed. John Preston and Mark Bishop, 51–69 (Oxford: Oxford University Press, 2002).

6. Samuel McNerney, "A Brief Guide to Embodied Cognition: Why You Are Not Your Brain," *Scientific American* (guest blog), November 4, 2011, https://blogs .scientificamerican.com/guest-blog/a-brief-guide-to-embodied-cognition-why-you -are-not-your-brain.

7. Arthur M. Glenberg, "Embodiment as a Unifying Perspective for Psychology," *Wiley Interdisciplinary Reviews: Cognitive Science* 1, no. 4 (2010): 586–96.

8. Arthur M. Glenberg and Michael P. Kaschak, "Grounding Language in Action," *Psychonomic Bulletin & Review* 9, no. 3 (2002): 558–65.

9. Max Louwerse, Sterling Hutchinson, Richard Tillman, and Gabriel Recchia, "Effect Size Matters: The Role of Language Statistics and Perceptual Simulation in Conceptual Processing," *Language, Cognition and Neuroscience* 30, no. 4 (2015): 430–47.

10. Giacomo Rizzolatti, Luciano Fadiga, Vittorio Gallese, and Leonardo Fogassi, "Premotor Cortex and the Recognition of Motor Actions," *Cognitive Brain Research* 3, no. 2 (1996): 131–41; Giacomo Rizzolatti and Laila Craighero, "The Mirror-Neuron System," *Annual Review of Neuroscience* 27 (2004): 169–92.

11. Wilder Penfield and Edwin Boldrey, "Somatic Motor and Sensory Representation in the Cerebral Cortex of Man as Studied by Electrical Stimulation," *Brain* 60, no. 4 (1937): 389–443.

12. James M. Kilner and Roger N. Lemon, "What We Know Currently about Mirror Neurons," *Current Biology* 23, no. 23 (2013): R1057–R62; Angelika Lingnau,

Benno Gesierich, and Alfonso Caramazza, "Asymmetric fMRI Adaptation Reveals No Evidence for Mirror Neurons in Humans," *Proceedings of the National Academy of Sciences* 106, no. 24 (2009): 9925–30.

13. Andrew N. Meltzoff and M. Keith Moore, "Imitation in Newborn Infants: Exploring the Range of Gestures Imitated and the Underlying Mechanisms," *Developmental Psychology* 25, no. 6 (1989): 954.

14. Tanya L. Chartrand and John A. Bargh, "The Chameleon Effect: The Perception–Behavior Link and Social Interaction," *Journal of Personality and Social Psychology* 76, no. 6 (1999): 893.

15. Obviously, we carefully controlled for chance by using a baseline of shuffled behavior.

16. Michael J. Spivey and Stephanie Huette, "Toward a Situated View of Language," in *Visually Situated Language Comprehension*, ed. Pia Knoeferle, Pirita Pyykkönen-Klauck, and Matthew W. Crocker, 1–30 (Amsterdam; Philadelphia: Benjamins, 2016).

17. Rick B. Van Baaren, Rob W. Holland, Bregje Steenaert, and Ad van Knippenberg, "Mimicry for Money: Behavioral Consequences of Imitation," *Journal of Experimental Social Psychology* 39, no. 4 (2003): 393–98.

18. Glenberg and Kaschak, "Grounding Language in Action."

19. Rolf A. Zwaan and Lawrence J. Taylor, "Seeing, Acting, Understanding: Motor Resonance in Language Comprehension," *Journal of Experimental Psychology General* 135, no. 1 (2006): 1–11.

20. Olaf Hauk, Ingrid Johnsrude, and Friedemann Pulvermüller, "Somatotopic Representation of Action Words in Human Motor and Premotor Cortex," *Neuron* 41, no. 2 (2004): 301–7.

21. Mark E. Wheeler, Steven E. Petersen, and Randy L. Buckner, "Memory's Echo: Vivid Remembering Reactivates Sensory-Specific Cortex," *Proceedings of the National Academy of Sciences* 97, no. 20 (2000): 11125–29.

22. David A. Havas, Arthur M. Glenberg, Karol A. Gutowski, Mark J. Lucarelli, and Richard J. Davidson, "Cosmetic Use of Botulinum Toxin-a Affects Processing of Emotional Language," *Psychological Science* 21, no. 7 (2010): 895–900.

23. Rolf A. Zwaan, Robert A. Stanfield, and Richard H. Yaxley, "Language Comprehenders Mentally Represent the Shapes of Objects," *Psychological Science* 13, no. 2 (2002): 168–71.

24. Robert A. Stanfield and Rolf A. Zwaan, "The Effect of Implied Orientation Derived from Verbal Context on Picture Recognition," *Psychological Science* 12, no. 2 (2001): 153–56.

25. Anna M. Borghi, Arthur M. Glenberg, and Michael P. Kaschak, "Putting Words in Perspective," *Memory & Cognition* 32, no. 6 (2004): 863–73.

26. Michael J. Spivey and Joy J. Geng, "Oculomotor Mechanisms Activated by Imagery and Memory: Eye Movements to Absent Objects," *Psychological Research* 65, no. 4 (2001): 235–41.

27. George Lakoff and Mark Johnson, *Philosophy in the Flesh: The Embodied Mind and Its Challenge to Western Thought* (New York: Basic Books, 1999); Eve Sweetser,

From Etymology to Pragmatics: Metaphorical and Cultural Aspects of Semantic Structure, vol. 54 (Cambridge: Cambridge University Press, 1990).

28. A. M. Glenberg and D. A. Robertson, "Symbol Grounding and Meaning: A Comparison of High-Dimensional and Embodied Theories of Meaning," *Journal of Memory and Language* 43, no. 3 (2000): 379–401.

29. This does not turn out to be the case, as I showed in Max Louwerse, "Symbolic or Embodied Representations: A Case for Symbol Interdependency," in *Handbook of Latent Semantic Analysis*, ed. Thomas K. Landauer, Danielle S. McNamara, Simon Dennis, and Walter Kintsch, 119–32 (Mahwah, NJ: Lawrence Erlbaum Associates, 2007). Computer models do allow for computing the differences between clothing, leaves, and water as a substitute for a pillow, but I leave that discussion for later chapters.

30. Michael P. Kaschak and Arthur M. Glenberg, "Constructing Meaning: The Role of Affordances and Grammatical Constructions in Sentence Comprehension," *Journal of Memory and Language* 43, no. 3 (2000): 508–29.

31. Glenberg and Kaschak, "Grounding Language in Action."

32. Stephen D. Goldinger, Megan H. Papesh, Anthony S. Barnhart, Whitney A. Hansen, and Michael C. Hout, "The Poverty of Embodied Cognition," *Psychonomic Bulletin & Review* 23, no. 4 (2016): 959–78; Bradford Z. Mahon and Alfonso Caramazza, "A Critical Look at the Embodied Cognition Hypothesis and a New Proposal for Grounding Conceptual Content," *Journal of Physiology—Paris* 102, no. 1–3 (2008): 59–70.

33. Jacob Cohen, "Things I Have Learned (So Far)," *American Psychologist* 45 (1990): 1304–12.

34. Andrew D. Wilson, "The Small Effect Size—Why Do We Put Up with Small Effects?" *Notes from Two Scientific Psychologists* (blog), August 17, 2012, http://psychsciencenotes.blogspot.com/2012/08/the-small-effect-size-effect-why-do-we.html.

35. Louwerse et al., "Effect Size Matters." It may be worth pointing out that the effect sizes for perceptual simulation effects were large, but for language statistics, they were even larger.

36. A. Z. Zeman, Michaela Dewar, and Sergio Della Sala, "Lives without Imagery—Congenital Aphantasia," *Cortex* 73 (2015): 378–80.

37. James Gallagher, "Aphantasia: A Life Without Mental Images," *BBC News*, August 25, 2015, www.bbc.com/news/health-34039054.

38. Leonid Rozenblit and Frank Keil, "The Misunderstood Limits of Folk Science: An Illusion of Explanatory Depth," *Cognitive Science* 26, no. 5 (2002): 521–62.

39. Mark Andrews, Gabriella Vigliocco, and David Vinson, "Integrating Experiential and Distributional Data to Learn Semantic Representations," *Psychological Review* 116, no. 3 (2009): 463–98; Lawrence W. Barsalou, "Perceptual Symbol Systems," *Behavioral and Brain Sciences* 22, no. 4 (1999): 577–660.

Granted, one could argue that describing a concept in all its visual details is different than having an automatic visual memory of a concept when reading a word, but the point is that grounding alone is an incomplete explanation for keeping those words in mind.

CHAPTER 8: SHORTCUT

1. Nick Chater, *The Mind Is Flat: The Illusion of Mental Depth and the Improvised Mind* (London: Allen Lane, 2018), 8.

2. P. Thompson, "Margaret Thatcher: A New Illusion," *Perception* 9, no. 4 (1980): 483–84.

3. Kimberly B. Weldon, Jessica Taubert, Carolynn L. Smith, and Lisa A. Parr, "How the Thatcher Illusion Reveals Evolutionary Differences in the Face Processing of Primates," *Animal Cognition* 16, no. 5 (2013): 691–700.

4. Solomon E. Asch and Harold Guetzkow, "Effects of Group Pressure Upon the Modification and Distortion of Judgments," *Organizational Influence Processes* (1951): 295–303.

5. One could argue that this is not cognitively lazy but cognitively smart. We are social animals, and it is considerably smarter to conform to others—while we know the others are wrong—than fight what we think is false. As we have seen already and will see later, this can also be found in language processing. Swimming with the current is easier than swimming against it. Whether it is cognitively lazy, or cognitively smart, it is certainly less cognitively taxing.

6. Keith Rayner, Alexander Pollatsek, Jane Ashby, and Charles Clifton Jr., *Psychology of Reading* (New York: Psychology Press, 2012).

7. Christopher F. Chabris and Daniel J. Simons, *The Invisible Gorilla: And Other Ways Our Intuitions Deceive Us*, 1st ed. (New York: Crown, 2010).

8. George A. Miller, "The Magical Number Seven, Plus or Minus Two: Some Limits on Our Capacity for Processing Information," *Psychological Review* 63, no. 2 (1956): 81–97.

9. Nobuyuki Kawai and Tetsuro Matsuzawa, "Numerical Memory Span in a Chimpanzee," *Nature* 403, no. 6765 (2000): 39–40.

10. One could raise the point that this is evidence in favor of a language instinct, but for language tasks, our performance turns out not to be that impressive either.

11. Daniel Kahneman, Barbara L. Fredrickson, Charles A. Schreiber, and Donald A. Redelmeier, "When More Pain Is Preferred to Less: Adding a Better End," *Psychological Science* 4, no. 6 (1993): 401–5.

12. Albert Stevens and Patty Coupe, "Distortions in Judged Spatial Relations," *Cognitive Psychology* 10, no. 4 (1978): 422–37.

13. Henry L. Roediger and Kathleen B. McDermott, "Creating False Memories: Remembering Words Not Presented in Lists," *Journal of Experimental Psychology: Learning, Memory, and Cognition* 21, no. 4 (1995): 803.

14. Esther Herrmann, Josep Call, María Victoria Hernández-Lloreda, Brian Hare, and Michael Tomasello, "Humans Have Evolved Specialized Skills of Social Cognition: The Cultural Intelligence Hypothesis," *Science* 317, no. 5843 (2007): 1360–66.

15. Amos Tversky and Daniel Kahneman, "Extensional Versus Intuitive Reasoning: The Conjunction Fallacy in Probability Judgment," *Psychological Review* 90, no. 4 (1983): 293.

16. Amos Tversky and Daniel Kahneman, "Judgment under Uncertainty: Heuristics and Biases," *Science* 185, no. 4157 (1974): 1124–31.

17. If you read the question as "Of all the countries that are in the UN, how many of them are African?" the actual answer is 28 percent. If you read the question as "Of all the countries in Africa, what percentage of them are in the UN?" the actual answer is 100 percent. But in either case, any answer you give—no matter how right or wrong—should not change because of a rigged spinning wheel.

18. If the description of Miss Johnson and Miss Pederson sounds familiar to you, it is the same as the one Emily Brontë uses for Miss Ingram in *Jane Eyre.*

19. Bertram R. Forer, "The Fallacy of Personal Validation; a Classroom Demonstration of Gullibility," *Journal of Abnormal Psychology* 44, no. 1 (1949): 120.

20. William Faulkner, *Absalom! Absalom!* Cited in Josh Jones, "When William Faulkner Set the World Record for Writing the Longest Sentence in Literature," *Open Culture*, March 14, 2019, www.openculture.com/2019/03/when-william-faulkner-set-the-world-record-for-writing-the-longest-sentence-in-literature.html.

21. Trevor A. Harley, *The Psychology of Language: From Data to Theory*, 3rd ed. (New York: Psychology Press, 2008).

22. Thomas D. Erickson and Mark E. Mattson, "From Words to Meaning: A Semantic Illusion," *Journal of Verbal Learning and Verbal Behavior* 20, no. 5 (1981): 540–51.

23. Daniel Kahneman, *Thinking, Fast and Slow*, 1st ed. (New York: Farrar, Straus and Giroux, 2011).

24. Gerd Gigerenzer, *Gut Feelings: The Intelligence of the Unconscious* (New York: Viking, 2007).

25. Chater, *The Mind Is Flat.*

26. Gigerenzer, *Gut Feelings.*

27. BBC, "The Code—the Wisdom of the Crowd," YouTube, 2011, video, 4:48, www.youtube.com/watch?v=iOucwX7Z1HU&t=2s.

28. Yuval Harari, "People Have Limited Knowledge. What's the Remedy? Nobody Knows," *New York Times*, April 18, 2017, www.nytimes.com/2017/04/18/books/review/knowledge-illusion-steven-sloman-philip-fernbach.html.

CHAPTER 9: PATTERNS

1. Daniel Kahneman, *Thinking, Fast and Slow*, 1st ed. (New York: Farrar, Straus and Giroux, 2011), 115.

2. Martin Gardner, *The Magic Numbers of Dr. Matrix* (Buffalo, NY: Prometheus Books, 1985); John Leavy, "Our Spooky Presidential Coincidences Contest," *Skeptical Inquirer* 16 (1992): 316–19.

3. Martin Hilbert, "Toward a Synthesis of Cognitive Biases: How Noisy Information Processing Can Bias Human Decision Making," *Psychological Bulletin* 138, no. 2 (2012): 211–37.

4. Raymond S. Nickerson, "Confirmation Bias: A Ubiquitous Phenomenon in Many Guises," *Review of General Psychology* 2, no. 2 (1998): 175–220.

5. E. Colin Cherry, "Some Experiments on the Recognition of Speech, with One and with Two Ears," *The Journal of the Acoustical Society of America* 25, no. 5 (1953): 975–79.

6. Kurt Koffka, *Principles of Gestalt Psychology* (New York: W. W. Norton, 1970).

7. Andreas Nieder, "Seeing More Than Meets the Eye: Processing of Illusory Contours in Animals," *Journal of Comparative Physiology A* 188, no. 4 (2002): 249–60.

8. Andreas Nieder and Hermann Wagner, "Perception and Neuronal Coding of Subjective Contours in the Owl," *Nature Neuroscience* 2, no. 7 (1999): 660–63.

9. Cats (Mary Bravo, Randolph Blake, and Sharon Morrison, "Cats See Subjective Contours," *Vision Research* 28, no. 8 [1988]: 861–65), monkeys (Rüdiger von der Heydt and Esther Peterhans, "Mechanisms of Contour Perception in Monkey Visual Cortex. I. Lines of Pattern Discontinuity," *Journal of Neuroscience* 9, no. 5 [1989]: 1731–48), barn owls (Nieder and Wagner, "Perception and Neuronal Coding").

10. David Premack, "Animal Cognition," *Annual Review of Psychology* 34, no. 1 (1983): 351–62.

11. Frans B. M. de Waal, *Are We Smart Enough to Know How Smart Animals Are?* 1st ed. (New York: W. W. Norton, 2016).

12. George Wolford, Michael B. Miller, and Michael Gazzaniga, "The Left Hemisphere's Role in Hypothesis Formation," *Journal of Neuroscience* 20, no. 6 (2000): RC64.

13. George Wolford, Sarah E. Newman, Michael B. Miller, and Gagan S. Wig, "Searching for Patterns in Random Sequences," *Canadian Journal of Experimental Psychology* 58, no. 4 (2004): 221.

14. C. Randy Gallistel, *The Organization of Learning*, Learning, Development, and Conceptual Change (Cambridge: MIT Press, 1990).

15. Nir Vulkan, "An Economist's Perspective on Probability Matching," *Journal of Economic Surveys* 14, no. 1 (2000): 101–18.

16. Michael S. Gazzaniga, *Nature's Mind: The Biological Roots of Thinking, Emotions, Sexuality, Language, and Intelligence* (New York: Basic Books, 1992); Michael S. Gazzaniga, *Who's in Charge?: Free Will and the Science of the Brain*, Gifford Lectures, 1st ed. (New York: HarperCollins, 2011).

17. Michael S. Gazzaniga, "Organization of the Human Brain," *Science* 245, no. 4921 (1989): 947–52.

18. Michael S. Gazzaniga, "Cerebral Specialization and Interhemispheric Communication: Does the Corpus Callosum Enable the Human Condition?" *Brain* 123, no. 7 (2000): 1293–326.

19. Michael S. Gazzaniga, *Who's in Charge?: Free Will and the Science of the Brain*, Gifford Lectures (New York: HarperCollins, 2011).

20. Janet Metcalfe, Margaret Funnell, and Michael S. Gazzaniga, "Right-Hemisphere Memory Superiority: Studies of a Split-Brain Patient," *Psychological Science* 6, no. 3 (1995): 157–64.

21. "The hemispheric difference in associating symbols with concepts and in extrapolating and applying rules may explain why the right hemisphere does not have

the same sort of interpretive capacity that the left hemisphere possesses." Margaret G. Funnell, "The Interpreting Hemispheres," in *The Cognitive Neuroscience of Mind: A Tribute to Michael S. Gazzaniga*, ed. Patricia Ann Reuter-Lorenz, Kathleen Baynes, George R. Mangun, and Elizabeth A. Phelps (Cambridge: MIT Press, 2010), 84.

22. Kristin Andrews, *The Animal Mind: An Introduction to the Philosophy of Animal Cognition* (New York: Routledge, 2020).

23. Bruce Hayes, Susan Curtiss, Anna Szabolcsi, Tim Stowell, Edward Stabler, Dominique Sportiche, Hilda Koopman, et al., *Linguistics: An Introduction to Linguistic Theory* (Hoboken, NJ: John Wiley & Sons, 2013); William O'Grady, Michael Dobrovolsky, and Francis Katamba, *Contemporary Linguistics* (New York: St. Martin's, 1997); William O'Grady, John Archibald, Mark Aronoff, and Janie Rees-Miller, *Contemporary Linguistics: An Introduction* (New York: St. Martin's Press, 2010).

CHAPTER 10: SOUND

1. Ferdinand de Saussure, *Cours de Linguistique Générale* (Paris: Payot, 1916), trans. in *Course in General Linguistics* (New York: Philosophical Library, 1959), 68.

2. Plato, *The Collected Dialogues of Plato*, ed. Edith Hamilton, Huntington Cairns, and Lane Cooper (Princeton: Princeton University Press, 1961).

3. William Shakespeare, *Romeo and Juliet*, Act II, Scene 2. William Shakespeare and Theobald, *The Works of Shakespeare: In Seven Volumes. Collated with the Oldest Copies, and Corrected*, 1st AMS ed., 7 vols. (New York: AMS Press, 1968).

4. In fact, the discussion on arbitrariness in language can be found throughout the centuries: Leonard Bloomfield, "Language [1933]," *Holt, New York* 56 (1962), 145; J. R. Firth, *The Tongues of Men, and Speech* (London: Oxford University Press, 1964), 181, 187; Charles Francis Hockett, *A Course in Modern Linguistics* (New York: Macmillan, 1958), 64; George A. Miller and Philip N. Johnson-Laird, *Language and Perception* (Cambridge: Belknap Press, 1976), 116; J. David Sapir, "Kujaama: Symbolic Separation among the Diola-Fogny 1," *American Anthropologist* 72, no. 6 (1970): 7.

5. de Saussure, *Cours de Linguistique Générale*, 100, trans. in *Course in General Linguistics*, 67.

6. One could perhaps make the argument that a sound-meaning relationship would be such grounding, but this is not the standard way that embodied cognition views grounding (Manuel de Vega, Arthur M. Glenberg, and Arthur C. Graesser, *Symbols and Embodiment: Debates on Meaning and Cognition* [Oxford; New York: Oxford University Press, 2008]).

7. Now there may be earlier examples of graphical expression. However, it is difficult to determine whether such expression is a picture, such as a cave painting, or an example of writing. The only difference between the two is likely the fact that there need to be repeated patterns in writing and not necessarily in images.

8. David Diringer, *Writing. Its Origins and Early History* (New York: Praeger, 1962).

9. Wendy Sandler, "Dedicated Gestures and the Emergence of Sign Language," *Gesture* 12, no. 3 (2012): 265–307.

10. Simon Kirby, Hannah Cornish, and Kenny Smith, "Cumulative Cultural Evolution in the Laboratory: An Experimental Approach to the Origins of Structure in Human Language," *Proceedings of the National Academy of Sciences* 105, no. 31 (2008): 10681–86.

11. Wolfgang Köhler, *Gestalt Psychology* (New York: New American Library, 1929).

12. This effect was initially reported by Sapir (1929) with *mil* and *mal*, *mil* sounding smaller and *mal* sounding larger. But with words such as *little* and *large*, *milli-* and *tall*, the effect may not be surprising. Edward Sapir, "A Study in Phonetic Symbolism," *Journal of Experimental Psychology* 12, no. 3 (1929): 225.

13. Patrick D. Thompson and Zachary Estes, "Sound Symbolic Naming of Novel Objects Is a Graded Function," *Quarterly Journal of Experimental Psychology* 64, no. 12 (2011): 2392–404.

14. Charles P. Davis, Hannah M. Morrow, and Gary Lupyan, "What Does a Horgous Look Like? Nonsense Words Elicit Meaningful Drawings," *Cognitive Science* 43, no. 10 (2019): e12791.

15. Daphne Maurer, Thanujeni Pathman, and Catherine J. Mondloch, "The Shape of Boubas: Sound–Shape Correspondences in Toddlers and Adults," *Developmental Science* 9, no. 3 (2006): 316–22.

16. Vanja Kovic, Kim Plunkett, and Gert Westermann, "The Shape of Words in the Brain," *Cognition* 114, no. 1 (2010): 19–28.

17. Nahyun Kwon, "Empirically Observed Iconicity Levels of English Phonaesthemes," *Public Journal of Semiotics* 7, no. 2 (2017): 73–93.

18. Padraic Monaghan, Morten H. Christiansen, and Nick Chater, "The Phonological-Distributional Coherence Hypothesis: Cross-Linguistic Evidence in Language Acquisition," *Cognitive Psychology* 55, no. 4 (2007): 259–305.

19. Time-stable concepts thus tend to be represented by nouns, and non-time-stable concepts tend to be represented by verbs (John Haiman, *Iconicity in Syntax: Proceedings of a Symposium on Iconicity in Syntax, Stanford, June 24–26, 1983*, Typological Studies in Language [Amsterdam; Philadelphia: J. Benjamins, 1985]; George Kingsley Zipf, *The Psycho-Biology of Language; an Introduction to Dynamic Philology* [Boston: Houghton Mifflin, 1935]).

20. Thomas A. Farmer, Morten H. Christiansen, and Padraic Monaghan, "Phonological Typicality Influences On-Line Sentence Comprehension," *Proceedings of the National Academy of Sciences* 103, no. 32 (2006): 12203–8.

21. Lynn K. Perry, Marcus Perlman, Bodo Winter, Dominic W. Massaro, and Gary Lupyan, "Iconicity in the Speech of Children and Adults," *Developmental Science* 21, no. 3 (2018): e12572.

22. Perry et al., "Iconicity in the Speech of Children and Adults," n.p.

23. Max Louwerse and Zhan Qu, "Estimating Valence from the Sound of a Word: Computational, Experimental, and Cross-Linguistic Evidence," *Psychonomic Bulletin & Review* 24, no. 3 (2017): 849–55.

24. Following the Principle of Parsimony or Occam's razor, not using more features without necessity.

25. Damián E. Blasi, Søren Wichmann, Harald Hammarström, Peter F. Stadler, and Morten H. Christiansen, "Sound–Meaning Association Biases Evidenced across Thousands of Languages," *Proceedings of the National Academy of Sciences* 113, no. 39 (2016): 10818–23.

26. Michael Gasser, "The Origins of Arbitrariness in Language," *Proceedings of the Annual Meeting of the Cognitive Science Society* (2004): 434–39.

27. Steven T. Piantadosi, Harry Tily, and Edward Gibson, "The Communicative Function of Ambiguity in Language," *Cognition* 122, no. 3 (2012): 280–91, for the advantages of ambiguity in the system; Paul A. Luce and David B. Pisoni, "Recognizing Spoken Words: The Neighborhood Activation Model," *Ear and Hearing* 19, no. 1 (1998): 36, for similar word forms; and Victoria A. Fromkin, "The Non-Anomalous Nature of Anomalous Utterances," *Language* (1971): 27–52, for different meanings. See also Michael Gasser, Nitya Sethuraman, and Stephen Hockema, "Iconicity in Expressives: An Empirical Investigation," in *Experimental and Empirical Methods* (Stanford, CA: CSLI Publications, 2005).

28. Bodo Winter, *Sensory Linguistics: Language, Perception and Metaphor*, vol. 20 (Amsterdam; Philadelphia: Benjamins, 2019).

29. Charles Egerton Osgood, George J. Suci, and Percy H. Tannenbaum, *The Measurement of Meaning* (Chicago: University of Illinois Press, 1957).

30. James Brand, Padraic Monaghan, and Peter Walker, "The Changing Role of Sound-Symbolism for Small Versus Large Vocabularies," *Cognitive Science* 42 (2018): 578–90.

CHAPTER 11: ORDER

1. John Robert Ross and William Edwin Cooper, "World Order," in *Papers from the Parasession on Functionalism*, ed. Robin E. Grossman, L. James San, and Timothy J. Vance (Chicago: Chicago Linguistic Society, 1975), 64.

2. Max Louwerse, "Embodied Relations Are Encoded in Language," *Psychonomic Bulletin & Review* 15, no. 4 (2008): 838–44.

3. Timothy A. Judge and Daniel M. Cable, "The Effect of Physical Height on Workplace Success and Income: Preliminary Test of a Theoretical Model," *Journal of Applied Psychology* 89, no. 3 (2004): 428–41.

4. Michelle M. Duguid and Jack A. Goncalo, "Living Large: The Powerful Overestimate Their Own Height," *Psychological Science* 23, no. 1 (2012): 36–40.

5. Brian P. Meier, and Michael D. Robinson, "Why the Sunny Side Is Up: Associations between Affect and Vertical Position," *Psychological Science* 15, no. 4 (2004): 243–47.

6. Sterling Hutchinson and Max Louwerse, "Language Statistics and Individual Differences in Processing Primary Metaphors," *Cognitive Linguistics* 24, no. 4 (2013): 667–87.

7. Richard Tillman and Max Louwerse, "Estimating Emotions through Language Statistics and Embodied Cognition," *Journal of Psycholinguistic Research* 47, no. 1 (2018): 159–67.

8. Here is the good news. If you go to Google n-gram viewer and watch the patterns of "men and women" and "women and men" over time, you'll find that since the 1960s, "women and men" becomes more frequent. Not more frequent than "men and women," which remains seven times more frequent, but compared to twenty times more frequent in the past, there has been a gradual improvement in the linguistic role of women.

9. Max Louwerse, Susanne Raisig, Richard Tillman, and Sterling Hutchinson, "Time after Time in Words: Chronology through Language Statistics," in *Proceedings of the 37th Annual Meeting of the Cognitive Science Society*, ed. D. C. Noelle et al., 1428–33 (Austin, TX: Cognitive Science Society, 2015).

10. Ross and Cooper, "World Order."

11. Sarah Bunin Benor and Roger Levy, "The Chicken or the Egg? A Probabilistic Analysis of English Binomials," *Language* (2006): 233–78.

12. Stanislas Dehaene, *The Number Sense: How the Mind Creates Mathematics* (New York: Allen Lane, 2011).

13. Sterling Hutchinson and Max M. Louwerse, "Language Statistics Explain the Spatial-Numerical Association of Response Codes," *Psychonomic Bulletin & Review* 21, no. 2 (2014): 470–78.

14. Max Louwerse and Patrick Jeuniaux, "The Linguistic and Embodied Nature of Conceptual Processing," *Cognition* 114, no. 1 (2010): 96–104.

15. Louwerse, "Embodied Relations Are Encoded in Language."

16. Max Louwerse and Louise Connell, "A Taste of Words: Linguistic Context and Perceptual Simulation Predict the Modality of Words," *Cognitive Science* 35, no. 2 (2011): 381–98.

17. Hutchinson and Louwerse, "Language Statistics and Individual Differences."

18. Talmy Givón, "Iconicity, Isomorphism and Non-Arbitrary Coding in Syntax," in *Iconicity in Syntax: Proceedings*, ed. John Haiman (Amsterdam: John Benjamins, 1985), 189.

19. Talmy Givón, *Syntax: An Introduction*, rev. ed., 2 vols (Amsterdam; Philadelphia: J. Benjamins, 2001).

20. Givón, "Iconicity, Isomorphism, and Non-Arbitrary Coding in Syntax," 197.

21. Max Louwerse, Patrick Jeuniaux, Bin Zhang, Jie Wu, and Mohammed E. Hoque, "The Interaction between Information and Intonation Structure: Prosodic Marking of Theme and Rheme," in *Proceedings of the 30th Annual Conference of the Cognitive Science Society*, ed. Brad C. Love, Ken McRae, and Vladimir M. Sloutsky, 1984–89 (Austin, TX: Cognitive Science Society, 2008).

22. Jared Diamond, *The Rise and Fall of the Third Chimpanzee: How Our Animal Heritage Affects the Way We Live* (New York: Random House, 2013).

23. Merriam-Webster Inc., *Merriam-Webster's Dictionary of English Usage* (Springfield, MA: Merriam-Webster, 1993), 720–21.

24. Filip Germeys and Géry d'Ydewalle, "The Psychology of Film: Perceiving beyond the Cut," *Psychological Research* 71, no. 4 (2007): 458–66.

25. Morten H. Christiansen and Nick Chater, "Language as Shaped by the Brain," *Behavioral and Brain Sciences* 31, no. 5 (2008): 489–509.

26. Talmy Givón, "Historical Syntax and Synchronic Morphology: An Archaeologist's Field Trip," *Chicago Linguistic Society* (1971), 413.

27. This process is called univerbation, combining a fixed expression of several words into a new single word.

28. Michael Tomasello, *Constructing a Language: A Usage-Based Theory of Language Acquisition* (Cambridge: Harvard University Press, 2003), 14.

CHAPTER 12: COMPANY

1. Zellig S. Harris, "Distributional Structure," *Word* 10, no. 2–3 (1954): 147.

2. J. R. Firth, *Papers in Linguistics, 1934–1951* (London; New York: Oxford University Press, 1957), 11.

3. *Kvelling* is an archaic Yiddish word for "happy and proud."

4. There are many such techniques, including Latent Semantic Analysis, Word-2Vec, Hyperspace Analog to Language, and other models of distributional semantics. See an extensive description of this method in Thomas K. Landauer, Simon Dennis, Danielle McNamara, and W. Kintsch, eds., *Handbook of Latent Semantic Analysis* (Mahwah, NJ: Lawrence Erlbaum, 2007).

5. I used the exact same parameters as outlined in Max Louwerse, "Symbol Interdependency in Symbolic and Embodied Cognition," *Topics in Cognitive Science* 3, no. 2 (2011): 273–302, and Max Louwerse, "Knowing the Meaning of a Word by the Linguistic and Perceptual Company It Keeps," *Topics in Cognitive Science* 10, no. 3 (2018): 573–89.

6. See Thomas K. Landauer and Susan Dumais, "A Solution to Plato's Problem: The Latent Semantic Analysis Theory of Acquisition, Induction, and Representation of Knowledge," *Psychological Review* 104, no. 2 (1997): 211–40, for empirical evidence of computationally passing the TOEFL test.

7. See Landauer et al., *Handbook of Latent Semantic Analysis*, for the general approach; see Max Louwerse and Willie Van Peer, "How Cognitive Is Cognitive Poetics? The Interaction between Symbolic and Embodied Cognition," *Cognitive Poetics: Goals, Gains and Gaps* 10 (2009): 423, for some concrete examples.

8. Multidimensional scaling. Joseph B. Kruskal, *Multidimensional Scaling* (Beverly Hills, CA: SAGE, 1978).

9. Louwerse, "Symbol Interdependency."

10. Max Louwerse and R. A. Zwaan, "Language Encodes Geographical Information," *Cognitive Science* 33, no. 1 (2009): 51–73.

11. Apparently not that ridiculous. Waldo Tobler, professor of geography and statistics at the University of California, Santa Barbara, and a member of the National Academy of Sciences of the United States, has proposed something similar in his First Law of Geography.

12. "It is important to note from the start that the similarity estimates derived by LSA are not simple contiguity frequencies, co-occurrence counts, or correlations in usage, but depend on a powerful mathematical analysis that is capable of correctly inferring much deeper relations (thus the phrase "Latent Semantic"), and as a consequence are often much better predictors of human meaning-based judgments and performance than are the surface level contingencies that have long been rejected . . . by linguists as the basis of language phenomena." Thomas K. Landauer, Peter W. Foltz, and Darrell Laham, "An Introduction to Latent Semantic Analysis," *Discourse Processes* 25, no. 2–3 (1998): 260.

13. Max Louwerse, Sterling Hutchinson, and Zhiqiang Cai, "The Chinese Route Argument: Predicting the Longitude and Latitude of Cities in China and the Middle East Using Statistical Linguistic Frequencies," in *Proceedings of the 34th Annual Conference of the Cognitive Science Society*, ed. N. Miyake, D. Peebles, and R. P. Cooper, 695–700 (Sapporo, Japan: Cognitive Science Society, 2012).

14. Some countries were not included because the Arabic notation of cities for those countries was unavailable (Saudi Arabia, Ethiopia, Eritrea, Somalia, Djibouti).

15. Gabriel Recchia and Max Louwerse, "Reproducing Affective Norms with Lexical Co-Occurrence Statistics: Predicting Valence, Arousal, and Dominance," *Quarterly Journal of Experimental Psychology* 68, no. 8 (2015): 1584–98.

16. Max Louwerse and Nick Benesh, "Representing Spatial Structure through Maps and Language: Lord of the Rings Encodes the Spatial Structure of Middle Earth," *Cognitive Science* 36, no. 8 (2012): 1556–69.

17. Sterling Hutchinson and Max Louwerse, "Extracting Social Networks from Language Statistics," *Discourse Processes* 55, no. 7 (2018): 607–18.

18. Landauer and Dumais, "A Solution to Plato's Problem."

19. Zellig S. Harris, "Distributional Structure," *Word* 10, no. 2–3 (1954): 146–62.

20. Martin Redington, Nick Chater, and Steven Finch, "Distributional Information: A Powerful Cue for Acquiring Syntactic Categories," *Cognitive Science* 22, no. 4 (1998): 425–69.

CHAPTER 13: BOOTSTRAPPING

1. Waldo R. Tobler, "A Computer Movie Simulating Urban Growth in the Detroit Region," *Economic Geography* 46, no. sup1 (1970): 236.

2. Rudolf Erich Raspe, William Strang, and Joseph Benwell Clark, *The Travels and Surprising Adventures of Baron Munchausen* (Brooklyn: Melville House Pub., 2012).

3. Jan Freeman, "Bootstraps and Baron Munchausen," *The Word* (blog), January 27, 2009, http://archive.boston.com/bostonglobe/ideas/theword/2009/01/bootstraps _and.html.

4. Indeed, that turns out to be the case. If one conducts a correlation between the x and y coordinates on this map and the actual distances between the cities in the

United States, the correlation is very high: .96 (where 0 is no correlation and 1 is a perfect correlation).

5. Max Louwerse, "Knowing the Meaning of a Word by the Linguistic and Perceptual Company It Keeps," *Topics in Cognitive Science* 10, no. 3 (2018): 573–89.

6. John Locke, *The Works of John Locke; a New Edition, Corrected* (London: Printed for Thomas Tegg, 1823), 4.21.4, p. 175.

7. I am simplifying de Saussure's theory, as for him the sound of the word *tree* is not an actual sound but the psychological perception of the sound in the hearer, and the reference of the actual tree in the real world is the mental construct of the concept of a tree. And, as we know from chapter 10, for de Saussure no intrinsic relationship existed between the signifier and the signified; their relationship was entirely arbitrary.

8. The Peirce Edition Project, School of Liberal Arts, Indiana University Indianapolis, aims to produce a thirty-volume edition of Peirce's writings from across the humanities and sciences.

9. In what follows (again), I wholeheartedly agree with Givón when he states, discussing the theories of Charles Sanders Peirce, "Like all traditions, one must weigh it dispassionately, adopt what is useful and discard without regret what seems to be orthodoxy for orthodoxy's sake." Talmy Givón, "Iconicity, Isomorphism and Non-Arbitrary Coding in Syntax," in *Iconicity in Syntax: Proceedings*, ed. John Haiman (Amsterdam: John Benjamins, 1985), 192.

10. I will not distinguish between the Immediate, Dynamic, and Final (or Normal) Interpretant. Nicole Everaert-Desmedt, "Peirce's Semiotics," Signo, 2011, www.signosemio.com/peirce/semiotics.asp.

11. See also Aristotle's *Metaphysics*: "And if the Ideas and the particulars that share in them have the same form, there will be something common to these. . . . But if they have not the same form, they must have only the name in common, and it is as if one were to call both Callias and a wooden image a 'man', without observing any community between them." Carlos G. Steel, Oliver Primavesi, and Aristotle, *Aristotle's Metaphysics Alpha: Symposium Aristotelicum*, 1st ed. (Oxford: Oxford University Press, 2012), book 1, part 9.

12. David Hume, *A Treatise of Human Nature* (Adelaide, South Australia: eBooks@Adelaide, 2006), https://web.archive.org/web/20060824185256/http://etext.library.adelaide.edu.au/h/hume/david/h92t/chapter4.html.

13. In English a "rooster" may be an animal; in Dutch it is a schedule or a barbeque.

14. Francesco Berna, Paul Goldberg, Liora Kolska Horwitz, James Brink, Sharon Holt, Marion Bamford, and Michael Chazan, "Microstratigraphic Evidence of in Situ Fire in the Acheulean Strata of Wonderwerk Cave, Northern Cape Province, South Africa," *Proceedings of the National Academy of Sciences* 109, no. 20 (2012): E1215–20.

15. This may remind you of chapter 10 ("Sound"), where we discuss the meaning of value.

16. David McNeill, *Hand and Mind: What Gestures Reveal about Thought* (Chicago: University of Chicago Press, 1992).

17. Public Domain Vectors, accessed November 12, 2020, https://publicdomain vectors.org/en/wild-animal-clipart-free.

18. Paul Bloom, *How Children Learn the Meanings of Words* (Cambridge: MIT Press, 2000).

19. Patrick Jeuniaux, Rick Dale, and Max M. Louwerse, "The Role of Feedback in Learning Form-Meaning Mapping," in *Proceedings of the 31th Annual Conference of the Cognitive Science Society*, ed. Niels A. Taatgen and Hedderik van Rijn, 488–93 (Austin, TX: Cognitive Science Society, 2009).

20. For completeness, in a first experiment where we presented objects differing in shape, size, and color, participants did well in the feedback condition, getting about 70 percent right, four times above chance level. In the no-feedback condition, participants did better than chance, but the performance was not deeply impressive. We wondered whether the reason may have been that participants had to keep three dimensions in mind. In a second experiment, we therefore cut one dimension.

21. Chen Yu and Linda B. Smith, "Rapid Word Learning under Uncertainty Via Cross-Situational Statistics," *Psychological Science* 18, no. 5 (2007): 414–20.

22. Andrew D. M. Smith and Kenny Smith, "Cross-Situational Learning," *Encyclopedia of the Sciences of Learning* (2012): 864–66.

23. Louwerse, "Knowing the Meaning of a Word."

24. Daniel Kahneman, *Thinking, Fast and Slow*, 1st ed. (New York: Farrar, Straus and Giroux, 2011).

25. Max Louwerse, "Symbolic or Embodied Representations: A Case for Symbol Interdependency," in *Handbook of Latent Semantic Analysis*, ed. Thomas K. Landauer, Danielle S. McNamara, Simon Dennis, and Walter Kintsch (Mahwah, NJ: Lawrence Erlbaum Associates, 2007), 120.

26. Donald O. Hebb, *The Organization of Behavior; a Neuropsychological Theory*, A Wiley Book in Clinical Psychology (New York: Wiley, 1949).

27. Kahneman, *Thinking, Fast and Slow*.

28. Michael Spivey, *The Continuity of Mind*, Oxford Psychology Series (Oxford; New York: Oxford University Press, 2007).

29. There is a growing body of evidence that patterns in the data result in a faster learning process. Devansh Arpit, Stanisław Jastrzębski, Nicolas Ballas, David Krueger, Emmanuel Bengio, Maxinder S. Kanwal, Tegan Maharaj, et al., "A Closer Look at Memorization in Deep Networks," in *Proceedings of the 34th International Conference on Machine Learning*, ed. Doina Precup and Yeewhye Teh, 233–42 (Sydney, Australia: PMLR 70).

30. I leave aside the question of whether that instinct must be innate, or whether it could also be acquired. According to the nativist view, a language instinct is built in, is innate, as shown in chapter 5.

31. Jean Berko, "The Child's Learning of English Morphology," *Word* 14, no. 2–3 (1958): 150–77.

32. Ramon Ferrer i Cancho, Oliver Riordan, and Béla Bollobás, "The Consequences of Zipf's Law for Syntax and Symbolic Reference," *Proceedings of the Royal Society B: Biological Sciences* 272, no. 1562 (2005): 561–65.

33. Lynn K. Perry, Marcus Perlman, Bodo Winter, Dominic W. Massaro, and Gary Lupyan, "Iconicity in the Speech of Children and Adults," *Developmental Science* 21, no. 3 (2018): e12572.

34. Dagmar Divjak, *Frequency in Language: Memory, Attention and Learning* (New York: Cambridge University Press, 2019).

35. Fernanda Ferreira, Karl G. D. Bailey, and Vittoria Ferraro, "Good-Enough Representations in Language Comprehension," *Current Directions in Psychological Science* 11, no. 1 (2002): 11–15.

36. After "there is another possibility that has been almost entirely overlooked, and it is the point of the remainder of this chapter to explore it. I think [many linguists] have articulated a central conundrum about language learning, but they offer an answer that inverts cause and effect. They assert that the source of prior support for language acquisition must originate from *inside* the brain, on the unstated assumption that there is no other possible source. But there is an alternative: that the extra support for language learning is vested neither in the brain of the child nor in the brains of parents or teachers, but outside the brains, in language itself." Terrence William Deacon, *The Symbolic Species: The Co-Evolution of Language and the Brain*, 1st ed. (New York: W. W. Norton, 1997), 105.

37. After "an ant, viewed as a behaving system, is quite simple. The apparent complexity of its behavior over time is largely a reflection of the complexity of the environment in which it finds itself." Herbert A. Simon, *The Sciences of the Artificial*, Karl Taylor Compton Lectures (Cambridge: MIT Press, 1969), 52.

CHAPTER 14: AVENUES

1. Albert Einstein, Leopold Infeld, and Rouben Mamoulian Collection (Library of Congress), *The Evolution of Physics: The Growth of Ideas from Early Concepts to Relativity and Quanta* (New York: Simon and Schuster, 1938), 27.

2. Allen J. Frances, "Science Is Not Just a Matter of Opinion," *Psychology Today*, December 2, 2016, www.psychologytoday.com/us/blog/saving-normal /201612/science-is-not-just-matter-opinion.

3. Max Louwerse and Zhan Qu, "Estimating Valence from the Sound of a Word: Computational, Experimental, and Cross-Linguistic Evidence," *Psychonomic Bulletin & Review* 24, no. 3 (2017): 849–55.

4. Max Louwerse, "Embodied Relations Are Encoded in Language," *Psychonomic Bulletin & Review* 15, no. 4 (August 2008): 838–44.

5. Max Louwerse, "Knowing the Meaning of a Word by the Linguistic and Perceptual Company It Keeps," *Topics in Cognitive Science* 10, no. 3 (2018): 573–89.

6. Max Louwerse and N. Benesh, "Representing Spatial Structure through Maps and Language: Lord of the Rings Encodes the Spatial Structure of Middle Earth," *Cognitive Science* 36, no. 8 (2012): 1556–69.

7. Richard K. Peach and Lewis P. Shapiro, *Cognition and Acquired Language Disorders: An Information Processing Approach* (St. Louis, MO: Elsevier, 2012).

8. S. Kevin Zhou, Hayit Greenspan, and Dinggang Shen, *Deep Learning for Medical Image Analysis*, Elsevier and Miccai Society Book Series (London; San Diego: Elsevier/Academic Press, 2017).

9. Marcel Adam Just, Vladimir L. Cherkassky, Sandesh Aryal, and Tom M. Mitchell, "A Neurosemantic Theory of Concrete Noun Representation Based on the Underlying Brain Codes," *PloS One* 5, no. 1 (2010): e8622; Karim S. Kassam, Amanda R. Markey, Vladimir L. Cherkassky, George Loewenstein, and Marcel Adam Just, "Identifying Emotions on the Basis of Neural Activation," *PloS One* 8, no. 6 (2013): e66032.

10. Marcel Adam Just, Lisa Pan, Vladimir L. Cherkassky, Dana L. McMakin, Christine Cha, Matthew K. Nock, and David Brent, "Machine Learning of Neural Representations of Suicide and Emotion Concepts Identifies Suicidal Youth," *Nature Human Behaviour* 1, no. 12 (2017): 911–19.

11. Frederick Jelinek, *Statistical Methods for Speech Recognition* (Cambridge: MIT Press, 1997).

12. Christopher D. Manning, Hinrich Schütze, and Prabhakar Raghavan, *Introduction to Information Retrieval* (Cambridge: Cambridge University Press, 2008).

13. A. C. Graesser, D. S. McNamara, M. M. Louwerse, and Z. Q. Cai, "Coh-Metrix: Analysis of Text on Cohesion and Language," *Behavior Research Methods Instruments & Computers* 36, no. 2 (2004): 193–202.

14. Dan Jurafsky and James H. Martin, *Speech and Language Processing: An Introduction to Natural Language Processing, Computational Linguistics, and Speech Recognition*, Prentice Hall Series in Artificial Intelligence (Upper Saddle River, NJ: Prentice Hall, 2000).

15. Benjamin Lee Whorf, *Language, Thought, and Reality: Selected Writings of Benjamin Lee Whorf* (Cambridge: MIT Press, 2012).

16. Dedre Gentner and Susan Goldin-Meadow, *Language in Mind: Advances in the Study of Language and Thought* (Cambridge: MIT Press, 2003); John J. Gumperz and Stephen C. Levinson, *Rethinking Linguistic Relativity*, Studies in the Social and Cultural Foundations of Language (Cambridge; New York: Cambridge University Press, 1996).

17. A. C. Graesser, S. L. Lu, G. T. Jackson, H. H. Mitchell, M. Ventura, A. Olney, and M. M. Louwerse, "Autotutor: A Tutor with Dialogue in Natural Language," *Behavior Research Methods Instruments & Computers* 36, no. 2 (2004): 180–92.

18. M. M. Louwerse, M. Nilsenova-Postma, H. A. T. van Limpt-Broers, T. T. de Back, A. M. Tinga, and M. Horden, "Beyond the Frontiers of Education: How Immersive Media Changes the Way We Learn," *ITU J. ICT Discover* 3 (2020): 43–51.

19. Louwerse et al., "Beyond the Frontiers of Education."

20. SpaceBuzz, "SpaceBuzz in Washington for Global Launch," YouTube, October 21, 2019, video, 1:54, www.youtube.com/watch?v=NuvLmlJurOo&feature =youtu.be.

Acknowledgments

"*You* must speak a lot of languages!" was the response people gave me in conversations at parties when I was obtaining my PhD in linguistics. "Oh dear, you then must be able to read my mind!" was the response people gave me in conversations at parties when I was a professor in psychology. "So you build computers that will take over my job!" was the response I got in conversations at parties as a professor in artificial intelligence. These responses motivated me to write this book. It would be too easy for me to ignore these responses because speaking a lot of languages, reading people's minds, and developing an AI-controlled world is not what linguists, psychologists, and artificial intelligence researchers do. But I also realized that too often scientists—and, to not offend any of my colleagues, I am happy to only be speaking for myself—tend to look down from the ivory tower and assume that the rest of the world will share the same fascination for a specific area of research as they do. Most nonscientists, however, will not. I realized that if I wanted to get others excited about what I am excited about, it would become my job to explain that fascination to others. Not in science jargon, but in popular science.

But this book has been written not just for the nonscientists among us who might be interested in language, cognition, and computation. It was also written for the young scientists among us, who might be interested in linguistics, psychology, and artificial intelligence, but would welcome an introduction to find out whether this is the field they want to explore further. A pile of journal articles might be intimidating, a textbook not immediately the most exciting read, but perhaps a popular science book may be a good primer. That primer could be read as an introduction to linguistics and psycholinguistics (chapters 1–3), as traditional explanations for language acquisition and language processing (chapters 4–7), or as an introduction to aspects of cognitive psychology (chapters 8–9) and computational psycholinguistics (chapters 10–13).

This book is written for the nonscientists wondering what happens in the ivory towers of academia and for the young scientists wondering whether those towers of academia are worth climbing. But of course, it is also for my colleagues in computational linguistics, psycholinguistics, cognitive and social psychology, computer science, and artificial intelligence. And for the reviewers who asked me to be more concrete in what I meant with a symbol interdependency hypothesis, or what I meant by the claim that language encodes perceptual information, or the claim that language comprehension is both symbolic and embodied. If it was not clear enough in my academic work, I hope it has become clearer in this book.

It is common practice for popular science books to provide recommendations on other popular science books related to the topic. This is a useful practice for this book too, as many of the references in the notes and bibliography excel in science, but not immediately in popular science (although sometimes they excel in both). In providing popular science recommendations, I struggle with the same hesitation as when referring to the bibliography of this book: what should be included and what should not. It is not difficult to answer the first question, but the second question—what to *not* include—is considerably harder to answer. With the same risk of not having included a reference in the bibliography that I should obviously have included, I will list some additional readings in popular science.

For a complete overview of language-related topics that are easy to read, David Crystal (2010) is a wonderful resource. There are many popular science books on language, Steven Pinker's (1994, 1999) work specifically. For an introduction into the psychology of language, please see Jean Aitchison (2007) and Gerry Altmann (1998). For a neuroscience perspective on language, Michael Gazzaniga (1992, 2011, 2018) provides nice introductions. Frans de Waal (2016) gives a wonderful overview of the field of animal cognition. Benjamin Bergen (2012) provides an accessible overview of the many experiments being conducted in the field of symbol grounding and embodied cognition. For more information on linguistic relativism, Guy Deutscher (2010) provides a valuable introduction. Cognitive shortcuts discussed in Nick Chater (2018), Gerd Gigerenzer (2007), and Daniel Kahneman (2011) are worthwhile, as well as Steve Sloman and Philip Fernbach (2017). Many examples of language analyses and what words can say about us can be found in James Pennebaker (2011). For more detail on algorithms, Brian Christian and Tom Griffiths (2016) provide an introduction to computer science and decision making. Terrence Deacon (1997) perhaps laid the foundation for the current book; it may not be the easiest read, though it provides a wealth of information on the evolution of keeping language in mind.

Acknowledgment sections are for people to say thanks to. There are too many people to thank to fit the pages of this book, for debating, discussing, and sharing ideas, as the ideas in this book have evolved over a significant stretch of time. I would like to thank colleagues, students, and staff (in chronological order) at Utrecht University, the University of Florida, the University of Edinburgh, the University of Memphis, and Tilburg University—but also those in those other places, those who I had the privilege to meet at conferences, invited talks, colloquia, and precious coffee breaks.

Thanks to the many undergraduate and graduate students in the United States, the United Kingdom, and the Netherlands for the discussions, arguments, questions, and answers—for being inquisitive, for being critical, and for collaborating in the process of understanding. I hope this book has answered some of your questions, but even more so, I hope this book has generated new questions that await being answered.

Thank you coauthors and collaborators Ellen Gurman Bard, Nick Benesh, Zhiqiang Cai, Louise Connell, Rick Dale, Vivek Datla, Art Graesser, Ehsan Hoque, Xianyou He, Xiangen Hu, Sterling Hutchinson, Patrick Jeuniaux, Gwyneth Lewis, Danielle McNamara, Andrew Olney, Zhan Qu, Gabriel Recchia, Rick Tillman, Matthew Ventura, Will van Peer, Fang Yang, and Rolf Zwaan (among many others) for working together on various publications on mental representations, language statistics, and symbolic embodied cognition. These collaborations directly or indirectly have shaped the contents of this book.

I am grateful to my agent, Giles Anderson. His comment on one of the first drafts of one of the chapters has been memorable and has shaped the tone of this book: "The first part of this chapter is great, but in the second part you really become that academician again!" (and "academician" was not meant as a compliment this time). I am also grateful to Jake Bonar, the acquisitions editor at Prometheus Books, for his encouragements and for believing in this book. Jessica Kastner Keene, Lara Hahn, and Kellie Hagan at the Rowman & Littlefield Publishing Group, thank you for keeping the pace and making sure that the book has become what it has become. And thank you to Tricia Currie-Knight, for the many stylistic suggestions that have made this book so much more consistent and more enjoyable for you, the reader.

Many of the chapters have undoubtedly improved greatly as a consequence of the comments and suggestions of those who dared to read the initial scribblings of the ideas presented here. A big thanks to Andrew Anderson, Gabriel Recchia, Julija Vaitonyte, and Hans IJzerman, and special thanks to Louise Connell, Eric Postma, and Will van Peer, for the valuable feedback they have provided on what have ultimately become the book chapters in front of you.

No words in this book could have been written down had it not been for my parents, who provided me with the training, the language instinct, the neural network, and the grounding skills to discover how language creates meaning, but who also raised me to be stubborn, critical, and perseverant. Without those skills, I would never have been able to complete this work.

Finally, I would like to thank Desirée, Quinten, and Eleane for their patience—patience for the many nights and weekends I walked up the stairs to my own personal ivory tower to write down how to keep those words in mind. Those are for you.

Bibliography

Aitchison, Jean. *The Articulate Mammal: An Introduction to Psycholinguistics.* New York: Routledge, 2007.

———. *Words in the Mind: An Introduction to the Mental Lexicon.* Oxford, UK; New York: Blackwell, 1987.

Akmajian, Adrian, Ann Kathleen Farmer, Lee Bickmore, Richard A. Demers, and Robert M. Harnish. *Linguistics: An Introduction to Language and Communication.* 7th ed. Cambridge: The MIT Press, 2017.

Allopenna, Paul D., James S. Magnuson, and Michael K. Tanenhaus. "Tracking the Time Course of Spoken Word Recognition Using Eye Movements: Evidence for Continuous Mapping Models." *Journal of Memory and Language* 38, no. 4 (1998): 419–39.

Altmann, Gerry T. M. *The Ascent of Babel: An Exploration of Language, Mind, and Understanding.* Oxford: Oxford University Press, 1998.

Anderson, James A. *An Introduction to Neural Networks.* Cambridge: MIT Press, 1995.

Andrews, Kristin. *The Animal Mind: An Introduction to the Philosophy of Animal Cognition.* New York: Routledge, 2020.

Andrews, Mark, Gabriella Vigliocco, and David Vinson. "Integrating Experiential and Distributional Data to Learn Semantic Representations." *Psychological Review* 116, no. 3 (2009): 463–98.

Arpit, Devansh, Stanisław Jastrzębski, Nicolas Ballas, David Krueger, Emmanuel Bengio, Maxinder S. Kanwal, Tegan Maharaj, et al. "A Closer Look at Memorization in Deep Networks." In *Proceedings of the 34th International Conference on Machine Learning,* edited by Doina Precup and Yeewhye Teh, 233–42. Sydney, Australia: PMLR 70.

Asch, Solomon E., and Harold Guetzkow. "Effects of Group Pressure Upon the Modification and Distortion of Judgments." *Organizational Influence Processes* (1951): 295–303.

Austin, John Langshaw. *How to Do Things with Words*. Vol. 88. Oxford: Oxford University Press, 1975.

Baker, Collin F., Charles J. Fillmore, and John B. Lowe. "The Berkeley FrameNet Project." Paper presented at the 36th Annual Meeting of the Association for Computational Linguistics and 17th International Conference on Computational Linguistics, volume 1, 1998.

Baker, Mark C. *The Atoms of Language*. 1st ed. New York: Basic Books, 2001.

Barsalou, Lawrence W. "Perceptual Symbol Systems." *Behavioral and Brain Sciences* 22, no. 4 (1999): 577–660.

Bauer, Richard H. "Lateralization of Neural Control for Vocalization by the Frog (Rana Pipiens)." *Psychobiology* 21, no. 3 (1993): 243–48.

BBC. "The Code—the Wisdom of the Crowd." YouTube. 2011. Video, 4:48. www .youtube.com/watch?v=iOucwX7Z1HU&t=2s.

BBC Earth Unplugged. "How Many Grains of Sand Are in the Sahara?" YouTube. December 3, 2014. Video, 4:12. www.youtube.com/watch?v=jQ41Gk80djs.

Benor, Sarah Bunin, and Roger Levy. "The Chicken or the Egg? A Probabilistic Analysis of English Binomials." *Language* (2006): 233–78.

Bergen, Benjamin K. *Louder Than Words: The New Science of How the Mind Makes Meaning*. New York: Basic Books, 2012.

Berko, Jean. "The Child's Learning of English Morphology." *Word* 14, no. 2–3 (1958): 150–77.

Berna, Francesco, Paul Goldberg, Liora Kolska Horwitz, James Brink, Sharon Holt, Marion Bamford, and Michael Chazan. "Microstratigraphic Evidence of in Situ Fire in the Acheulean Strata of Wonderwerk Cave, Northern Cape Province, South Africa." *Proceedings of the National Academy of Sciences* 109, no. 20 (2012): E1215–20.

Berwick, Robert C., and Noam Chomsky. *Birdsong, Speech, and Language: Exploring the Evolution of Mind and Brain*. Cambridge: MIT Press, 2013.

Blancke, Stefaan. "Lord Monboddo's Ourang-Outang and the Origin and Progress of Language." In *The Evolution of Social Communication in Primates*, 31–44. Cham, Switzerland: Springer, 2014.

Blasi, Damián E., Søren Wichmann, Harald Hammarström, Peter F. Stadler, and Morten H. Christiansen. "Sound–Meaning Association Biases Evidenced across Thousands of Languages." *Proceedings of the National Academy of Sciences* 113, no. 39 (2016): 10818–23.

Bloom, Paul. *How Children Learn the Meanings of Words*. Cambridge: MIT Press, 2000.

Bloomfield, Leonard. "Language [1933]." *Holt, New York* 56 (1962).

Bolhuis, Johan J., and Martin Everaert. *Birdsong, Speech, and Language: Exploring the Evolution of Mind and Brain*. Cambridge: MIT Press, 2013.

Borghi, Anna M., Arthur M. Glenberg, and Michael P. Kaschak. "Putting Words in Perspective." *Memory & Cognition* 32, no. 6 (2004): 863–73.

Braine, Martin D. S. "On Two Types of Models of the Internalization of Grammars." *The Ontogenesis of Grammar* (1971): 153–86.

Brand, James, Padraic Monaghan, and Peter Walker. "The Changing Role of Sound-Symbolism for Small Versus Large Vocabularies." *Cognitive Science* 42 (2018): 578–90.

Bravo, Mary, Randolph Blake, and Sharon Morrison. "Cats See Subjective Contours." *Vision Research* 28, no. 8 (1988): 861–65.

Broadbent, D. E. "Review of Verbal Behavior." *British Journal of Psychology* 50 (1959): 371–73.

Brysbaert, Marc, Michaël Stevens, Pawel Mandera, and Emmanuel Keuleers. "How Many Words Do We Know? Practical Estimates of Vocabulary Size Dependent on Word Definition, the Degree of Language Input and the Participant's Age." *Frontiers in Psychology* 7 (2016): 1116.

Carroll, Sean B. "Genetics and the Making of Homo Sapiens." *Nature* 422, no. 6934 (2003): 849–57.

Cattell, James McKeen. "The Time It Takes to See and Name Objects." *Mind* 11, no. 41 (1886): 63–65.

Chabris, Christopher F., and Daniel J. Simons. *The Invisible Gorilla: And Other Ways Our Intuitions Deceive Us.* 1st ed. New York: Crown, 2010.

Chartrand, Tanya L., and John A. Bargh. "The Chameleon Effect: The Perception–Behavior Link and Social Interaction." *Journal of Personality and Social Psychology* 76, no. 6 (1999): 893.

Chater, Nick. *The Mind Is Flat: The Illusion of Mental Depth and the Improvised Mind.* London: Allen Lane, 2018.

Cherry, E. Colin. "Some Experiments on the Recognition of Speech, with One and with Two Ears." *The Journal of the Acoustical Society of America* 25, no. 5 (1953): 975–79.

Chomsky, Noam. *The Architecture of Language.* New Delhi: Oxford University Press, 2000.

———. *Aspects of the Theory of Syntax.* Massachusetts Institute of Technology Research Laboratory of Electronics Special Technical Report. Cambridge: MIT Press, 1965.

———. *Current Issues in Linguistic Theory (Janua Linguarum 38).* The Hague: Mouton, 1964.

———. *Language and Problems of Knowledge: The Managua Lectures.* Vol. 16. Cambridge: MIT Press, 1988.

———. *Syntactic Structures.* Janua Linguarum. The Hague: Mouton, 1965.

———. "Three Factors in Language Design: Background and Prospects." Paper presented at the invited address at the 78th annual meeting of the Linguistic Society of America, Boston, MA, 2004.

Chomsky, Noam, Nirmalangshu Mukherji, B. N. Patnaik, and Rama Kant Agnihotri. *The Architecture of Language.* New Delhi; New York: Oxford University Press, 2000.

Christian, Brian, and Tom Griffiths. *Algorithms to Live By: The Computer Science of Human Decisions.* 1st ed. New York: Henry Holt, 2016.

Christiansen, Morten H., and Nick Chater. "Language as Shaped by the Brain." *Behavioral and Brain Sciences* 31, no. 5 (2008): 489–509.

Clark, Herbert H. *Using Language.* Cambridge, UK; New York: Cambridge University Press, 1996.

Cohen, Jacob. "Things I Have Learned (So Far)." *American Psychologist* 45 (1990): 1304–12.

Collins, Allan M., and Elizabeth F. Loftus. "A Spreading-Activation Theory of Semantic Processing." *Psychological Review* 82, no. 6 (1975): 407.

Collins, Allan M., and M. Ross Quillian. "Retrieval Time from Semantic Memory." *Journal of Verbal Learning and Verbal Behavior* 8, no. 2 (1969): 240–47.

Collins, John. *Chomsky: A Guide for the Perplexed.* London; New York: Continuum, 2008.

Conselice, Christopher J., Aaron Wilkinson, Kenneth Duncan, and Alice Mortlock. "The Evolution of Galaxy Number Density at Z< 8 and Its Implications." *The Astrophysical Journal* 830, no. 2 (2016): 83.

Cooper, John O., Timothy E. Heron, and William L. Heward. *Applied Behavior Analysis.* 3rd ed. Hoboken, NJ: Pearson, 2019.

Corballis, Michael C. "The Uniqueness of Human Recursive Thinking: The Ability to Think About Thinking May Be the Critical Attribute That Distinguishes Us from All Other Species." *American Scientist* 95, no. 3 (2007): 240–48.

Crain, Stephen, and Diane C. Lillo-Martin. *An Introduction to Linguistic Theory and Language Acquisition.* Malden, MA: Blackwell, 1999.

Crystal, David. *The Cambridge Encyclopedia of Language.* 2nd ed. Cambridge, UK; New York: Cambridge University Press, 1997.

———. *The Cambridge Encyclopedia of Language.* Cambridge, UK; New York: Cambridge University Press, 2010.

———. *The Cambridge Encyclopedia of the English Language.* Cambridge, UK; New York: Cambridge University Press, 1995.

Curtiss, Susan. "Abnormal Language Acquisition and the Modularity of Language." *Linguistics: The Cambridge Survey* 2 (1989): 96–116.

———. "The Case of Chelsea: The Effects of Late Age at Exposure to Language on Language Performance and Evidence for the Modularity of Language and Mind." In *Connectedness: Papers by and for Sarah Vanwagenen,* edited by T. Carson and Linnaea Stockall Schütze, 115–46. UCLA Working Papers in Linguistics, 2014.

———. *Genie: A Psycholinguistic Study of a Modern-Day "Wild Child."* Perspectives in Neurolinguistics and Psycholinguistics. New York: Academic Press, 1977.

Davis, Charles P., Hannah M. Morrow, and Gary Lupyan. "What Does a Horgous Look Like? Nonsense Words Elicit Meaningful Drawings." *Cognitive Science* 43, no. 10 (2019): e12791.

Deacon, Terrence William. *The Symbolic Species: The Co-Evolution of Language and the Brain.* 1st ed. New York: W. W. Norton, 1997.

Dehaene, Stanislas. *The Number Sense: How the Mind Creates Mathematics.* New York: Allen Lane, 2011.

Dehaene-Lambertz, Ghislaine, Stanislav Dehaene, and Lucie Hertz-Pannier. "Functional Neuroimaging of Speech Perception in Infants." *Science* 298, no. 5600 (2002): 2013–15.

Dennett, D. C. *Consciousness Explained.* 1st ed. Boston: Little, Brown, 1991.

Deutscher, Guy. *Through the Language Glass: Why the World Looks Different in Other Languages.* New York: Metropolitan Books, 2010.

Diamond, Jared. *The Rise and Fall of the Third Chimpanzee: How Our Animal Heritage Affects the Way We Live.* New York: Random House, 2013.

Dick, Joel. "Time Magazine's All-TIME 100 Nonfiction Books." List Challenges. www.listchallenges.com/time-magazines-all-time-100-nonfiction-books.

Diringer, David. *Writing. Its Origins and Early History.* New York: Praeger, 1962.

Divjak, Dagmar. *Frequency in Language: Memory, Attention and Learning.* New York: Cambridge University Press, 2019.

Duffy, Bobby. *The Perils of Perception: Why We're Wrong about Nearly Everything.* London: Atlantic Books, 2018.

Duguid, Michelle M., and Jack A. Goncalo. "Living Large: The Powerful Overestimate Their Own Height." *Psychological Science* 23, no. 1 (2012): 36–40.

Eco, Umberto. *A Theory of Semiotics.* Advances in Semiotics. Bloomington: Indiana University Press, 1976.

Efron, Bradley, and Ronald Thisted. "Estimating the Number of Unseen Species: How Many Words Did Shakespeare Know?" *Biometrika* 63, no. 3 (1976): 435–47.

Einstein, Albert, Leopold Infeld, and Rouben Mamoulian Collection (Library of Congress). *The Evolution of Physics: The Growth of Ideas from Early Concepts to Relativity and Quanta.* New York: Simon and Schuster, 1938.

Enard, Wolfgang, Sabine Gehre, Kurt Hammerschmidt, Sabine M. Hölter, Torsten Blass, Mehmet Somel, Martina K. Brückner, et al. "A Humanized Version of Foxp2 Affects Cortico-Basal Ganglia Circuits in Mice." *Cell* 137, no. 5 (2009): 961–71.

Erickson, Thomas D., and Mark E. Mattson. "From Words to Meaning: A Semantic Illusion." *Journal of Verbal Learning and Verbal Behavior* 20, no. 5 (1981): 540–51.

Everaert-Desmedt, Nicole. "Peirce's Semiotics." Signo, 2011. www.signosemio.com /peirce/semiotics.asp.

Eysenck, Michael W., and Mark T. Keane. *Cognitive Psychology: A Student's Handbook.* 5th ed. Hove, UK; New York: Psychology Press, 2005.

Farmer, Thomas A., Morten H. Christiansen, and Padraic Monaghan. "Phonological Typicality Influences On-Line Sentence Comprehension." *Proceedings of the National Academy of Sciences* 103, no. 32 (2006): 12203–8.

Fernald, Anne. "Four-Month-Old Infants Prefer to Listen to Motherese." *Infant Behavior and Development* 8, no. 2 (1985): 181–95.

Fernández, Eva M., and Helen Smith Cairns. *Fundamentals of Psycholinguistics.* Fundamentals of Linguistics. Chichester, UK; Malden, MA: Wiley-Blackwell, 2011.

Ferreira, Fernanda, Karl G. D. Bailey, and Vittoria Ferraro. "Good-Enough Representations in Language Comprehension." *Current Directions in Psychological Science* 11, no. 1 (2002): 11–15.

Ferrer i Cancho, Ramon, Oliver Riordan, and Béla Bollobás. "The Consequences of Zipf's Law for Syntax and Symbolic Reference." *Proceedings of the Royal Society B: Biological Sciences* 272, no. 1562 (2005): 561–65.

Ferrigno, Stephen, Samuel J. Cheyette, Steven T. Piantadosi, and Jessica F. Cantlon. "Recursive Sequence Generation in Monkeys, Children, US Adults, and Native Amazonians." *Science Advances* 6, no. 26 (2020): eaaz1002.

Fillenbaum, Samuel. "Memory for Gist: Some Relevant Variables." *Language and Speech* 9, no. 4 (1966): 217–27.

Firth, J. R. *Papers in Linguistics, 1934–1951*. London; New York: Oxford University Press, 1957.

———. *The Tongues of Men, and Speech*. London: Oxford University Press, 1964.

Fodor, Janet Dean, and William Gregory Sakas. "Evaluating Models of Parameter Setting." Paper presented at the Proceedings of the 28th Annual Boston University Conference on Language Development, Boston, MA, 2004.

Forer, Bertram R. "The Fallacy of Personal Validation; a Classroom Demonstration of Gullibility." *Journal of Abnormal Psychology* 44, no. 1 (1949): 118–23.

Frances, Allen J. "Science Is Not Just a Matter of Opinion." *Psychology Today*, December 2, 2016. www.psychologytoday.com/us/blog/saving-normal/201612 /science-is-not-just-matter-opinion.

Freeman, Jan. "Bootstraps and Baron Munchausen." *The Word* (blog), January 27, 2009. http://archive.boston.com/bostonglobe/ideas/theword/2009/01/bootstraps _and.html.

Fromkin, Victoria A. "The Non-Anomalous Nature of Anomalous Utterances." *Language* (1971): 27–52.

Fromkin, Victoria, Stephen Krashen, Susan Curtiss, David Rigler, and Marilyn Rigler. "The Development of Language in Genie: A Case of Language Acquisition Beyond the 'Critical Period.'" *Brain and Language* 1, no. 1 (1974): 81–107.

Funnell, Margaret G. "The Interpreting Hemispheres." In *The Cognitive Neuroscience of Mind: A Tribute to Michael S. Gazzaniga*, edited by Patricia Ann Reuter-Lorenz, Kathleen Baynes, George R. Mangun, and Elizabeth A. Phelps, 73–86. Cambridge: MIT Press, 2010.

Gallagher, James. "Aphantasia: A Life Without Mental Images." *BBC News*, August 25, 2015. www.bbc.com/news/health-34039054.

Gallistel, C. Randy. *The Organization of Learning*. Learning, Development, and Conceptual Change. Cambridge: MIT Press, 1990.

Gannon, Patrick J., Ralph L. Holloway, Douglas C. Broadfield, and Allen R. Braun. "Asymmetry of Chimpanzee Planum Temporale: Humanlike Pattern of Wernicke's Brain Language Area Homolog." *Science* 279, no. 5348 (1998): 220–22.

Gardner, Martin. *The Magic Numbers of Dr. Matrix*. Buffalo, NY: Prometheus Books, 1985.

Gardner, R. Allen, and Beatrice T. Gardner. "Teaching Sign Language to a Chimpanzee." *Science* 165, no. 3894 (1969): 664–72.

Gardner, R. Allen, Beatrix T. Gardner, and Thomas E. Van Cantfort. *Teaching Sign Language to Chimpanzees*. Albany: SUNY Press, 1989.

Gasser, Michael. "The Origins of Arbitrariness in Language." *Proceedings of the Annual Meeting of the Cognitive Science Society* (2004): 434–39.

Gasser, Michael, Nitya Sethuraman, and Stephen Hockema. "Iconicity in Expressives: An Empirical Investigation." *Experimental and Empirical Methods.* Stanford, CA: CSLI Publications, 2005.

Gazzaniga, Michael S. "Cerebral Specialization and Interhemispheric Communication: Does the Corpus Callosum Enable the Human Condition?" *Brain* 123, no. 7 (2000): 1293–326.

———. *The Consciousness Instinct: Unraveling the Mystery of How the Brain Makes the Mind.* 1st ed. New York: Farrar, Straus and Giroux, 2018.

———. *Nature's Mind: The Biological Roots of Thinking, Emotions, Sexuality, Language, and Intelligence.* New York: Basic Books, 1992.

———. "Organization of the Human Brain." *Science* 245, no. 4921 (1989): 947–52.

———. *Who's in Charge?: Free Will and the Science of the Brain.* Gifford Lectures. 1st ed. New York: HarperCollins, 2011.

Gazzaniga, Michael S., Todd F. Heatherton, and Diane F. Halpern. *Psychological Science.* New York: W. W. Norton, 2010.

Gentner, Dedre, and Susan Goldin-Meadow. *Language in Mind: Advances in the Study of Language and Thought.* Cambridge: MIT Press, 2003.

Germeys, Filip, and Géry d'Ydewalle. "The Psychology of Film: Perceiving beyond the Cut." *Psychological Research* 71, no. 4 (2007): 458–66.

Gernsbacher, Morton Ann, and Talmy Givón. *Coherence in Spontaneous Text.* Typological Studies in Language. Amsterdam; Philadelphia: J. Benjamins, 1995.

Gibbs, Raymond W. *Embodiment and Cognitive Science.* Cambridge; New York: Cambridge University Press, 2006.

Gigerenzer, Gerd. *Gut Feelings: The Intelligence of the Unconscious.* New York: Viking, 2007.

Givón, Talmy. "Coherence in Text, Coherence in Mind." *Pragmatics & Cognition* 1, no. 2 (1993): 171–227.

———. "Coherence in Text vs. Coherence in Mind." In *Coherence in Spontaneous Text*, edited by Morton Ann Gernsbacher and Talmy Givón, 59–115. Amsterdam: Benjamins, 1995.

———. *English Grammar: A Function-Based Introduction.* 2 vols. Amsterdam; Philadelphia: J. Benjamins Pub. Co., 1993.

———. "Historical Syntax and Synchronic Morphology: An Archaeologist's Field Trip." Paper presented at the Chicago Linguistic Society, 1971.

———. "Iconicity, Isomorphism and Non-Arbitrary Coding in Syntax." In *Iconicity in Syntax: Proceedings*, edited by John Haiman. Amsterdam: John Benjamins, 1985.

———. *Syntax: An Introduction.* Rev. ed. 2 vols. Amsterdam; Philadelphia: J. Benjamins, 2001.

Glenberg, Arthur M. "Embodiment as a Unifying Perspective for Psychology." *Wiley Interdisciplinary Reviews: Cognitive Science* 1, no. 4 (2010): 586–96.

Glenberg, Arthur M., and Michael P. Kaschak. "Grounding Language in Action." *Psychonomic Bulletin & Review* 9, no. 3 (2002): 558–65.

Glenberg, A. M., and D. A. Robertson. "Symbol Grounding and Meaning: A Comparison of High-Dimensional and Embodied Theories of Meaning." *Journal of Memory and Language* 43, no. 3 (2000): 379–401.

Goldinger, Stephen D., Megan H. Papesh, Anthony S. Barnhart, Whitney A. Hansen, and Michael C. Hout. "The Poverty of Embodied Cognition." *Psychonomic Bulletin & Review* 23, no. 4 (2016): 959–78.

Goodfellow, Ian, Yoshua Bengio, and Aaron Courville. *Deep Learning.* Adaptive Computation and Machine Learning. Cambridge: The MIT Press, 2016.

Goodglass, Harold. "Agrammatism." In *Studies in Neurolinguistics,* edited by Haiganoosh Whitaker and Harry A. Whitaker. New York: Academic Press, 1976.

Goodglass, Harold, and Edith Kaplan. *The Assessment of Aphasia and Related Disorders.* Philadelphia: Lea & Febiger, 1972.

Goodglass, Harold, and Norman Geschwind. "Language Disorders (Aphasia)." In *Handbook of Perception,* edited by Edward C. Carterette and Morton P. Friedman, 389–428. New York: Academic Press, 1976.

Goodman, Kenneth S. "Reading: A Psycholinguistic Guessing Game." *Literacy Research and Instruction* 6, no. 4 (1967): 126–35.

Graesser, A. C., D. S. McNamara, M. M. Louwerse, and Z. Q. Cai. "Coh-Metrix: Analysis of Text on Cohesion and Language." *Behavior Research Methods Instruments & Computers* 36, no. 2 (2004): 193–202.

Graesser, A. C., S. L. Lu, G. T. Jackson, H. H. Mitchell, M. Ventura, A. Olney, and M. M. Louwerse. "Autotutor: A Tutor with Dialogue in Natural Language." *Behavior Research Methods Instruments & Computers* 36, no. 2 (2004): 180–92.

Grice, Herbert P. "Logic and Conversation." In *Syntax and Semantics 3: Speech Acts,* edited by Peter Cole and Jerry L. Morgan, 41–58. New York: Academic Press, 1975.

Gross, Charles G. "Genealogy of the 'Grandmother Cell.'" *The Neuroscientist* 8, no. 5 (2002): 512–18.

Grossman, Robin E., L. James San, Timothy J. Vance, and Chicago Linguistic Society. *Papers from the Parasession on Functionalism, April 17, 1975.* 1st ed. Chicago: Chicago Linguistic Society, 1975.

Gumperz, John J., and Stephen C. Levinson. *Rethinking Linguistic Relativity.* Studies in the Social and Cultural Foundations of Language. Cambridge; New York: Cambridge University Press, 1996.

Haber, Ralph Norman, and Maurice Hershenson. *The Psychology of Visual Perception.* 2nd ed. New York: Holt, Rinehart and Winston, 1980.

Haggbloom, Steven J., Renee Warnick, Jason E. Warnick, Vinessa K. Jones, Gary L. Yarbrough, Tenea M. Russell, Chris M. Borecky, et al. "The 100 Most Eminent Psychologists of the 20th Century." *Review of General Psychology* 6, no. 2 (2002): 139–52.

Haiman, John. *Iconicity in Syntax: Proceedings of a Symposium on Iconicity in Syntax, Stanford, June 24–26, 1983.* Typological Studies in Language. Amsterdam; Philadelphia: J. Benjamins, 1985.

Hammarström, Harald. "Linguistic Diversity and Language Evolution." *Journal of Language Evolution* 1, no. 1 (2016): 19–29.

Harari, Yuval. "People Have Limited Knowledge. What's the Remedy? Nobody Knows." *New York Times,* April 18, 2017. www.nytimes.com/2017/04/18/books /review/knowledge-illusion-steven-sloman-philip-fernbach.html.

Harley, Trevor A. *The Psychology of Language: From Data to Theory.* 3rd ed. New York: Psychology Press, 2008.

Harris, Zellig S. "Distributional Structure." *Word* 10, no. 2–3 (1954): 146–62.

Hart, Betty, and Todd R. Risley. *Meaningful Differences in the Everyday Experience of Young American Children.* Baltimore: Paul H. Brookes, 1995.

Haspelmath, Martin. "Optimality and Diachronic Adaptation." *Zeitschrift für Sprachwissenschaft* 18, no. 2 (1999): 180–205.

Hauk, Olaf, Ingrid Johnsrude, and Friedemann Pulvermüller. "Somatotopic Representation of Action Words in Human Motor and Premotor Cortex." *Neuron* 41, no. 2 (2004): 301–7.

Hauser, Marc D., Noam Chomsky, and W. Tecumseh Fitch. "The Faculty of Language: What Is It, Who Has It, and How Did It Evolve?" *Science* 298, no. 5598 (2002): 1569–79.

Havas, David A., Arthur M. Glenberg, Karol A. Gutowski, Mark J. Lucarelli, and Richard J. Davidson. "Cosmetic Use of Botulinum Toxin-a Affects Processing of Emotional Language." *Psychological Science* 21, no. 7 (2010): 895–900.

Haviland, William A., Harald E. L. Prins, Bunny McBride, and Dana Walrath. *Cultural Anthropology: The Human Challenge.* Boston: Cengage Learning, 2013.

Hayes, Bruce, Susan Curtiss, Anna Szabolcsi, Tim Stowell, Edward Stabler, Dominique Sportiche, Hilda Koopman, et al. *Linguistics: An Introduction to Linguistic Theory.* Hoboken, NJ: John Wiley & Sons, 2013.

Hayes, Keith J., and Catherine H. Nissen. "Higher Mental Functions of a Home-Raised Chimpanzee." In *Behavior of Nonhuman Primates*, edited by Allan M. Schrier, Harry F. Harlow, and Fred Stollnitz, 59–115. New York: Academic Press, 1971.

Hebb, Donald O. *The Organization of Behavior; a Neuropsychological Theory.* A Wiley Book in Clinical Psychology. New York: Wiley, 1949.

Herrmann, Esther, Josep Call, María Victoria Hernández-Lloreda, Brian Hare, and Michael Tomasello. "Humans Have Evolved Specialized Skills of Social Cognition: The Cultural Intelligence Hypothesis." *Science* 317, no. 5843 (2007): 1360–66.

Hilbert, Martin. "Toward a Synthesis of Cognitive Biases: How Noisy Information Processing Can Bias Human Decision Making." *Psychological Bulletin* 138, no. 2 (2012): 211–37.

Hockett, Charles Francis. *A Course in Modern Linguistics.* New York: Macmillan, 1958.

Hume, David. *A Treatise of Human Nature.* Adelaide, South Australia: eBooks @Adelaide, 2006. https://web.archive.org/web/20060824185256/http://etext.library.adelaide.edu.au/h/hume/david/h92t/chapter4.html.

Hutchinson, Sterling, and Max Louwerse. "Extracting Social Networks from Language Statistics." *Discourse Processes* 55, no. 7 (2018): 607–18.

———. "Language Statistics and Individual Differences in Processing Primary Metaphors." *Cognitive Linguistics* 24, no. 4 (2013): 667–87.

Hutchinson, S., and M. M. Louwerse. "Language Statistics Explain the Spatial-Numerical Association of Response Codes." *Psychonomic Bulletin & Review* 21, no. 2 (2014): 470–78.

Ikeda, Mitsuo, and Shinya Saida. "Span of Recognition in Reading." *Vision Research* 18, no. 1 (1978): 83–88.

Inhoff, A. W., and W. M. Liu. "The Perceptual Span and Oculomotor Activity During the Reading of Chinese Sentences." *Journal of Experimental Psychology: Human Perception and Performance* 24, no. 1 (1998): 20–34.

Jackendoff, Ray. *Foundations of Language: Brain, Meaning, Grammar, Evolution.* New York: Oxford University Press, 2002.

Jaensch, Erich Rudolf, and Wilhelm Neuhaus. *Grundformen Menschlichen Seins.* Berlin: Otto Elsner, 1929.

James, William. *The Principles of Psychology.* 2 vols. New York: H. Holt, 1902.

Jelinek, Frederick. *Statistical Methods for Speech Recognition.* Cambridge: MIT Press, 1997.

Jeuniaux, Patrick, Rick Dale, and Max M. Louwerse. "The Role of Feedback in Learning Form-Meaning Mapping." In *Proceedings of the 31th Annual Conference of the Cognitive Science Society*, edited by Niels A. Taatgen and Hedderik van Rijn, 488–93. Austin, TX: Cognitive Science Society, 2009.

Johnson, Jacqueline S., and Elissa L. Newport. "Critical Period Effects in Second Language Learning: The Influence of Maturational State on the Acquisition of English as a Second Language." *Cognitive Psychology* 21, no. 1 (1989): 60–99.

Jones, Josh. "When William Faulkner Set the World Record for Writing the Longest Sentence in Literature." *Open Culture*, March 14, 2019. www.openculture.com/2019/03/when-william-faulkner-set-the-world-record-for-writing-the-longest-sentence-in-literature.html.

Judge, Timothy A., and Daniel M. Cable. "The Effect of Physical Height on Workplace Success and Income: Preliminary Test of a Theoretical Model." *Journal of Applied Psychology* 89, no. 3 (2004): 428–41.

Jurafsky, Dan, and James H. Martin. *Speech and Language Processing: An Introduction to Natural Language Processing, Computational Linguistics, and Speech Recognition.* Prentice Hall Series in Artificial Intelligence. Upper Saddle River, NJ: Prentice Hall, 2000.

Just, Marcel Adam, Lisa Pan, Vladimir L. Cherkassky, Dana L. McMakin, Christine Cha, Matthew K. Nock, and David Brent. "Machine Learning of Neural Representations of Suicide and Emotion Concepts Identifies Suicidal Youth." *Nature Human Behavior* 1, no. 12 (2017): 911–19.

Just, Marcel Adam, Vladimir L. Cherkassky, Sandesh Aryal, and Tom M. Mitchell. "A Neurosemantic Theory of Concrete Noun Representation Based on the Underlying Brain Codes." *PloS One* 5, no. 1 (2010): e8622.

Kahneman, Daniel. *Thinking, Fast and Slow.* 1st ed. New York: Farrar, Straus and Giroux, 2011.

Kahneman, Daniel, Barbara L. Fredrickson, Charles A. Schreiber, and Donald A. Redelmeier. "When More Pain Is Preferred to Less: Adding a Better End." *Psychological Science* 4, no. 6 (1993): 401–5.

Kaschak, Michael P., and Arthur M. Glenberg. "Constructing Meaning: The Role of Affordances and Grammatical Constructions in Sentence Comprehension." *Journal of Memory and Language* 43, no. 3 (2000): 508–29.

Kassam, Karim S., Amanda R. Markey, Vladimir L. Cherkassky, George Loewenstein, and Marcel Adam Just. "Identifying Emotions on the Basis of Neural Activation." *PloS One* 8, no. 6 (2013): e66032.

Kawai, Nobuyuki, and Tetsuro Matsuzawa. "Numerical Memory Span in a Chimpanzee." *Nature* 403, no. 6765 (2000): 39–40.

Keenan, Janice M., Brian MacWhinney, and Deborah Mayhew. "Pragmatics in Memory: A Study of Natural Conversation." *Journal of Verbal Learning and Verbal Behavior* 16, no. 5 (1977): 549–60.

Kilner, James M., and Roger N. Lemon. "What We Know Currently about Mirror Neurons." *Current Biology* 23, no. 23 (2013): R1057–R62.

Kintsch, Walter, David Welsch, Franz Schmalhofer, and Susan Zimny. "Sentence Memory: A Theoretical Analysis." *Journal of Memory and Language* 29, no. 2 (1990): 133–59.

Kintsch, Walter, and Teun A. van Dijk. "Toward a Model of Text Comprehension and Production." *Psychological Review* 85, no. 5 (1978): 363–94.

Kirby, Simon, Hannah Cornish, and Kenny Smith. "Cumulative Cultural Evolution in the Laboratory: An Experimental Approach to the Origins of Structure in Human Language." *Proceedings of the National Academy of Sciences* 105, no. 31 (2008): 10681–86.

Koffka, Kurt. *Principles of Gestalt Psychology*. New York: W. W. Norton, 1970.

Komatsu, Lloyd K. "Recent Views of Conceptual Structure." *Psychological Bulletin* 112, no. 3 (1992): 500–26.

Kovic, Vanja, Kim Plunkett, and Gert Westermann. "The Shape of Words in the Brain." *Cognition* 114, no. 1 (2010): 19–28.

Köhler, Wolfgang. *Gestalt Psychology*. New York: New American Library, 1929.

Kroll, Judith F., and Gretchen Sunderman. "Cognitive Processes in Second Language Learners and Bilinguals: The Development of Lexical and Conceptual Representations." In *The Handbook of Second Language Acquisition*, edited by Catherine J. Doughty and Michael H. Long, 104–129. Oxford: Blackwell, 2003.

Kruskal, Joseph B. *Multidimensional Scaling*. Beverly Hills, CA: SAGE, 1978.

Kwon, Nahyun. "Empirically Observed Iconicity Levels of English Phonaesthemes." *Public Journal of Semiotics* 7, no. 2 (2017): 73–93.

Lai, Cecilia S. L., Simon E. Fisher, Jane A. Hurst, Faraneh Vargha-Khadem, and Anthony P. Monaco. "A Forkhead-Domain Gene Is Mutated in a Severe Speech and Language Disorder." *Nature* 413, no. 6855 (2001): 519–23.

Lakoff, George. *Women, Fire, and Dangerous Things: What Categories Reveal about the Mind*. Chicago: University of Chicago Press, 1987.

Lakoff, George, and Mark Johnson. *Metaphors We Live By*. Chicago: University of Chicago Press, 1980.

———. *Philosophy in the Flesh: The Embodied Mind and Its Challenge to Western Thought*. New York: Basic Books, 1999.

Landauer, Thomas K. "LSA as a Theory of Meaning." In *Handbook of Latent Semantic Analysis*, edited by Thomas K. Landauer, Dennis S. McNamara, and W. Kintsch, 32. Mahwah, NJ: Lawrence Erlbaum, 2007.

Landauer, Thomas K., Simon Dennis, Danielle McNamara, and Walter Kintsch, eds. *Handbook of Latent Semantic Analysis*. Mahwah, NJ: Lawrence Erlbaum, 2007.

Landauer, Thomas K., and Jonathan L. Freedman. "Information Retrieval from Long-Term Memory: Category Size and Recognition Time." *Journal of Verbal Learning and Verbal Behavior* 7, no. 2 (1968): 291–95.

Landauer, Thomas K., Peter W. Foltz, and Darrell Laham. "An Introduction to Latent Semantic Analysis." *Discourse Processes* 25, no. 2–3 (1998): 259–84.

Landauer, Thomas K., and Susan Dumais. "A Solution to Plato's Problem: The Latent Semantic Analysis Theory of Acquisition, Induction, and Representation of Knowledge." *Psychological Review* 104, no. 2 (1997): 211–40.

Leavy, John. "Our Spooky Presidential Coincidences Contest." *Skeptical Inquirer* 16 (1992): 316–19.

Lenat, Douglas B. "Cyc: A Large-Scale Investment in Knowledge Infrastructure." *Communications of the ACM* 38, no. 11 (1995): 33–38.

———. "What AI Can Learn from Romeo & Juliet." *Forbes*, July 3, 2019. www .forbes.com/sites/cognitiveworld/2019/07/03/what-ai-can-learn-from-romeo --juliet/?sh=7bec33861bd0.

Lightfoot, David. *The Development of Language: Acquisition, Change, and Evolution.* Blackwell/Maryland Lectures in Language and Cognition. Malden, MA: Blackwell, 1999.

Lingnau, Angelika, Benno Gesierich, and Alfonso Caramazza. "Asymmetric Fmri Adaptation Reveals No Evidence for Mirror Neurons in Humans." *Proceedings of the National Academy of Sciences* 106, no. 24 (2009): 9925–30.

Locke, John. *The Works of John Locke; a New Edition, Corrected.* London: Printed for Thomas Tegg, 1823.

Louwerse, Max. "An Analytic and Cognitive Parametrization of Coherence Relations." *Cognitive Linguistics* 12, no. 3 (2001): 291–316.

———. "Bits and Pieces: Toward an Interactive Classification of Folktales." *Journal of Folklore Research* (1997): 245–49.

———. "Embodied Relations Are Encoded in Language." *Psychonomic Bulletin & Review* 15, no. 4 (2008): 838–44.

———. "Knowing the Meaning of a Word by the Linguistic and Perceptual Company It Keeps." *Topics in Cognitive Science* 10, no. 3 (2018): 573–89.

———. "Stormy Seas and Cloudy Skies: Conceptual Processing Is (Still) Linguistic and Perceptual." *Frontiers in Psychology* 2 (2011): 105.

———. "Symbol Interdependency in Symbolic and Embodied Cognition." *Topics in Cognitive Science* 3, no. 2 (2011): 273–302.

———. "Symbolic or Embodied Representations: A Case for Symbol Interdependency." In *Handbook of Latent Semantic Analysis*, edited by Thomas K. Landauer, Danielle S. McNamara, Simon Dennis, and Walter Kintsch, 119–32. Mahwah, NJ: Lawrence Erlbaum Associates, 2007.

Louwerse, Max, and Louise Connell. "A Taste of Words: Linguistic Context and Perceptual Simulation Predict the Modality of Words." *Cognitive Science* 35, no. 2 (2011): 381–98.

Louwerse, Max, and Matthew Ventura. "How Children Learn the Meaning of Words and How LSA Does It (Too)." *Journal of the Learning Sciences* 14, no. 2 (2005): 301–9.

Louwerse, Max, and Nick Benesh. "Representing Spatial Structure through Maps and Language: Lord of the Rings Encodes the Spatial Structure of Middle Earth." *Cognitive Science* 36, no. 8 (2012): 1556–69.

Louwerse, Max M., Marie Nilsenova-Postma, H. Anna T. van Limpt-Broers, Tycho T. de Back, Angelique M. Tinga, and Maarten Horden. "Beyond the Frontiers of Education: How Immersive Media Changes the Way We Learn." *ITU Journal ICT Discover* 3 (2020): 43–51.

Louwerse, Max, and P. Jeuniaux. "The Linguistic and Embodied Nature of Conceptual Processing." *Cognition* 114, no. 1 (2010): 96–104.

Louwerse, Max, Patrick Jeuniaux, Bin Zhang, Jie Wu, and Mohammed E. Hoque. "The Interaction between Information and Intonation Structure: Prosodic Marking of Theme and Rheme." In *Proceedings of the 30th Annual Conference of the Cognitive Science Society*, edited by Brad C. Love, Ken McRae, and Vladimir M. Sloutsky, 1984–89. Austin, TX: Cognitive Science Society, 2008.

Louwerse, Max, and R. A. Zwaan. "Language Encodes Geographical Information." *Cognitive Science* 33, no. 1 (2009): 51–73.

Louwerse, Max, R. Dale, E. G. Bard, and P. Jeuniaux. "Behavior Matching in Multimodal Communication Is Synchronized." *Cognitive Science* 36, no. 8 (2012): 1404–26.

Louwerse, Max, and Sterling Hutchinson. "Neurological Evidence Linguistic Processes Precede Perceptual Simulation in Conceptual Processing." *Frontiers in Psychology* 3 (2012): 385.

Louwerse, Max, Sterling Hutchinson, Richard Tillman, and Gabriel Recchia. "Effect Size Matters: The Role of Language Statistics and Perceptual Simulation in Conceptual Processing." *Language, Cognition and Neuroscience* 30, no. 4 (2015): 430–47.

Louwerse, Max, Sterling Hutchinson, and Zhiqiang Cai. "The Chinese Route Argument: Predicting the Longitude and Latitude of Cities in China and the Middle East Using Statistical Linguistic Frequencies." In *Proceedings of the 34th Annual Conference of the Cognitive Science Society*, edited by N. Miyake, D. Peebles, and R. P. Cooper, 695–700 (Sapporo, Japan: Cognitive Science Society, 2012).

Louwerse, Max, Susanne Raisig, Richard Tillman, and Sterling Hutchinson. "Time after Time in Words: Chronology through Language Statistics." In *Proceedings of the 37th Annual Meeting of the Cognitive Science Society*, edited by D. C. Noelle et al., 1428–33. Austin, TX: Cognitive Science Society, 2015.

Louwerse, Max, and Willie Van Peer. "How Cognitive Is Cognitive Poetics? The Interaction between Symbolic and Embodied Cognition." *Cognitive Poetics: Goals, Gains and Gaps* 10 (2009): 423.

———. *Thematics: Interdisciplinary Studies.* Vol. 3. Amsterdam: Benjamins, 2002.

Louwerse, Max, and Zhan Qu. "Estimating Valence from the Sound of a Word: Computational, Experimental, and Cross-Linguistic Evidence." *Psychonomic Bulletin & Review* 24, no. 3 (2017): 849–55.

Luce, Paul A., and David B. Pisoni. "Recognizing Spoken Words: The Neighborhood Activation Model." *Ear and Hearing* 19, no. 1 (1998): 36.

MacCorquodale, Kenneth. "On Chomsky's Review of Skinner's Verbal Behavior." *Journal of the Experimental Analysis of Behavior* 13, no. 1 (1970): 83.

Mahon, Bradford Z., and Alfonso Caramazza. "A Critical Look at the Embodied Cognition Hypothesis and a New Proposal for Grounding Conceptual Content." *Journal of Physiology—Paris* 102, no. 1–3 (2008): 59–70.

Mandler, Jean M., Patricia J. Bauer, and Laraine McDonough. "Separating the Sheep from the Goats: Differentiating Global Categories." *Cognitive Psychology* 23, no. 2 (1991): 263–98.

Manning, Christopher D., Hinrich Schütze, and Prabhakar Raghavan. *Introduction to Information Retrieval*. Cambridge: Cambridge University Press, 2008.

Marcus, Gary F., and Simon E. Fisher. "FOXP2 in Focus: What Can Genes Tell Us About Speech and Language?" *Trends in Cognitive Sciences* 7, no. 6 (2003): 257–62.

Markman, Arthur B. *Knowledge Representation*. Mahwah, NJ: L. Erlbaum, 1999.

Marsh, James, dir. *Project Nim*. Santa Monica, CA: Lionsgate, 2011.

Maurer, Daphne, Thanujeni Pathman, and Catherine J. Mondloch. "The Shape of Boubas: Sound–Shape Correspondences in Toddlers and Adults." *Developmental Science* 9, no. 3 (2006): 316–22.

McClelland, James L., David E. Rumelhart, and Geoffrey E. Hinton. "The Appeal of Parallel Distributed Processing." In *Parallel Distributed Processing. Explorations in the Microstructure of Cognition.*, edited by James L. McClelland, David E. Rumelhart, and PDP Research Group, 3–44. Cambridge: MIT Press, 1986.

McNamara, Danielle S., Max M. Louwerse, Philip M. McCarthy, and Arthur C. Graesser. "Coh-Metrix: Capturing Linguistic Features of Cohesion." *Discourse Processes* 47, no. 4 (2010): 292–330.

McNamara, Timothy P. *Semantic Priming: Perspectives from Memory and Word Recognition*. New York: Psychology Press, 2005.

McNerney, Samuel. "A Brief Guide to Embodied Cognition: Why You Are Not Your Brain." *Scientific American* (guest blog), November 4, 2011. https://blogs.scientificamerican.com/guest-blog/a-brief-guide-to-embodied-cognition-why-you-are-not-your-brain.

McNeill, David. *Hand and Mind: What Gestures Reveal about Thought*. Chicago: University of Chicago Press, 1992.

Meier, Brian P., and Michael D. Robinson. "Why the Sunny Side Is Up: Associations between Affect and Vertical Position." *Psychological Science* 15, no. 4 (2004): 243–47.

Meltzoff, Andrew N., and M. Keith Moore. "Imitation in Newborn Infants: Exploring the Range of Gestures Imitated and the Underlying Mechanisms." *Developmental Psychology* 25, no. 6 (1989): 954.

Merriam-Webster Inc. *Merriam-Webster's Dictionary of English Usage*. Springfield, MA: Merriam-Webster, 1993.

Metcalfe, Janet, Margaret Funnell, and Michael S. Gazzaniga. "Right-Hemisphere Memory Superiority: Studies of a Split-Brain Patient." *Psychological Science* 6, no. 3 (1995): 157–64.

Meyer, David E., and Roger W. Schvaneveldt. "Facilitation in Recognizing Pairs of Words: Evidence of a Dependence between Retrieval Operations." *Journal of Experimental Psychology* 90, no. 2 (Oct 1971): 227–34.

Miller, G. A. "The Cognitive Revolution: A Historical Perspective." *Trends in Cognive Science* 7, no. 3 (2003): 141–44.

Miller, George A. "The Magical Number Seven, Plus or Minus Two: Some Limits on Our Capacity for Processing Information." *Psychological Review* 63, no. 2 (1956): 81–97.

———. *The Science of Words.* New York: Scientific American Library, 1991.

———. *Wordnet: An Electronic Lexical Database.* Cambridge: MIT Press, 1998.

Miller, George A., and Jennifer A. Selfridge. "Verbal Context and the Recall of Meaningful Material." *The American Journal of Psychology* 63, no. 2 (1950): 176–85.

Miller, George A., and Philip N. Johnson-Laird. *Language and Perception.* Cambridge: Belknap Press, 1976.

Monaghan, Padraic, Morten H. Christiansen, and Nick Chater. "The Phonological-Distributional Coherence Hypothesis: Cross-Linguistic Evidence in Language Acquisition." *Cognitive Psychology* 55, no. 4 (2007): 259–305.

Moon, Christine, Hugo Lagercrantz, and Patricia K. Kuhl. "Language Experienced in Utero Affects Vowel Perception after Birth: A Two-Country Study." *Acta Paediatrica* 102, no. 2 (2013): 156–60.

Murphy, Gregory L., and Douglas L. Medin. "The Role of Theories in Conceptual Coherence." *Psychological Review* 92, no. 3 (1985): 289–316.

Musso, Mariacristina, Andrea Moro, Volkmar Glauche, Michel Rijntjes, Jürgen Reichenbach, Christian Buchel, and Cornelius Weiller. "Broca's Area and the Language Instinct." *Nature Neuroscience* 6, no. 7 (2003): 774–81.

Nagy, William E., and Patricia A. Herman. "Breadth and Depth of Vocabulary Knowledge: Implications for Acquisition and Instruction." *The Nature of Vocabulary Acquisition* 19 (1987): 35.

Nagy, William E., and Richard C. Anderson. "How Many Words Are There in Printed School English?" *Reading Research Quarterly* (1984): 304–30.

Neely, James H. "Semantic Priming Effects in Visual Word Recognition: A Selective Review of Current Findings and Theories." *Basic Processes in Reading: Visual Word Recognition* 11, no. 1 (1991): 264–336.

Newport, Elissa L. "Maturational Constraints on Language Learning." *Cognitive Science* 14, no. 1 (1990): 11–28.

Nickerson, Raymond S. "Confirmation Bias: A Ubiquitous Phenomenon in Many Guises." *Review of General Psychology* 2, no. 2 (1998): 175–220.

Nieder, Andreas. "Seeing More Than Meets the Eye: Processing of Illusory Contours in Animals." *Journal of Comparative Physiology A* 188, no. 4 (2002): 249–60.

Nieder, Andreas, and Hermann Wagner. "Perception and Neuronal Coding of Subjective Contours in the Owl." *Nature Neuroscience* 2, no. 7 (1999): 660–63.

Nova Science Now. "Irene Pepperberg & Alex." YouTube. November 13, 2011. Video, 11:55. www.youtube.com/watch?v=cO6XuVlcEO4.

Ober, Beth A., and Gregory K. Shenaut. "Semantic Memory." In *Handbook of Psycholinguistics*, edited by Matthew J. Traxler and Morton Ann Gernsbacher, 403–53. Amsterdam; Boston: Elsevier, 2006.

O'Grady, William. *Syntactic Development*. Chicago: University of Chicago Press, 2007.

O'Grady, William, John Archibald, Mark Aronoff, and Janie Rees-Miller. *Contemporary Linguistics: An Introduction*. New York: St. Martin's Press, 2010.

O'Grady, William, Michael Dobrovolsky, and Francis Katamba. *Contemporary Linguistics*. New York: St. Martin's, 1997.

Oller, D. Kimbrough. "Underpinnings for a Theory of Communicative Evolution." In *Evolution of Communication Systems: A Comparative Approach*, edited by D. Kimbrough Oller and Ulrike Griebel, 49–65. Cambridge: MIT Press, 2004.

Osaka, Naoyuki, and Koichi Oda. "Effective Visual Field Size Necessary for Vertical Reading during Japanese Text Processing." *Bulletin of the Psychonomic Society* 29, no. 4 (1991): 345–47.

Osgood, Charles Egerton. *The Measurement of Meaning*. Urbana: University of Illinois Press, 1957.

———. "Verbal Behavior, by BF Skinner." *Contemporary Psychology* 3 (1958): 209–12.

Osgood, Charles Egerton, George J. Suci, and Percy H. Tannenbaum. *The Measurement of Meaning*. Chicago: University of Illinois Press, 1957.

Pauen, Sabina. "Evidence for Knowledge-Based Category Discrimination in Infancy." *Child Development* 73, no. 4 (2002): 1016–33.

Peach, Richard K., and Lewis P. Shapiro. *Cognition and Acquired Language Disorders: An Information Processing Approach*. St. Louis, MO: Elsevier, 2012.

Pecher, Diane, and Rolf A. Zwaan. *Grounding Cognition: The Role of Perception and Action in Memory, Language, and Thinking*. New York: Cambridge University Press, 2005.

Peirce, Charles S. *Collected Papers of Charles Sanders Peirce*. 8 vols. Cambridge: Harvard University Press, 1931.

Penfield, Wilder, and Edwin Boldrey. "Somatic Motor and Sensory Representation in the Cerebral Cortex of Man as Studied by Electrical Stimulation." *Brain* 60, no. 4 (1937): 389–443.

Pennebaker, James W. *The Secret Life of Pronouns: What Our Words Say about Us*. New York: Bloomsbury, 2011.

Pepperberg, Irene M. *The Alex Studies: Cognitive and Communicative Abilities of Grey Parrots*. Cambridge: Harvard University Press, 2009.

Pepperberg, Irene M. "Evolution of Communication from an Avian Perspective." In *Evolution of Communication Systems: A Comparative Approach*, edited by D. Kimbrough Oller and Ulrike Griebel, 171–92. Cambridge: MIT Press, 2004.

Perry, Lynn K., Marcus Perlman, Bodo Winter, Dominic W. Massaro, and Gary Lupyan. "Iconicity in the Speech of Children and Adults." *Developmental Science* 21, no. 3 (2018): e12572.

Piantadosi, Steven T., Harry Tily, and Edward Gibson. "The Communicative Function of Ambiguity in Language." *Cognition* 122, no. 3 (2012): 280–91.

Pinker, Steven. *The Language Instinct.* 1st ed. New York: W. Morrow, 1994.

———. *Words and Rules: The Ingredients of Language.* 1st ed. New York: Basic Books, 1999.

Plato. *The Collected Dialogues of Plato.* Edited by Edith Hamilton, Huntington Cairns, and Lane Cooper. Princeton: Princeton University Press, 1961.

Pollatsek, Alexander, Shmuel Bolozky, Arnold D. Well, and Keith Rayner. "Asymmetries in the Perceptual Span for Israeli Readers." *Brain and Language* 14, no. 1 (1981): 174–80.

Premack, David. "Animal Cognition." *Annual Review of Psychology* 34, no. 1 (1983): 351–62.

Preston, John, and Mark Bishop. *Views into the Chinese Room: New Essays on Searle and Artificial Intelligence.* Oxford: Oxford University Press, 2002.

Propp, Vladimir I. A. *Morphology of the Folktale.* International Journal of American Linguistics. Bloomington: Research Center, Indiana University, 1958.

Public Domain Vectors. Accessed November 12, 2020. https://publicdomainvectors. org/en/wild-animal-clipart-free.

Quillian, M. Ross. "Word Concepts: A Theory and Simulation of Some Basic Semantic Capabilities." *Behavioral Science* 12, no. 5 (1967): 410–30.

Quine, W. V. *Word and Object.* Studies in Communication. Cambridge: Technology Press of the Massachusetts Institute of Technology, 1960.

Quiroga, R. Q., L. Reddy, G. Kreiman, C. Koch, and I. Fried. "Invariant Visual Representation by Single Neurons in the Human Brain." *Nature* 435, no. 7045 (2005): 1102–7.

Raspe, Rudolf Erich, William Strang, and Joseph Benwell Clark. *The Travels and Surprising Adventures of Baron Munchausen.* Brooklyn: Melville House, 2012.

Rayner, Keith, and Alexander Pollatsek. *The Psychology of Reading.* Englewood Cliffs, NJ: Prentice Hall, 1989.

Rayner, Keith, Alexander Pollatsek, Jane Ashby, and Charles Clifton Jr. *Psychology of Reading.* New York: Psychology Press, 2012.

Rayner, Keith, and George W. McConkie. "Perceptual Processes in Reading: The Perceptual Spans." In *Toward a Psychology of Reading*, edited by Arthur S. Reber and City University, 104–23. Hillsdale, NJ: Erlbaum, 1977.

Recchia, Gabriel, and Max Louwerse. "Archaeology through Computational Linguistics: Inscription Statistics Predict Excavation Sites of Indus Valley Artifacts." *Cognitive Science* 40, no. 8 (2016): 2065–80.

———. "Reproducing Affective Norms with Lexical Co-Occurrence Statistics: Predicting Valence, Arousal, and Dominance." *Quarterly Journal of Experimental Psychology* 68, no. 8 (2015): 1584–98.

Reder, Lynne M., and Gail W. Kusbit. "Locus of the Moses Illusion: Imperfect Encoding, Retrieval, or Match?" *Journal of Memory and Language* 30, no. 4 (1991): 385–406.

Redington, Martin, Nick Chater, and Steven Finch. "Distributional Information: A Powerful Cue for Acquiring Syntactic Categories." *Cognitive Science* 22, no. 4 (1998): 425–69.

Reicher, Gerald M. "Perceptual Recognition as a Function of Meaningfulness of Stimulus Material." *Journal of Experimental Psychology* 81, no. 2 (1969): 275.

Rizzolatti, Giacomo, and Laila Craighero. "The Mirror-Neuron System." *Annual Review of Neuroscience* 27 (2004): 169–92.

Rizzolatti, Giacomo, Luciano Fadiga, Vittorio Gallese, and Leonardo Fogassi. "Premotor Cortex and the Recognition of Motor Actions." *Cognitive Brain Research* 3, no. 2 (1996): 131–41.

Roediger, Henry L., and Kathleen B. McDermott. "Creating False Memories: Remembering Words Not Presented in Lists." *Journal of Experimental Psychology: Learning, Memory, and Cognition* 21, no. 4 (1995): 803.

Rogers, Timothy T., and James L. McClelland. *Semantic Cognition: A Parallel Distributed Processing Approach.* Cambridge: MIT Press, 2004.

Rosch, Eleanor. "Principles of Categorization." In *Cognition and Categorization,* edited by E. Rosch and B. B. Lloyd. Hillsdale, NJ: Erlbaum, 1978.

Ross, John Robert, and William Edwin Cooper. "World Order." In *Papers from the Parasession on Functionalism,* edited by Robin E. Grossman, L. James San, and Timothy J. Vance, 63–111. Chicago: Chicago Linguistic Society, 1975.

Rozenblit, Leonid, and Frank Keil. "The Misunderstood Limits of Folk Science: An Illusion of Explanatory Depth." *Cognitive Science* 26, no. 5 (2002): 521–62.

Rubin, Philip, Michael T. Turvey, and Peter Van Gelder. "Initial Phonemes Are Detected Faster in Spoken Words Than in Spoken Nonwords." *Perception & Psychophysics* 19, no. 5 (1976): 394–98.

Rumelhart, David E., James L. McClelland, and University of California San Diego PDP Research Group. *Parallel Distributed Processing: Explorations in the Microstructure of Cognition.* Computational Models of Cognition and Perception. 2 vols. Cambridge: MIT Press, 1986.

Sampson, Geoffrey. *Educating Eve: The "Language Instinct" Debate.* Open Linguistics Series. London; Washington, DC: Cassell, 1997.

———. *The "Language Instinct" Debate.* Rev. ed. London; New York: Continuum, 2005.

Samuelson, Larissa K., and Linda B. Smith. "Children's Attention to Rigid and Deformable Shape in Naming and Non-Naming Tasks." *Child Development* 71, no. 6 (2000): 1555–70.

Sandler, Wendy. "Dedicated Gestures and the Emergence of Sign Language." *Gesture* 12, no. 3 (2012): 265–307.

Sapir, Edward. "A Study in Phonetic Symbolism." *Journal of Experimental Psychology* 12, no. 3 (1929): 225.

Sapir, J. David. "Kujaama: Symbolic Separation among the Diola-Fogny 1." *American Anthropologist* 72, no. 6 (1970): 1330–48.

Saussure, Ferdinand de. *Cours de Linguistique Générale.* Paris: Payot, 1916. Translated in *Course in General Linguistics.* New York: Philosophical Library, 1959.

Schaeffer, Benson, and Richard Wallace. "Semantic Similarity and the Comparison of Word Meanings." *Journal of Experimental Psychology* 82, no. 2 (1969): 3.

Schank, Roger C., and Robert P. Abelson. *Scripts, Plans, Goals, and Understanding: An Inquiry into Human Knowledge Structures.* The Artificial Intelligence Series. Hillsdale, NJ; New York: L. Erlbaum Associates, 1977.

Schuler, Karin Kipper. "VerbNet: A Broad-Coverage, Comprehensive Verb Lexicon." PhD dissertation, University of Pennsylvania, 2005. https://repository.upenn.edu /dissertations/AAI3179808.

Searle, John R. "Minds, Brains, and Programs." *Behavioral and Brain Sciences* 3 (1980): 417–57.

———. "Twenty-One Years in the Chinese Room." In *Views into the Chinese Room: New Essays on Searle and Artificial Intelligence*, edited by John Preston and Mark Bishop, 51–69. Oxford: Oxford University Press, 2002.

Semin, Gün R., and Eliot R. Smith. *Embodied Grounding: Social, Cognitive, Affective, and Neuroscientific Approaches.* Cambridge; New York: Cambridge University Press, 2008.

Shakespeare, William, and Theobald. *The Works of Shakespeare: In Seven Volumes. Collated with the Oldest Copies, and Corrected.* 1st AMS ed. 7 vols. New York: AMS Press, 1968.

Shang, Miles. "Javascript/Canvas Linguistics Syntax Tree Generator." 2011. https:// github.com/mshang/syntree.

Shannon, Claude Elwood, and Warren Weaver. *The Mathematical Theory of Communication.* Urbana: University of Illinois Press, 1962.

———. *The Mathematical Theory of Communication.* Urbana: University of Illinois Press, 1949.

Simon, Herbert A. *The Sciences of the Artificial.* Karl Taylor Compton Lectures. Cambridge: MIT Press, 1969.

Skinner, B. F. *Verbal Behavior.* The Century Psychology Series. New York: Appleton-Century-Crofts, 1957.

Sloman, Steven A., and Philip Fernbach. *The Knowledge Illusion: Why We Never Think Alone.* New York: Riverhead Books, 2017.

Smith, Andrew D. M., and Kenny Smith. "Cross-Situational Learning." *Encyclopedia of the Sciences of Learning* (2012): 864–66.

SpaceBuzz. "SpaceBuzz in Washington for Global Launch." YouTube. October 21, 2019. Video, 1:54. www.youtube.com/watch?v=NuvLmlJur0o&feature=youtu.be.

Spivey, Michael. *The Continuity of Mind.* Oxford Psychology Series. Oxford; New York: Oxford University Press, 2007.

Spivey, Michael J., and Joy J. Geng. "Oculomotor Mechanisms Activated by Imagery and Memory: Eye Movements to Absent Objects." *Psychological Research* 65, no. 4 (2001): 235–41.

Spivey, Michael J., and Stephanie Huette. "Toward a Situated View of Language." In *Visually Situated Language Comprehension*, edited by Pia Knoeferle, Pirita Pyykkönen-Klauck, and Matthew W. Crocker, 1–30. Amsterdam; Philadelphia: Benjamins, 2016.

Spocter, Muhammad A., William D. Hopkins, Amy R. Garrison, Amy L. Bauern-feind, Cheryl D. Stimpson, Patrick R. Hof, and Chet C. Sherwood. "Wernicke's Area Homologue in Chimpanzees (Pan Troglodytes) and Its Relation to the Appearance of Modern Human Language." *Proceedings of the Royal Society B: Biological Sciences* 277, no. 1691 (2010): 2165–74.

SRF Kultur. "«Gavagai»—the Philosophical Thought Experiment." YouTube. April 13, 2018. Video, 2:06. www.youtube.com/watch?v=0YY4qxkqm3o.

Stanfield, Robert A., and Rolf A. Zwaan. "The Effect of Implied Orientation Derived from Verbal Context on Picture Recognition." *Psychological Science* 12, no. 2 (2001): 153–56.

Steel, Carlos G., Oliver Primavesi, and Aristotle. *Aristotle's Metaphysics Alpha: Symposium Aristotelicum.* 1st ed. Oxford: Oxford University Press, 2012.

Stevens, Albert, and Patty Coupe. "Distortions in Judged Spatial Relations." *Cognitive Psychology* 10, no. 4 (1978): 422–37.

Stroop, J. Ridley. "Studies of Interference in Serial Verbal Reactions." *Journal of Experimental Psychology* 18, no. 6 (1935): 643.

Sweetser, Eve. *From Etymology to Pragmatics: Metaphorical and Cultural Aspects of Semantic Structure.* Vol. 54. Cambridge: Cambridge University Press, 1990.

Swiggers, Pierre. "How Chomsky Skinned Quine, or What 'Verbal Behavior' Can Do." *Language Sciences* 17, no. 1 (1995): 1–18.

Terrace, Herbert S. *Why Chimpanzees Can't Learn Language and Only Humans Can.* New York: Columbia University Press, 2019.

Terrace, Herbert S., Laura Ann Petitto, Richard Jay Sanders, and Thomas G. Bever. "Can an Ape Create a Sentence?" *Science* 206, no. 4421 (1979): 891–902.

Thompson, P. "Margaret Thatcher: A New Illusion." *Perception* 9, no. 4 (1980): 483–84.

Thompson, Patrick D., and Zachary Estes. "Sound Symbolic Naming of Novel Objects Is a Graded Function." *Quarterly Journal of Experimental Psychology* 64, no. 12 (2011): 2392–404.

Tillman, Richard, and Max Louwerse. "Estimating Emotions through Language Statistics and Embodied Cognition." *Journal of Psycholinguistic Research* 47, no. 1 (2018): 159–67.

Tillman, Richard, Vivek Datla, Sterling Hutchinson, and Max Louwerse. "From Head to Toe: Embodiment through Statistical Linguistic Frequencies." *Proceedings of the Annual Meeting of the Cognitive Science Society* (2012): 2434–39.

Tobler, Waldo R. "A Computer Movie Simulating Urban Growth in the Detroit Region." *Economic Geography* 46, no. sup1 (1970): 234–40.

Tolkien, J. R. R. *The Lord of the Rings.* 3 vols. London: Allen & Unwin, 1954.

Tomasello, Michael. *Constructing a Language: A Usage-Based Theory of Language Acquisition.* Cambridge: Harvard University Press, 2003.

———. "What Kind of Evidence Could Refute the UG Hypothesis?: Commentary on Wunderlich." *Studies in Language* 28, no. 3 (2004): 642–45.

Townsend, David J., and Thomas G. Bever. *Sentence Comprehension: The Integration of Rules and Habits.* Cambridge: MIT Press, 2001.

Traxler, Matthew J., and Morton Ann Gernsbacher. *Handbook of Psycholinguistics.* 2nd ed. Boston: Elsevier, 2006.

Turing, Alan M. "Computing Machinery and Intelligence." *Mind* 59, no. 236 (1950): 433–60.

Tversky, Amos, and Daniel Kahneman. "Extensional Versus Intuitive Reasoning: The Conjunction Fallacy in Probability Judgment." *Psychological Review* 90, no. 4 (1983): 293.

———. "Judgment under Uncertainty: Heuristics and Biases." *Science* 185, no. 4157 (1974): 1124–31.

Van Baaren, Rick B., Rob W. Holland, Bregje Steenaert, and Ad van Knippenberg. "Mimicry for Money: Behavioral Consequences of Imitation." *Journal of Experimental Social Psychology* 39, no. 4 (2003): 393–98.

Van Dijk, Teun Adrianus. *Some Aspects of Text Grammars. A Study in Theoretical Linguistics and Poetics.* Janua Linguarum Series Maior. The Hague: Mouton, 1972.

Van Dijk, Teun Adrianus, and Walter Kintsch. *Strategies of Discourse Comprehension.* New York: Academic Press, 1983.

Vega, Manuel de, Arthur M. Glenberg, and Arthur C. Graesser. *Symbols and Embodiment: Debates on Meaning and Cognition.* Oxford; New York: Oxford University Press, 2008.

von der Heydt, Riidiger, and Esther Peterhans. "Mechanisms of Contour Perception in Monkey Visual Cortex. I. Lines of Pattern Discontinuity." *Journal of Neuroscience* 9, no. 5 (1989): 1731–48.

Vulkan, Nir. "An Economist's Perspective on Probability Matching." *Journal of Economic Surveys* 14, no. 1 (2000): 101–18.

Waal, Frans B. M. de. *Are We Smart Enough to Know How Smart Animals Are?* 1st ed. New York: W. W. Norton, 2016.

Wanner, Eric. *On Remembering, Forgetting, and Understanding Sentences.* The Hague: Mouton, 1974.

Warren, Richard M. "Perceptual Restoration of Missing Speech Sounds." *Science* 167, no. 3917 (1970): 392–93.

Weldon, Kimberly B., Jessica Taubert, Carolynn L. Smith, and Lisa A. Parr. "How the Thatcher Illusion Reveals Evolutionary Differences in the Face Processing of Primates." *Animal Cognition* 16, no. 5 (2013): 691–700.

West, Geoffrey B. *Scale: The Universal Laws of Growth, Innovation, Sustainability, and the Pace of Life in Organisms, Cities, Economies, and Companies.* New York: Penguin, 2017.

Wheeler, Daniel D. "Processes in Word Recognition." *Cognitive Psychology* 1, no. 1 (1970): 59–85.

Wheeler, Mark E., Steven E. Petersen, and Randy L. Buckner. "Memory's Echo: Vivid Remembering Reactivates Sensory-Specific Cortex." *Proceedings of the National Academy of Sciences* 97, no. 20 (2000): 11125–29.

Whorf, Benjamin Lee. *Language, Thought, and Reality: Selected Writings of Benjamin Lee Whorf.* Cambridge: MIT Press, 2012.

Wilson, Andrew D. "The Small Effect Size—Why Do We Put Up with Small Effects?" *Notes from Two Scientific Psychologists* (blog), August 17, 2012. http://psych sciencenotes.blogspot.com/2012/08/the-small-effect-size-effect-why-do-we.html.

Winter, Bodo. *Sensory Linguistics: Language, Perception and Metaphor.* Vol. 20. Amsterdam; Philadelphia: Benjamins, 2019.

Wittgenstein, Ludwig. *Philosophical Investigations.* New York: Macmillan, 1953.

Wolford, George, Michael B. Miller, and Michael Gazzaniga. "The Left Hemisphere's Role in Hypothesis Formation." *Journal of Neuroscience* 20, no. 6 (2000): RC64.

Wolford, George, Sarah E. Newman, Michael B. Miller, and Gagan S. Wig. "Searching for Patterns in Random Sequences." *Canadian Journal of Experimental Psychology* 58, no. 4 (2004): 221.

Wunderlich, Dieter. "Why Assume UG." In *What Counts as Evidence in Linguistics: The Case of Innateness,* edited by Martina Penke and Anette Rosenbach, 147–74. Amsterdam: John Benjamins, 2007.

Yang, Fang, Lun Mo, and Max M. Louwerse. "Effects of Local and Global Context on Processing Sentences with Subject and Object Relative Clauses." *Journal of Psycholinguistic Research* 42, no. 3 (2013): 227–37.

Yee, Eiling, and Julie C. Sedivy. "Eye Movements to Pictures Reveal Transient Semantic Activation During Spoken Word Recognition." *Journal of Experimental Psychology: Learning, Memory, and Cognition* 32, no. 1 (2006): 1–14.

Yu, Chen, and Linda B. Smith. "Rapid Word Learning under Uncertainty Via Cross-Situational Statistics." *Psychological Science* 18, no. 5 (2007): 414–20.

Zeman, A. Z., Michaela Dewar, and Sergio Della Sala. "Lives without Imagery—Congenital Aphantasia." *Cortex* 73 (2015): 378–80.

Zhou, S. Kevin, Hayit Greenspan, and Dinggang Shen. *Deep Learning for Medical Image Analysis.* Elsevier and Miccai Society Book Series. London; San Diego: Elsevier/Academic Press, 2017.

Zipf, George Kingsley. *Human Behavior and the Principle of Least Effort; an Introduction to Human Ecology.* Cambridge: Addison-Wesley Press, 1949.

———. *The Psycho-Biology of Language; an Introduction to Dynamic Philology.* Boston: Houghton Mifflin, 1935.

Zwaan, Rolf A., and David N. Rapp. "Discourse Comprehension." In *Handbook of Psycholinguistics,* edited by Matthew J. Traxler and Morton Ann Gernsbacher, 725–64. Boston: Elsevier, 2006.

Zwaan, Rolf A., and Lawrence J. Taylor. "Seeing, Acting, Understanding: Motor Resonance in Language Comprehension." *Journal of Experimental Psychology General* 135, no. 1 (2006): 1–11.

Zwaan, Rolf A., and Richard H. Yaxley. "Spatial Iconicity Affects Semantic Relatedness Judgments." *Psychonomic Bulletin & Review* 10, no. 4 (2003): 954–58.

Zwaan, Rolf A., Robert A. Stanfield, and Richard H. Yaxley. "Language Comprehenders Mentally Represent the Shapes of Objects." *Psychological Science* 13, no. 2 (2002): 168–71.

Index

ABBA (band), 168
abstract (abstract, amodal, arbitrary),
    124, 134, 136
acronym, 21
action ladder, 75
adjective, 27, 48, 197, 210, 250, 280,
    287n13; distinguishing in vocabulary,
    25–26; permutations on sentences we
    know, 35; syntactic structures, 83
adverb, 84, 197, 212, 250, 287n13;
    distinguishing in vocabulary, 25–26;
    permutations on sentences we know,
    35; syntactic structures, 83–84. *See
    also* grammatical item
affordance, 122, 132–35, 138, 156, 268
age of acquisition (word acquisition),
    47–48
Aitchison, Jean, 314
Alex (gray parrot), 67–68, 74
algorithm, 7, 117, 314; in applications,
    278–79, 283; and distributional
    semantics, 233, 241, 243, 250
alphabet, 40, 42, 49, 164
Altmann, Gerry T. M., 314
ambiguity, 29, 201, 202
American Sign Language, 64
amodal (abstract, amodal, arbitrary),
    124, 134, 136

animacy (word animacy), 47, 48, 216,
    217
animal cognition, 67–69, 96, 160, 174–
    77, 273, 314
animal communication, 77–78
animal psychology, 67
Aniston, Jennifer (Jennifer Aniston
    neuron), 108
Ansari, Anousheh, 284
anthropology, 9, 256, 284, 292n8
antonym, 24, 228
Apalaí language, 224
aphantasia, 134
applied research (vs. basic research), 277
Arabic language, 223, 242, 252, 282,
    307n14
arbitrariness, 14, 120, 122, 188, 221,
    242, 256, 280; abstract, amodal,
    arbitrary, 124, 134, 136; explanation
    for, 200–202; sound-meaning, 124,
    183, 185–87, 201, 248, 256, 259,
    302nn4–6, 308n7; and symbol
    interdependency, 267, 268, 270, 272
arbitrariness (word order), 204, 207, 214
archeology, 242, 243, 244
Aristotle, 256, 308n11
artificial intelligence (discipline), 7,
    10–12, 14, 160, 284, 292n8, 295n16,

313–14; and artificial neural network, 99, 117; and symbol grounding, 121, 124, 125; and syntactic structure, 84–85

artificial mind, 7, 85, 99, 112, 116–17, 120, 133, 283–84

artificial neural network, 11, 111–18, 180, 278, 283, 309n29; and human neural network, 140, 142; and symbol grounding, 122, 125; and symbol interdependency, 269–70

Asch, Solomon E., 141

ASL. *See* American Sign Language

Aspects of the Theory of Syntax, 43

Assyrian script, 189, 200

auditory modality (sound), 124, 197, 198, 268

Austronesian language, 224

AutoTutor, 283. *See also* intelligent tutoring system

auxiliary verb, 41, 85, 250. *See also* grammatical item

Ayumu (chimp), 144

backpropagation, 110, 114

Baron Munchausen, 251–53, 254, 255

basic research (vs. applied research), 276

behaviorism, 69–74, 75, 76, 79

Bergen, Benjamin, 314

Bible, 155, 233

bipedalism, 293n29

bird, 96, 293n29, 294n35

bird song, 91, 294n35

blank slate, 10, 74, 76, 82, 111

Bloom, Paul, 262

Bohemian Rhapsody (song), 168

bonobo, 175, 179

Bontius, Jacobus, 66

bootstrapping, 251–55, 267, 269, 271

Botox (botulinum toxin A), 129

bottom-up process, 44, 61

brain, 81–82, 147, 213, 225, 275, 278, 284; and artificial neural networks, 11, 107–17, 181–82; animal brain, 66, 81, 125, 147; brain activity, 7, 93;

brain damage, 92; brain imaging, 93, 194, 278; EEG study on linguistic and perceptual activation, 220, 221; and language instinct, 91–92, 96, 181–82; and split-brain patients, 178–79; and symbol grounding, 122, 127, 128, 181–82; and symbol interdependency, 270, 272, 273

A Brief History of Time, 82

Broca, Pierre P., 92

Broca's aphasia, 92

Broca's area, 92, 93, 96, 127, 128, 220

Brontë, Emily J., 300n18

Bunker, Archie, 213

Caesar, G. Julius, 211, 212

Capitalism and Freedom, 82

Cariban language, 224

cat, 77, 174, 179, 230, 261

Cattell, James M., 42

central nervous system, 114

Chater, Nick, 137, 158, 314

Chelsea, 90, 94, 95

chess (board game), 76, 77, 79

child-directed speech, 94, 250

chimpanzee, 75, 147–48, 175–76; and learning language, 64–68, 95–96; and memory tasks, 143–44; and pattern-matching skills, 179–81; and reverted images, 140–41. *See also* primate

Chinese language, 52, 86, 223, 242, 252, 277, 282; and valence study, 198

Chinese room argument, 119–22, 125, 135, 242, 252, 254

Chomsky, A. Noam, 43, 81–96, 124, 249, 250, 291n22; and behaviorism, 64, 75–76

Christin, Brian, 314

Chrystal, David, 314

clinical psychology, 278

Closure, Law of, 174

cocktail party effect, 167

cognition, 135, 147, 157, 158, 160, 313; and cognitive shortcut,

137–38; deficient cognition, 95; and grounding, 118, 125, 128; semantic, 113, 116, 249

cognitive effort, 45, 145, 154, 262

cognitive fallacy, 171

cognitive laziness (path of least cognitive resistance), 138, 139, 141–47, 150–61, 254, 299n5. *See also* cognitive shortcut

cognitive psychology, 14, 76, 245, 314

cognitive revolution, 133

cognitive science, 85, 112, 256, 284, 292n8

cognitive shortcut, 138–61, 181, 248, 264, 273, 277, 314; and arbitrariness, 201; archeology, 244; distributional semantics, 237–38, 248; and estimating valence, 199; geographical estimates, 238–42; and left-hemisphere interpreter, 179; sound and meaning, 192–94; word order, 204–24; writing system, 189

cognitive smartness, 299n5

coherence, 39, 44, 133, 163, 279

coin flip, 45, 168, 181, 182

Collected Works of William Shakespeare, 18–19

comprehension (language), 7, 19, 45, 74, 79, 92, 125, 160, 314; and context, 237, 250; and grounding, 131, 135, 137, 269, 273; picture, 129; process, 29, 197; sentence, 27, 34, 135; skill, 92; speech, 5, 39; and symbol interdependency, 254; vervet monkey calls, 78; word, 47, 48, 49, 188; and word order, 207, 211

computational linguistics, 29, 105, 121, 124, 196, 244, 250, 314; and application, 279, 283; distributional semantics, 245, 250, 252

computer model, 7, 160, 241, 269, 298n29; and applications, 276, 278; and embodied cognition, 124–25, 132

computer science, 9, 14, 84, 99, 104, 124–25, 241, 314

concreteness (word concreteness), 47, 48

confirmation bias, 6

conformity, 141

conjunction fallacy, 149

connectionism, 111, 112, 117

Connell, Louise, 220

consciousness, 42, 122

consonant, 193

content word, 41, 50

context, 61, 78, 202, 228, 230, 239, 272; and distributional semantics, 227, 229, 231, 236–42, 249, 250; linguistic and perceptual, 280, 281; linguistic, 37, 79, 97, 105, 155, 217, 255; and Principle of Contiguity, 266–69; understanding garden-path sentences, 54–56; understanding speech, 60

perceptual, 268; sound, 58; spatiotemporal, 258, 260; stimulus, 263

contiguity, 257–62, 265, 268, 269

Continuation, Law of, 174

contract (communication contract), 32–33

convention, 259; in communication, 76; in form and meaning, 260; in language, 210, 225, 257; sign and meaning relation, 189; sound meaning relationship, 256

Cooper, William E., 203

corpus callosum, 178

corpus linguistics, 196, 197

cortex, 125, 221; language cortex, 221; motor cortex, 125, 127, 128; sensory cortex, 91, 125; visual cortex, 91, 220, 221

cosine (measure of semantic similarity), 231, 233, 279

Cratylus (character), 185–86, 199

Cratylus (dialog), 256

critical period, 86, 89–90, 94, 95–96

cross-situational learning, 264–65
cuneiform, 189, 242–43
Curtiss, Susan, 90, 94–95
Cyc, 106, 107
cycology, 134–35

Dale, Rick, 263
Dancing Queen (song), 168
data-driven process, 44
Deacon, Terrence W., 13–14, 268, 273, 314
decision making, 158, 314
deep learning, 117
deep structure, 86–87, 93
deixis, 260
dementia, 117
Descartes, René, 122
desire path, 159, 160
determiner, 35, 83, 88. *See also* grammatical item
Deutscher, Guy, 314
dictionary, 41
Diringer, David, 189
disambiguity, 41, 265
discourse psychology, 55
disfluency (speech), 75, 88
distributional semantics, 241, 250, 254, 265, 306n4
dog, 69, 71, 72, 73, 77
dollar bill, 144, 163–65, 180, 259
dolphin, 10, 13, 179
Duffy, Bobby, 146
Dutch language, 26, 52, 66, 86, 159, 187, 196, 308n13; valence study, 198–99
Dwarvish language (fictional), 18

economics, 292n8
educated guess, 45–46, 56, 59, 60, 174
education, 86, 148, 277, 283, 284, 292n8
Educational Testing Service, 233
EEG *See* electroencephalography
Einstein, Albert, 275

electroencephalography, 7, 221
emancipation, 280
embodied cognition, 122–29, 269, 302n6, 314; and artificial neural network, 132–33, 135, 137
embodiment, 122, 124, 135, 211, 284
emotion, 129; emotion words, 210, 237, 238, 278
encyclopedia, 101, 234
ESA. *See* European Space Agency
Eskimo, 280
Eskimo language, 280
ETS. *See* Educational Testing Service
European Space Agency, 283
evolution, 114, 315; brain, 14; evolutionary theory, 14; language, 189, 191, 200, 221, 225; money, 191; writing systems, 189
excavation site, 243, 244
exemplar theory, 294n4
expectation bias, 165
eye tracking, 7, 49–50, 54; eye fixation, 43, 50–52, 59, 142; eye movements, 50, 130–31; eye trackers, 49–50, 58

facial expression, 126, 129, 191
facial recognition, 109, 117
Faulkner, William C., 154
Fellowship of the Ring, 245, 246
Fernbach, Philip, 160, 314
Finish language, 187, 199
First Law of Geography, 306n11
Firth, John R., 227–29, 234, 255, 261, 265
Flemish language, 187
Forer, Bertram R., 152–53
FOX2P gene, 91, 96
FrameNet, 105–6
French language, 49, 52, 92, 159, 187, 199, 223, 281
frequency, word pairs, 215, 218, 219, 230, 234. *See also* word frequency
frequency matching, 176–77
Friedman, Milton, 82

Frisian language, 199
frog, 96
Fromkin, Victoria A., 94

galaxy (vocabulary size estimate), 36–37
Gallistel, Charles R., 177
gambler's fallacy, 172
Game of Thrones (television series), 248
garden-path sentence, 53–55, 97, 154–56
Gardner, Allen, 64, 67
Gardner, Beatrix T., 64, 67
gavagai (reference problem), 8–11, 14, 263
Gazzaniga, Michael S., 177–79, 314
genetics (basis for language), 91, 96
Genie, 89, 90, 94, 95
geography, 238; geographical knowledge, 145, 239; geographical location, 145, 239–44, 252, 254; geographical map, 247, 254, 282. *See also* excavation site
German language, 52, 86, 93, 159, 196, 198, 199
gesture, 8, 9, 126, 260; deictic, 260; iconic, 191, 225
gibbon, 293n29
Gigerenzer, Gerd, 158, 314
Givón, Talmy, 221–22, 225, 229, 308n9
Goblin script (fictional), 18
van Gogh, Vincent W., 257
Google, 124, 279; n-gram corpus, 205, 305n8
Graesser, Arthur C., 283
grammar: generative grammar, 81, 89; sentence grammar, 6, 10, 30–31, 56, 60, 63, 77, 124, 214, 222; sentence grammar and language instinct, 82, 85, 87, 90, 94–96; sound grammar, 30; story grammar, 6, 56, 57
grammatical item, 41, 43, 50, 174, 259, 271
grammatical word. *See* grammatical item
grandmother cell, 108

Greek language (ancient Greek), 24, 107, 256
grey parrot, 67
Griffiths, Thomas L., 314
grounding, 11, 13, 119–37, 156, 160, 180, 182, 188, 277, 281, 314, 298n29, 302n6; and bootstrapping, 252–55, 262, 265–69, 272, 273; and distributional semantics, 231, 232, 250; reference problem, 9; and word order, 204, 208, 220, 221
guessing game, 44, 45, 52, 56, 57, 60
gustatory modality (taste), 11, 124, 131, 168, 197, 198, 268
gut feeling, 158

HAL. *See* Hyperspace Analog to Language
Harnad, Stevan R., 121
Harris, Zellig S., 83, 227, 250
Harry Potter, 247, 248
Hausa language, 186, 199
Hawaiian language, 187
Hawking, Stephen W., 82
healthcare, 283, 284
hearing: hearing route, 41; impairment, 90; sound perception, 69. *See also* speech perception
Hebrew language, 52, 187
hemisphere, 91, 107, 178, 180; left hemisphere, 91–93, 96, 127, 177–81, 220, 294n35, 302n21; right hemisphere, 91, 93, 177–80, 301n21
Hermogenes (character), 185–86, 199, 256
heuristics, 158, 265; anchoring and adjustment, 151, 170
hidden layer, 111, 114–17. *See also* artificial neural network
Hindi language, 187, 223
Hinton, Geoffrey E., 99
Hixkaryana language, 224
The Hobbit, 245, 246
holonym, 24, 104

homo diurnus, 66
homo erectus, 259
homo nocturnus, 66
homo sapiens, 250
homonym, 196
homophone, 30, 31
homunculus, 7, 105, 114, 213
Hopi language, 280
Hopi Native Americans, 280
horoscope, 170
hot hand fallacy, 172
How Children Learn the Meaning of Words, 262
How to Do Things with Words, 74
Hume, David, 256, 258, 261, 262
Hungarian language, 187, 199
Hutchinson, Sterling, 215, 221
Hyperspace Analog to Language, 306n4
hypernym, 100, 104
hyponym, 24, 104

IBM Watson, 105, 124
Icelandic language, 187
icon (Peirce), 257–60, 262, 267
iconicity, 188, 197–98, 229, 260, 272;
    iconicity principle, 225, 229; and
    word order, 221, 222, 225
ideogram, 188, 189
image recognition, 118
imagery, 134
index (Peirce), 257, 258–62, 267, 268
Indus script, 242–44, 252
Indus Valley Civilization, 242–43, 282
Infeld, Leopold, 275
inference, 55, 106, 107, 147, 180
innateness, 309n30
instinct (language instinct), 9–13,
    81–97, 118, 180, 181, 182, 188,
    214, 299n10, 309n30; and cognitive
    shortcut, 136, 137, 154, 156,
    160; and distributional semantics,
    231, 232, 249, 250; and symbol
    interdependency, 270, 273, 277
intelligent tutoring system, 7, 283
intention, 6, 9, 74, 75, 78, 163, 283

interdependency (symbol
    interdependency), 48, 250, 266,
    268–72, 280, 314
interpreter; left-brain interpreter, 178–
    79, 180; right-brain interpreter, 179
introspection, 68, 69
IQ test, 78
Irish language, 223
ISL. *See* Israeli Sign Language
Israeli Sign Language, 189, 200, 202,
    225
Italian language, 93, 187

Jaensch, Erich R., 46
James, William, 1
Jane Eyre, 300n18
Japanese language, 52, 86, 93, 187, 196,
    223
jay (scrub jay), 179
Jeuniaux, Patrick P. J. M. H., 217, 263
Johnson, Andrew, 164
Johnson, Lyndon B., 164
Juliet (character), 106, 107, 186
Jurafsky, Daniel, 28
Just, Marcel, 278

Kahneman, Daniel, 148, 151, 158, 163,
    314
kangaroo, 293n29
Kennedy, John F., 164, 165, 180
King, Martin Luther Jr., 82
Kintsch, Walter, 55, 105
Kirby, Simon M., 191
Knowledge Illusion, 160
Köhler, Wolfgang, 192
Korean language, 86, 187, 223
Kuipers, André, 283

Lady and the Tramp (movie), 24
language acquisition, 9–14, 41,
    64, 65, 73, 180, 202, 313; and
    bootstrapping, 271, 273; and
    language instinct, 81, 86, 87, 89, 90,
    94, 95
Language Instinct, 82

language organ, 93

language processing, 13–14, 40, 141, 174, 180–82, 313; and cognitive shortcut, 154, 156; and distributional semantics, 204, 210, 217, 220, 221; and educated guesses, 57, 59; and grounding, 121, 127, 128, 134, 135; and language instinct, 82, 85, 91, 92, 96

language statistics, 210, 220, 269, 277, 298n35

language use, 31, 72, 74, 76, 222, 269, 271

language-acquisition device, 81, 87, 88, 93, 96, 97

Latent Semantic Analysis, 306 n4, 307n12

law (law firm), 279

learn, 94

learning, 68, 73, 86, 118, 147, 260, 264, 272, 281; in animals, 68, 69, 70, 71`; animals learning behavior, 78, 95; animals learning shapes, 175; animals learning sign language, 64, 65, 74; artificial neural network, 109–11, 113, 116–18, 180, 236, 270, 283; associative, 71, 72, 73; behavior, 10, 13, 72; birds learning language, 74; concepts, 101; cross-situational, 264, 265; game of chess, 76, 77, 79; knowledge, 7, 277, 283

learning language, 6, 9–14, 58, 128, 281, 284; and arbitrariness, 192, 194, 201; and bootstrapping, 262, 263, 268, 271–73; and distributional semantics, 249, 250; and language instinct, 81–82, 86, 87, 88, 89, 94, 95, 96; one-shot, 265; primates learning language, 64; primates learning sign language, 63, 64; process, 309n29; pronounce, 5; reading, 58; school grammar, 30, 31; sign language, 200; situational, 268; sounds, 58; speaking, 10; swimming,

94; and training, 72–75, 78. *See also* language acquisition

lemma, 25

Lenat, Douglas Bruce, 106

lexical item, 41, 174, 259

lexical semantics, 33

Lincoln, Abraham, 164, 165, 180

linguistic relativism, 314. *See also* Sapir-Whorf hypothesis

linguistics, 12, 14, 43–44, 187, 256, 284, 313, 292n8; distributional linguistics, 249; forensic linguistics, 282; and language instinct, 75, 93

Linnaeus, Carl, 65

Lisala (bonobo), 175

literature (literary), 18, 20, 154

little Albert, 69, 70

Locke, John, 256

Lord Monboddo, 67

Lord of the Rings, 18, 21, 245, 277, 282

Lord of the Rings (movie), 21, 247

Los Angeles Times, 239, 240

Loulis (chimp), 64

Lowery, Bill (character Wordplay), 1–11, 14, 21, 281

LSA. *See* Latent Semantic Analysis

Magnetic Resonance Imaging, 127

magnitude (word magnitude), 215, 216, 217

Mannish language (fictional), 18

Martin, James, 28

matrix algebra, 230, 232, 241

maximizing, 177, 179

McClelland, James L., 99, 112, 113

McConkie, George, 50, 51

medicine, 148

memory, 78, 101, 143, 179, 182, 200, 273; for change in meaning, 54; in chimps, 144; and cognitive shortcut, 151, 153, 156–57, 160; connectionism, 113; eye tracking, 54; guessing game, 44, 60; human vs. chimp, 144, 145; long-term, 120,

231, 232, 233; modality-specific memory; semantic, 278; semantic network, 101; spatial, 145, 246; visual memory, 298n39

mental dictionary, 40–42, 48, 52, 59, 228

mental lexicon, 169, 228, 230

mental process, 61, 68, 69, 122

mental representation, 7, 42, 106, 133, 228, 257, 259

meronym, 24, 104

Merriam-Webster dictionary, 40, 228

metacognition, 134

Metaphysics, 308n11

metaphor, 131, 132, 135, 208, 211

Middle Earth, 18, 245–47, 277, 282

Miller, George A., 85, 104, 106

mimicry, 10, 126–27

mind-body problem, 122

modality shift experiment, 131

morpheme, 26

morphology, 25–26, 30–31, 33, 61, 90, 141, 183, 196, 204, 225; Moses illusion. *See* semantic illusion

Motherese, 88, 89

MRI. *See* Magnetic Resonance Imaging, 127

NASA. *See* National Aeronautics and Space Administration

National Aeronautics and Space Administration, 284

National Safety Council, 150

nativism, 82, 85, 96–97, 309n30

Natural and Medical History of the Indies, 66

natural language processing, 7

network, 9, 11, 99, 125, 136, 156, 160, 180, 182, 188, 277; and bootstrapping, 272, 273; and distributional semangics, 231, 232, 250; propositional network, 105, 123. *See also* artificial neural network

neural network, 11, 107–11, 137, 140–42, 144, 181, 236, 265. *See also* artificial neural network

neurobiology, 14

neurogenerative diseases, 278

neuroscience, 292n8

neuron, 107–9, 114, 117, 125; interneurons, 114, 115; mirror neuron, 125; motor neurons, 114; sensory neurons, 114

neuroscience, 14, 96, 177, 284, 314

New York Times, 112, 160, 239, 240

Nim Chimpsky (chimp), 64, 65, 67, 74, 95, 96

Nirvana (band), 168

nonsense word, 88, 115, 194, 197, 263

nonword, 20, 21, 48, 51, 52, 58

noun, 27, 34–36, 47, 48, 73, 250, 271, 287n13; distinguishing in vocabulary, 25–26; identifying based on sound, 196–97, 267; permutations on sentences we know, 34–36; syntactic structures, 83–84; temporal order, 212. *See also* grammatical item

NSC. *See* National Safety Council

object, grammatical, 63, 65, 86, 223, 224

Occam's razor, 304n24

olfactory modality (smell), 122, 124, 186, 197, 198, 268

onomatopoeia, 187, 197, 200, 258–60, 267

orangutan, 66

owl (barn owl), 175, 179

Oxford English dictionary, 22, 40, 228

parallel distributed processing, 112, 113

parrot (grey parrot), 67, 75

parsing (sentence parsing), 153, 154

pattern, 42, 163–202, 250, 254, 270, 272, 309n29; animal responses, 176, 179; in distributional semantics, 237, 241, 247–50, 268, 270, 273; language patterns, 14, 182–97, 206, 277, 280, 281; pattern matching, 166–68, 179, 181, 250; pattern-matching skill, 165, 169–70, 176,

179–81, 270, 272; pattern of sound, 73; perceptual patterns, 172, 174, 207; sound-meaning patterns, 199, 201–3, 248, 249, 254, 270; in stories, 56; in word order, 216, 217, 220–22; word patterns, 222
patterns of activation, 108, 109, 111, 112, 116, 270. *See also* artificial neural network
Pavlov, Ivan P., 69
PDP. *See* parallel distributed processing
Peirce, Charles Sanders, 256, 257, 258, 259, 261, 262, 268, 308n9
Penfield, Wilder G., 125
Pennebaker, James W., 314
Pepperberg, Irene, 67, 68, 74
perception, 13, 113, 124, 143, 147, 157, 160, 173, 269, 273, 280; in reading, 43, 57; veridical, 179
perceptual experience, 11, 122, 132–36, 188, 249, 269
perceptual simulation, 11, 13, 122–35, 180, 298n35; and bootstrapping, 267, 269; and cognitive shortcut, 140, 141, 144, 153, 156; and word order, 204, 207, 218, 221, 224
Perils of Perception, 146
permutation (vocabulary size), 35, 36
Persian language, 86
personality, 152, 153
pervasiveness of language, 46
philosophy, 9, 256, 292n8
phoneme, 30, 58, 59, 60, 198
phonetics, 204
phonology, 30–31, 59–61, 141, 183, 189, 204, 294n35
physiological processes, 128
Picasso, Pablo R., 259
pictogram, 188, 189
pictograph, 188, 189, 200, 225, 243
pigeon, 176, 177, 181
Pinker, Steven, 82, 85, 87, 95, 314
pitch (speech), 88
planum temporale, 92, 93
Plato, 185, 199, 249, 256

Plato's problem, 248, 249
plenum temporale, 96
poverty of the stimulus, 88–89, 93–94, 96, 181, 249, 250
pragmatics, 33, 61, 74, 75, 95, 141, 204
preposition, 27, 41, 157, 271, 287n13; permutations on sentences we know, 34–36; syntactic structures, 83
primate, 64, 66, 147, 293n33
priming, 48, 49, 55
Principle of Contiguity, 261, 262, 263, 265, 267
Principle of Parsimony, 304n24
probability, 13, 46, 149, 177, 181, 182
production (language), 19, 137, 207, 211, 237, 250, 269, 273
production (speech), 5
Project Nim (documentary), 65
pronoun, 41, 87, 155, 223, 250, 258, 259, 267, 271, 287n13
permutations on sentences we know, 34–36
proposition, 105, 106, 107
Propp, Vladimir, 56
prototype, 101, 294n4
prototype theory, 294n4
Proust, Marcel, 233
proximity; geographical, 243; of shapes, 173; word proximity, 225, 229
Proximity, Law of, 173
psycholinguistics, 44, 54, 58, 75, 76
psychology, 12, 46, 68, 104, 284, 313; behaviorism, 69–70; introspection, 68; language instinct, 81
psychology of language, 75, 241, 314. *See also* psycholinguistics
punctuation marker (in sentences), 57, 58
punishment, 71, 72, 74, 76, 86, 118, 181

Queen (band), 168
Quenyatic script (fictional), 18
Quillian, M. Ross, 112
Quine, Willard Van Orman, 9

rat, 70, 72, 176, 177
Rayner, Keith, 50, 51
readability formula, 279
reading, 24, 39, 58, 179, 220, 289n31; and the brain, 221; and educated guesses, 40–45; eye tracking experiment, 50–52, 142; process, 43, 57, 58, 61, 157, 197; reading experiment, 246; reading process, 40, 44; reading route, 41; reading skill, 21; reading speed, 48; reading time experiment, 129, 197; recognition experiment, 55; self-paced reading time experiment, 7, 49; skill, 21, 50; speed, 49, 52, 57, 60, 142, 143; story reading, 129, 223
Recchia, Gabriel, 242, 243
recursion, 83, 84, 293n33
reenactment, 127, 128, 140, 182
reference, 132, 254, 257–59, 262, 264, 265–69, 272
reference problem. *See* gavagai (reference problem)
reinforcement, 86, 137, 144, 180–81, 250; artificial neural networks, 114, 117, 118; in behaviorism, 63, 70, 72–78; and bootstrapping, 262–63
Remembrance of Past Times, 233
reward, 10, 12, 13, 118, 144, 148, 175, 181; in behaviorism, 70–72, 74, 75
Romeo (character), 106, 107
Romeo and Juliet (play), 106, 186
Ross, John R., 203
rule-of-thumb, 158, 265
Rumelhart, David E., 99, 112
Russian language, 187, 223

saccades, 50
Sahara Desert (vocabulary size estimate), 36–37
Sapir, Edward, 280
Sapir-Whorf hypothesis, 280. *See also* linguistic relativism
de Saussure, Ferdinand, 76, 185, 187, 199, 214, 256, 257, 280, 308n7

The Sciences of the Artificial, 273
scientific process, 276
Screen of Death, 70
sealings, 243–44
seals, 243
Searle, John R., 121
second language, 81, 89, 271
second language learning, 281
self-paced reading time (button press), 7, 49, 127, 129, 206–9, 215–18
semantic cognition, 113, 116, 249
semantic illusion, 155
semantic network, 100–101, 104–7, 112, 122–23, 131, 249, 294n4; features, 100–102, 107, 117, 118, 122, 194, 261; hierarchical, 100–101, 103, 107; prototype, 103, 122; theory theory, 122
semantic relations, 24, 29, 37, 59, 206, 254, 265; applications of distributional semantics, 278–79; in word order, 219, 229
semantics, 31, 61, 97, 121, 141, 228, 249, 250
semiotics, 14, 256
sentence structure, 27, 53, 55, 56, 61; impaired, 92. *See also* grammar
sexism (sexism in language), 155, 210, 305n8. *See also* emancipation
Shakespeare, William, 18, 19, 20, 21, 32, 37, 186
sign language, 63, 64, 67, 74, 95, 191, 200
similarity, 257, 258, 259, 260; of shapes, 173
Similarity, Law of, 173
Simmons, Daniel, 142
Simon, Herbert A., 85, 273
Simpson, Homer, 158, 213, 214
Skinner box, 70
Skinner, B. F., 63, 70–76, 78, 290n12, 291n22
slip of the tongue, 88
Sloman, Steven, 160, 314
Smells Like Teen Spirit (song), 168

SNARC (spatial-numerical association of response codes), 215–17
social cognition, 126
social media, 37, 282
social network, 247, 248, 249, 282
social psychology, 314
socioeconomic status, 85, 86
Socrates (character), 185, 186, 256
Song of Ice and Fire, 248
SpaceBuzz, 283–84
Spanish language, 86, 87
speech act, 75
Speech and Language Processing, 28
speech organ, 66
speech pathology, 5
speech perception, 30, 39, 57, 59, 89, 127, 191; speech perception and educated guesses, 58, 59, 61; speech perception and verbal behavior, 73, 78; speech perception experiment, 59, 60, 128; speech perception in songs, 168
speech recognition, 112, 117, 278, 279, 284
spelling, 57, 87
split-brain patient, 177, 178, 179
statistical learning, 265
statistics, 19, 133, 234, 260, 276
Stroop effect, 46
Stroop, John R., 46
subject, grammatical, 63, 65, 86, 223, 224
Sumerian script, 188–91, 200, 225, 242–43
surface structure, 87
symbol (Peirce), 257–60, 267, 268
symbol grounding. *See* Chinese room argument; grounding
symbolic merry-go-round, 122, 137, 252, 272
Symbolic Species, 13, 268, 273
synapse, 109, 117
synonym, 11, 24, 201, 202, 228
Syntactic Structures, 82, 84
syntactic tree, 84, 87

syntax, 43, 48, 61, 183, 294n35; and acquisition in chimpanzees, 63, 65, 132, 133; biological basis, 90, 91, 93–97; and cognitive shortcut, 141, 153–56; and computational linguistics, 99, 106; and distributional semantics, 249, 250; and embodied cognition, 121, 124; and garden-path sentence, 52, 53, 55; and language structure, 30, 31, 33, 34; predicting based on sound, 196, 198; syntactic trees, 83, 84, 88; and word order, 204, 225. *See also* grammar
Systema Naturae, 66

tachistoscope, 49
tactile modality (touch), 124, 197, 198, 268
Tanenhaus, Michael, 58
teaching of English as a Foreign Language test, 233, 306n6
telepathy, 169
Telephone Game, 191
Terrace, Herbert S., 64, 65, 67, 95, 96
Thatcher, Margaret H., 139, 140
theory theory, 101. *See also* semantic network
theory-driven process, 44
Thinking, Fast and Slow, 158
Thompson, Peter, 139
Tobler, Waldo R., 251, 261, 306n11
TOEFL. *See* Teaching of English as a Foreign Language test
Tolkien, John R. R., 18, 19, 21, 245, 246
top-down process, 44, 61
training, 9–13, 63–79, 136, 180, 182, 188, 277; after speech deprivation, 90; in artificial neural networks, 110–11, 118; and bootstrapping, 270, 272, 273; and cognitive shortcut, 137, 141, 142, 144, 156, 160; and distributional semantics, 231, 232, 236, 250; and language instinct, 97

Treatise of Human Nature, 258, 261
Trump, Donald J., 87
Tulp, Nicolaas, 66
Turing, Alan M., 119
Turkish language, 86
Tversky, Amos N., 148, 151
Twilight Zone (television series), 2, 142, 326
typo, 30, 43, 58
Tyson, Edward, 66

United Nations, 284
univerbation, 306n27
universal grammar, 86–88, 93, 96
Urdu language, 223

valence, 197–99, 201, 228, 267, 277; and word order, 203, 211, 213, 215
Valmaric script (fictional), 18
van Dijk, Teun A., 105
vector (word vector), 231, 239, 241, 245
verb, 25–26, 27, 47, 65, 73, 86, 88, 93, 267, 287n13; distinguishing in vocabulary, 25–26; identifying based on sound, 196–97, 267; permutations on sentences we know, 34–36; syntactic structures, 83–84
temporal order, 212
verbal behavior, 10, 63, 72–79, 95
Verbal Behavior, 72, 75
VerbNet, 106
veridical perception, 179
vervet monkey, 77, 78
Viki (chimp), 64
visual field, 178
visual modality (image), 124, 129, 131, 198
visual representation, 141, 247
vocabulary, 17, 18, 20, 21, 25, 26, 31, 34, 78, 202, 203; development, 202; size, 17, 18, 20, 21, 24–27, 29; test, 95, 64
vowel, 5, 193, 198

de Waal, Frans, 175, 314
Wall Street Journal, 239, 240
Warao language, 224
Washoe (chimp), 64–65, 67, 95
Watson, John B., 69, 70
Welsh language, 186
Wernicke, Carl, 92
Wernicke's aphasia, 92
Wernicke's area, 96, 128, 220
Whitcomb, James, 117
Whorf, Benjamin Lee, 280
Why Chimpanzees Can't Learn Language and Only Humans Can, 96
Why We Can't Wait, 82
wisdom of the crowd, 160
Wittgenstein, Ludwig, 39
Woolf, Virginia, 33, 35
Word2Vec, 306n4
word frequency, 47, 48, 53, 205, 207, 216, 271
word length, 47, 48
word order, 36, 44, 86, 203–25, 228, 248, 273, 284; gender, 211, 214, 222, 305n8; perceptual, 206, 207, 218, 219, 220, 221; power, 207, 210, 214; syntactic (SOV), 86, 93; syntactic (SVO), 86, 93; temporal, 212, 213, 223; valence, 204, 209, 210, 214, 222; vertical, 206, 208, 210, 222
word token, 18
word type, 18, 19, 20
WordNet, 104, 105, 106, 107
Wordplay (Twilight Zone episode), 2–4, 6, 8
word-superiority effect, 42, 57
writing, 19

Yiddish language, 306 n3

Zipf, Georg Kingsley, 17, 271
Zipf's Law, 271
Zulu language, 186
Zwaan, Rolf A., 239